MUSASHI #9

volume 3

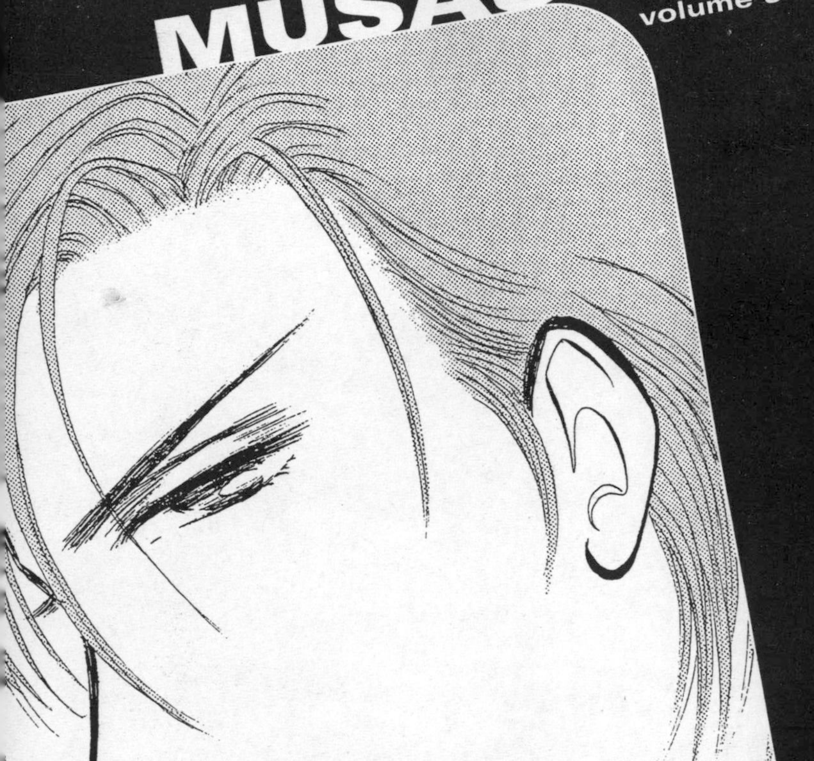

by Takahashi Miyuki

The history of mankind has
been one of wars. Race.
Religion. Philosophy.
The causes are untold.

The combatants have their own
justifications, but on occasion,
some create a volatile
situation that threatens to
destroy the world.

Ultimate Blue.

An organization shrouded in
complete secrecy. Also known
as "the other United Nations."
Nobody knows when it was
created. Nobody knows
where it is based.

The Blue of the Seas.
The Blue of the Skies.
The Blue of the Earth.

The last line of defense against chaos.

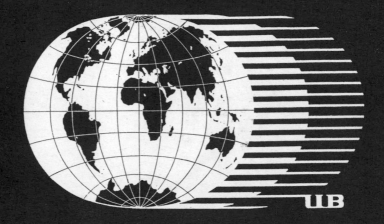

MUSASHI
(SHINOZUKA KOU)

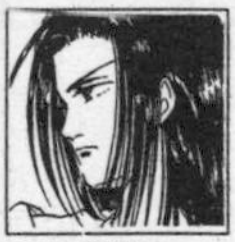

TACHIBANA
SHINGO

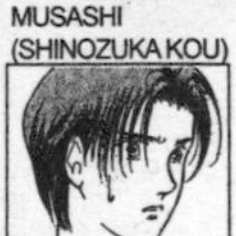

LONTON

The story so far...

The history of mankind has been one of wars. Relentless hostilities would have doomed the planet to annihilation were it not for Ultimate Blue, a secret organization, also known as "the other United Nations," and its team of super agents. Musashi Number Nine, or Shinozuka Kou, as she is known, is one of them.
A politician crusading against gun smuggling is cut down by a sniper's bullet. A teen who unwittingly photographed the fatal scene comes to a similar and tragic end. The evidence passes into the hands of Tachibana Shingo, the dead teen's best friend. But, with the evidence comes the attention of the gun smugglers "White Dragon" and its assassin, Lonton. Musashi reveals her true gender to Shingo to gain his trust. Together, they apprehend Lonton and succeed in securing the evidence needed to destroy the White Dragon. But, until White Dragon is destroyed and the threat of any revenge neutralized, Musashi must stand guard. However, things spin into a more complex web than Musashi could ever have imagined...

WAIT...
WAIT A MIN-UTE...
YOU... YOU... HAVE...
He's... I mean she's...
THAT IS THE WAY IT IS.
I WORK FOR A CERTAIN ORGANIZATION.
I WAS ORDERED HERE.
I'M A GIRL, BUT I WAS SENT TO THIS BOY'S SCHOOL WITH GOOD REASON.
I'M HERE TO PROTECT YOU.
AND I'M HERE TO FIND THE EVIDENCE THAT WILL PUT HIM AWAY.

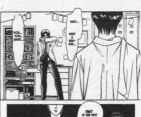

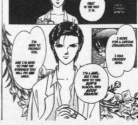

contents

MUSASHI #9

3

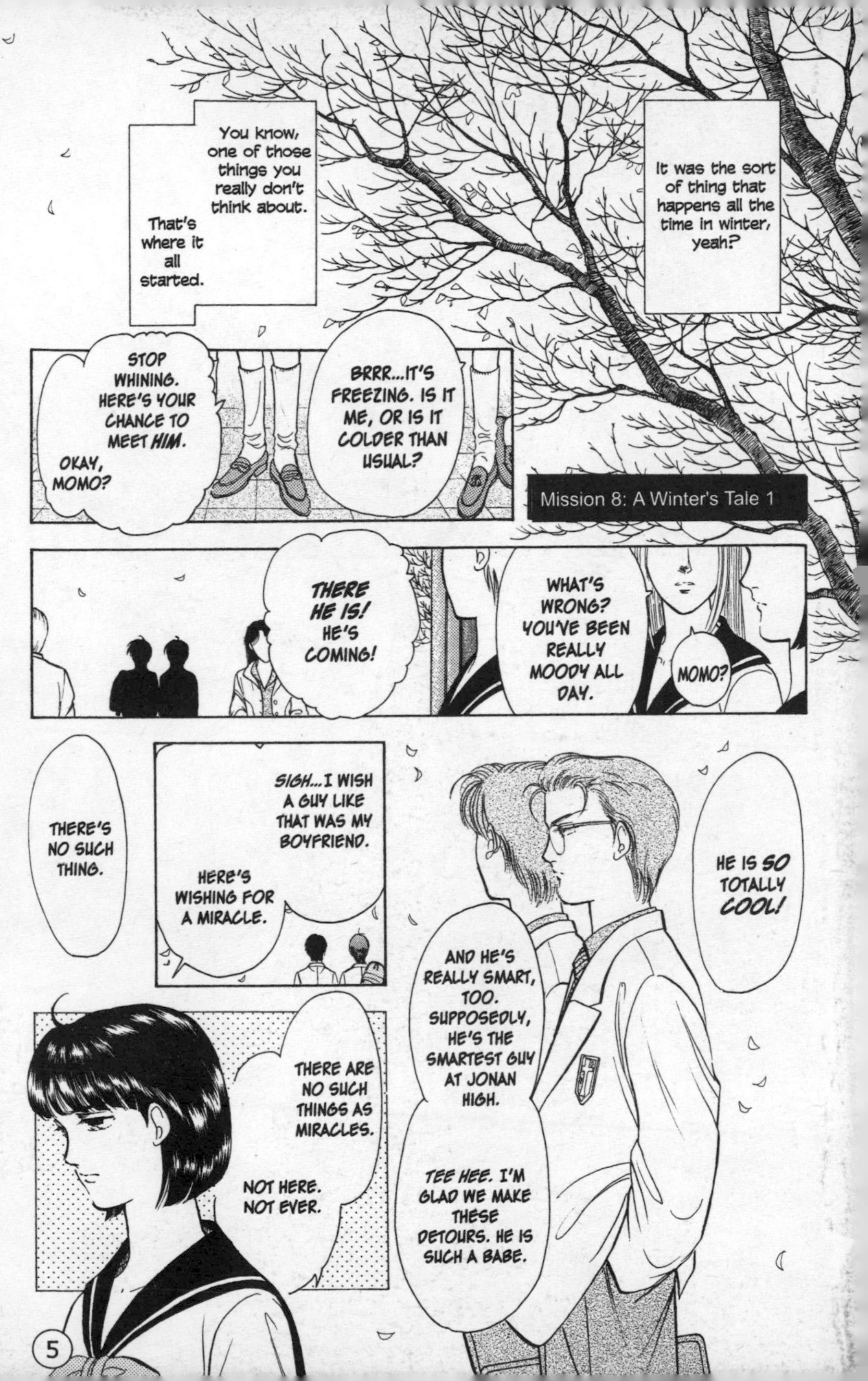

It was the sort of thing that happens all the time in winter, yeah?
You know, one of those things you really don't think about.
That's where it all started.
Mission 8: A Winter's Tale 1
BRRR...IT'S FREEZING. IS IT ME, OR IS IT COLDER THAN USUAL?
STOP WHINING. HERE'S YOUR CHANCE TO MEET *HIM*.
OKAY, MOMO?
WHAT'S WRONG? YOU'VE BEEN REALLY MOODY ALL DAY.
MOMO?
THERE HE IS! HE'S COMING!
HE IS *SO* TOTALLY *COOL!*
AND HE'S REALLY SMART, TOO. SUPPOSEDLY, HE'S THE SMARTEST GUY AT JONAN HIGH.
TEE HEE. I'M GLAD WE MAKE THESE DETOURS. HE IS SUCH A BABE.
*SIGH...*I WISH A GUY LIKE THAT WAS MY BOYFRIEND.
HERE'S WISHING FOR A MIRACLE.
THERE'S NO SUCH THING.
THERE ARE NO SUCH THINGS AS MIRACLES.
NOT HERE. NOT EVER.

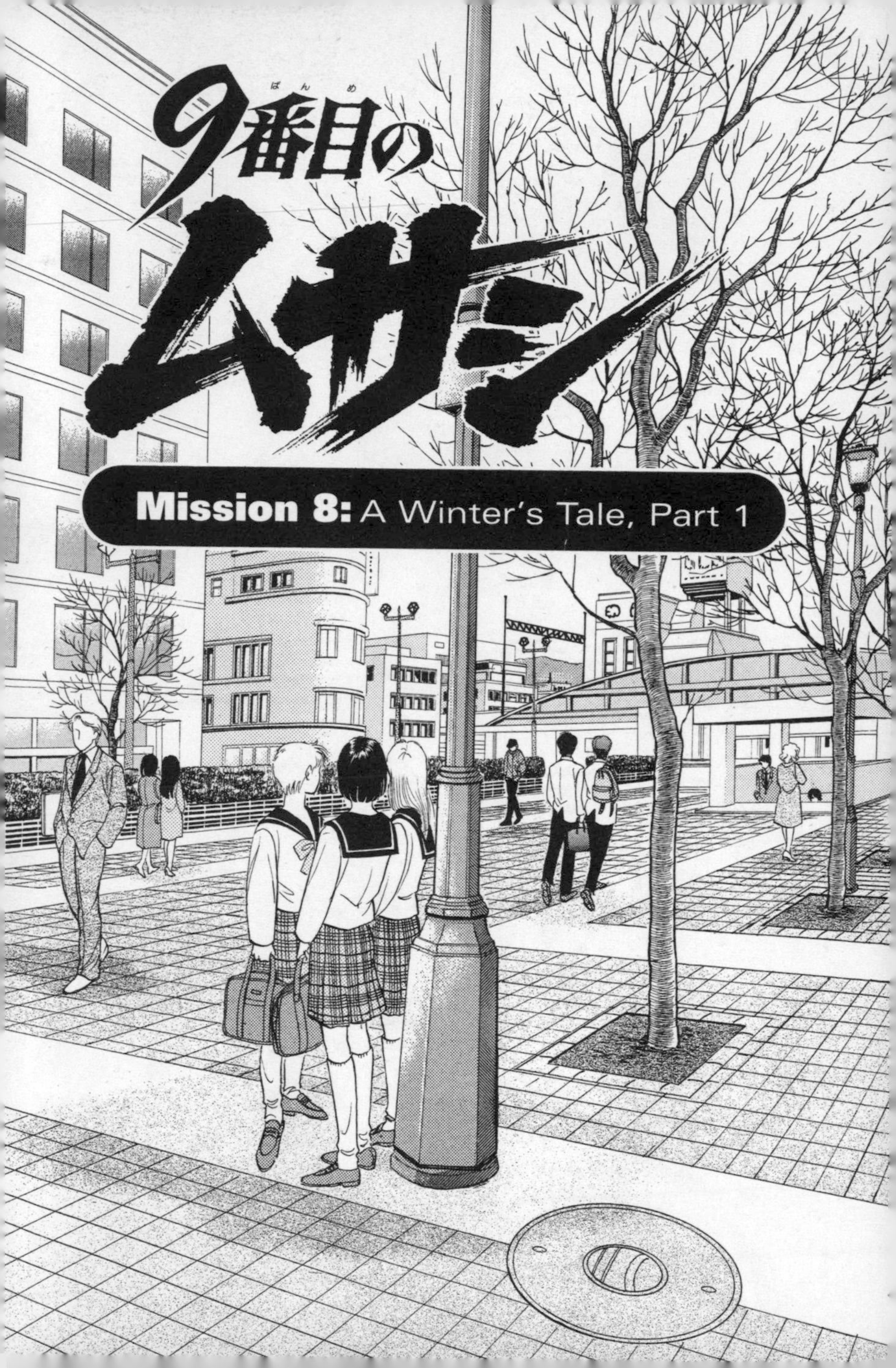
9番目のムサシ
Mission 8: A Winter's Tale, Part 1

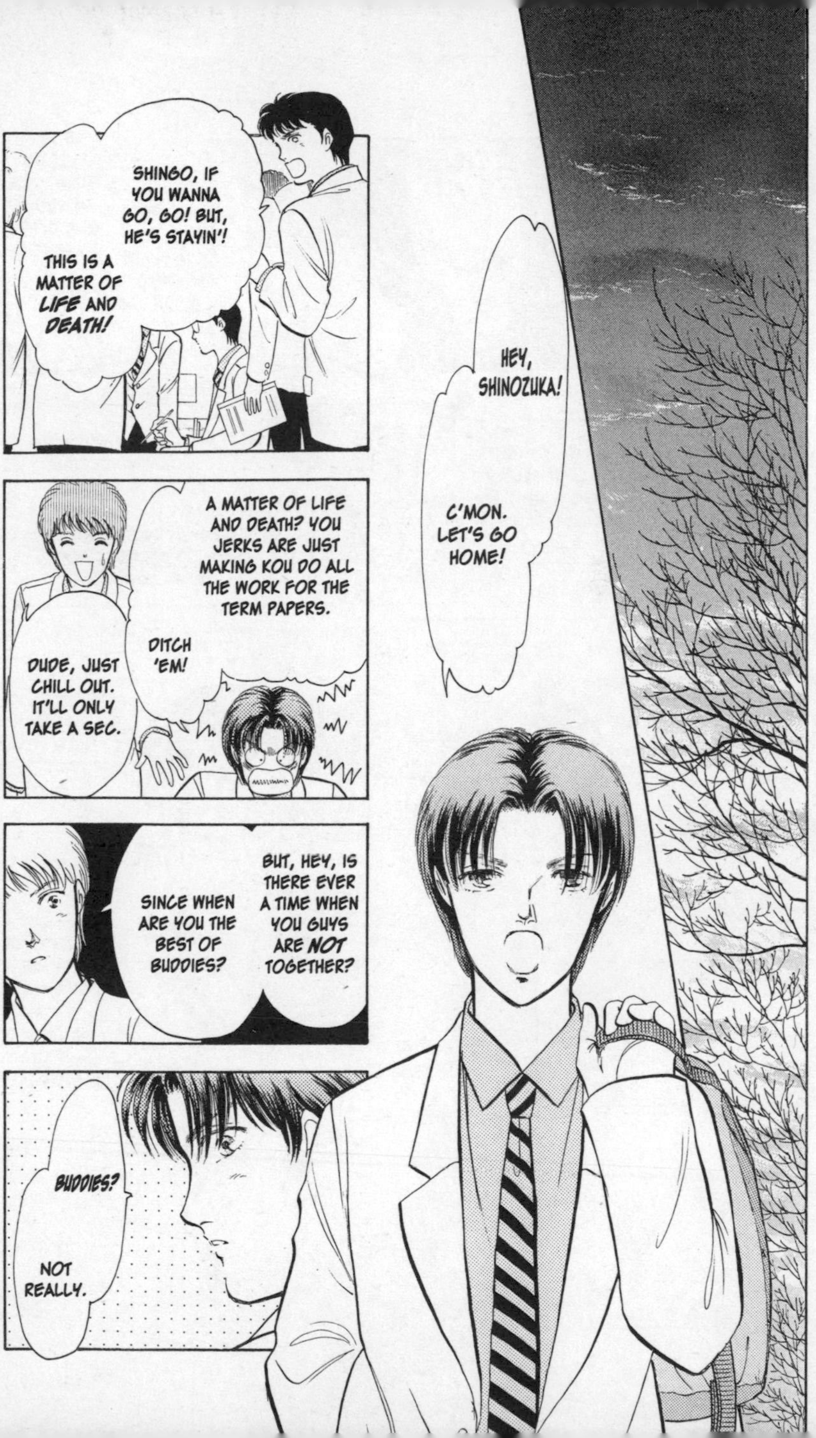
HEY, SHINOZUKA!
C'MON. LET'S GO HOME!
SHINGO, IF YOU WANNA GO, GO! BUT, HE'S STAYIN'!
THIS IS A MATTER OF LIFE AND DEATH!
A MATTER OF LIFE AND DEATH? YOU JERKS ARE JUST MAKING KOU DO ALL THE WORK FOR THE TERM PAPERS.
DITCH 'EM!
DUDE, JUST CHILL OUT. IT'LL ONLY TAKE A SEC.
BUT, HEY, IS THERE EVER A TIME WHEN YOU GUYS ARE NOT TOGETHER?
SINCE WHEN ARE YOU THE BEST OF BUDDIES?
BUDDIES?
NOT REALLY.

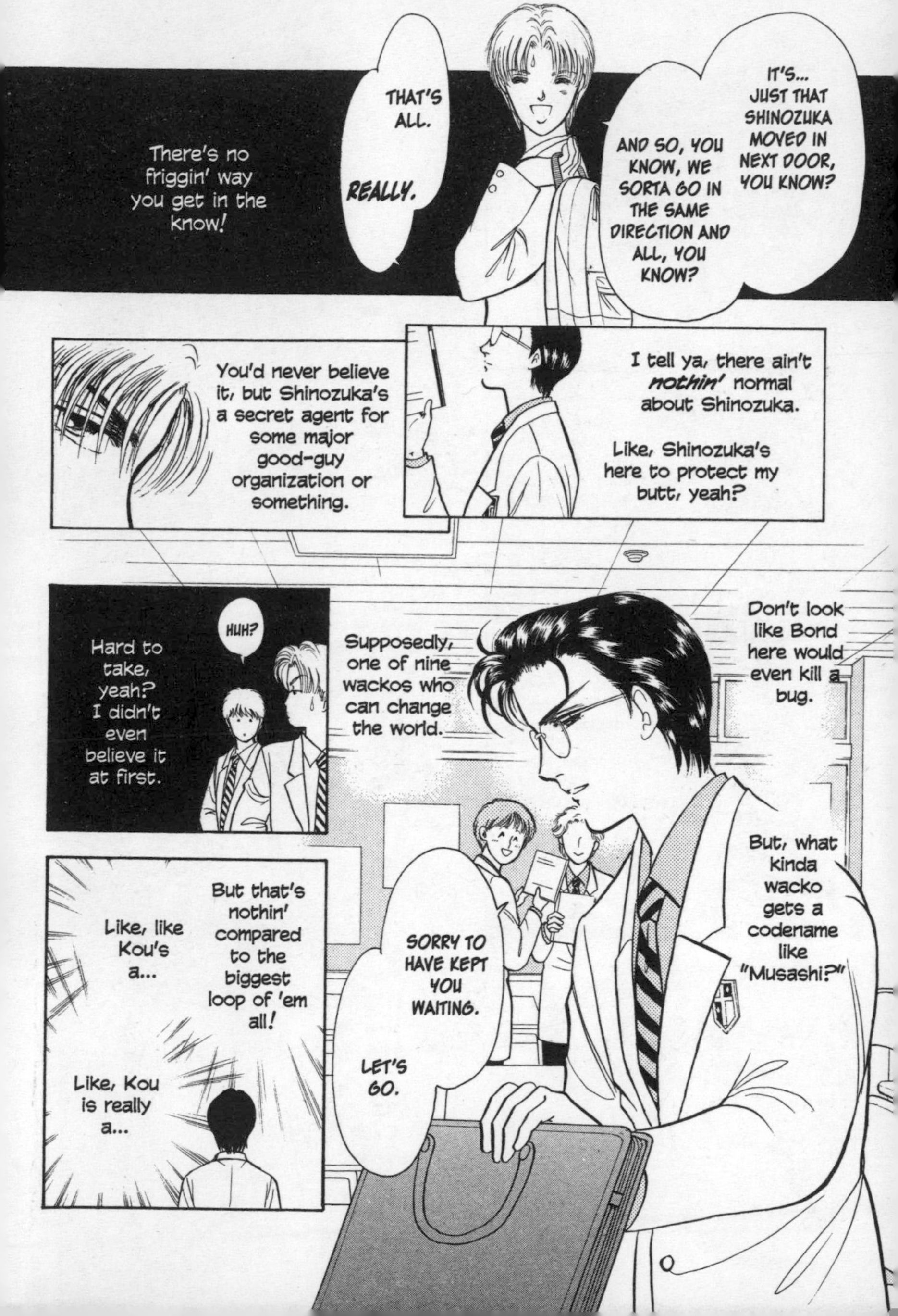
IT'S... JUST THAT SHINOZUKA MOVED IN NEXT DOOR, YOU KNOW?
AND SO, YOU KNOW, WE SORTA GO IN THE SAME DIRECTION AND ALL, YOU KNOW?
THAT'S ALL.
REALLY.
There's no friggin' way you get in the know!
I tell ya, there ain't *nothin'* normal about Shinozuka.
Like, Shinozuka's here to protect my butt, yeah?
You'd never believe it, but Shinozuka's a secret agent for some major good-guy organization or something.
Don't look like Bond here would even kill a bug.
Supposedly, one of nine wackos who can change the world.
But, what kinda wacko gets a codename like "Musashi?"
SORRY TO HAVE KEPT YOU WAITING.
LET'S GO.
HUH?
Hard to take, yeah? I didn't even believe it at first.
But that's nothin' compared to the biggest loop of 'em all!
Like, like Kou's a...
Like, Kou is really a...

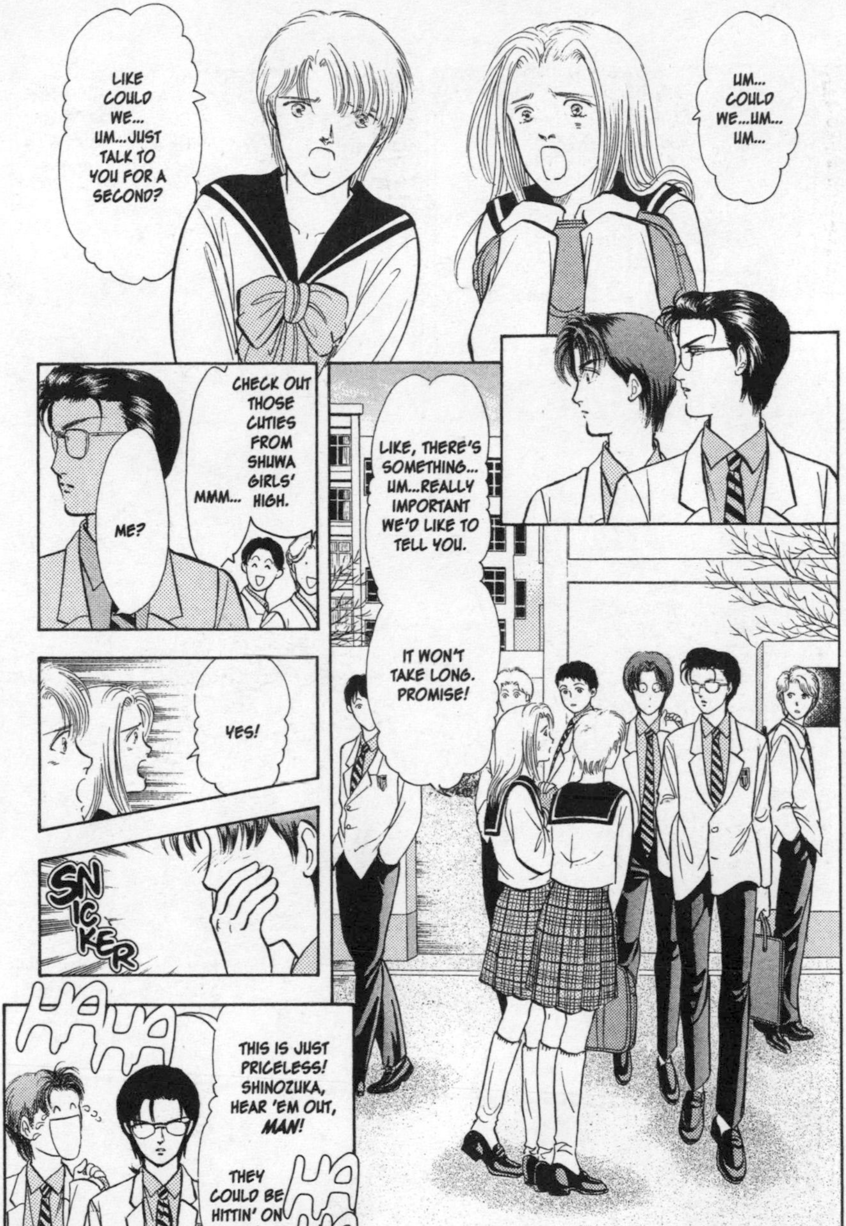
UM... COULD WE...UM... UM...
LIKE COULD WE... UM...JUST TALK TO YOU FOR A SECOND?
LIKE, THERE'S SOMETHING... UM...REALLY IMPORTANT WE'D LIKE TO TELL YOU.
IT WON'T TAKE LONG. PROMISE!
CHECK OUT THOSE CUTIES FROM SHUWA GIRLS' HIGH.
MMM...
ME?
YES!
SNICKER
HAHA
THIS IS JUST PRICELESS! SHINOZUKA, HEAR 'EM OUT, MAN!
THEY COULD BE HITTIN' ON YA!
HA HA

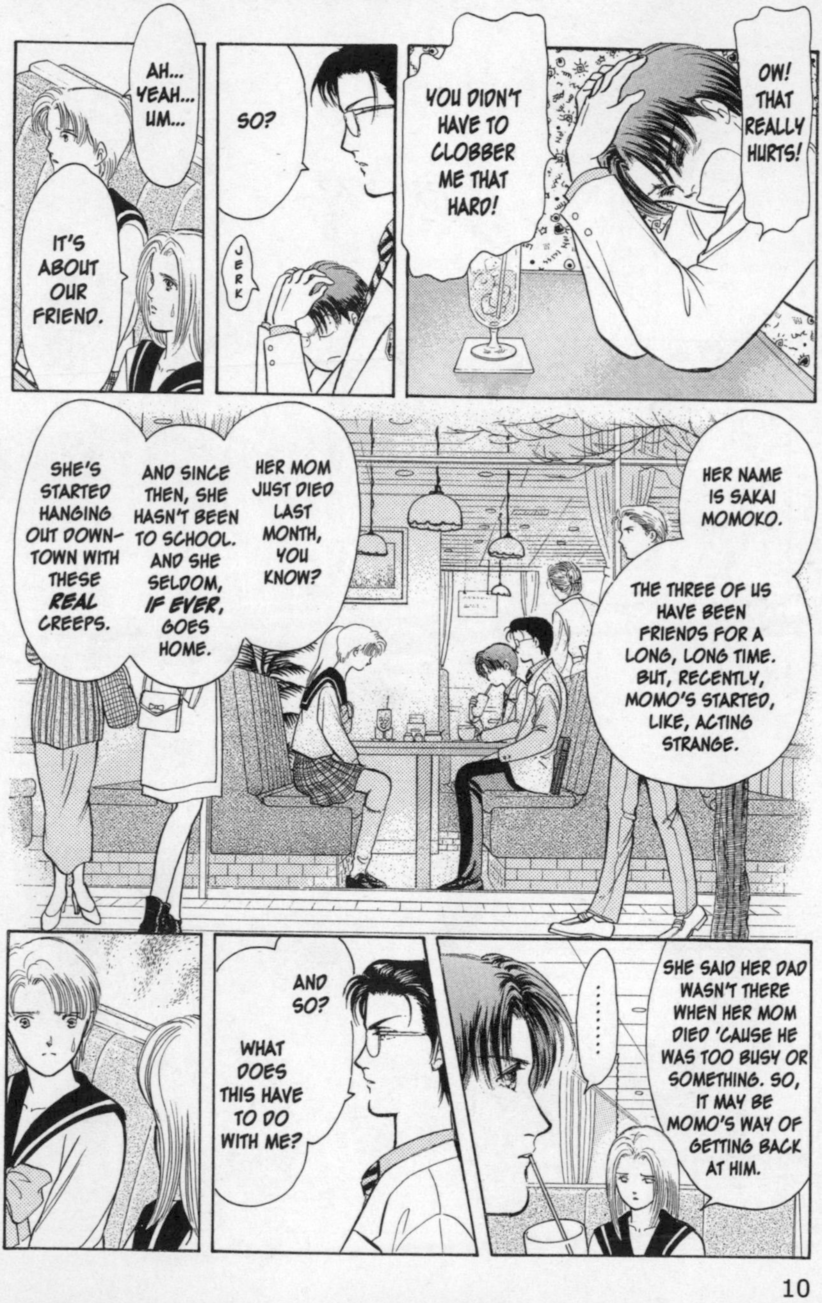
OW! THAT REALLY HURTS!
YOU DIDN'T HAVE TO CLOBBER ME THAT HARD!
SO?
JERK
AH... YEAH... UM...
IT'S ABOUT OUR FRIEND.
HER NAME IS SAKAI MOMOKO.
THE THREE OF US HAVE BEEN FRIENDS FOR A LONG, LONG TIME. BUT, RECENTLY, MOMO'S STARTED, LIKE, ACTING STRANGE.
HER MOM JUST DIED LAST MONTH, YOU KNOW?
AND SINCE THEN, SHE HASN'T BEEN TO SCHOOL. AND SHE SELDOM, IF EVER, GOES HOME.
SHE'S STARTED HANGING OUT DOWN-TOWN WITH THESE REAL CREEPS.
SHE SAID HER DAD WASN'T THERE WHEN HER MOM DIED 'CAUSE HE WAS TOO BUSY OR SOMETHING. SO, IT MAY BE MOMO'S WAY OF GETTING BACK AT HIM.
......
AND SO?
WHAT DOES THIS HAVE TO DO WITH ME?

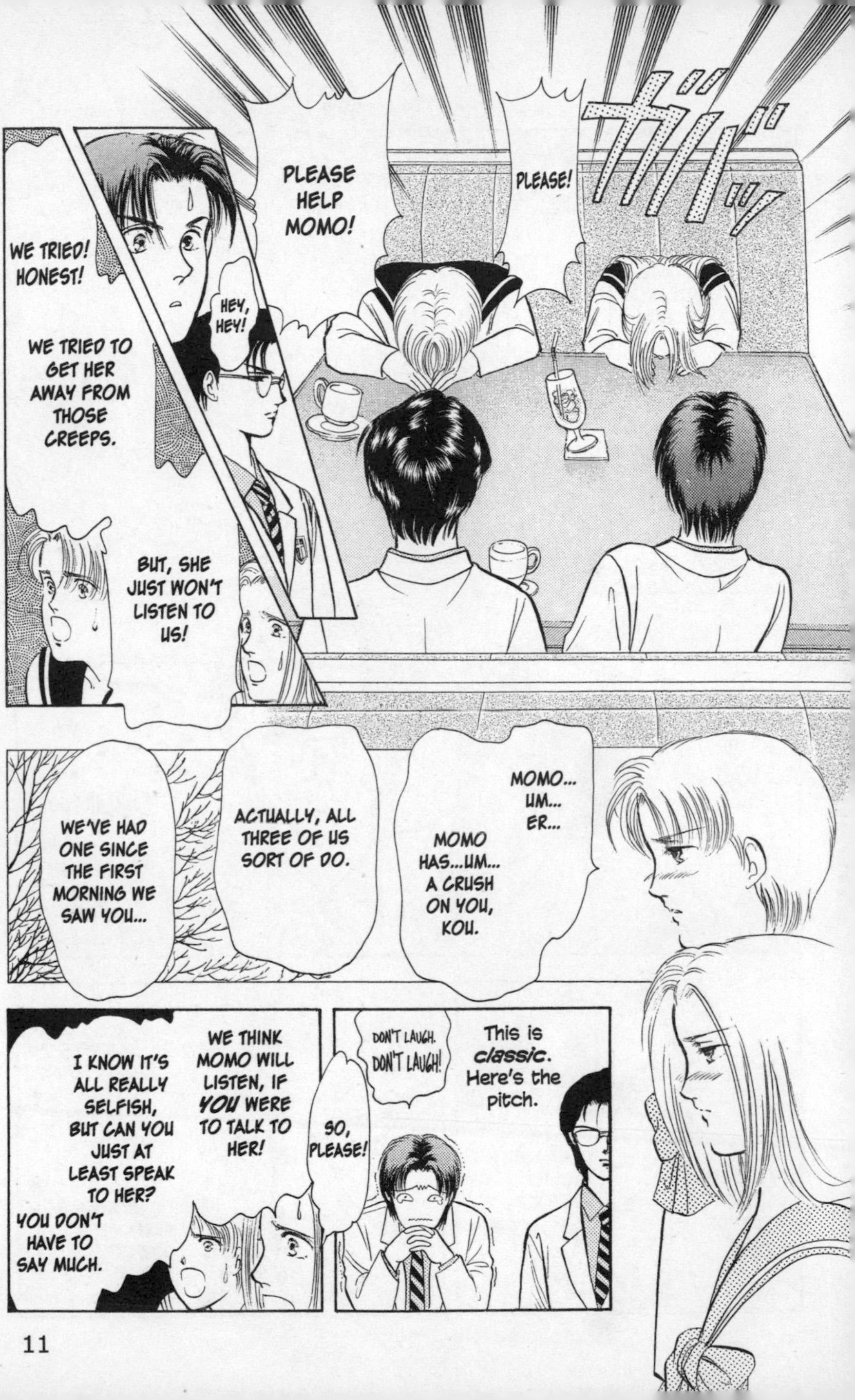
ガバッ
PLEASE!
PLEASE HELP MOMO!
HEY, HEY!
WE TRIED! HONEST!
WE TRIED TO GET HER AWAY FROM THOSE CREEPS.
BUT, SHE JUST WON'T LISTEN TO US!
MOMO... UM... ER...
MOMO HAS...UM... A CRUSH ON YOU, KOU.
ACTUALLY, ALL THREE OF US SORT OF DO.
WE'VE HAD ONE SINCE THE FIRST MORNING WE SAW YOU...
This is *classic*. Here's the pitch.
DON'T LAUGH. DON'T LAUGH!
SO, PLEASE!
WE THINK MOMO WILL LISTEN, IF *YOU* WERE TO TALK TO HER!
I KNOW IT'S ALL REALLY SELFISH, BUT CAN YOU JUST AT LEAST SPEAK TO HER?
YOU DON'T HAVE TO SAY MUCH.

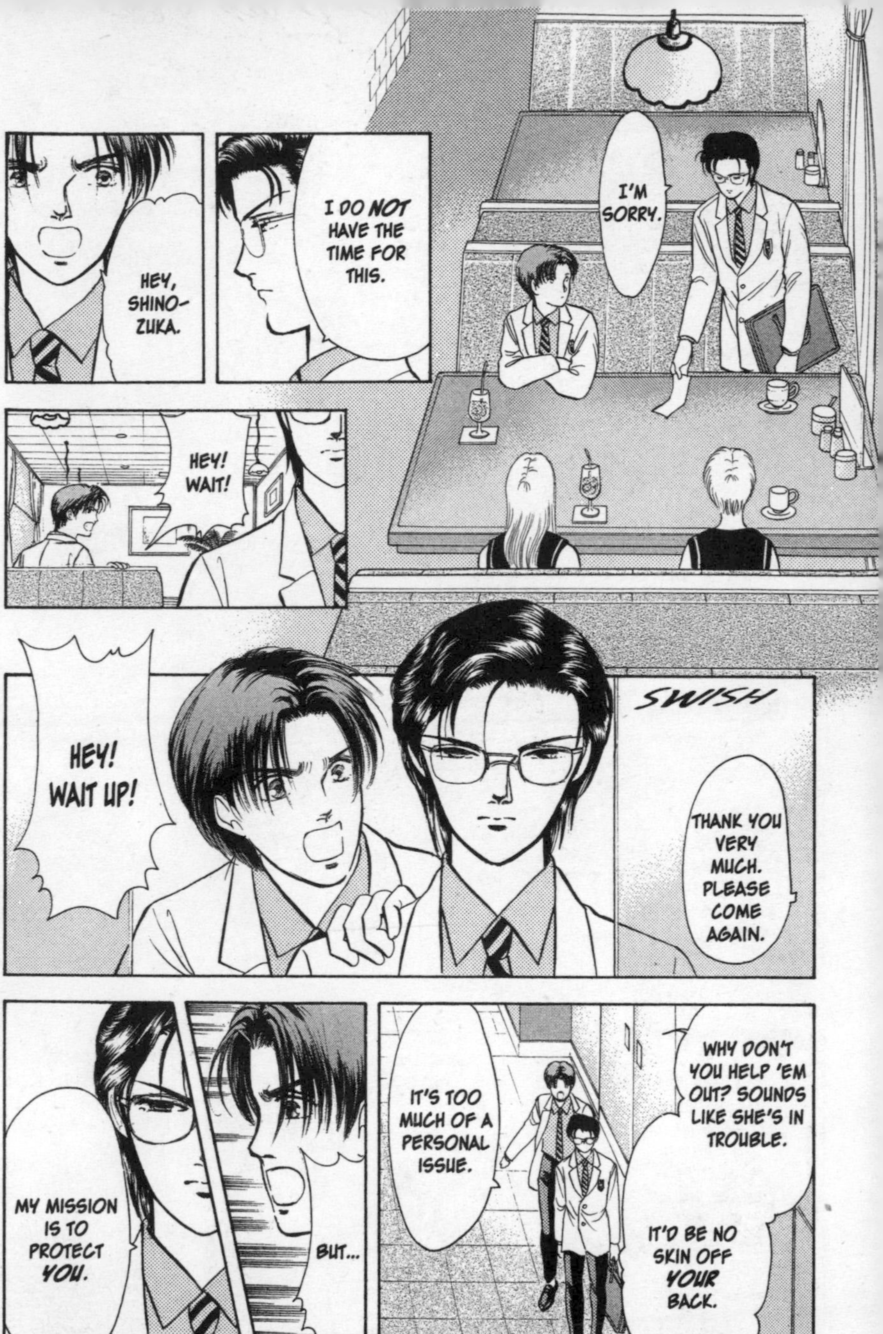
I'M SORRY.
I DO NOT HAVE THE TIME FOR THIS.
HEY, SHINOZUKA.
HEY! WAIT!
SWISH
THANK YOU VERY MUCH. PLEASE COME AGAIN.
HEY! WAIT UP!
WHY DON'T YOU HELP 'EM OUT? SOUNDS LIKE SHE'S IN TROUBLE.
IT'D BE NO SKIN OFF YOUR BACK.
IT'S TOO MUCH OF A PERSONAL ISSUE.
BUT...
MY MISSION IS TO PROTECT YOU.

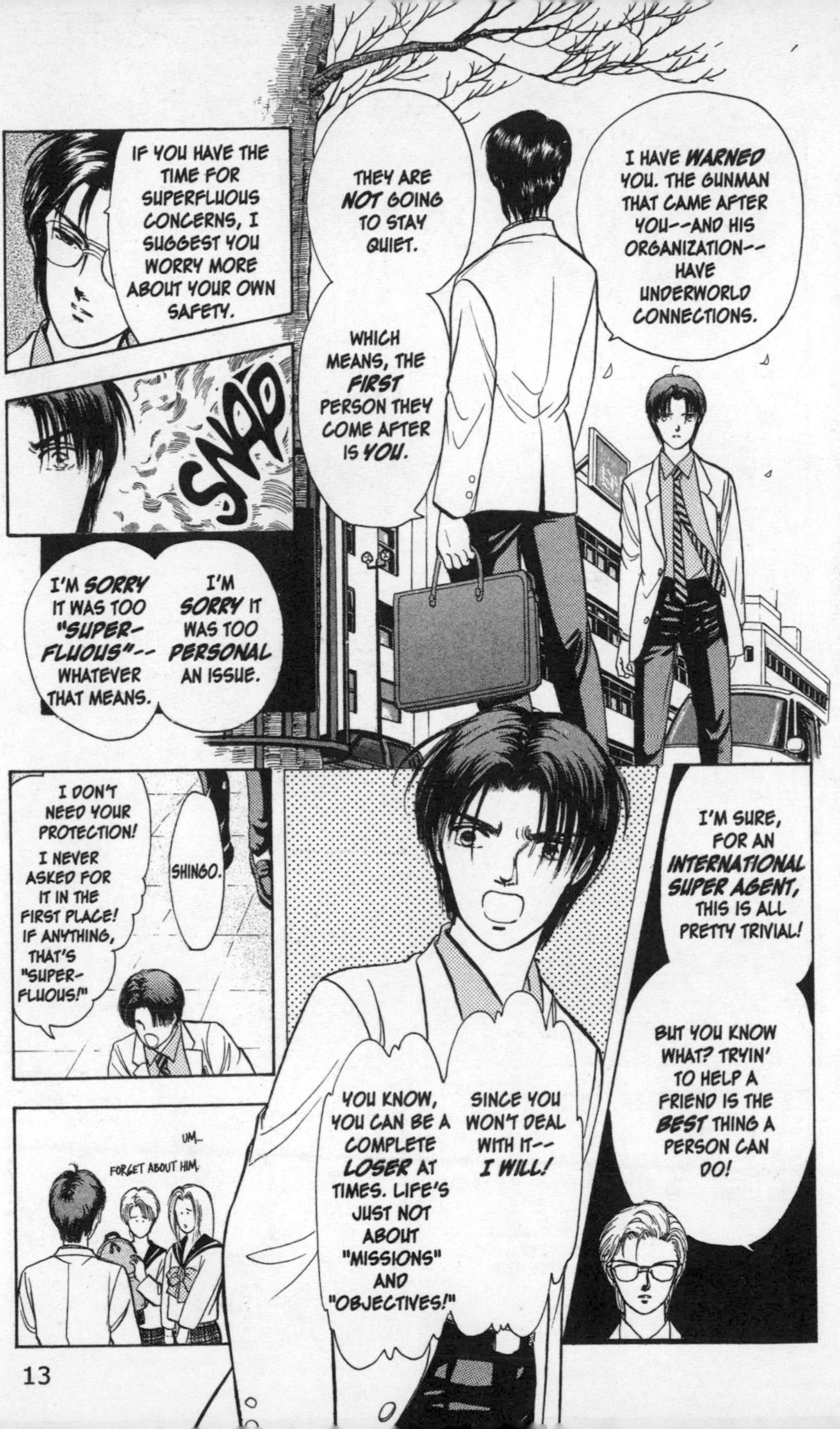
I HAVE WARNED YOU. THE GUNMAN THAT CAME AFTER YOU--AND HIS ORGANIZATION--HAVE UNDERWORLD CONNECTIONS.
THEY ARE NOT GOING TO STAY QUIET.
WHICH MEANS, THE FIRST PERSON THEY COME AFTER IS YOU.
IF YOU HAVE THE TIME FOR SUPERFLUOUS CONCERNS, I SUGGEST YOU WORRY MORE ABOUT YOUR OWN SAFETY.
SNAP
I'M SORRY IT WAS TOO PERSONAL AN ISSUE.
I'M SORRY IT WAS TOO "SUPERFLUOUS"--WHATEVER THAT MEANS.
I'M SURE, FOR AN INTERNATIONAL SUPER AGENT, THIS IS ALL PRETTY TRIVIAL!
BUT YOU KNOW WHAT? TRYIN' TO HELP A FRIEND IS THE BEST THING A PERSON CAN DO!
SINCE YOU WON'T DEAL WITH IT-- I WILL!
YOU KNOW, YOU CAN BE A COMPLETE LOSER AT TIMES. LIFE'S JUST NOT ABOUT "MISSIONS" AND "OBJECTIVES!"
SHINGO.
I DON'T NEED YOUR PROTECTION! I NEVER ASKED FOR IT IN THE FIRST PLACE! IF ANYTHING, THAT'S "SUPERFLUOUS!"
UM...
FORGET ABOUT HIM.

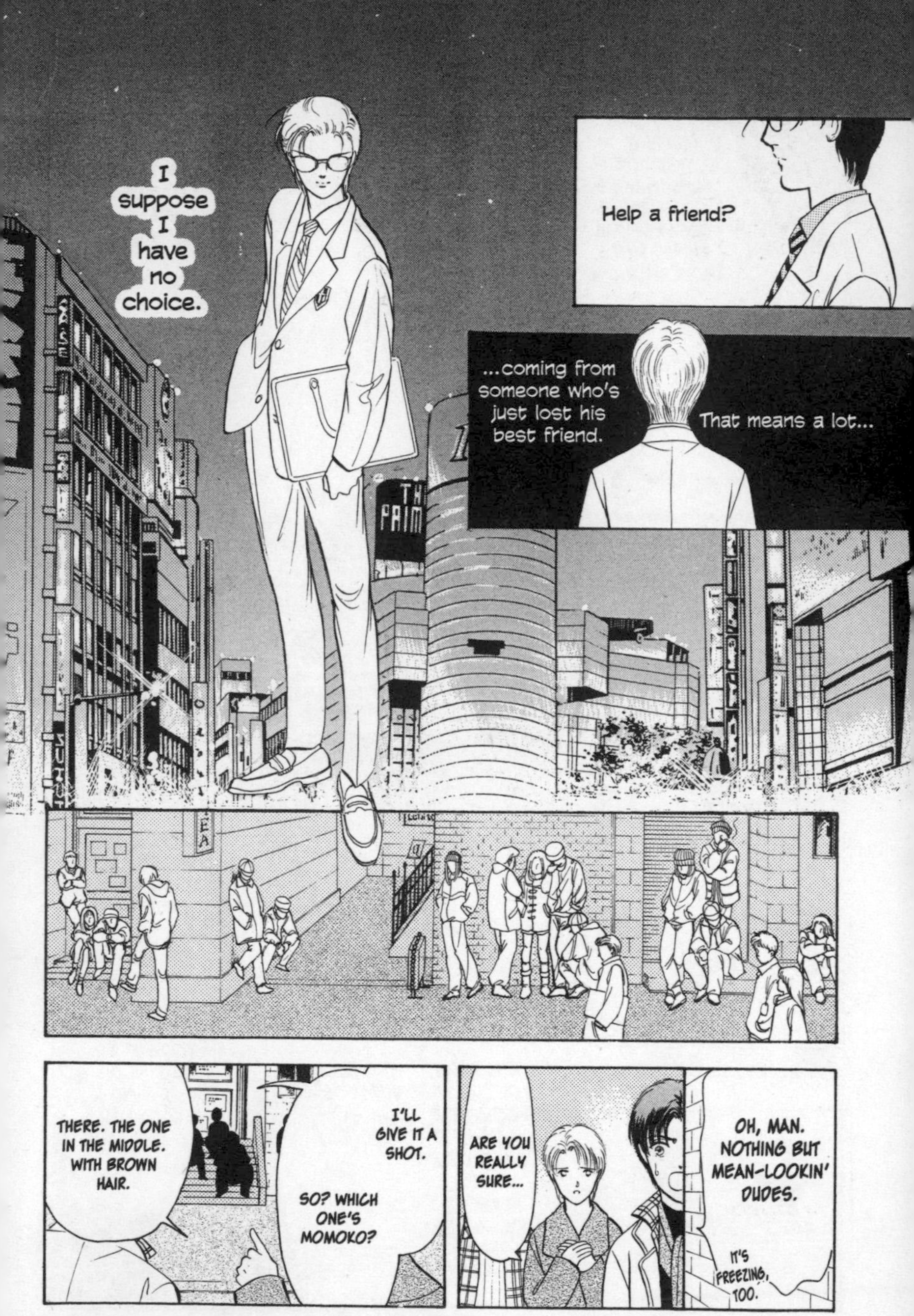
Help a friend?
That means a lot...
...coming from someone who's just lost his best friend.
I suppose I have no choice.
OH, MAN. NOTHING BUT MEAN-LOOKIN' DUDES.
IT'S FREEZING, TOO.
ARE YOU REALLY SURE...
I'LL GIVE IT A SHOT.
SO? WHICH ONE'S MOMOKO?
THERE. THE ONE IN THE MIDDLE. WITH BROWN HAIR.

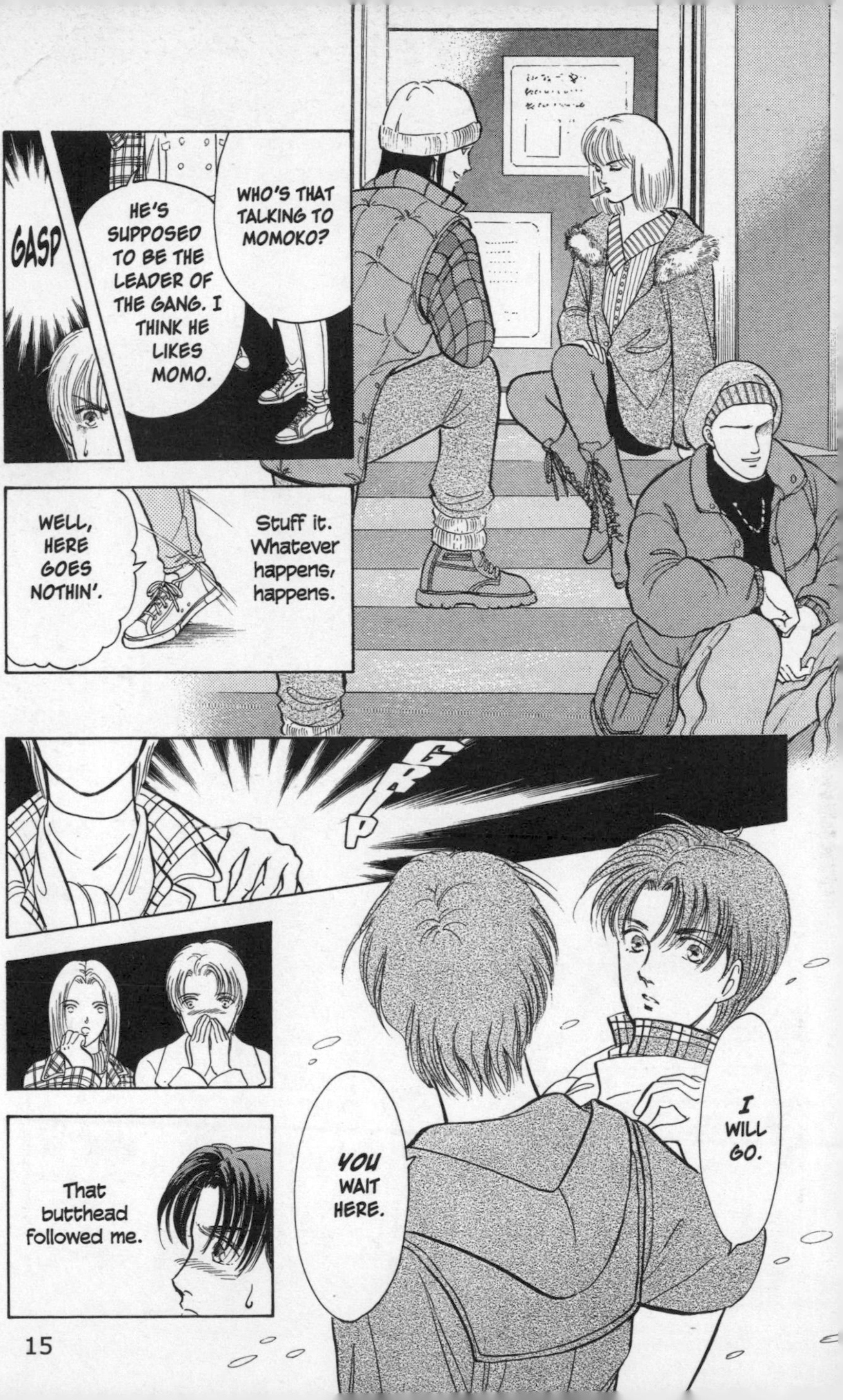
WHO'S THAT TALKING TO MOMOKO?
HE'S SUPPOSED TO BE THE LEADER OF THE GANG. I THINK HE LIKES MOMO.
GASP
Stuff it. Whatever happens, happens.
WELL, HERE GOES NOTHIN'.
GRIP
I WILL GO.
YOU WAIT HERE.
That butthead followed me.

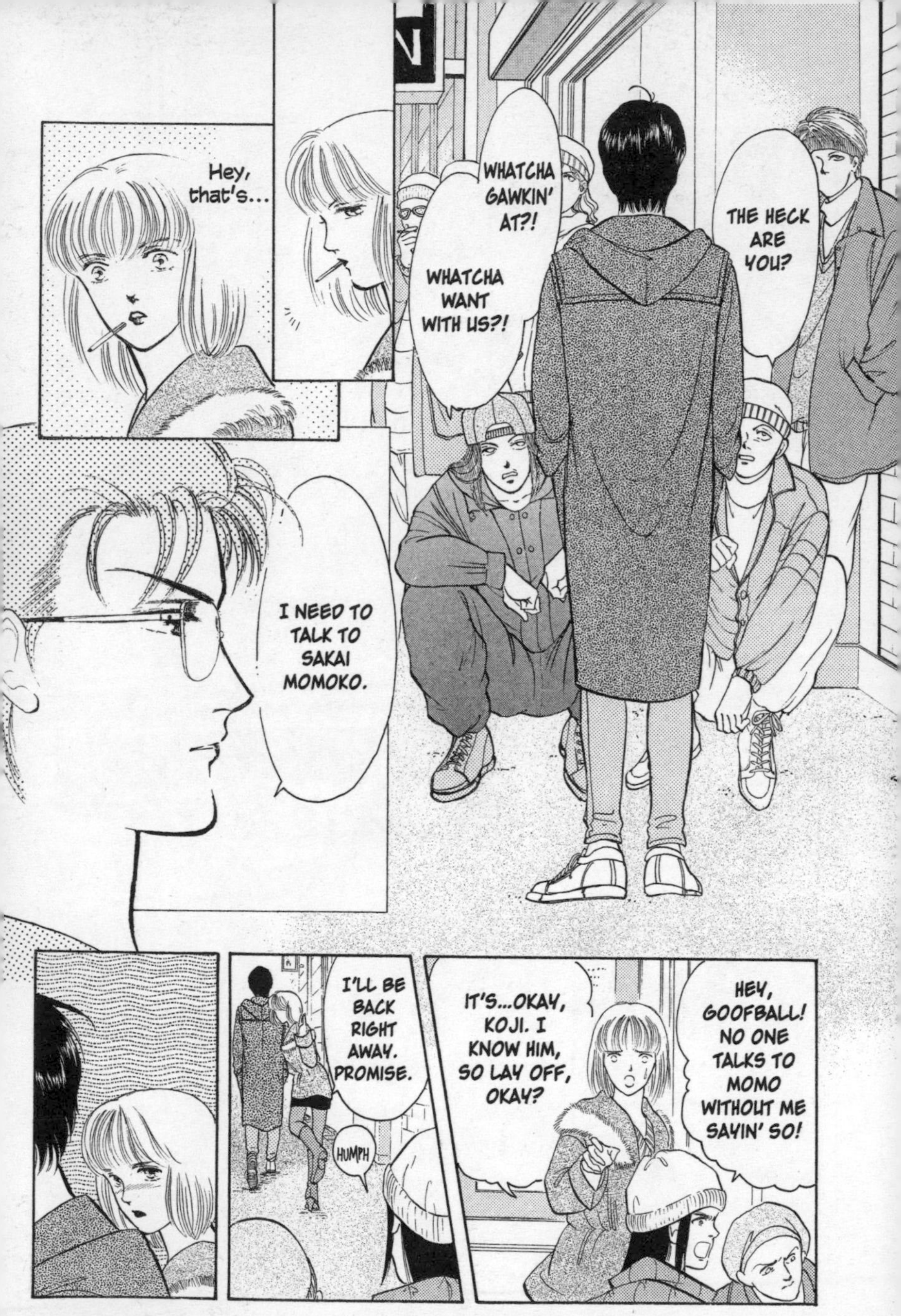
THE HECK ARE YOU?
WHATCHA GAWKIN' AT?!
WHATCHA WANT WITH US?!
Hey, that's...
I NEED TO TALK TO SAKAI MOMOKO.
HEY, GOOFBALL! NO ONE TALKS TO MOMO WITHOUT ME SAYIN' SO!
IT'S...OKAY, KOJI. I KNOW HIM, SO LAY OFF, OKAY?
I'LL BE BACK RIGHT AWAY. PROMISE.
HUMPH

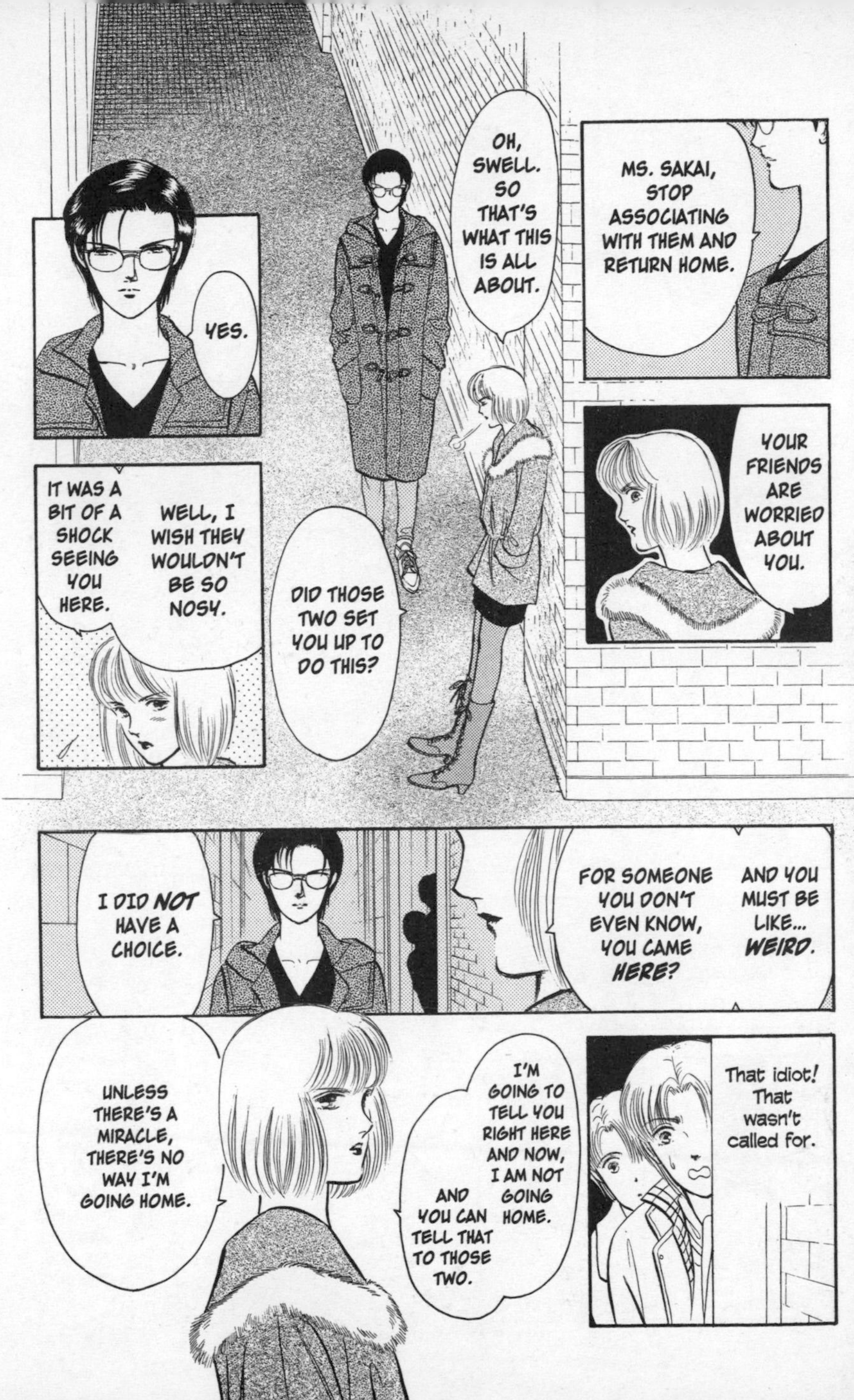
MS. SAKAI, STOP ASSOCIATING WITH THEM AND RETURN HOME.
YOUR FRIENDS ARE WORRIED ABOUT YOU.
OH, SWELL. SO THAT'S WHAT THIS IS ALL ABOUT.
DID THOSE TWO SET YOU UP TO DO THIS?
YES.
WELL, I WISH THEY WOULDN'T BE SO NOSY.
IT WAS A BIT OF A SHOCK SEEING YOU HERE.
AND YOU MUST BE LIKE... WEIRD.
FOR SOMEONE YOU DON'T EVEN KNOW, YOU CAME HERE?
I DID NOT HAVE A CHOICE.
That idiot! That wasn't called for.
I'M GOING TO TELL YOU RIGHT HERE AND NOW, I AM NOT GOING HOME.
AND YOU CAN TELL THAT TO THOSE TWO.
UNLESS THERE'S A MIRACLE, THERE'S NO WAY I'M GOING HOME.

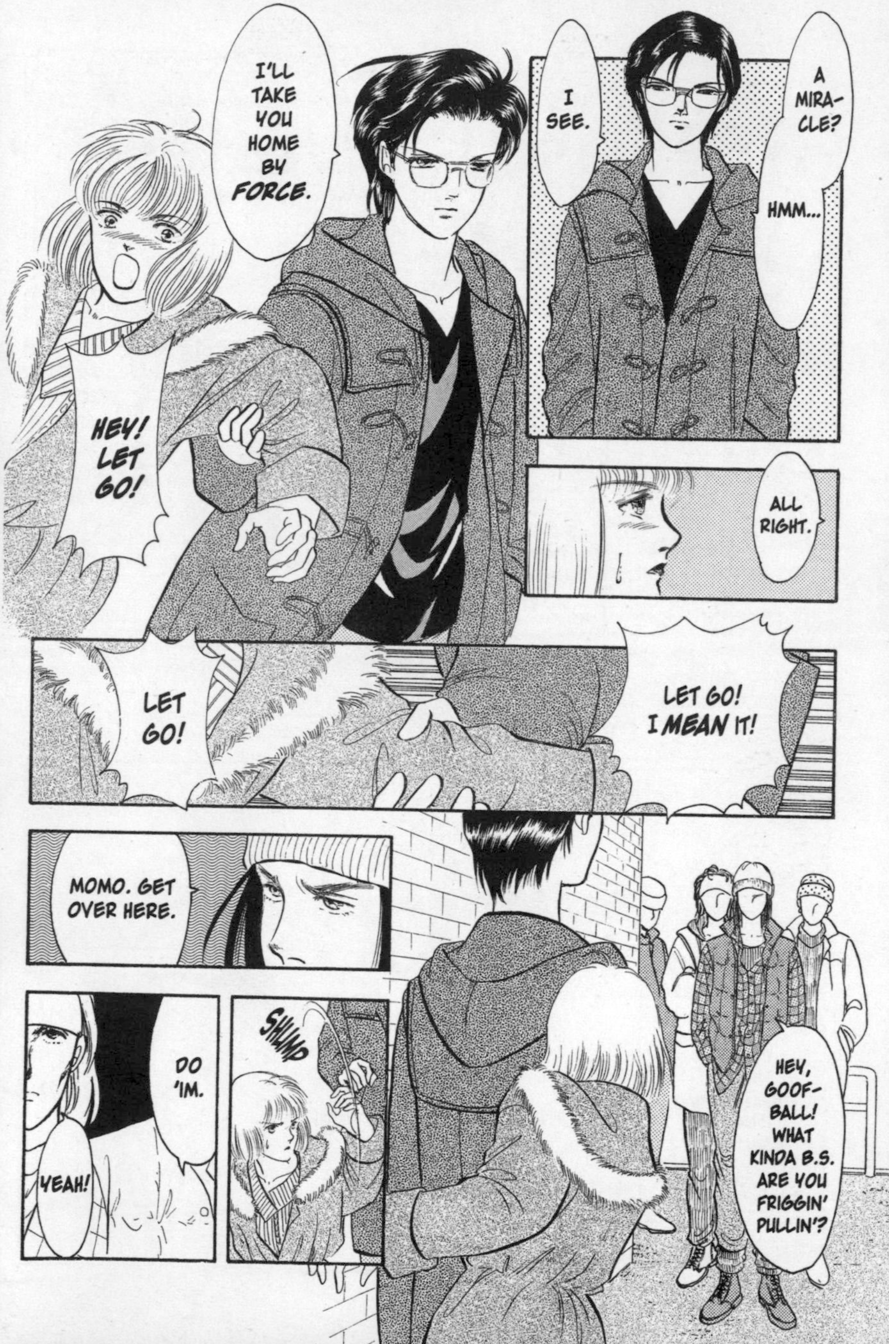
A MIRA-CLE?
HMM...
I SEE.
ALL RIGHT.
I'LL TAKE YOU HOME BY FORCE.
HEY! LET GO!
LET GO! I MEAN IT!
LET GO!
HEY, GOOF-BALL! WHAT KINDA B.S. ARE YOU FRIGGIN' PULLIN'?
MOMO. GET OVER HERE.
SHUMP
DO 'IM.
YEAH!

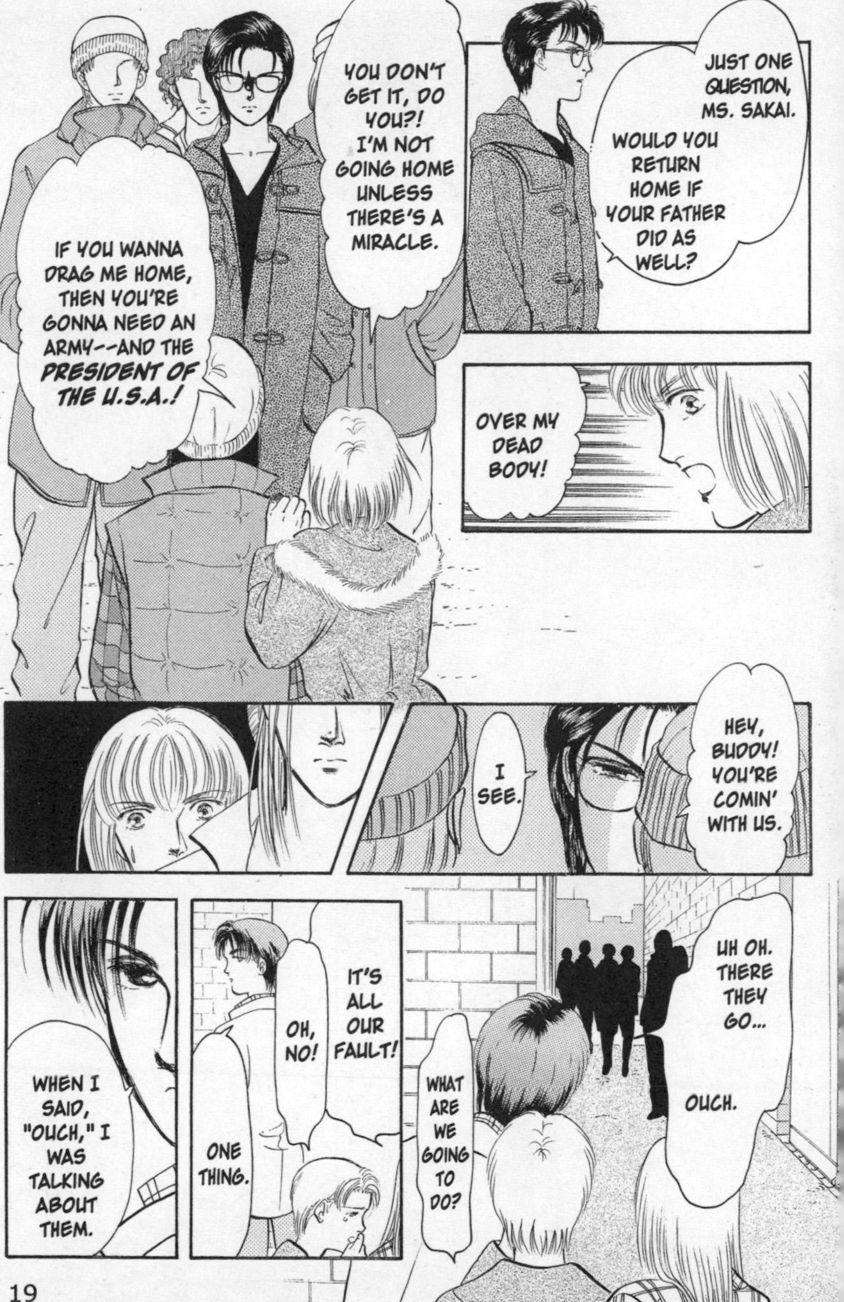
YOU DON'T GET IT, DO YOU?! I'M NOT GOING HOME UNLESS THERE'S A MIRACLE.
IF YOU WANNA DRAG ME HOME, THEN YOU'RE GONNA NEED AN ARMY--AND THE *PRESIDENT OF THE U.S.A.!*
JUST ONE QUESTION, MS. SAKAI.
WOULD YOU RETURN HOME IF YOUR FATHER DID AS WELL?
OVER MY DEAD BODY!
HEY, BUDDY! YOU'RE COMIN' WITH US.
I SEE.
UH OH. THERE THEY GO...
OUCH.
WHAT ARE WE GOING TO DO?
IT'S ALL OUR FAULT!
OH, NO!
ONE THING.
WHEN I SAID, "OUCH," I WAS TALKING ABOUT THEM.

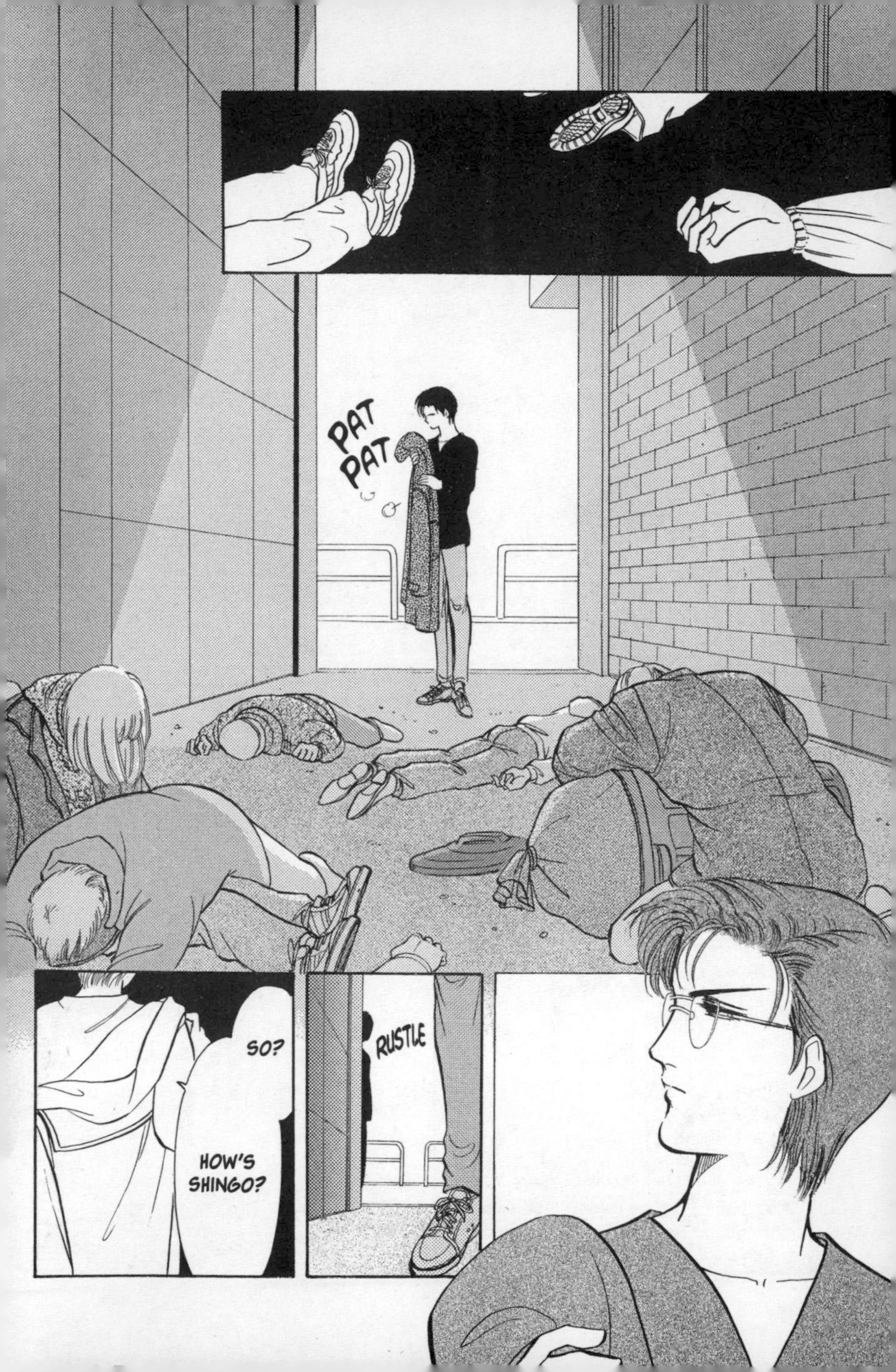
PAT PAT
RUSTLE
SO?
HOW'S SHINGO?

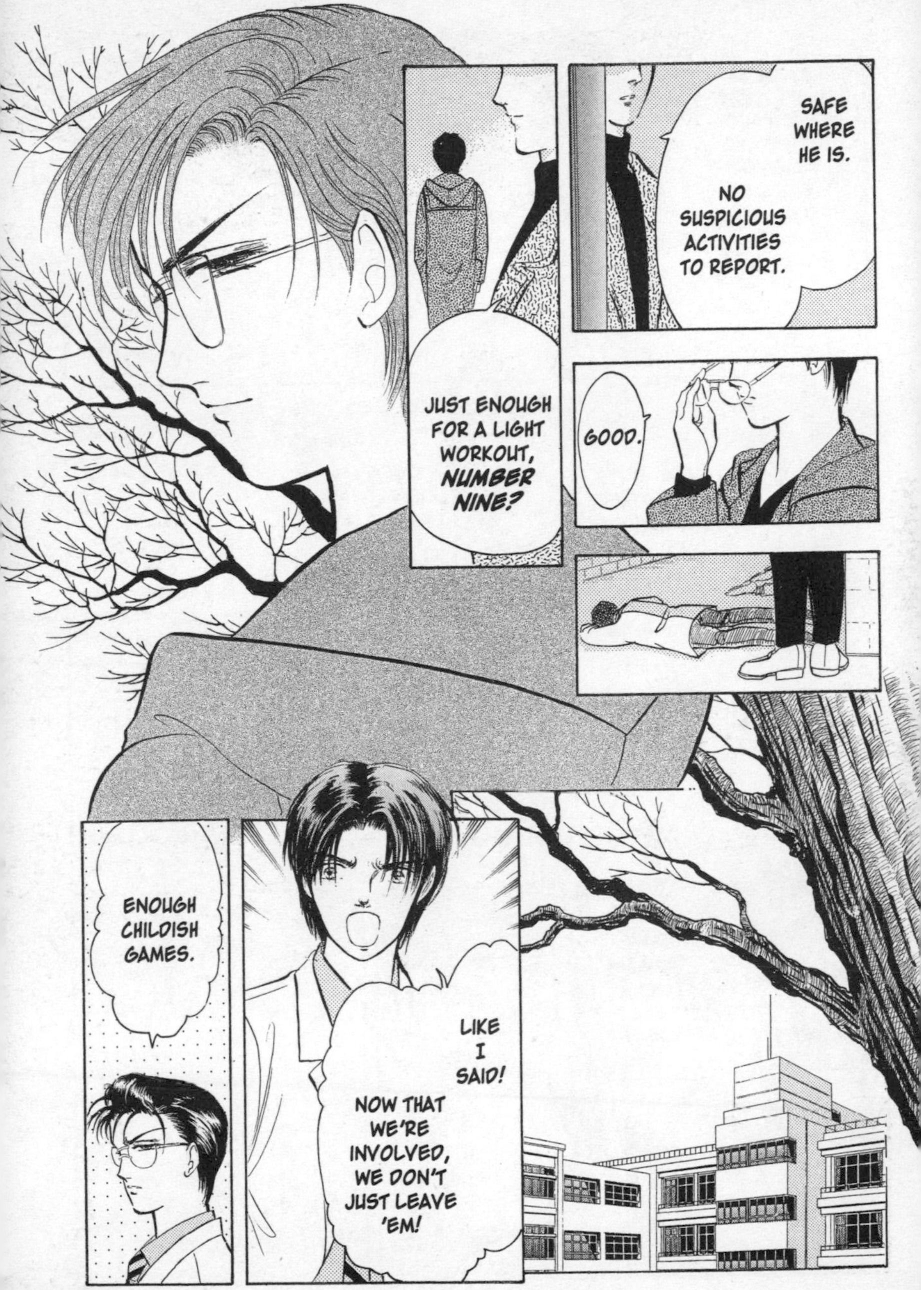
SAFE WHERE HE IS.
NO SUSPICIOUS ACTIVITIES TO REPORT.
JUST ENOUGH FOR A LIGHT WORKOUT, NUMBER NINE?
GOOD.
LIKE I SAID!
NOW THAT WE'RE INVOLVED, WE DON'T JUST LEAVE 'EM!
ENOUGH CHILDISH GAMES.

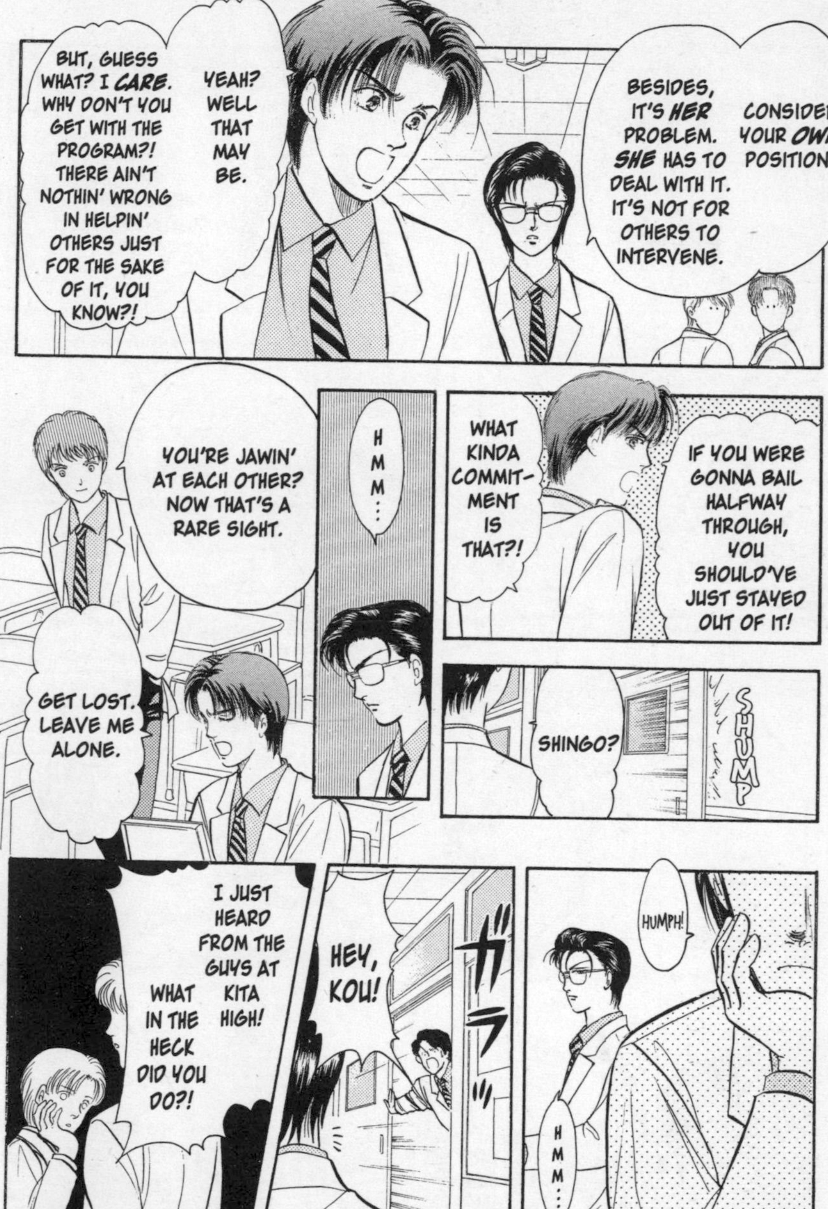
CONSIDER YOUR OWN POSITION.
BESIDES, IT'S HER PROBLEM. SHE HAS TO DEAL WITH IT. IT'S NOT FOR OTHERS TO INTERVENE.
YEAH? WELL THAT MAY BE.
BUT, GUESS WHAT? I CARE. WHY DON'T YOU GET WITH THE PROGRAM?! THERE AIN'T NOTHIN' WRONG IN HELPIN' OTHERS JUST FOR THE SAKE OF IT, YOU KNOW?!
IF YOU WERE GONNA BAIL HALFWAY THROUGH, YOU SHOULD'VE JUST STAYED OUT OF IT!
WHAT KINDA COMMITMENT IS THAT?!
SHUMP
SHINGO?
HMM...
YOU'RE JAWIN' AT EACH OTHER? NOW THAT'S A RARE SIGHT.
GET LOST. LEAVE ME ALONE.
HUMPH!
HMM...
ガラ
HEY, KOU!
I JUST HEARD FROM THE GUYS AT KITA HIGH!
WHAT IN THE HECK DID YOU DO?!

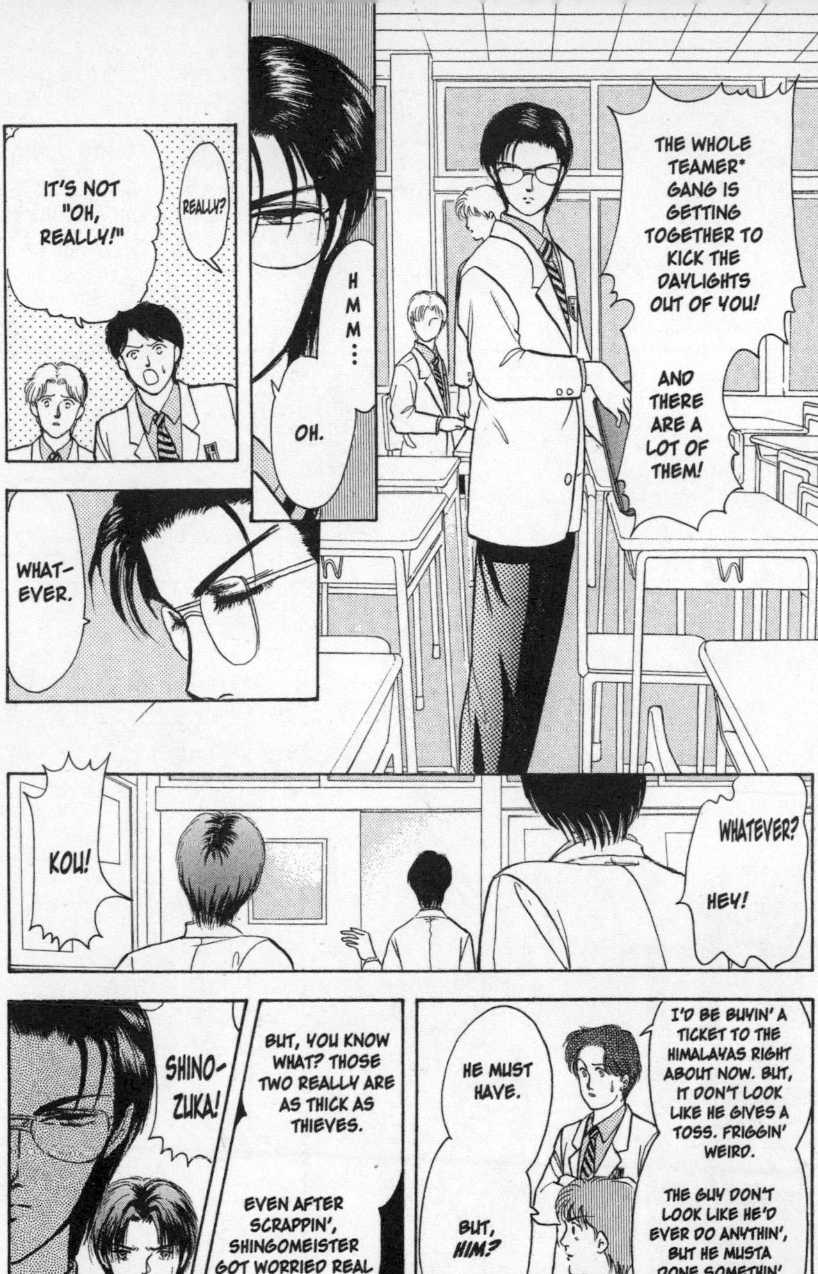
THE WHOLE TEAMER* GANG IS GETTING TOGETHER TO KICK THE DAYLIGHTS OUT OF YOU!
AND THERE ARE A LOT OF THEM!
HMM...
OH.
REALLY?
IT'S NOT "OH, REALLY!"
WHAT-EVER.
WHATEVER?
HEY!
KOU!
I'D BE BUYIN' A TICKET TO THE HIMALAYAS RIGHT ABOUT NOW. BUT, IT DON'T LOOK LIKE HE GIVES A TOSS. FRIGGIN' WEIRD.
HE MUST HAVE.
THE GUY DON'T LOOK LIKE HE'D EVER DO ANYTHIN', BUT HE MUSTA DONE SOMETHIN' TO REALLY CHEESE THEM OFF.
BUT, *HIM?*
BUT, YOU KNOW WHAT? THOSE TWO REALLY ARE AS THICK AS THIEVES.
EVEN AFTER SCRAPPIN', SHINGOMEISTER GOT WORRIED REAL QUICK.
SHINO-ZUKA!

*Teamer: Japanese street gang member.

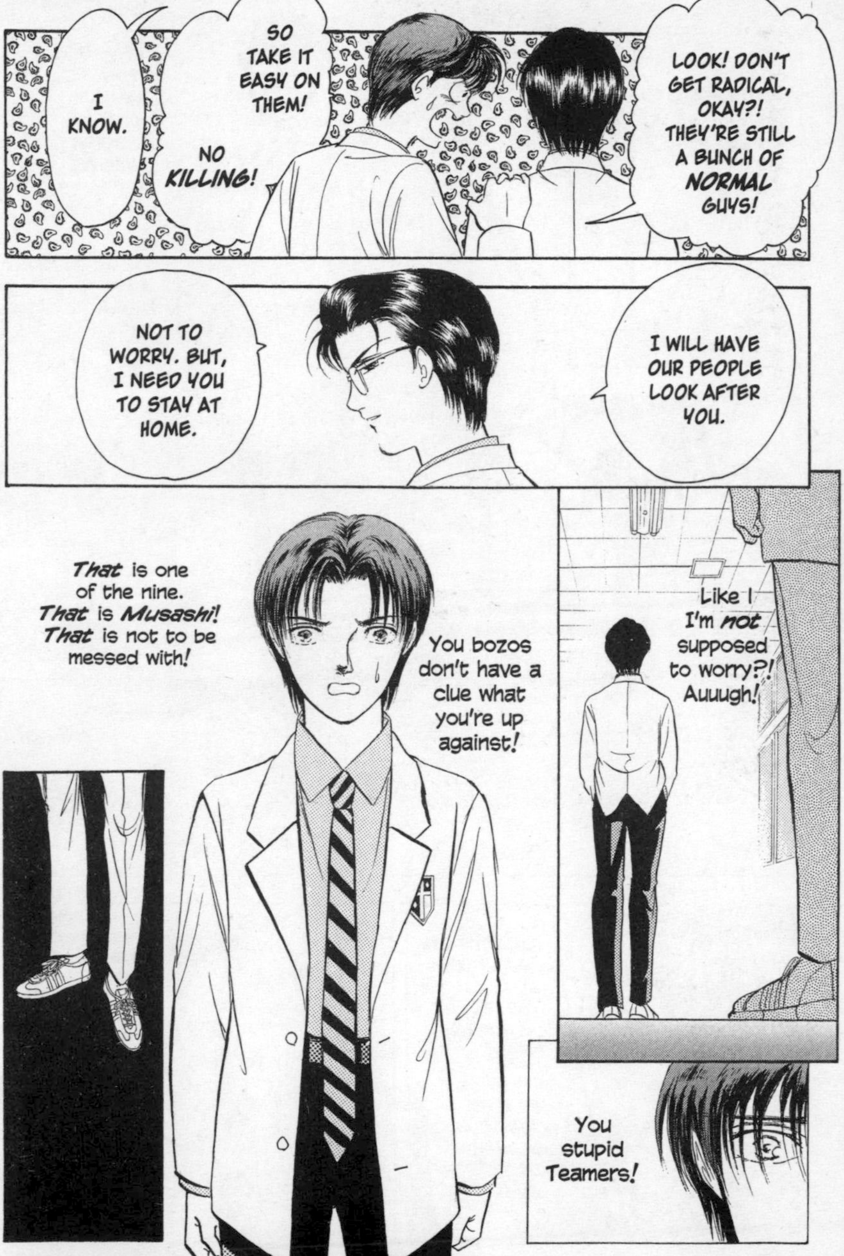
LOOK! DON'T GET RADICAL, OKAY?! THEY'RE STILL A BUNCH OF **NORMAL** GUYS!
SO TAKE IT EASY ON THEM!
NO **KILLING!**
I KNOW.
I WILL HAVE OUR PEOPLE LOOK AFTER YOU.
NOT TO WORRY. BUT, I NEED YOU TO STAY AT HOME.
Like I'm ***not*** supposed to worry?! Auuugh!
You stupid Teamers!
You bozos don't have a clue what you're up against!
That is one of the nine. ***That*** is ***Musashi!*** ***That*** is not to be messed with!

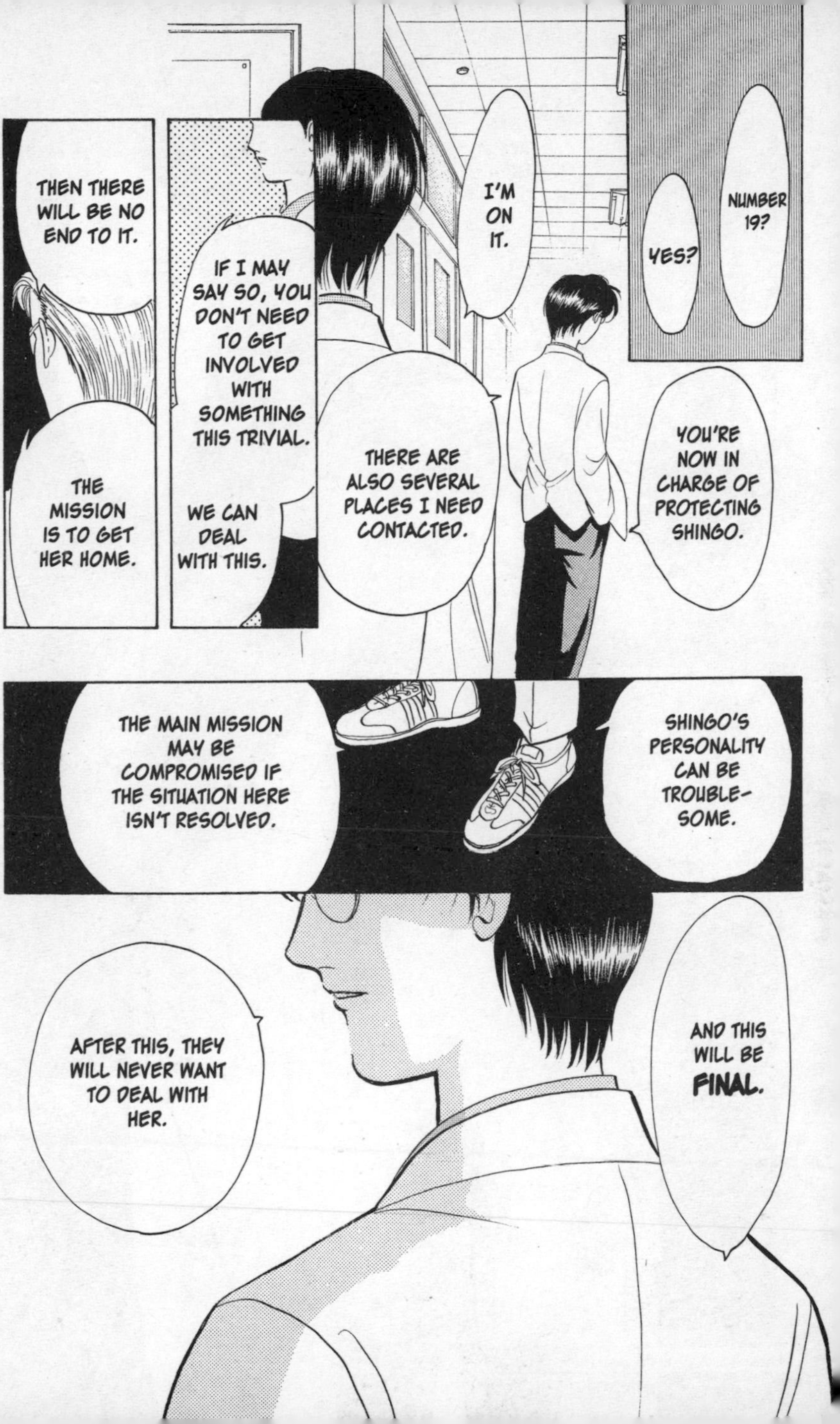
NUMBER 19?
YES?
I'M ON IT.
YOU'RE NOW IN CHARGE OF PROTECTING SHINGO.
THERE ARE ALSO SEVERAL PLACES I NEED CONTACTED.
IF I MAY SAY SO, YOU DON'T NEED TO GET INVOLVED WITH SOMETHING THIS TRIVIAL.
WE CAN DEAL WITH THIS.
THEN THERE WILL BE NO END TO IT.
THE MISSION IS TO GET HER HOME.
SHINGO'S PERSONALITY CAN BE TROUBLE-SOME.
THE MAIN MISSION MAY BE COMPROMISED IF THE SITUATION HERE ISN'T RESOLVED.
AND THIS WILL BE **FINAL.**
AFTER THIS, THEY WILL NEVER WANT TO DEAL WITH HER.

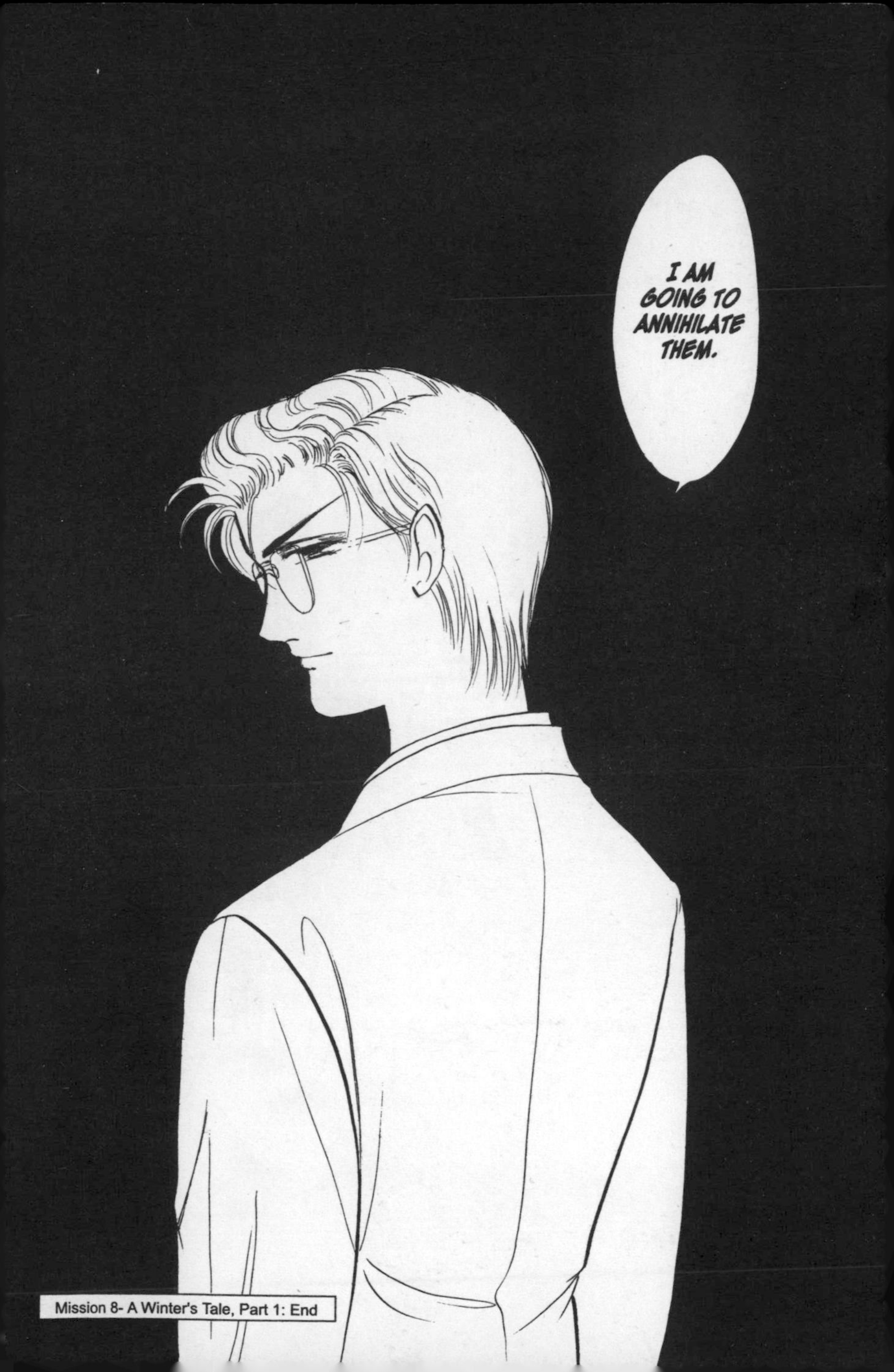
I AM GOING TO ANNIHILATE THEM.
Mission 8- A Winter's Tale, Part 1: End

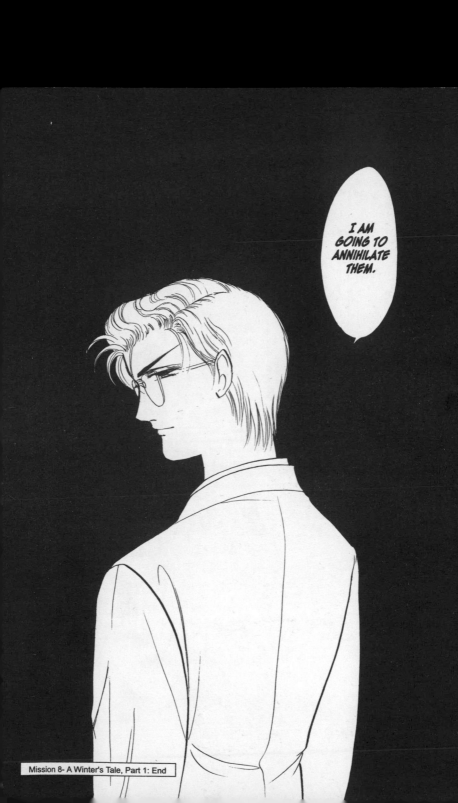

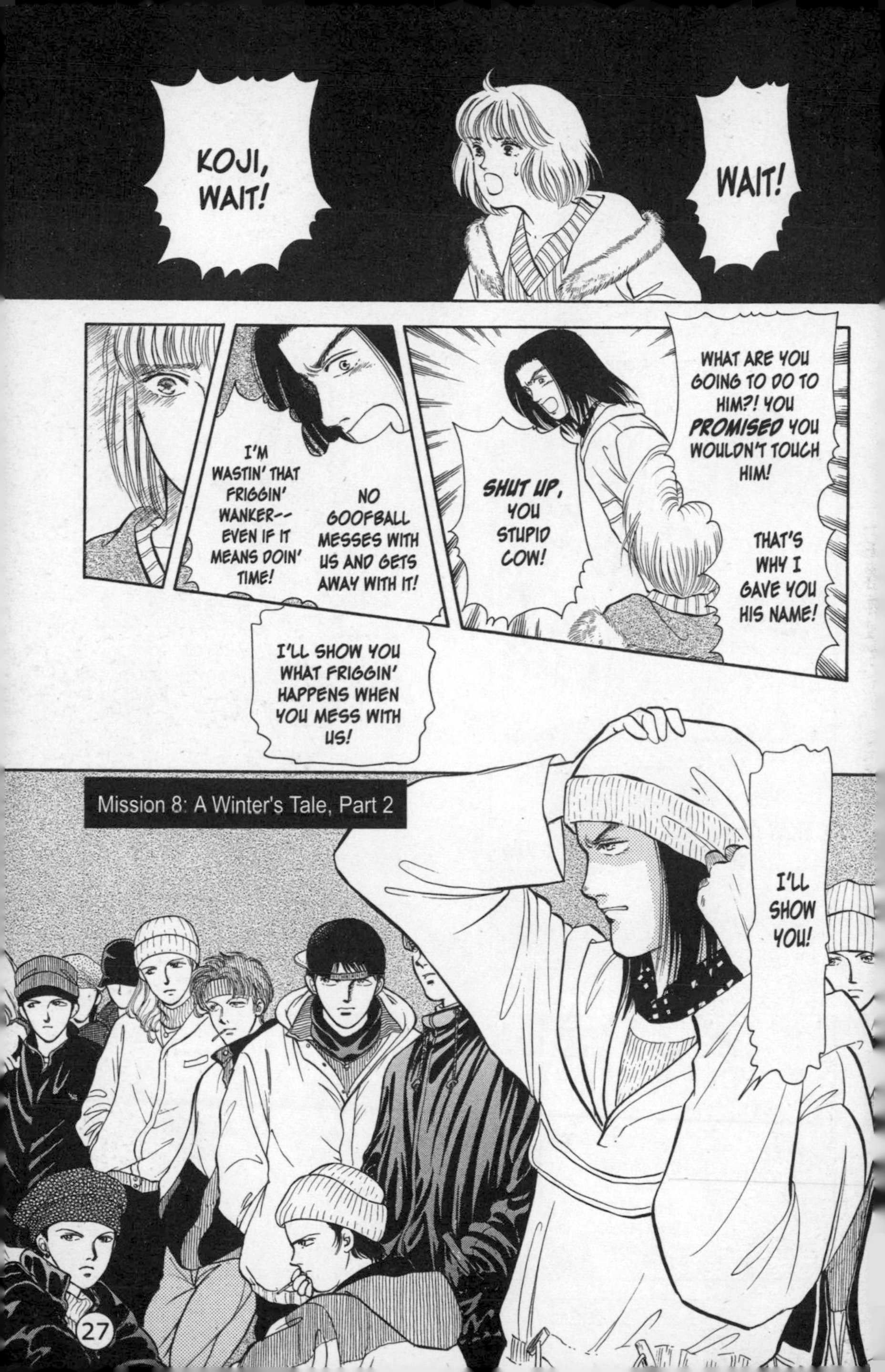
WAIT!
KOJI, WAIT!
WHAT ARE YOU GOING TO DO TO HIM?! YOU PROMISED YOU WOULDN'T TOUCH HIM!
THAT'S WHY I GAVE YOU HIS NAME!
SHUT UP, YOU STUPID COW!
NO GOOFBALL MESSES WITH US AND GETS AWAY WITH IT!
I'M WASTIN' THAT FRIGGIN' WANKER-- EVEN IF IT MEANS DOIN' TIME!
I'LL SHOW YOU WHAT FRIGGIN' HAPPENS WHEN YOU MESS WITH US!
I'LL SHOW YOU!
Mission 8: A Winter's Tale, Part 2

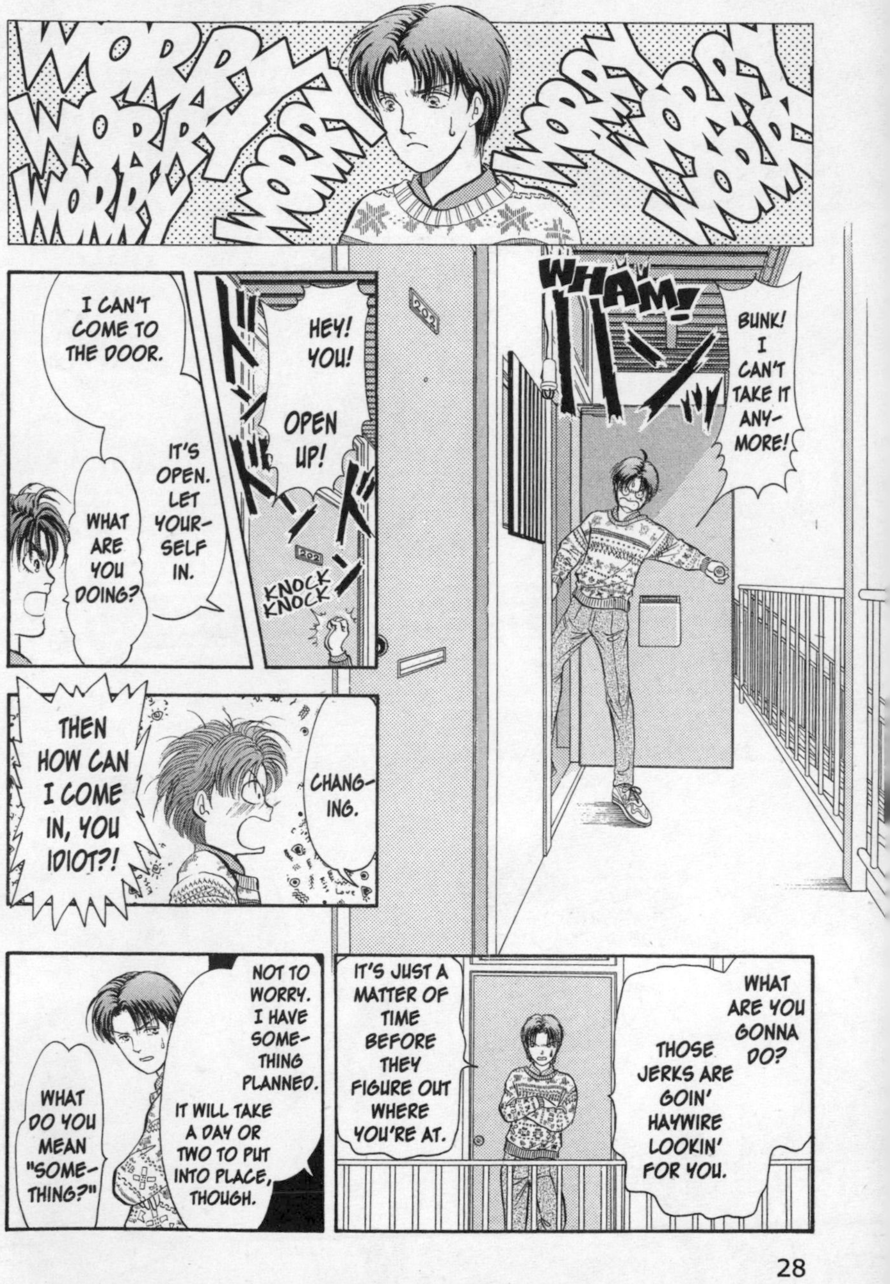
WORRY WORRY WORRY WORRY WORRY WORRY WORRY
WHAM!
BUNK! I CAN'T TAKE IT ANYMORE!
HEY! YOU!
OPEN UP!
KNOCK KNOCK
IT'S OPEN. LET YOURSELF IN.
I CAN'T COME TO THE DOOR.
WHAT ARE YOU DOING?
CHANGING.
THEN HOW CAN I COME IN, YOU IDIOT?!
WHAT ARE YOU GONNA DO?
THOSE JERKS ARE GOIN' HAYWIRE LOOKIN' FOR YOU.
IT'S JUST A MATTER OF TIME BEFORE THEY FIGURE OUT WHERE YOU'RE AT.
NOT TO WORRY. I HAVE SOMETHING PLANNED.
IT WILL TAKE A DAY OR TWO TO PUT INTO PLACE, THOUGH.
WHAT DO YOU MEAN "SOMETHING?"

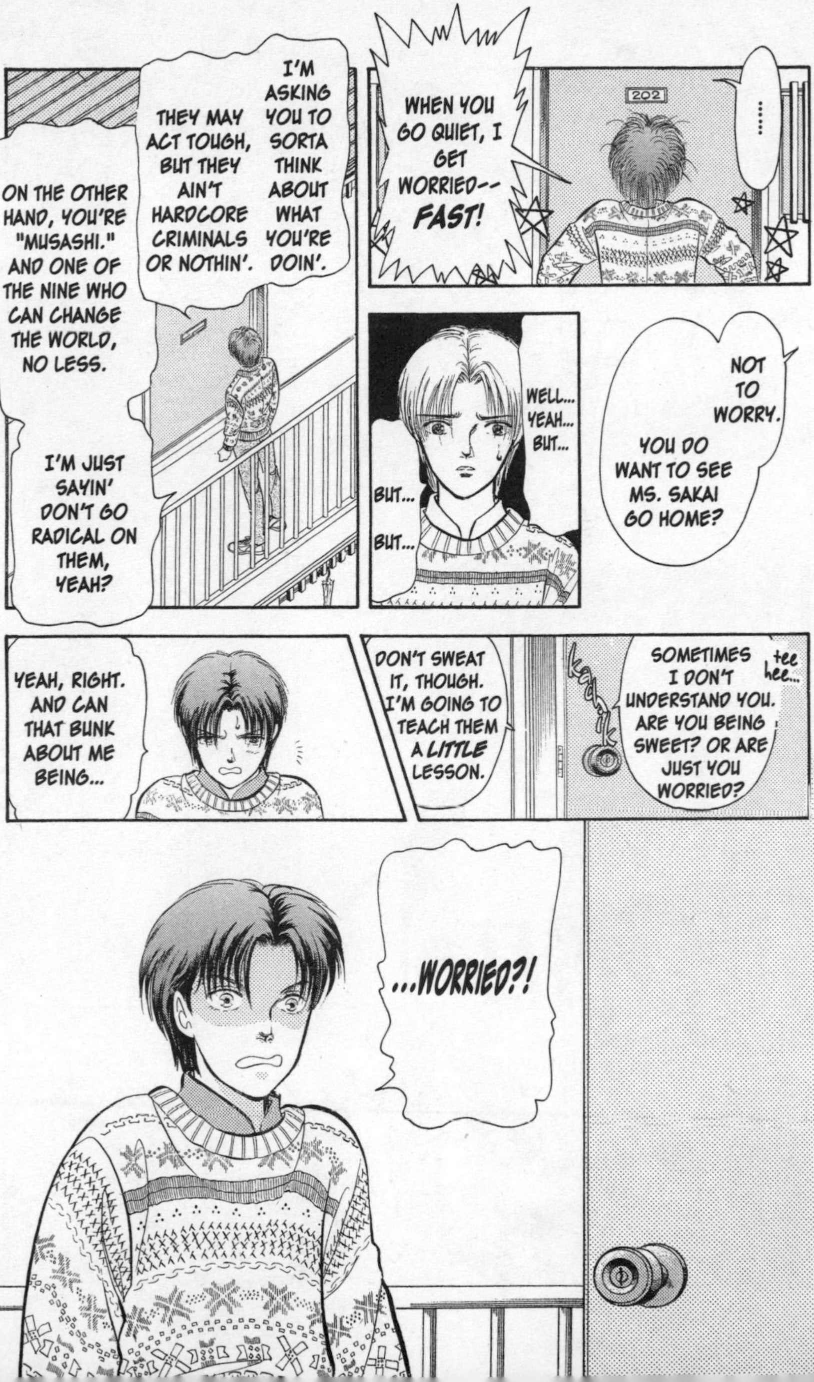
......
WHEN YOU GO QUIET, I GET WORRIED--*FAST!*
NOT TO WORRY.
YOU DO WANT TO SEE MS. SAKAI GO HOME?
WELL... YEAH... BUT...
BUT...
BUT...
I'M ASKING YOU TO SORTA THINK ABOUT WHAT YOU'RE DOIN'.
THEY MAY ACT TOUGH, BUT THEY AIN'T HARDCORE CRIMINALS OR NOTHIN'.
ON THE OTHER HAND, YOU'RE "MUSASHI." AND ONE OF THE NINE WHO CAN CHANGE THE WORLD, NO LESS.
I'M JUST SAYIN' DON'T GO RADICAL ON THEM, YEAH?
tee hee...
SOMETIMES I DON'T UNDERSTAND YOU. ARE YOU BEING SWEET? OR ARE JUST YOU WORRIED?
DON'T SWEAT IT, THOUGH. I'M GOING TO TEACH THEM A *LITTLE* LESSON.
YEAH, RIGHT. AND CAN THAT BUNK ABOUT ME BEING...
...WORRIED?!

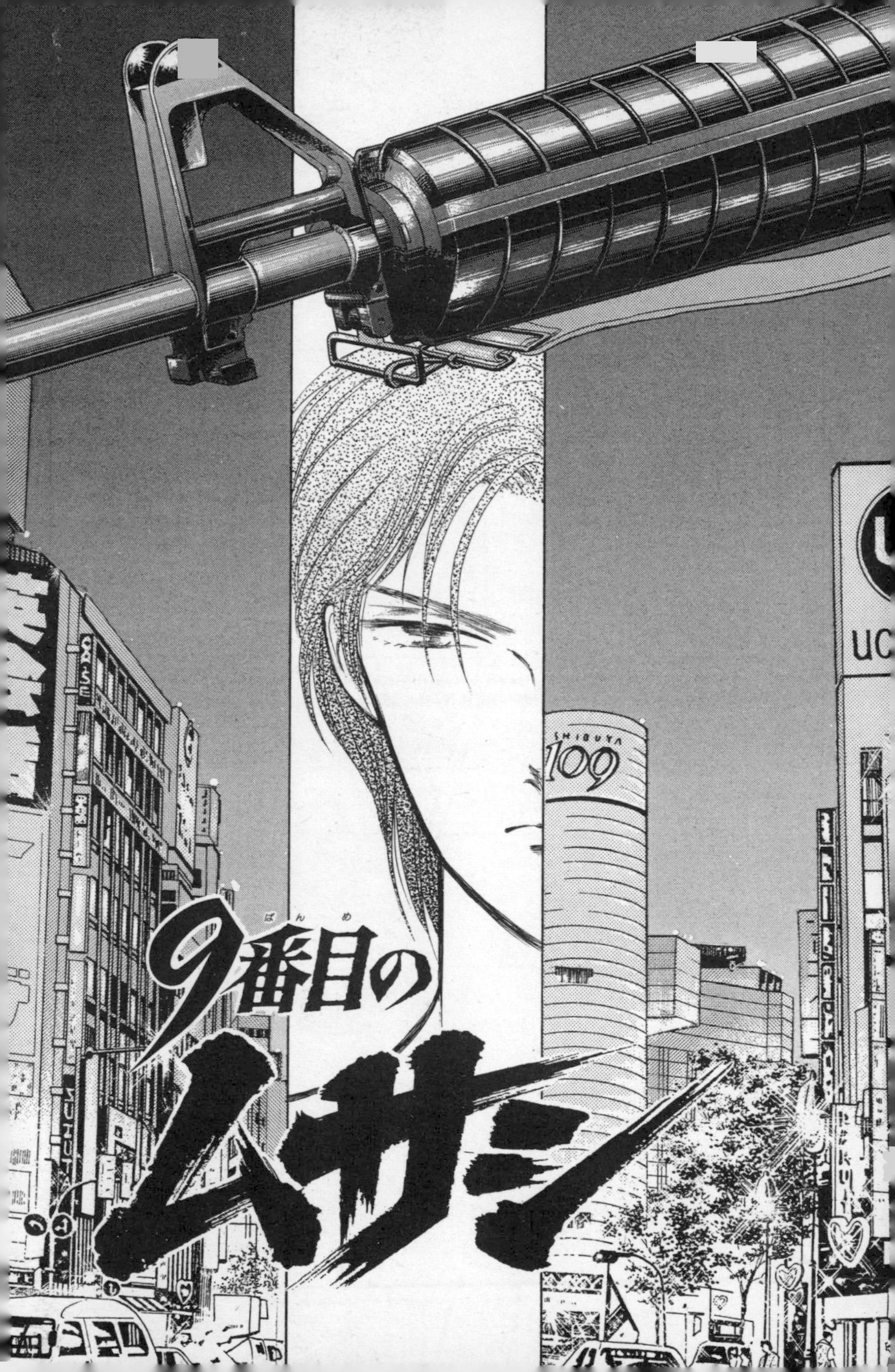
9番目のムサシ
ばんめ
SHIBUYA
109
UC

Mission 8: A Winter's Tale, Part 2

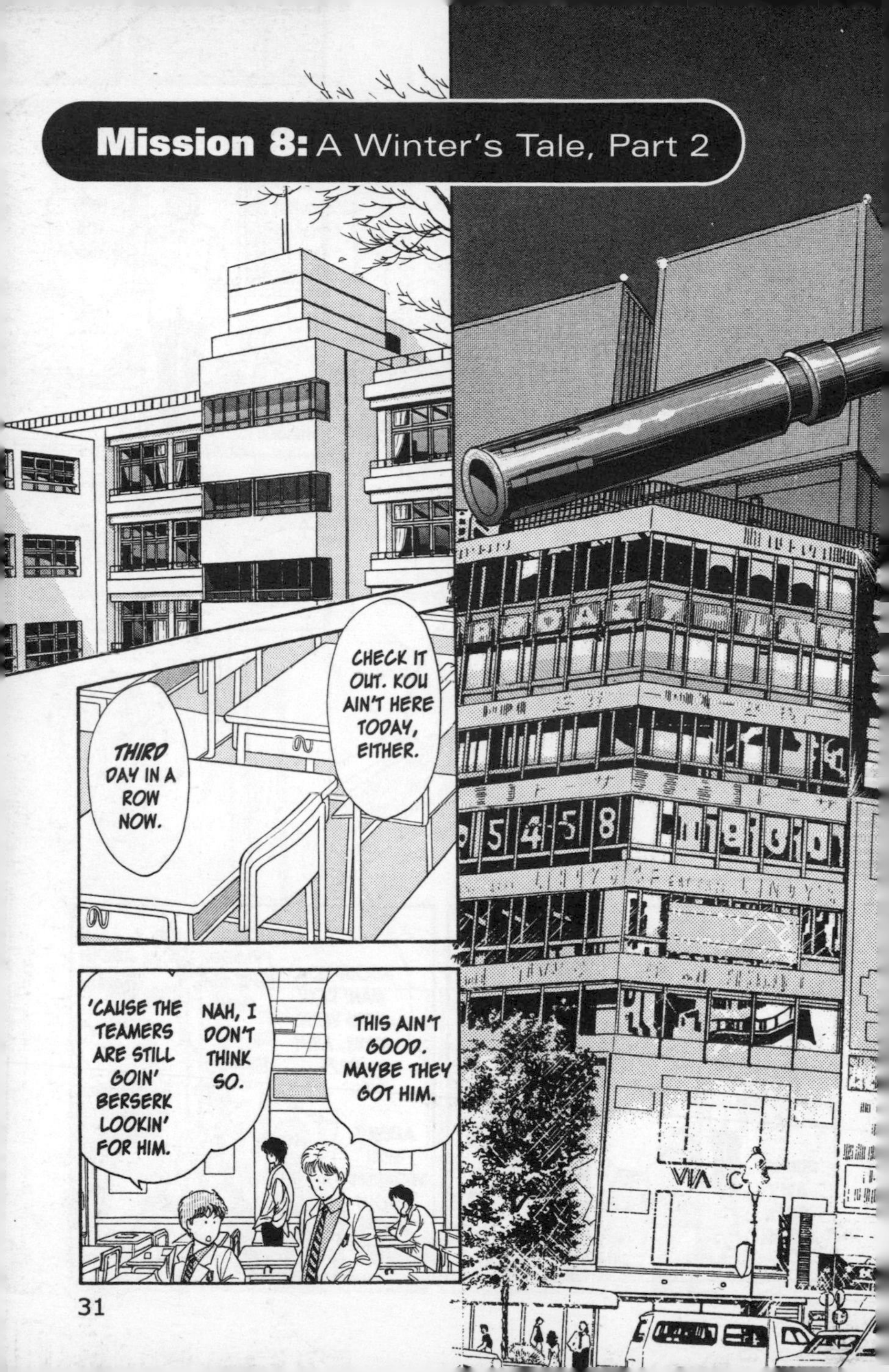
CHECK IT OUT. KOU AIN'T HERE TODAY, EITHER.
THIRD DAY IN A ROW NOW.
THIS AIN'T GOOD. MAYBE THEY GOT HIM.
NAH, I DON'T THINK SO.
'CAUSE THE TEAMERS ARE STILL GOIN' BERSERK LOOKIN' FOR HIM.

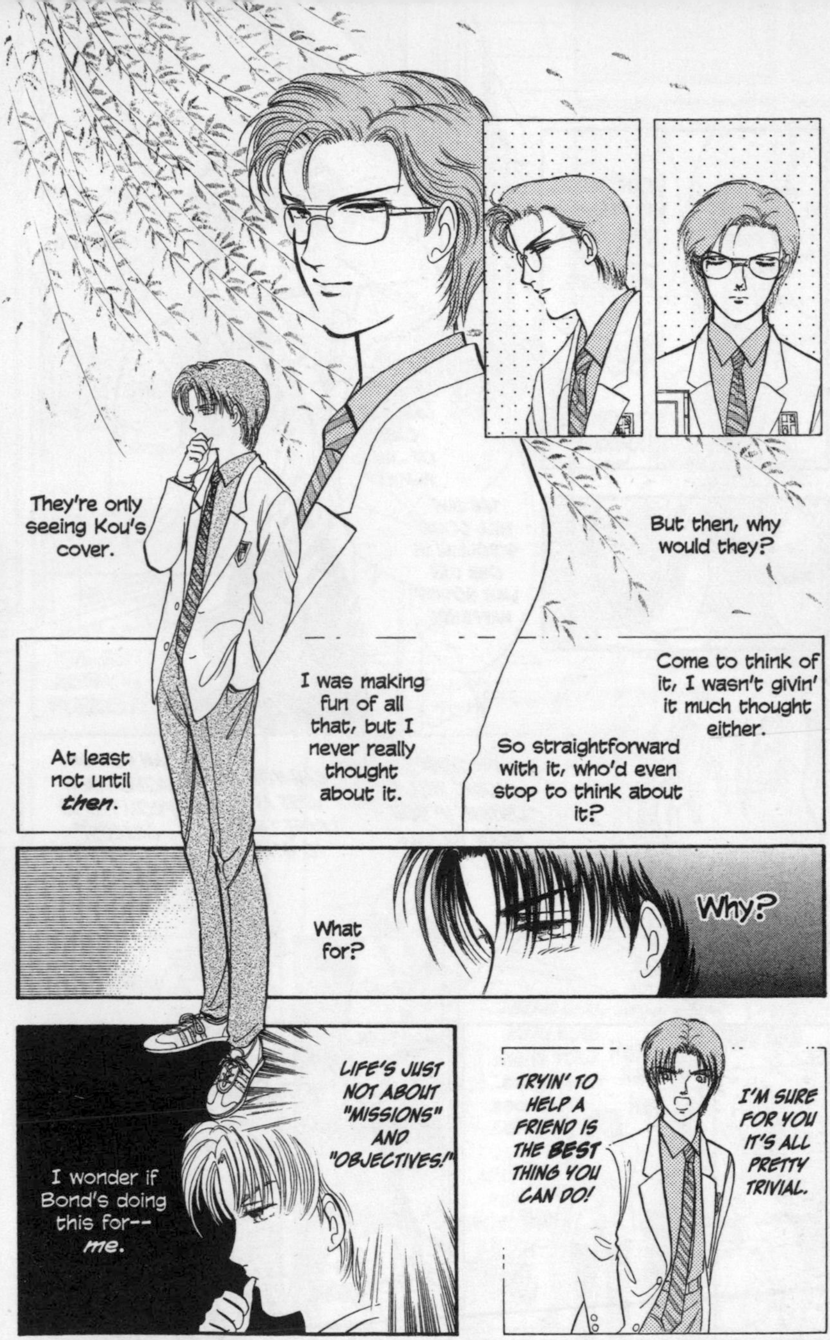
But then, why would they?
They're only seeing Kou's cover.
Come to think of it, I wasn't givin' it much thought either.
So straightforward with it, who'd even stop to think about it?
I was making fun of all that, but I never really thought about it.
At least not until *then*.
Why?
What for?
I'M SURE FOR YOU IT'S ALL PRETTY TRIVIAL.
TRYIN' TO HELP A FRIEND IS THE **BEST** THING YOU CAN DO!
LIFE'S JUST NOT ABOUT "MISSIONS" AND "OBJECTIVES!"
I wonder if Bond's doing this for-- *me*.

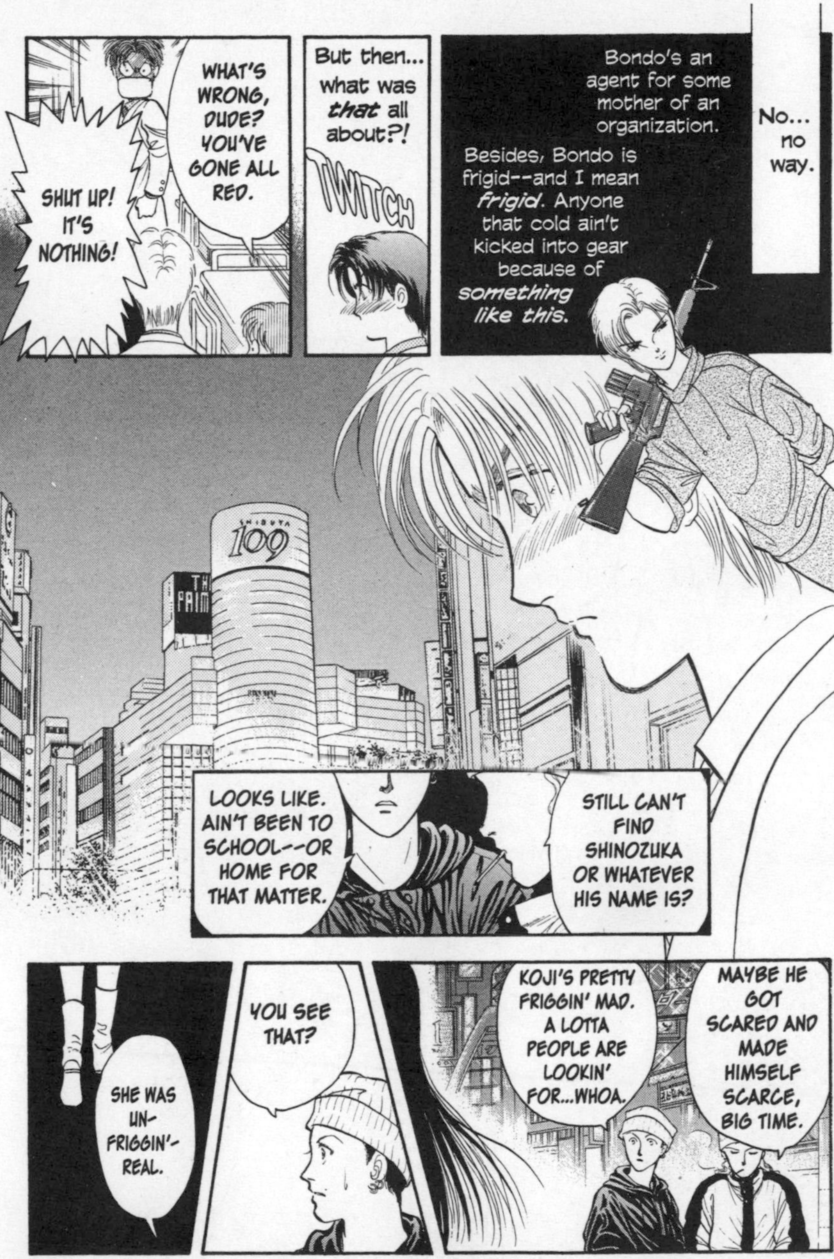
No... no way.
Bondo's an agent for some mother of an organization.
Besides, Bondo is frigid--and I mean *frigid*. Anyone that cold ain't kicked into gear because of *something like this*.
But then... what was *that* all about?!
TWITCH
WHAT'S WRONG, DUDE? YOU'VE GONE ALL RED.
SHUT UP! IT'S NOTHING!
STILL CAN'T FIND SHINOZUKA OR WHATEVER HIS NAME IS?
LOOKS LIKE. AIN'T BEEN TO SCHOOL--OR HOME FOR THAT MATTER.
MAYBE HE GOT SCARED AND MADE HIMSELF SCARCE, BIG TIME.
KOJI'S PRETTY FRIGGIN' MAD. A LOTTA PEOPLE ARE LOOKIN' FOR...WHOA.
YOU SEE THAT?
SHE WAS UN-FRIGGIN'-REAL.

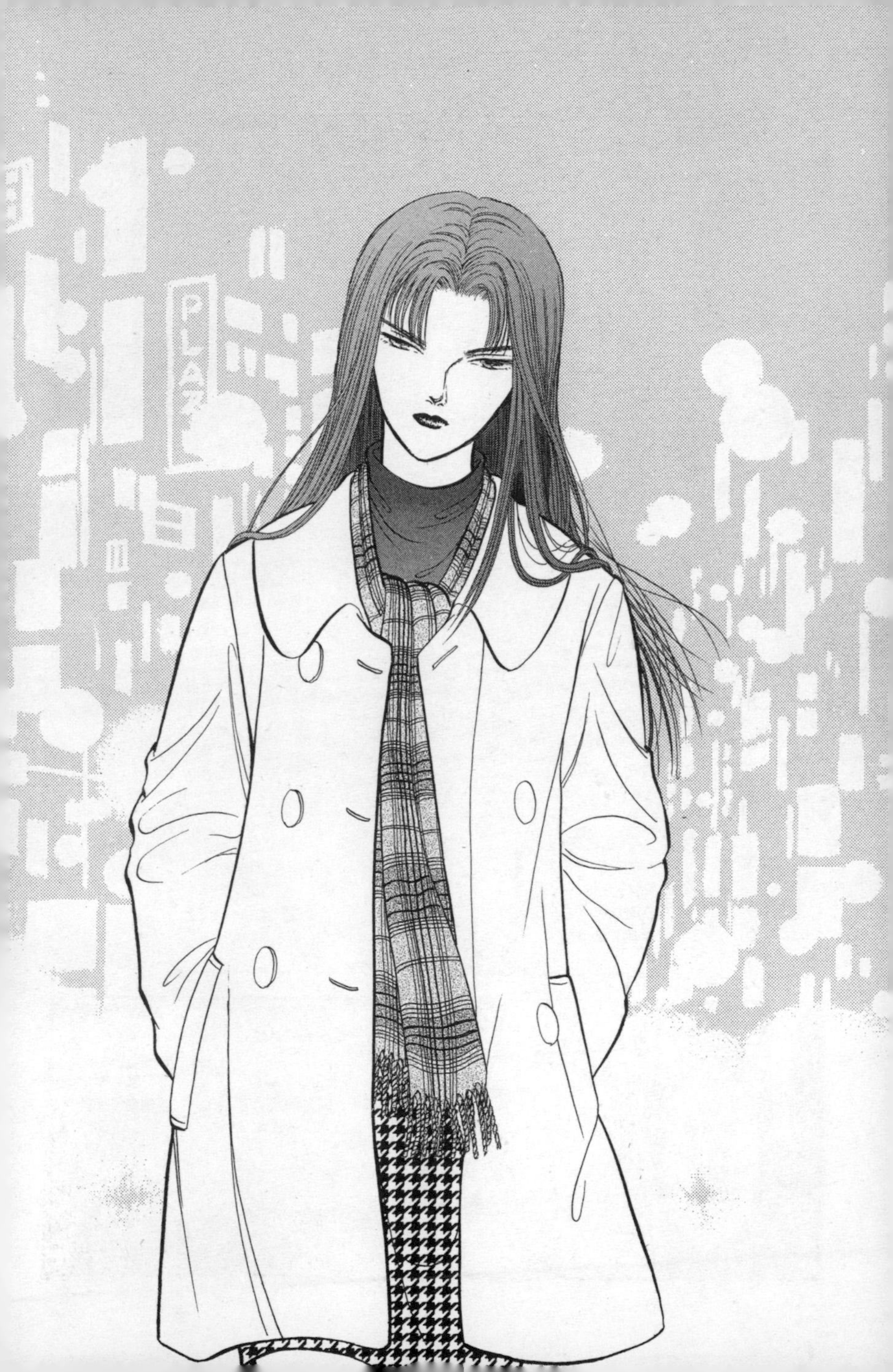

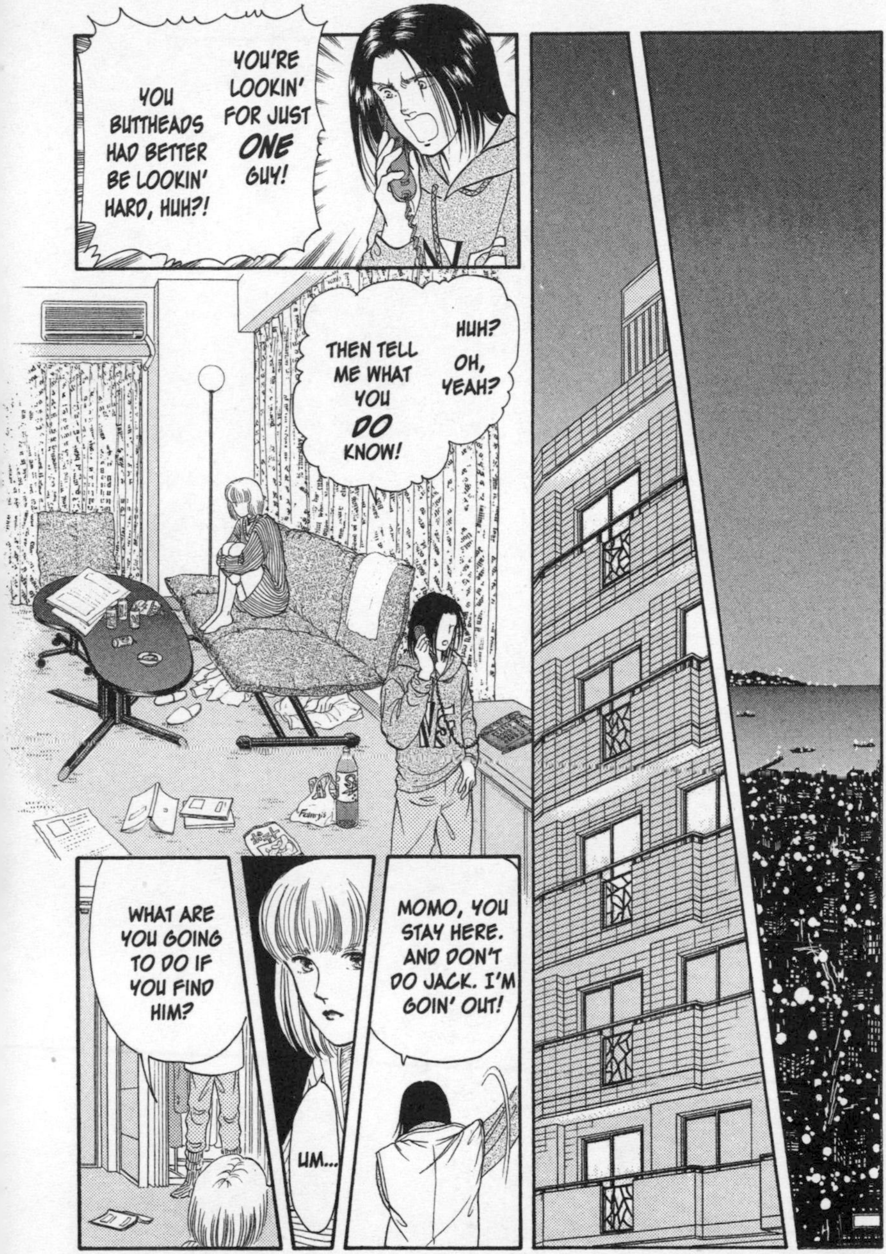
YOU'RE LOOKIN' FOR JUST ONE GUY!
YOU BUTTHEADS HAD BETTER BE LOOKIN' HARD, HUH?!
HUH?
OH, YEAH?
THEN TELL ME WHAT YOU DO KNOW!
MOMO, YOU STAY HERE. AND DON'T DO JACK. I'M GOIN' OUT!
UM...
WHAT ARE YOU GOING TO DO IF YOU FIND HIM?

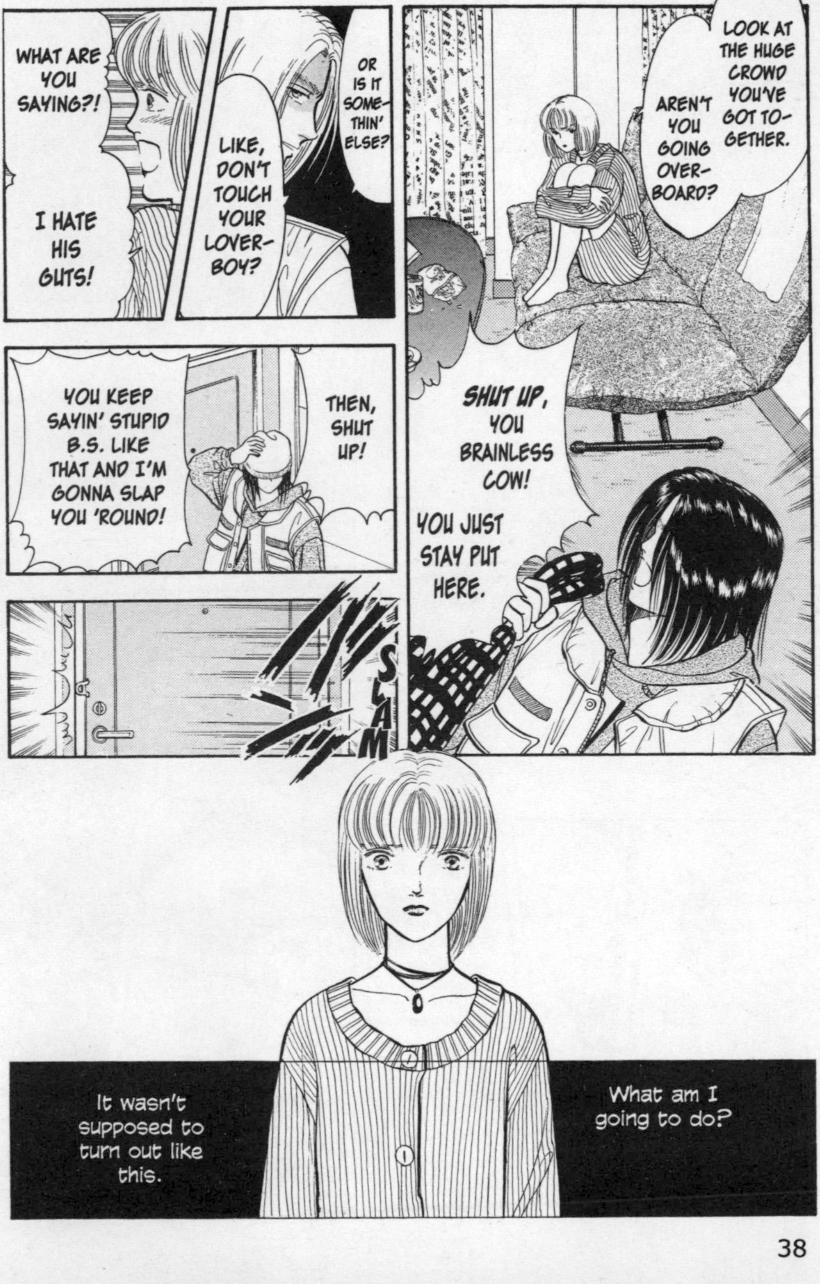

LOOK AT THE HUGE CROWD YOU'VE GOT TO-GETHER.
AREN'T YOU GOING OVER-BOARD?
SHUT UP, YOU BRAINLESS COW!
YOU JUST STAY PUT HERE.
OR IS IT SOME-THIN' ELSE?
LIKE, DON'T TOUCH YOUR LOVER-BOY?
WHAT ARE YOU SAYING?!
I HATE HIS GUTS!
THEN, SHUT UP!
YOU KEEP SAYIN' STUPID B.S. LIKE THAT AND I'M GONNA SLAP YOU 'ROUND!
SLAM
What am I going to do?
It wasn't supposed to turn out like this.

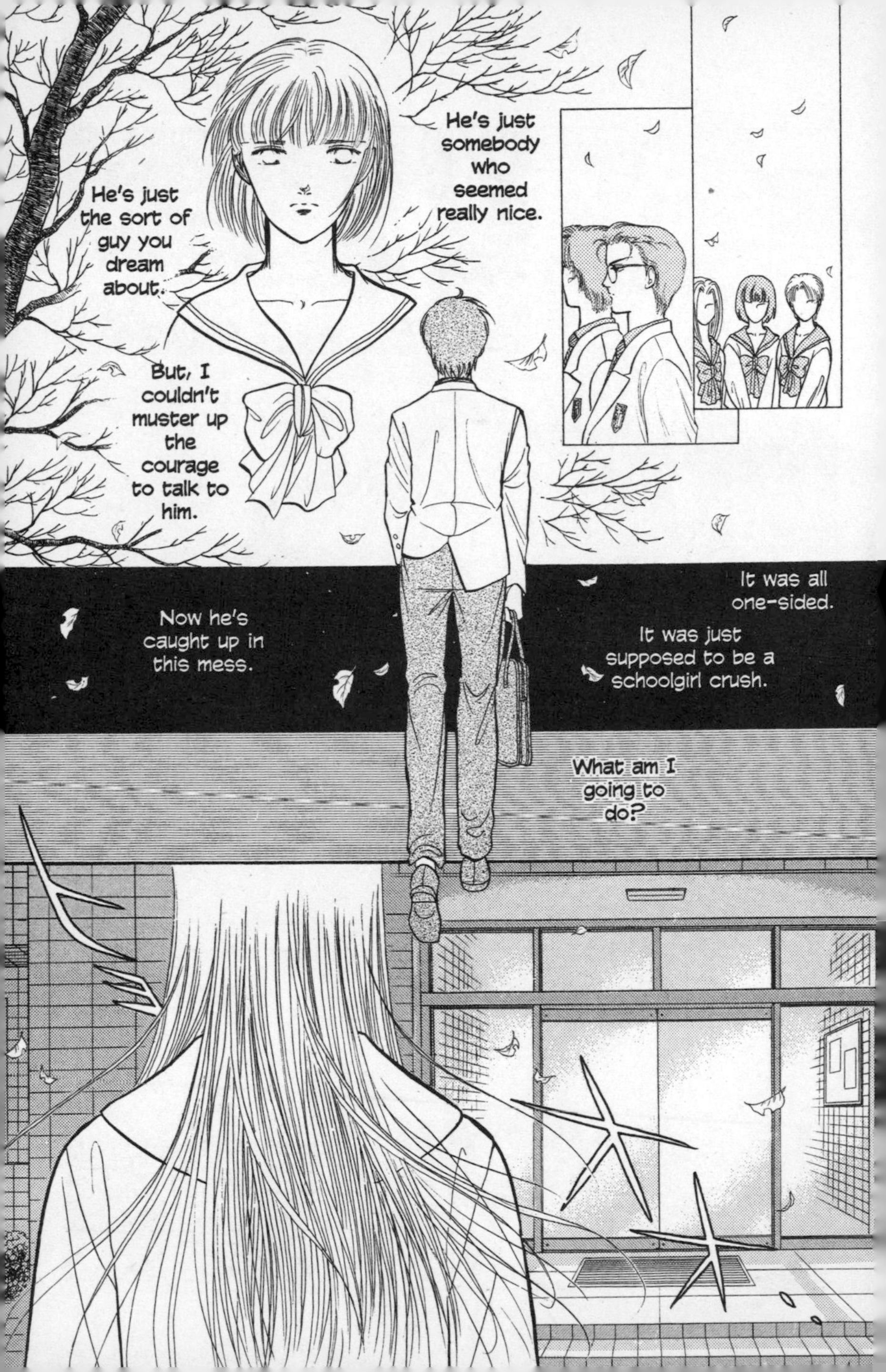
He's just somebody who seemed really nice.
He's just the sort of guy you dream about.
But, I couldn't muster up the courage to talk to him.
It was all one-sided.
It was just supposed to be a schoolgirl crush.
Now he's caught up in this mess.
What am I going to do?

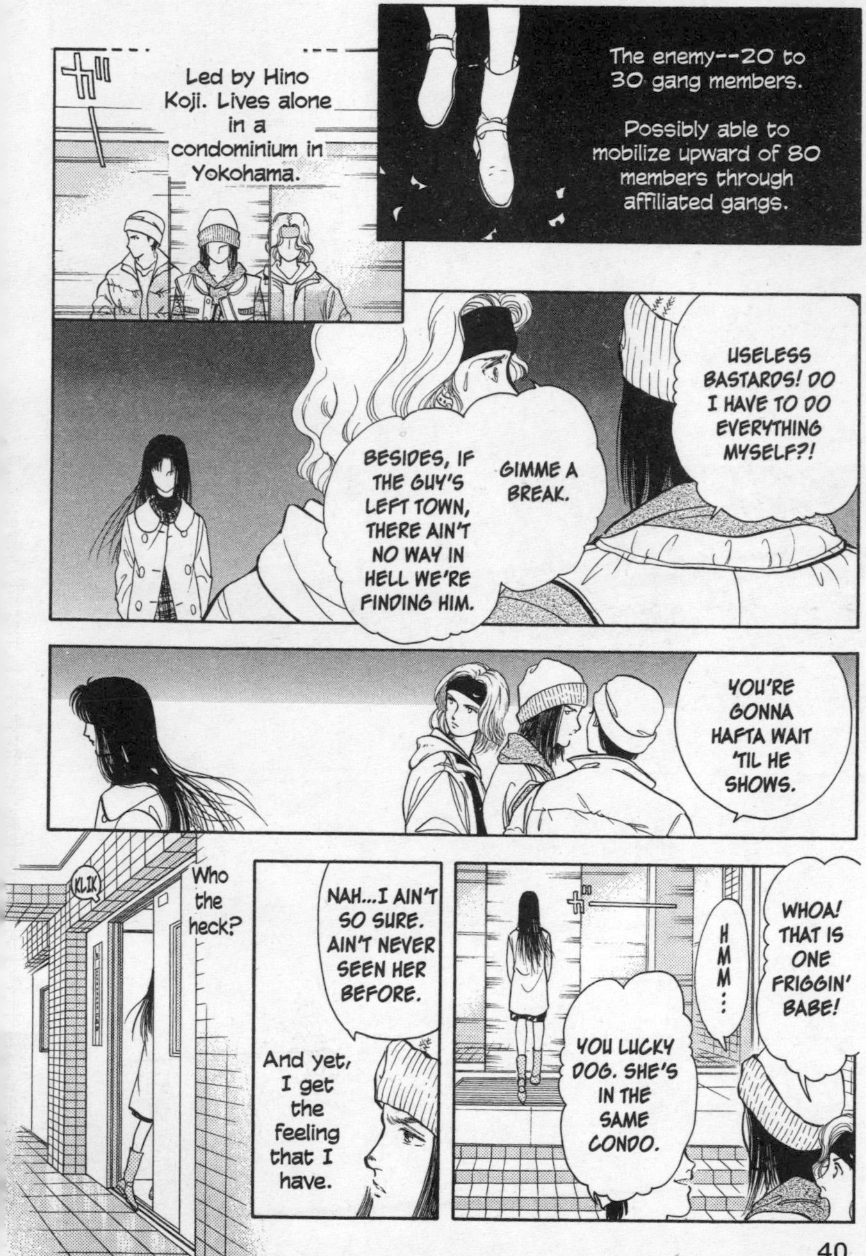
The enemy--20 to 30 gang members.
Possibly able to mobilize upward of 80 members through affiliated gangs.
Led by Hino Koji. Lives alone in a condominium in Yokohama.
USELESS BASTARDS! DO I HAVE TO DO EVERYTHING MYSELF?!
GIMME A BREAK.
BESIDES, IF THE GUY'S LEFT TOWN, THERE AIN'T NO WAY IN HELL WE'RE FINDING HIM.
YOU'RE GONNA HAFTA WAIT 'TIL HE SHOWS.
WHOA! THAT IS ONE FRIGGIN' BABE!
HMM...
YOU LUCKY DOG. SHE'S IN THE SAME CONDO.
NAH...I AIN'T SO SURE. AIN'T NEVER SEEN HER BEFORE.
And yet, I get the feeling that I have.
KLIK
Who the heck?

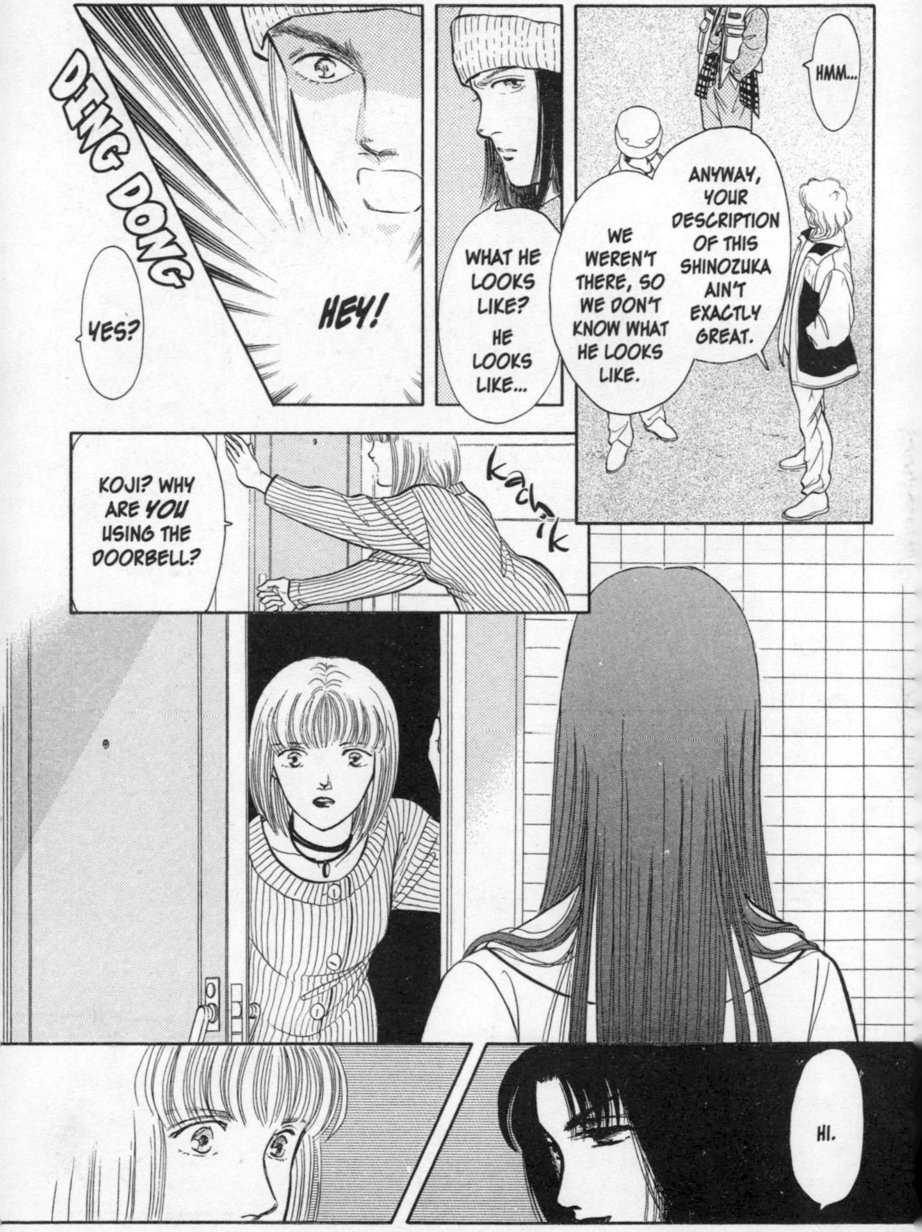
HMM...
ANYWAY, YOUR DESCRIPTION OF THIS SHINOZUKA AIN'T EXACTLY GREAT.
WE WEREN'T THERE, SO WE DON'T KNOW WHAT HE LOOKS LIKE.
WHAT HE LOOKS LIKE?
HE LOOKS LIKE...
DING DONG
HEY!
YES?
kachik
KOJI? WHY ARE *YOU* USING THE DOORBELL?
HI.

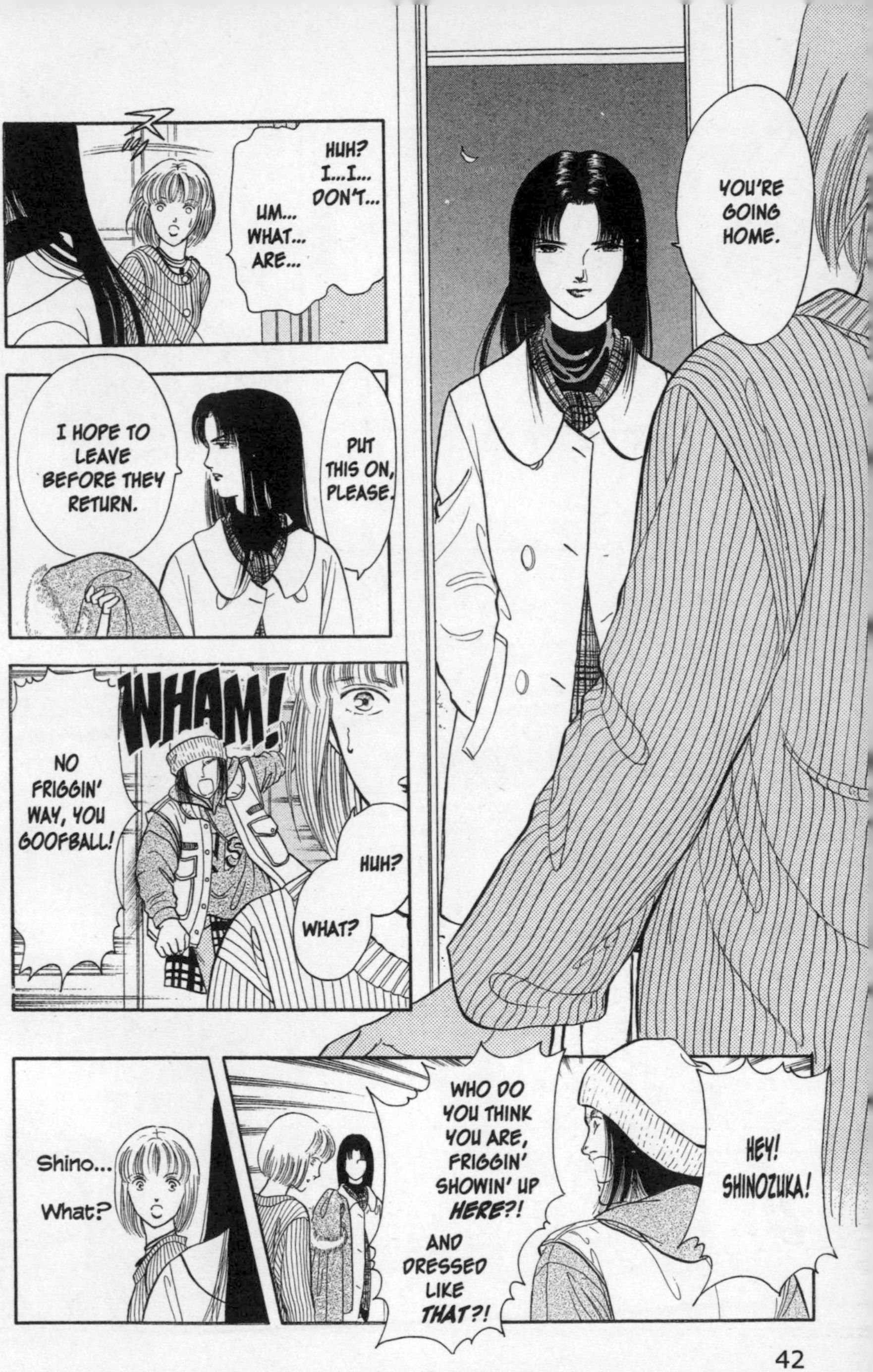
YOU'RE GOING HOME.
HUH? I...I... DON'T...
UM... WHAT... ARE...
PUT THIS ON, PLEASE.
I HOPE TO LEAVE BEFORE THEY RETURN.
WHAM!
NO FRIGGIN' WAY, YOU GOOFBALL!
HUH?
WHAT?
HEY! SHINOZUKA!
WHO DO YOU THINK YOU ARE, FRIGGIN' SHOWIN' UP *HERE*?!
AND DRESSED LIKE *THAT*?!
Shino...
What?

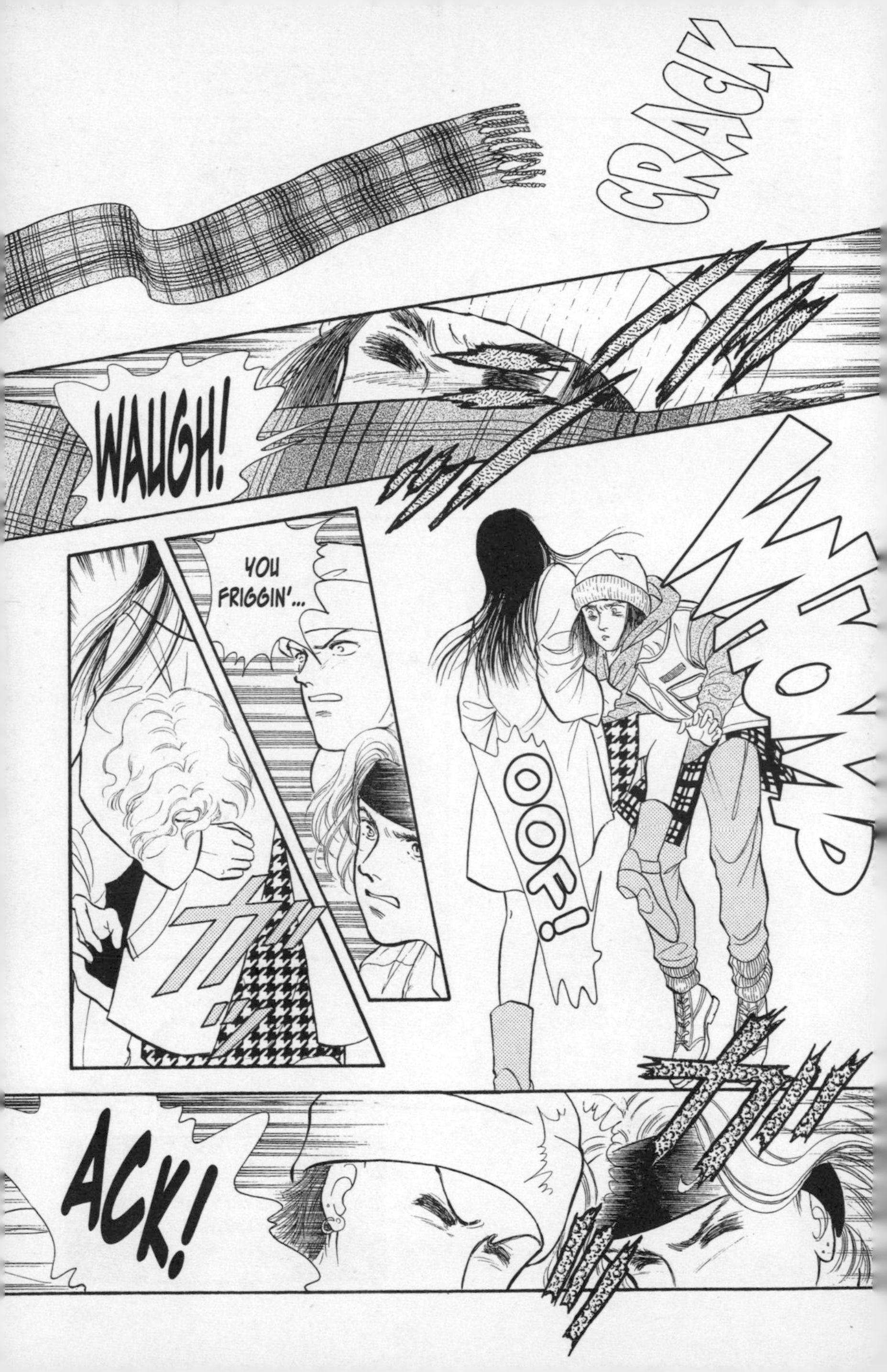
CRACK
WAUGH!
WHOMP
OOF!
YOU FRIGGIN'...
ACK!

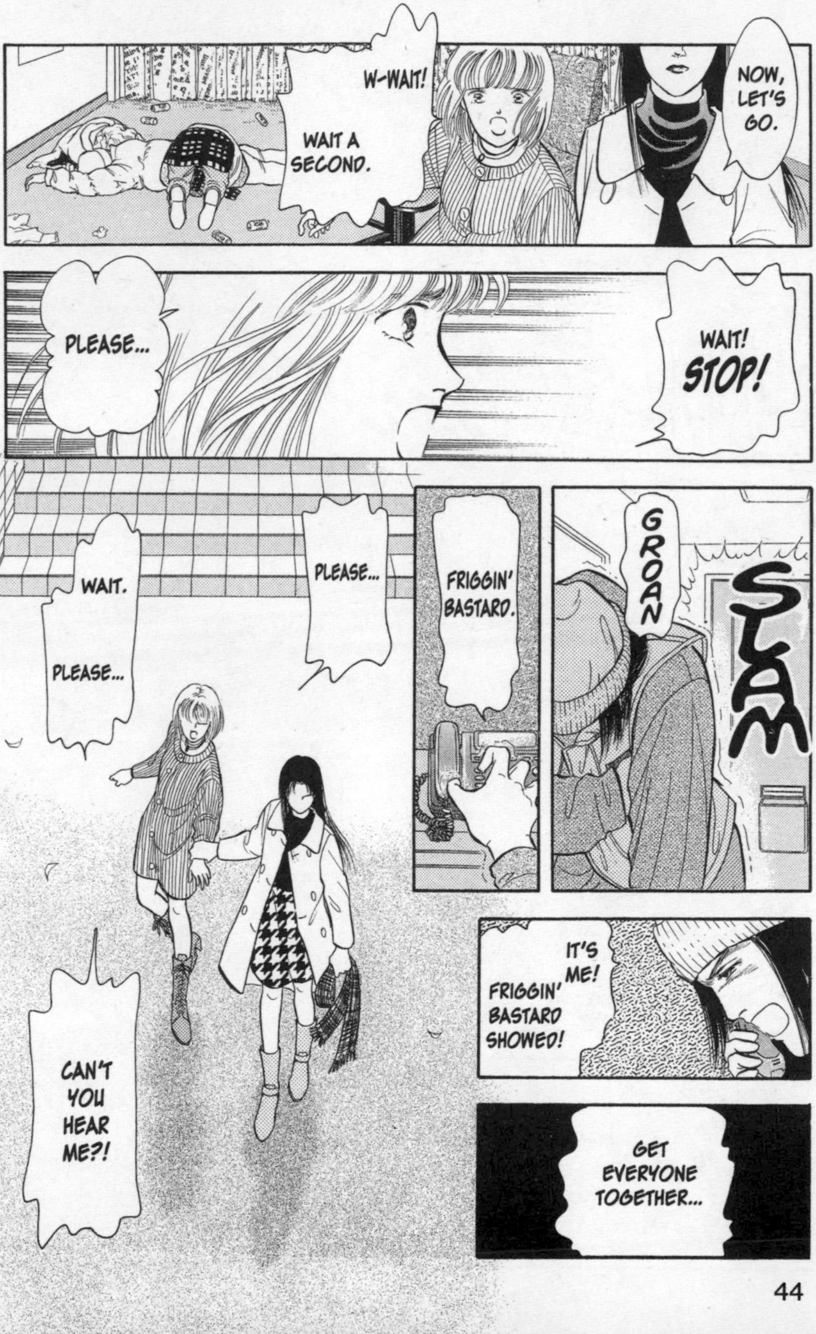
NOW, LET'S GO.
W-WAIT!
WAIT A SECOND.
WAIT! STOP!
PLEASE...
GROAN
SLAM
FRIGGIN' BASTARD.
IT'S ME!
FRIGGIN' BASTARD SHOWED!
GET EVERYONE TOGETHER...
PLEASE...
WAIT.
PLEASE...
CAN'T YOU HEAR ME?!

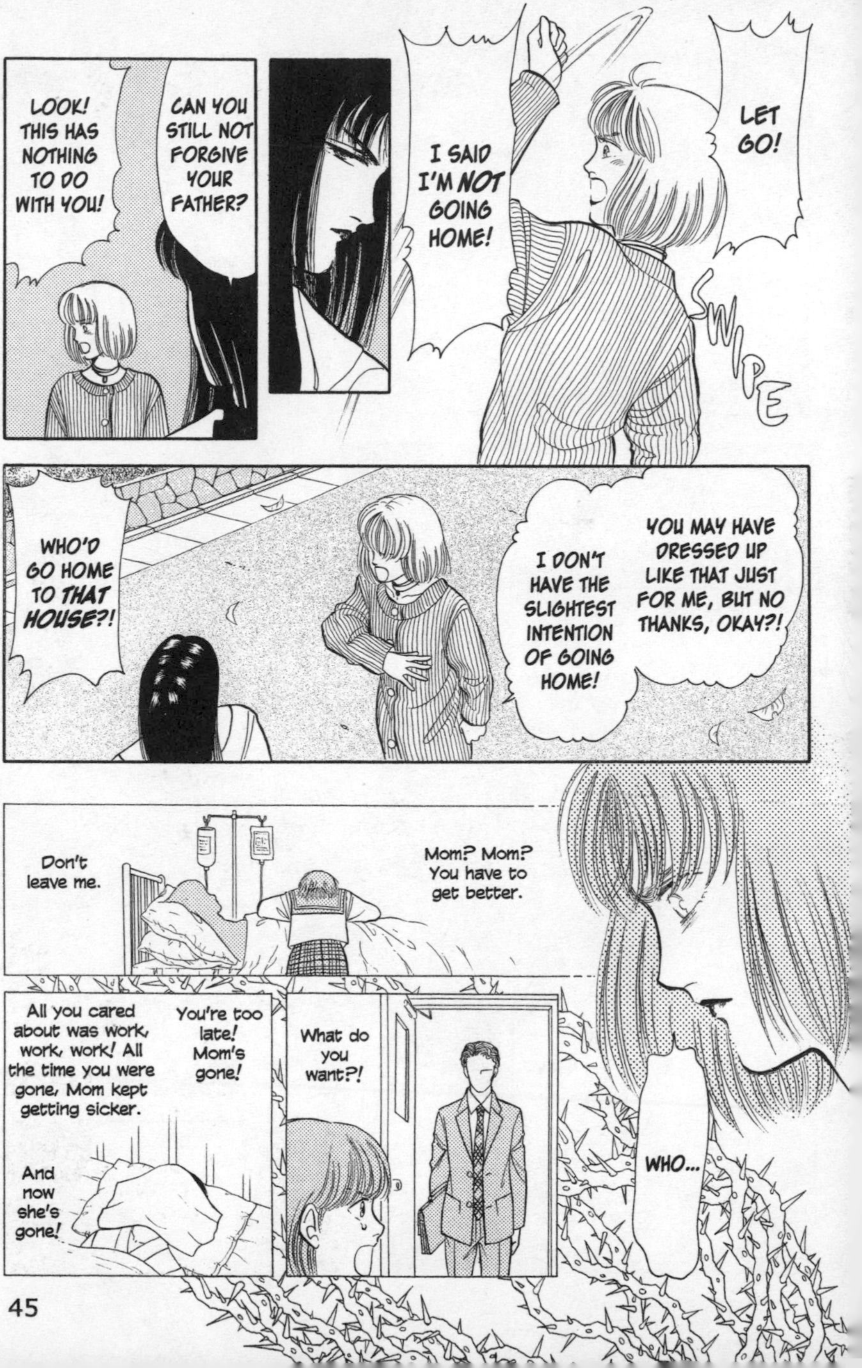
LET GO!
I SAID I'M ***NOT*** GOING HOME!
SWIPE
CAN YOU STILL NOT FORGIVE YOUR FATHER?
LOOK! THIS HAS NOTHING TO DO WITH YOU!
YOU MAY HAVE DRESSED UP LIKE THAT JUST FOR ME, BUT NO THANKS, OKAY?!
I DON'T HAVE THE SLIGHTEST INTENTION OF GOING HOME!
WHO'D GO HOME TO ***THAT HOUSE?!***
WHO...
Mom? Mom? You have to get better.
Don't leave me.
What do you want?!
You're too late! Mom's gone!
All you cared about was work, work, work! All the time you were gone, Mom kept getting sicker.
And now she's gone!

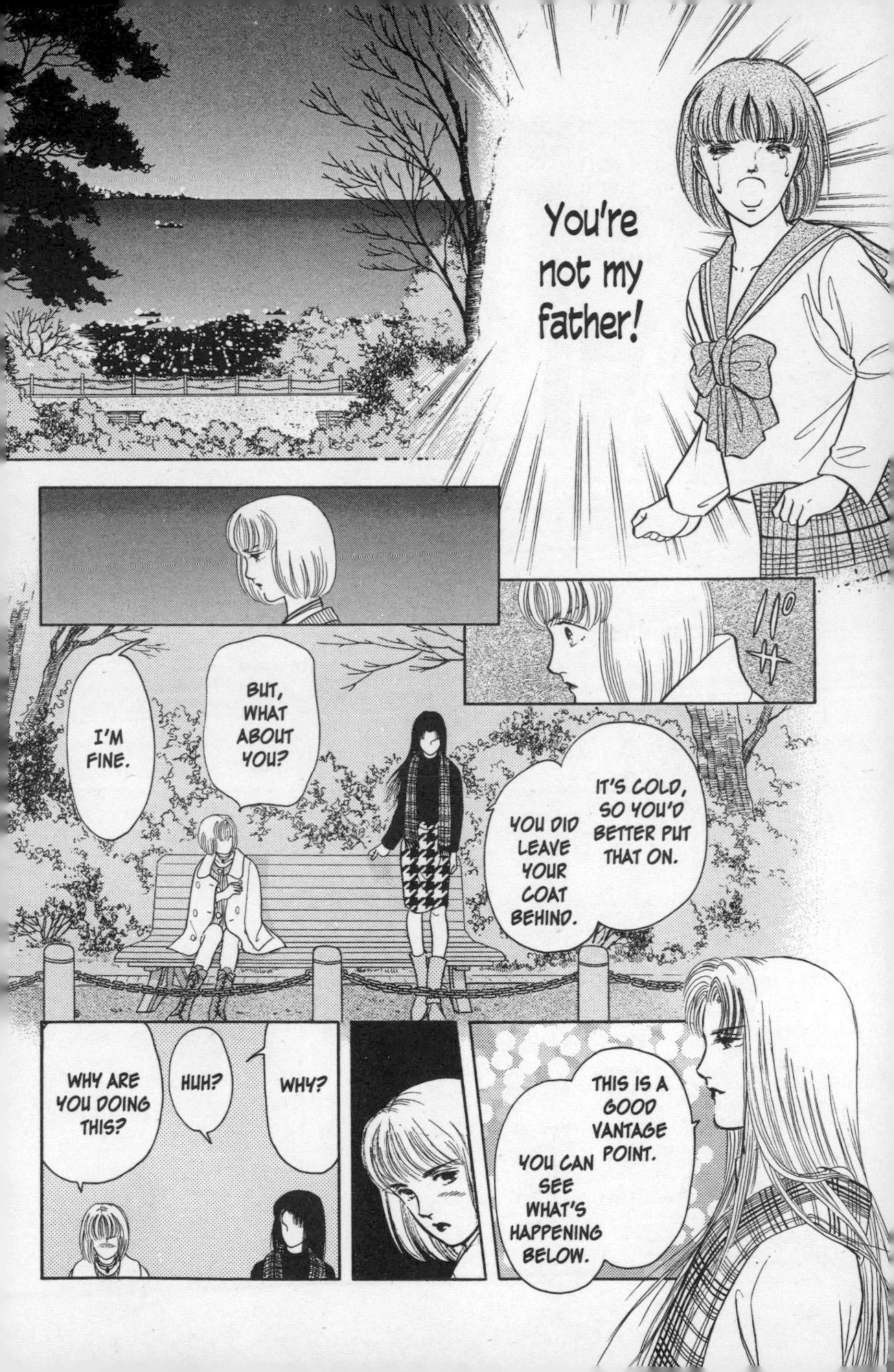
You're not my father!
It's cold, so you'd better put that on.
You did leave your coat behind.
But, what about you?
I'm fine.
This is a good vantage point.
You can see what's happening below.
Why?
Huh?
Why are you doing this?

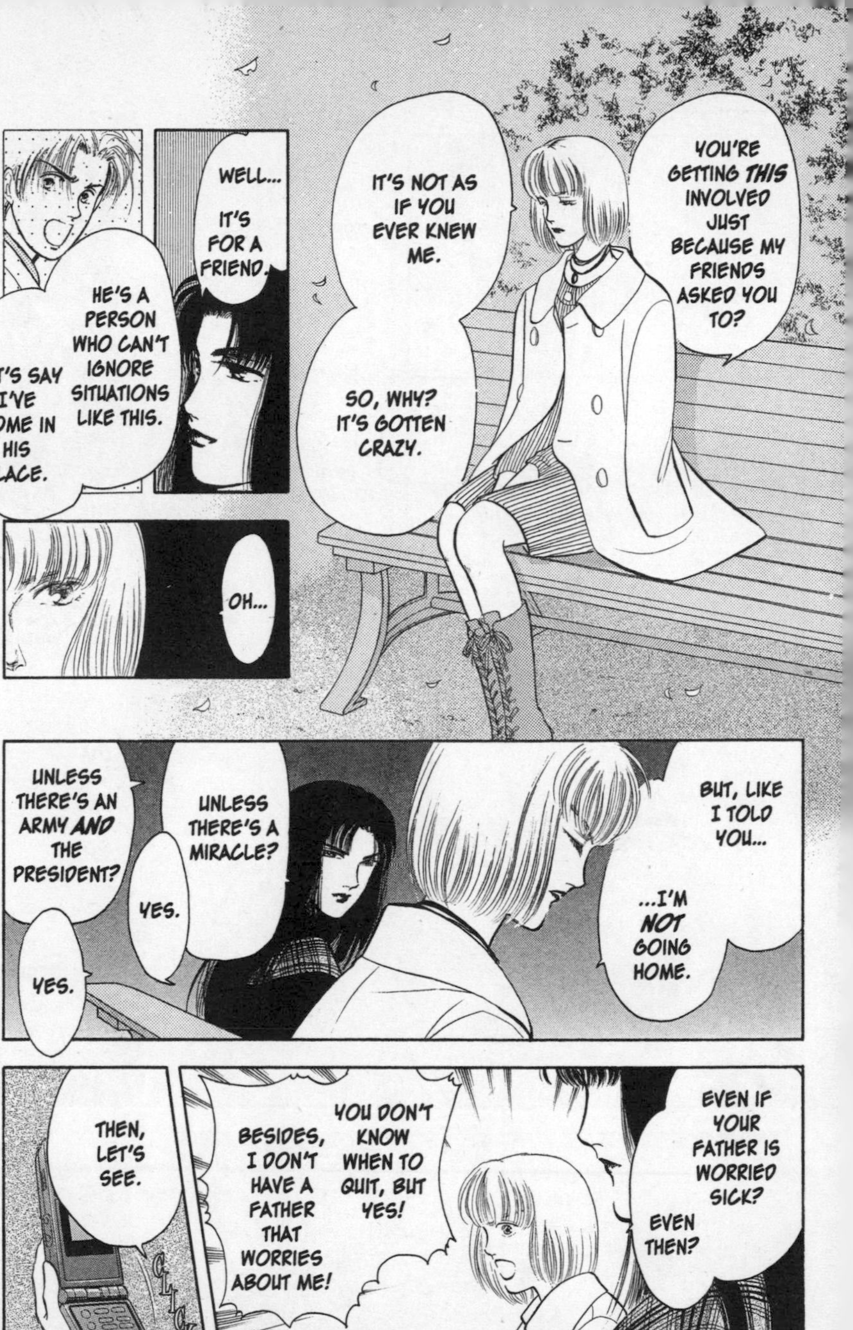
YOU'RE GETTING *THIS* INVOLVED JUST BECAUSE MY FRIENDS ASKED YOU TO?
IT'S NOT AS IF YOU EVER KNEW ME.
SO, WHY? IT'S GOTTEN CRAZY.
WELL... IT'S FOR A FRIEND.
HE'S A PERSON WHO CAN'T IGNORE SITUATIONS LIKE THIS.
LET'S SAY I'VE COME IN HIS PLACE.
OH...
BUT, LIKE I TOLD YOU...
...I'M *NOT* GOING HOME.
UNLESS THERE'S A MIRACLE?
YES.
UNLESS THERE'S AN ARMY *AND* THE PRESIDENT?
YES.
EVEN IF YOUR FATHER IS WORRIED SICK?
EVEN THEN?
YOU DON'T KNOW WHEN TO QUIT, BUT YES!
BESIDES, I DON'T HAVE A FATHER THAT WORRIES ABOUT ME!
THEN, LET'S SEE.
CLICK

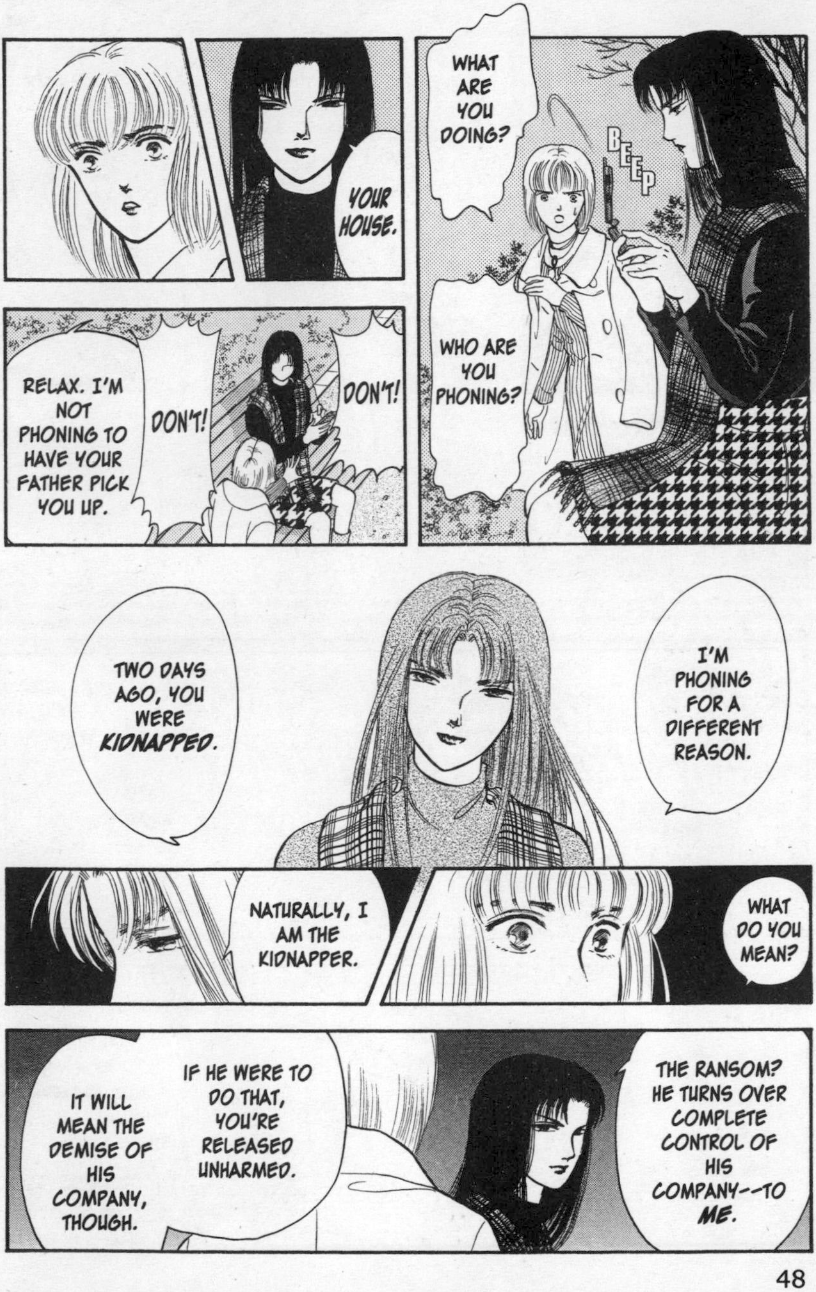
WHAT ARE YOU DOING?
BEEEP
WHO ARE YOU PHONING?
YOUR HOUSE.
DON'T!
DON'T!
RELAX. I'M NOT PHONING TO HAVE YOUR FATHER PICK YOU UP.
I'M PHONING FOR A DIFFERENT REASON.
TWO DAYS AGO, YOU WERE *KIDNAPPED*.
WHAT DO YOU MEAN?
NATURALLY, I AM THE KIDNAPPER.
THE RANSOM? HE TURNS OVER COMPLETE CONTROL OF HIS COMPANY--TO *ME*.
IF HE WERE TO DO THAT, YOU'RE RELEASED UNHARMED.
IT WILL MEAN THE DEMISE OF HIS COMPANY, THOUGH.

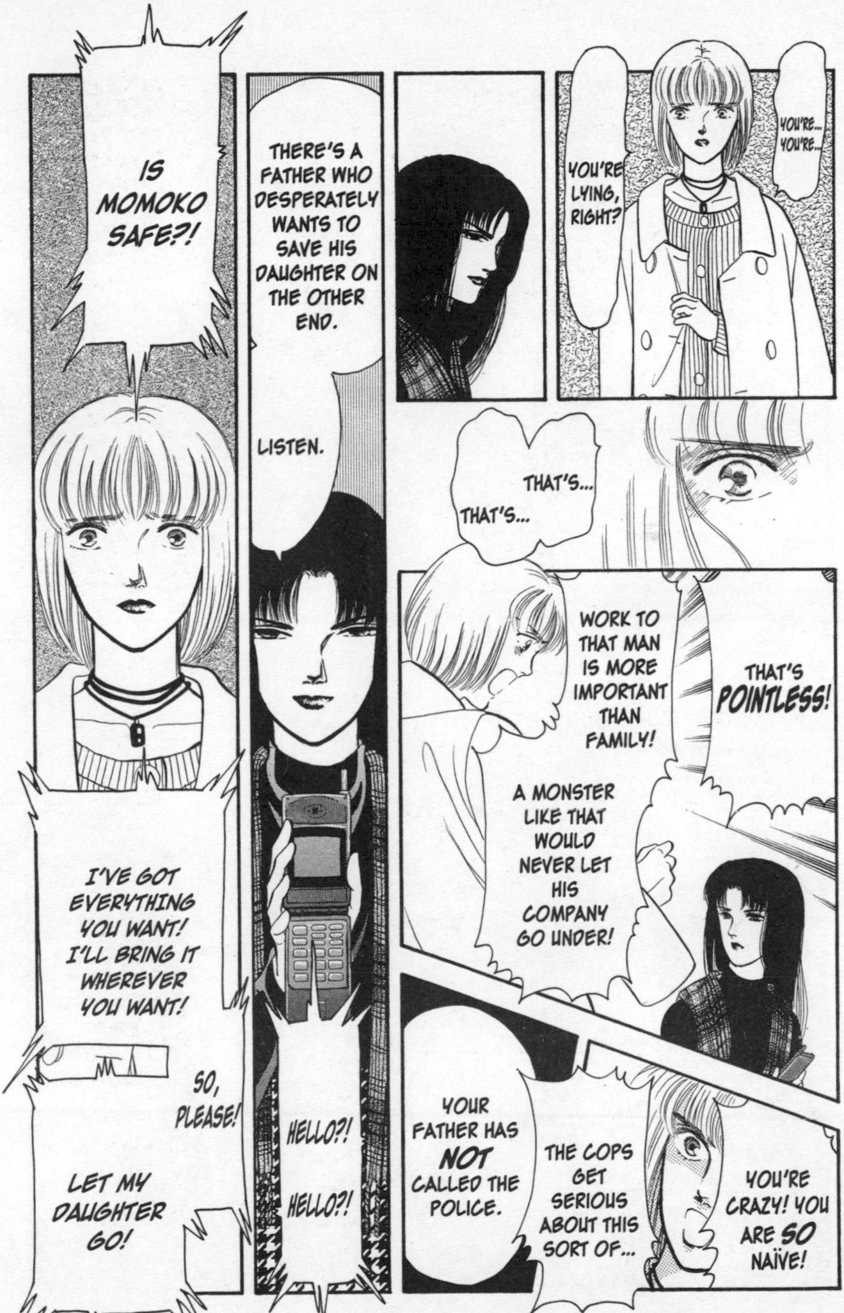

YOU'RE... YOU'RE...
YOU'RE LYING, RIGHT?
THAT'S... THAT'S...
THAT'S POINTLESS!
WORK TO THAT MAN IS MORE IMPORTANT THAN FAMILY!
A MONSTER LIKE THAT WOULD NEVER LET HIS COMPANY GO UNDER!
YOU'RE CRAZY! YOU ARE SO NAÏVE!
THE COPS GET SERIOUS ABOUT THIS SORT OF...
YOUR FATHER HAS NOT CALLED THE POLICE.
THERE'S A FATHER WHO DESPERATELY WANTS TO SAVE HIS DAUGHTER ON THE OTHER END.
LISTEN.
HELLO?!
HELLO?!
IS MOMOKO SAFE?!
I'VE GOT EVERYTHING YOU WANT! I'LL BRING IT WHEREVER YOU WANT!
SO, PLEASE!
LET MY DAUGHTER GO!

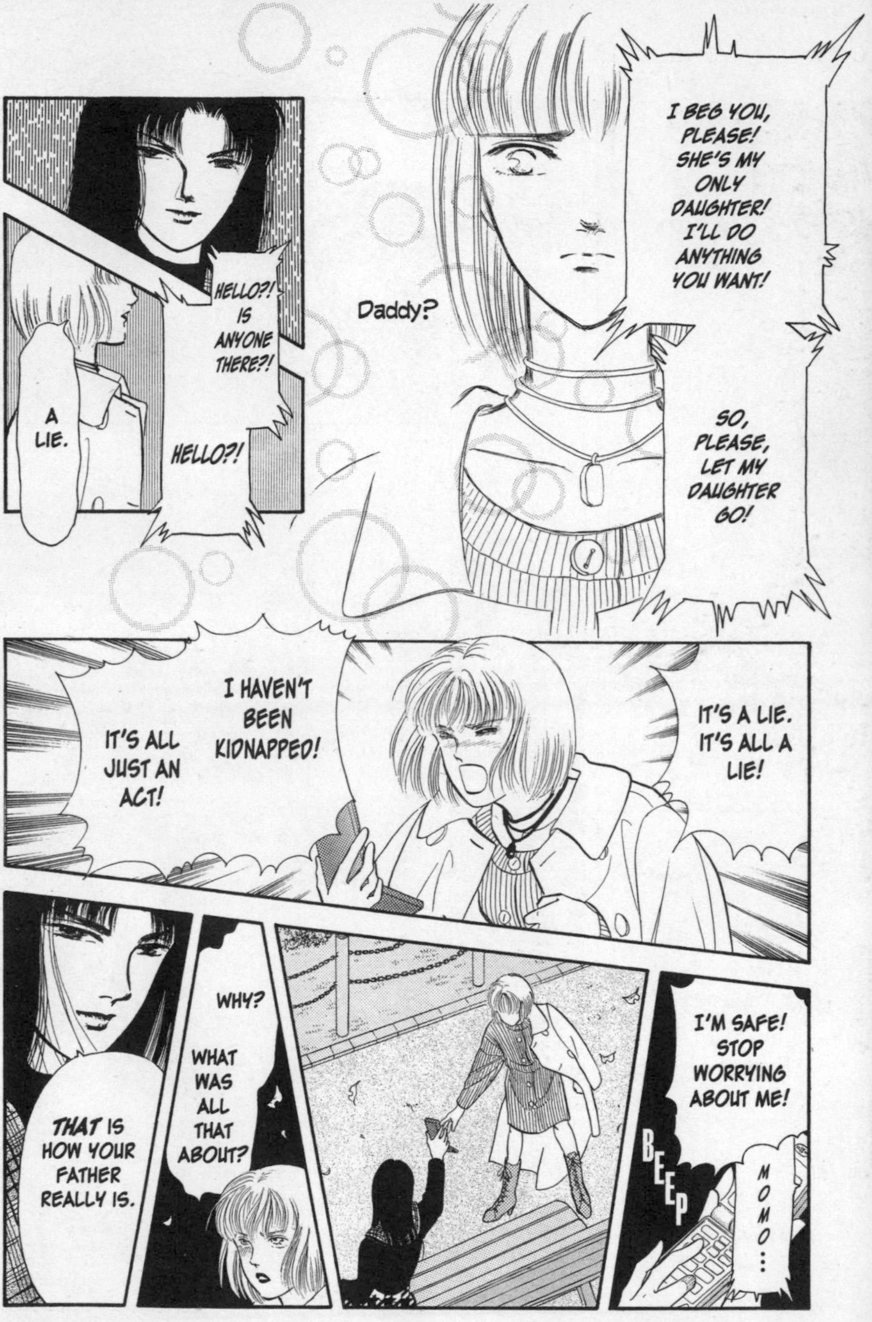

Daddy?
I BEG YOU, PLEASE! SHE'S MY ONLY DAUGHTER! I'LL DO ANYTHING YOU WANT!
SO, PLEASE, LET MY DAUGHTER GO!
HELLO?! IS ANYONE THERE?!
HELLO?!
A LIE.
IT'S A LIE. IT'S ALL A LIE!
I HAVEN'T BEEN KIDNAPPED!
IT'S ALL JUST AN ACT!
I'M SAFE! STOP WORRYING ABOUT ME!
BEEEP
MOMO...
WHY?
WHAT WAS ALL THAT ABOUT?
THAT IS HOW YOUR FATHER REALLY IS.

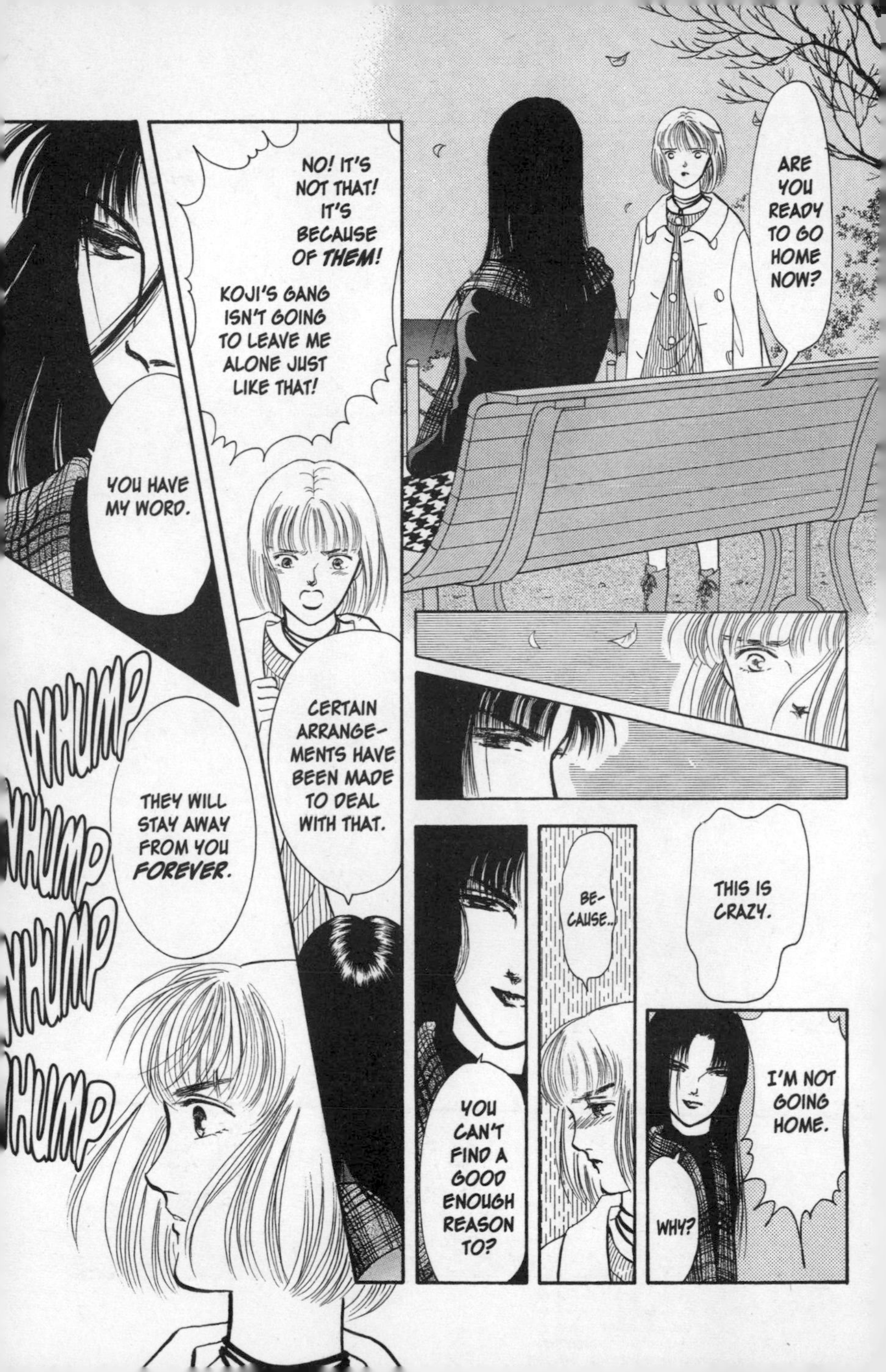

ARE YOU READY TO GO HOME NOW?
THIS IS CRAZY.
I'M NOT GOING HOME.
WHY?
BE-CAUSE...
YOU CAN'T FIND A GOOD ENOUGH REASON TO?
NO! IT'S NOT THAT! IT'S BECAUSE OF *THEM*!
KOJI'S GANG ISN'T GOING TO LEAVE ME ALONE JUST LIKE THAT!
CERTAIN ARRANGE-MENTS HAVE BEEN MADE TO DEAL WITH THAT.
THEY WILL STAY AWAY FROM YOU *FOREVER*.
YOU HAVE MY WORD.
WHUMP
WHUMP
WHUMP
WHUMP

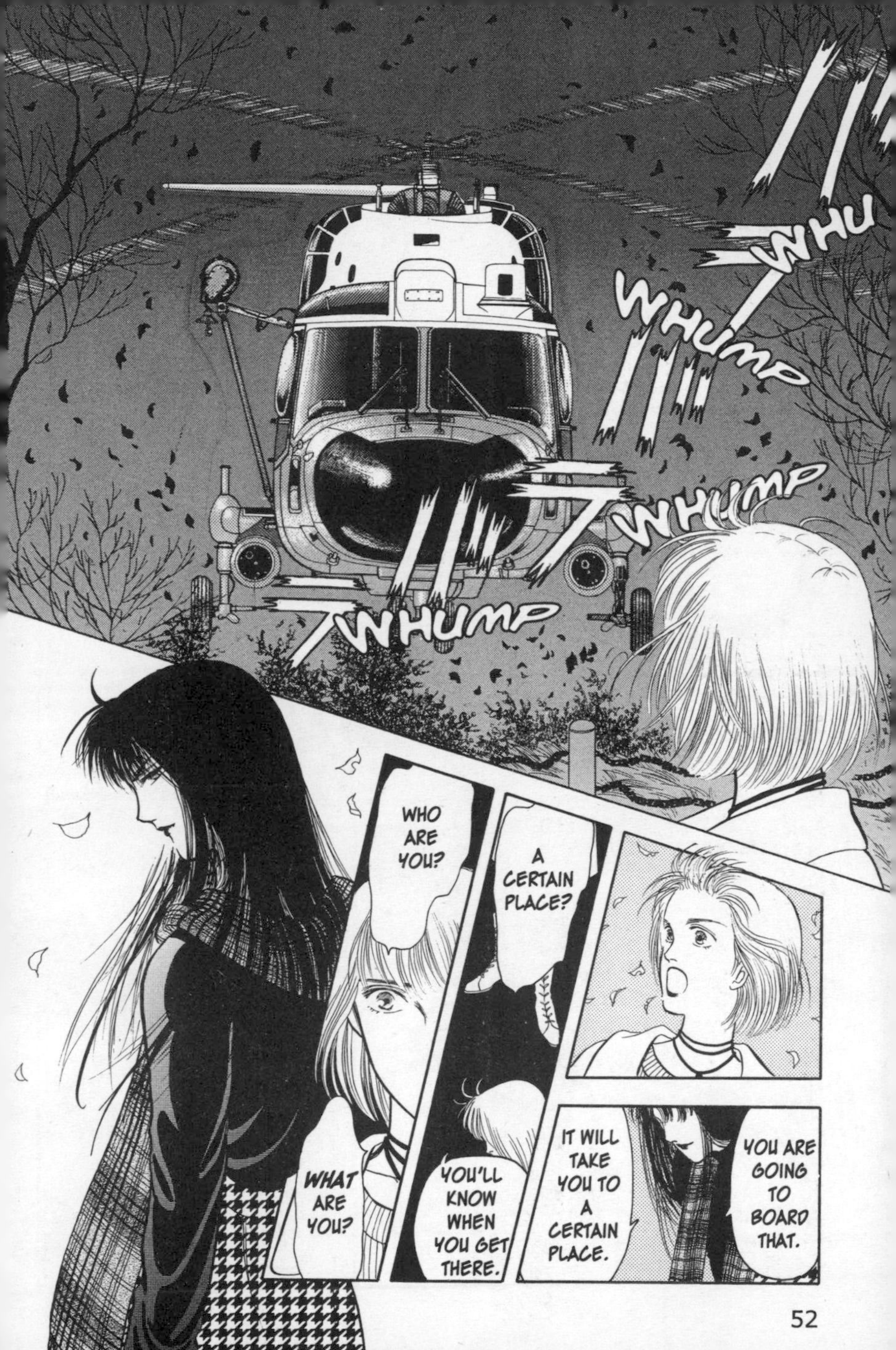
WHU
WHUMP
WHUMP
WHUMP
YOU ARE GOING TO BOARD THAT.
IT WILL TAKE YOU TO A CERTAIN PLACE.
A CERTAIN PLACE?
YOU'LL KNOW WHEN YOU GET THERE.
WHO ARE YOU?
WHAT ARE YOU?

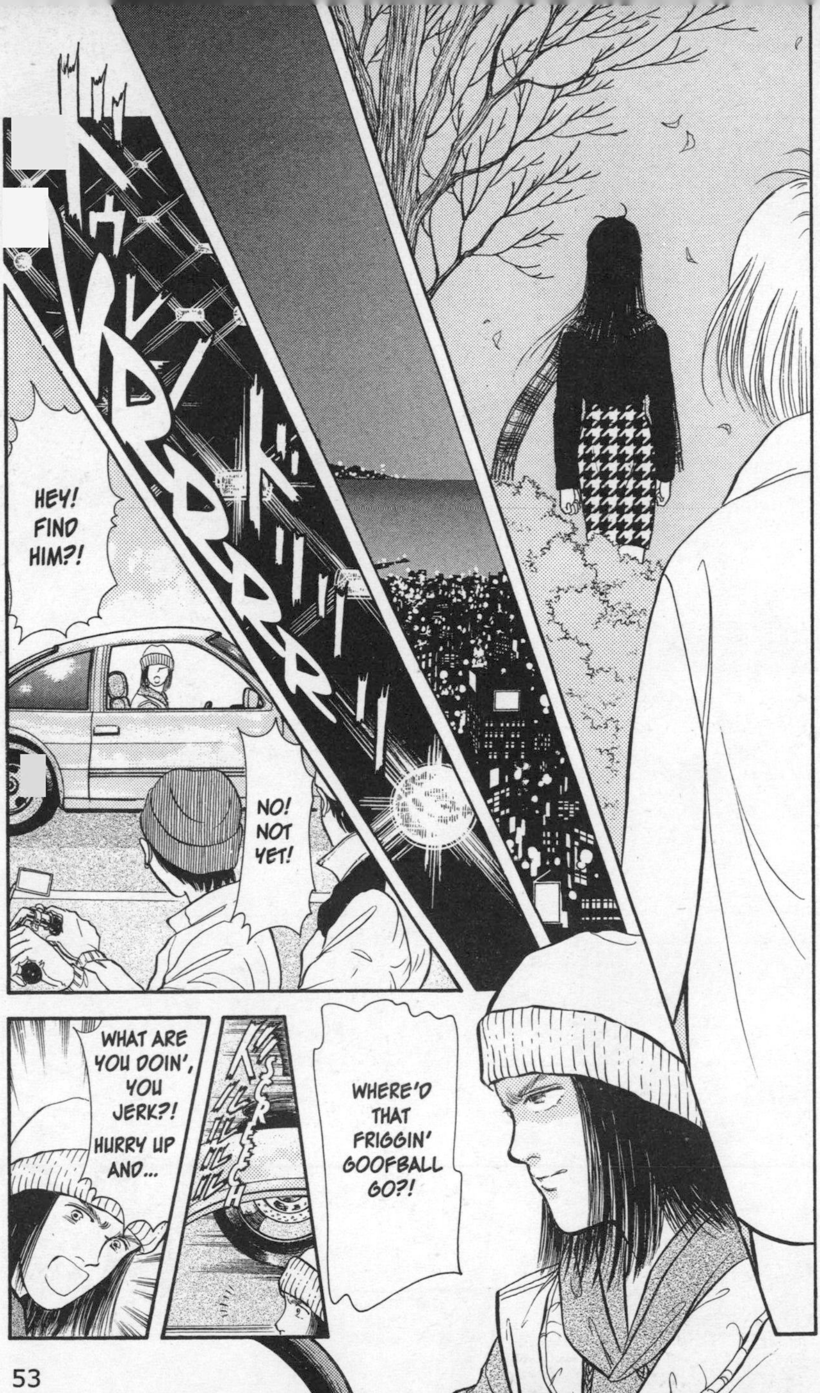
HEY! FIND HIM?!
NO! NOT YET!
WHERE'D THAT FRIGGIN' GOOFBALL GO?!
WHAT ARE YOU DOIN', YOU JERK?!
HURRY UP AND...

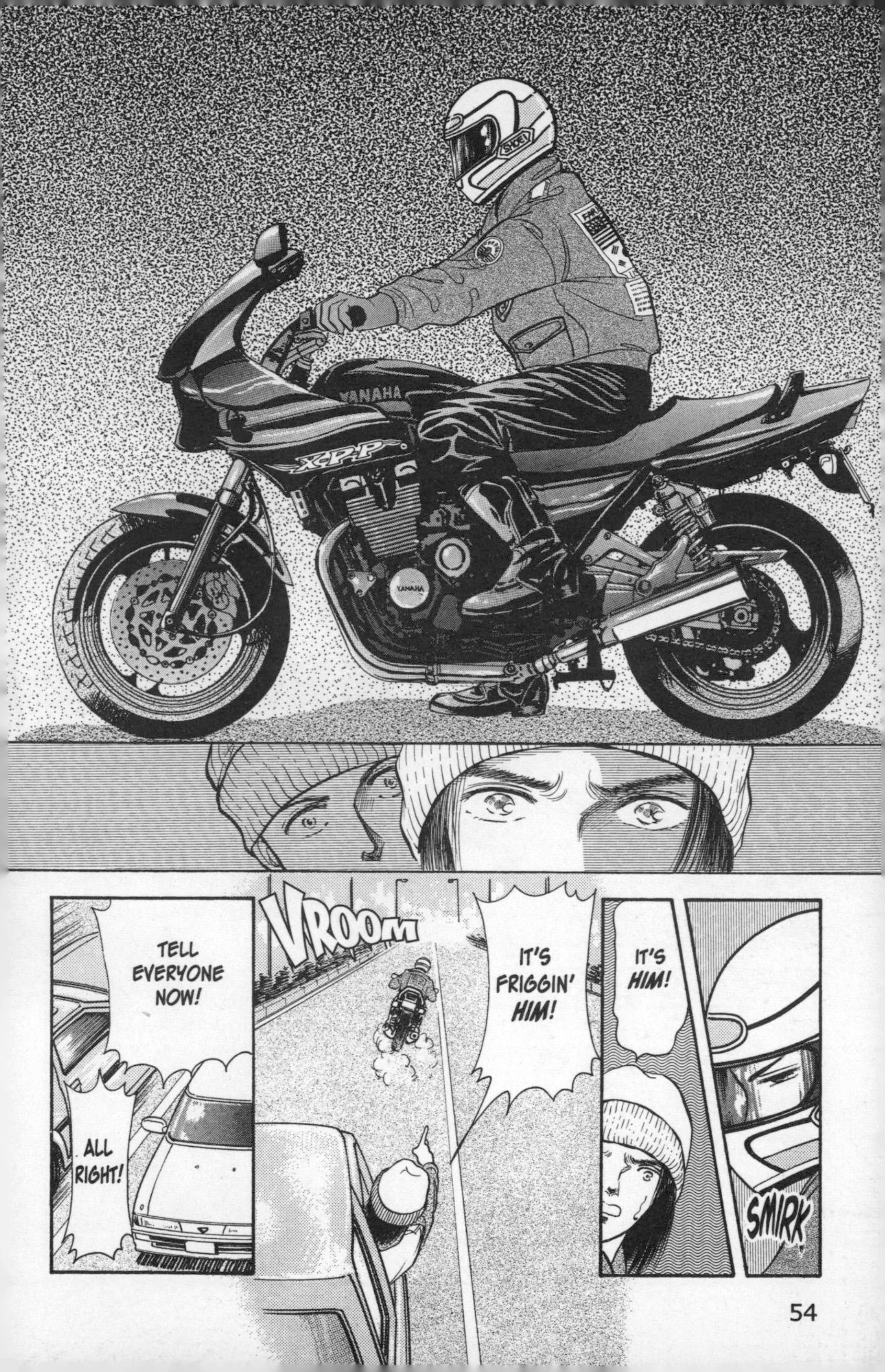
YAMAHA
IT'S HIM!
SMIRK
VROOM
IT'S FRIGGIN' HIM!
TELL EVERYONE NOW!
ALL RIGHT!

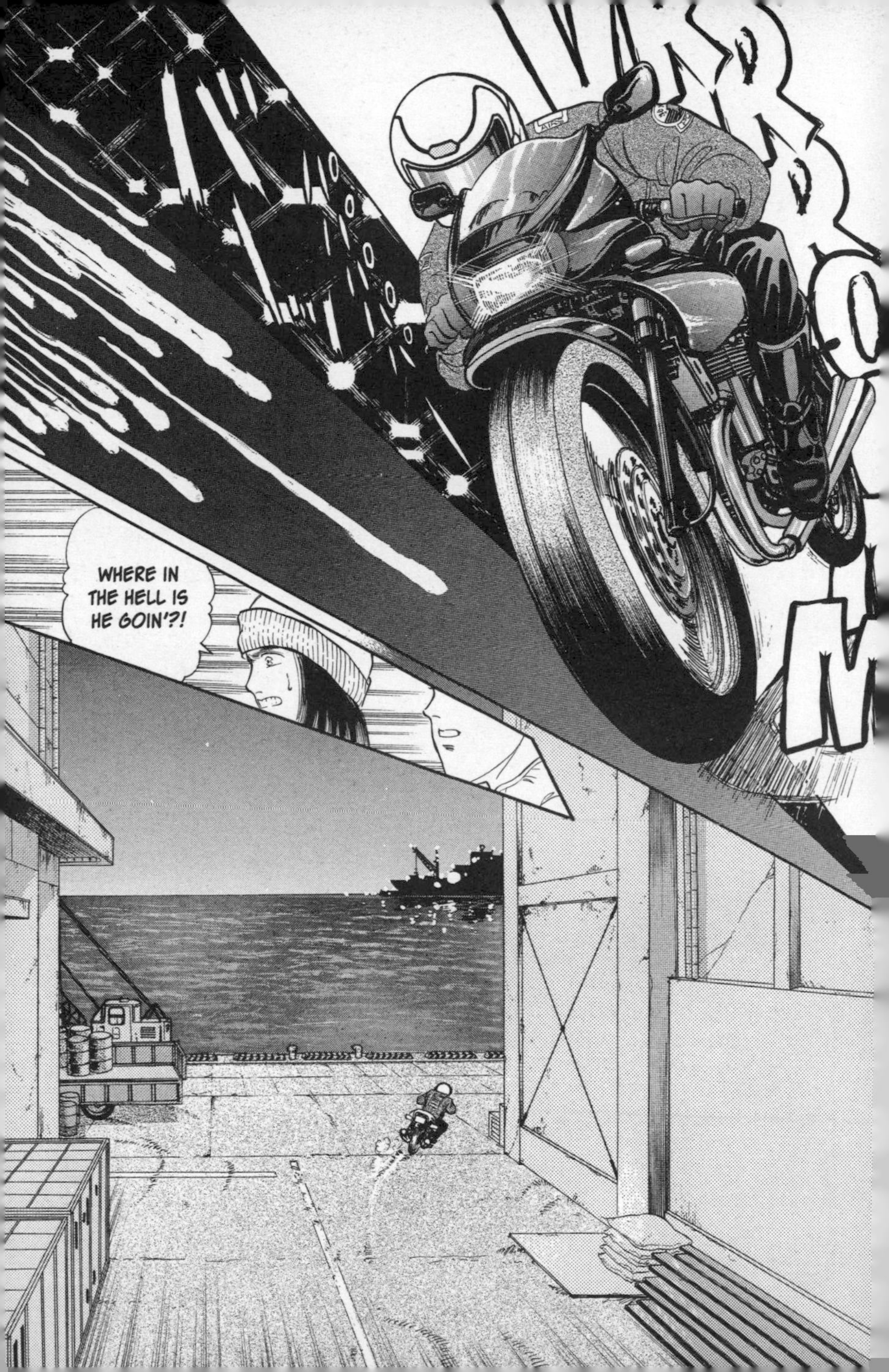
WHERE IN THE HELL IS HE GOIN'?!

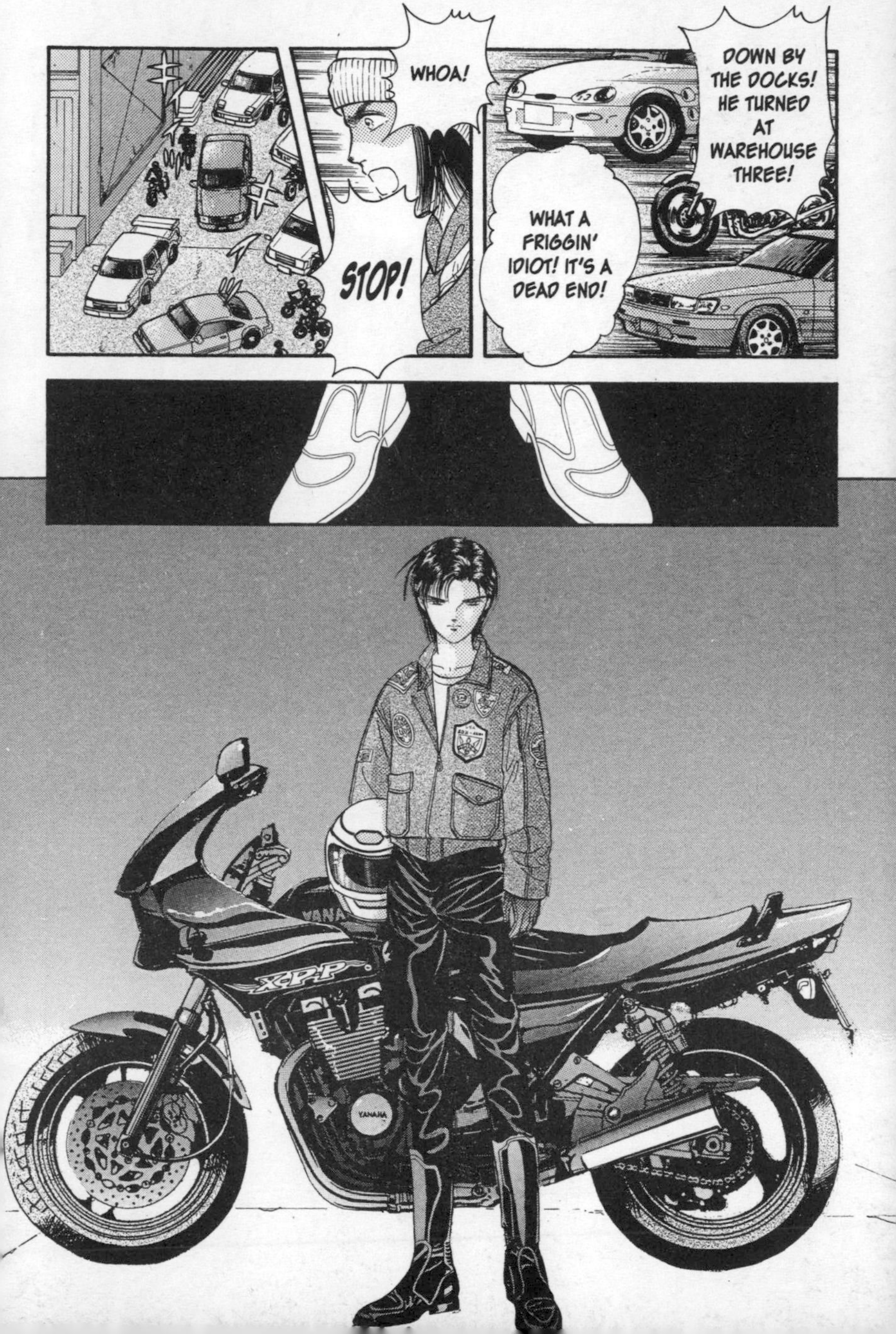
DOWN BY THE DOCKS! HE TURNED AT WAREHOUSE THREE!
WHAT A FRIGGIN' IDIOT! IT'S A DEAD END!
WHOA!
STOP!

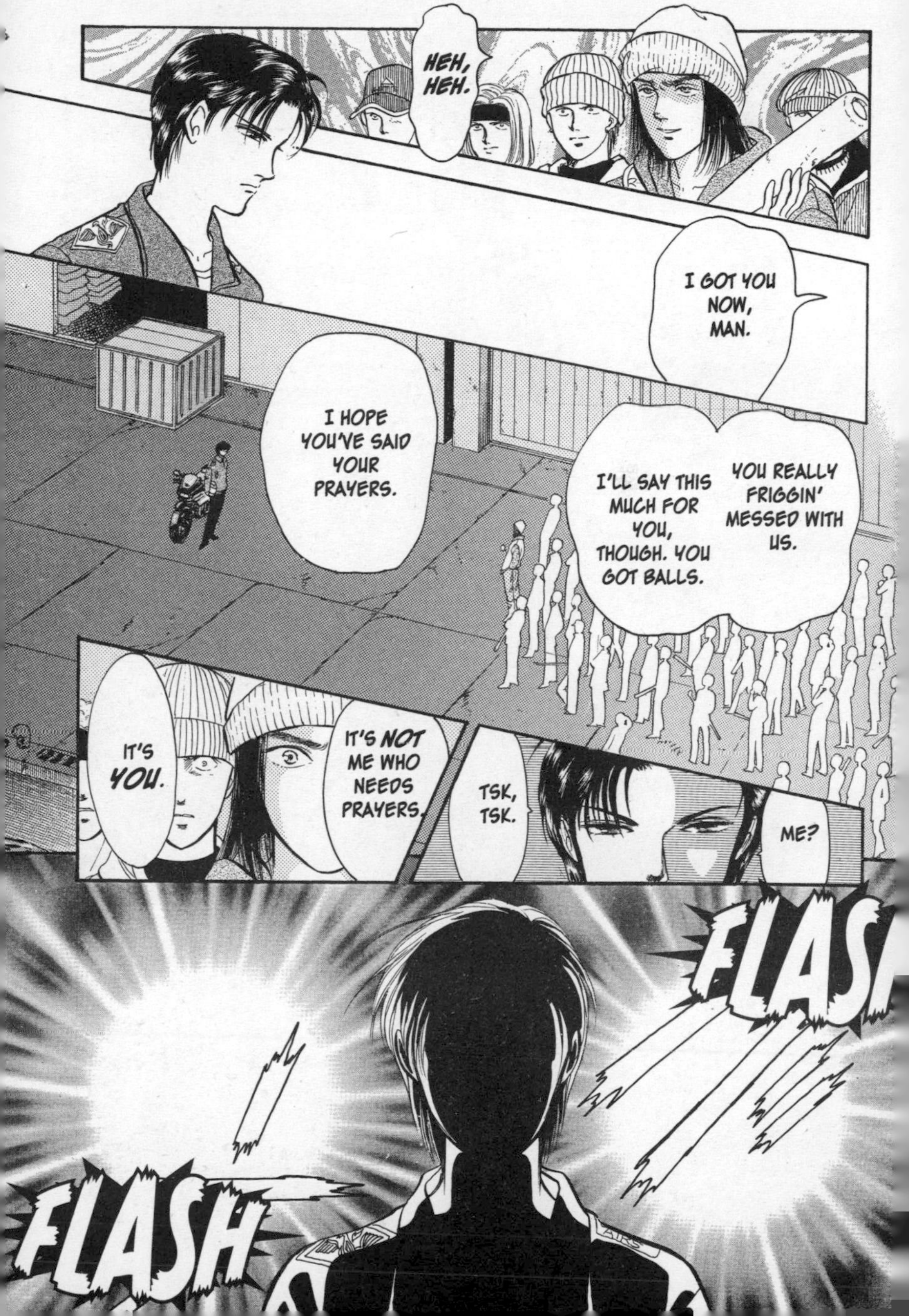
HEH, HEH.
I GOT YOU NOW, MAN.
YOU REALLY FRIGGIN' MESSED WITH US.
I'LL SAY THIS MUCH FOR YOU, THOUGH. YOU GOT BALLS.
I HOPE YOU'VE SAID YOUR PRAYERS.
ME?
TSK, TSK.
IT'S NOT ME WHO NEEDS PRAYERS.
IT'S YOU.
FLASH
FLASH

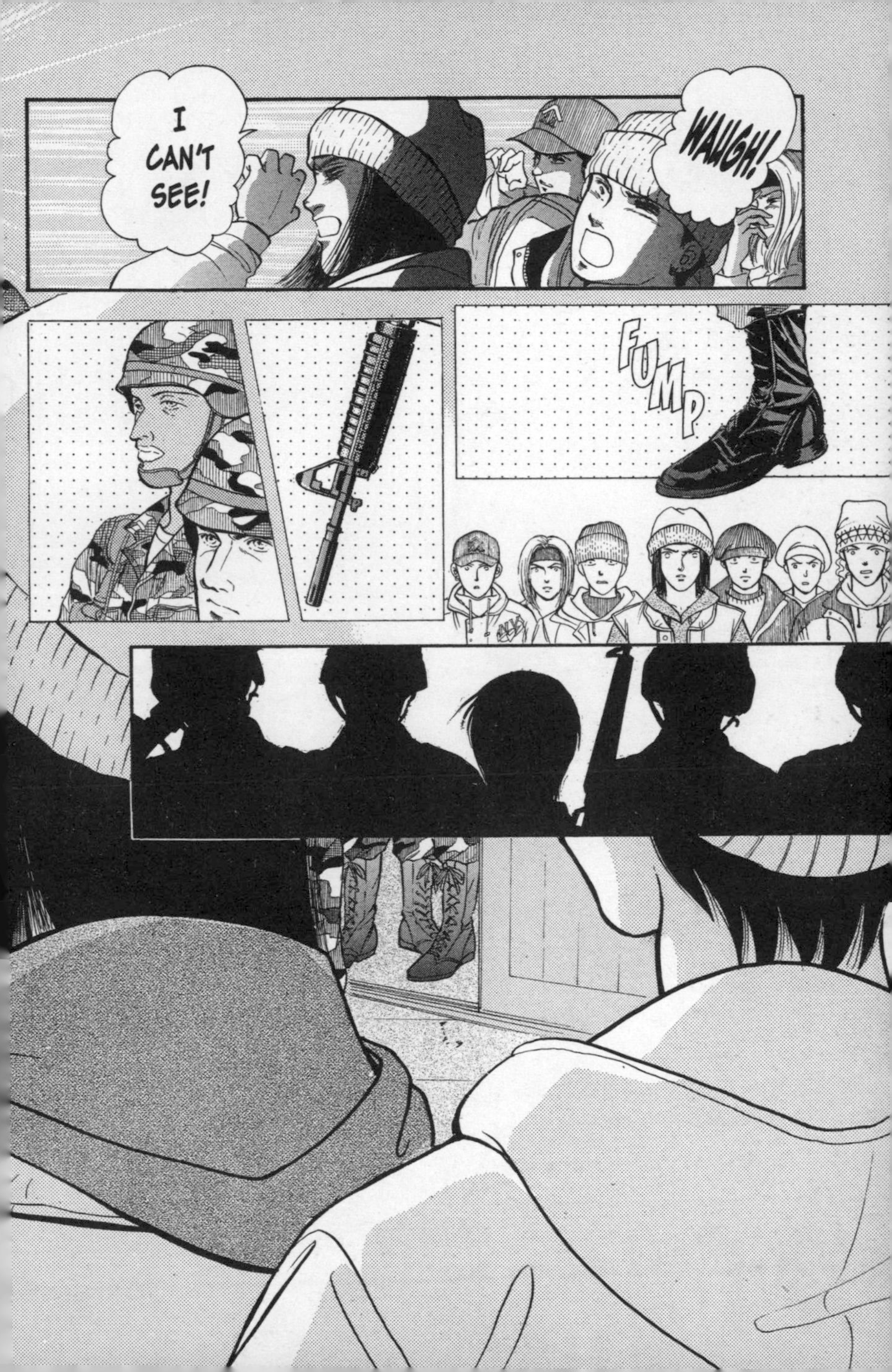
WAUGH!
I CAN'T SEE!
FUMP

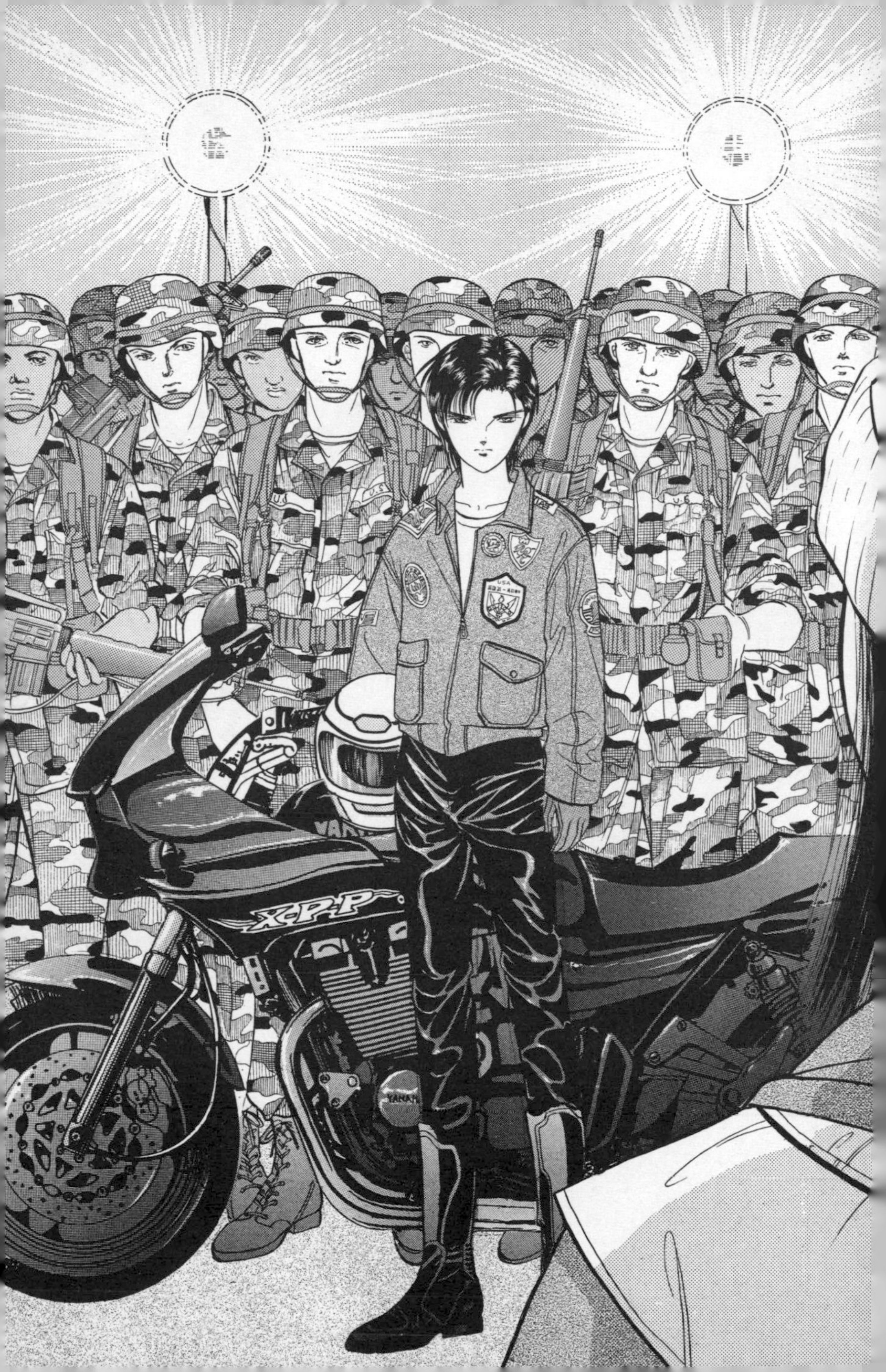
X-P-P

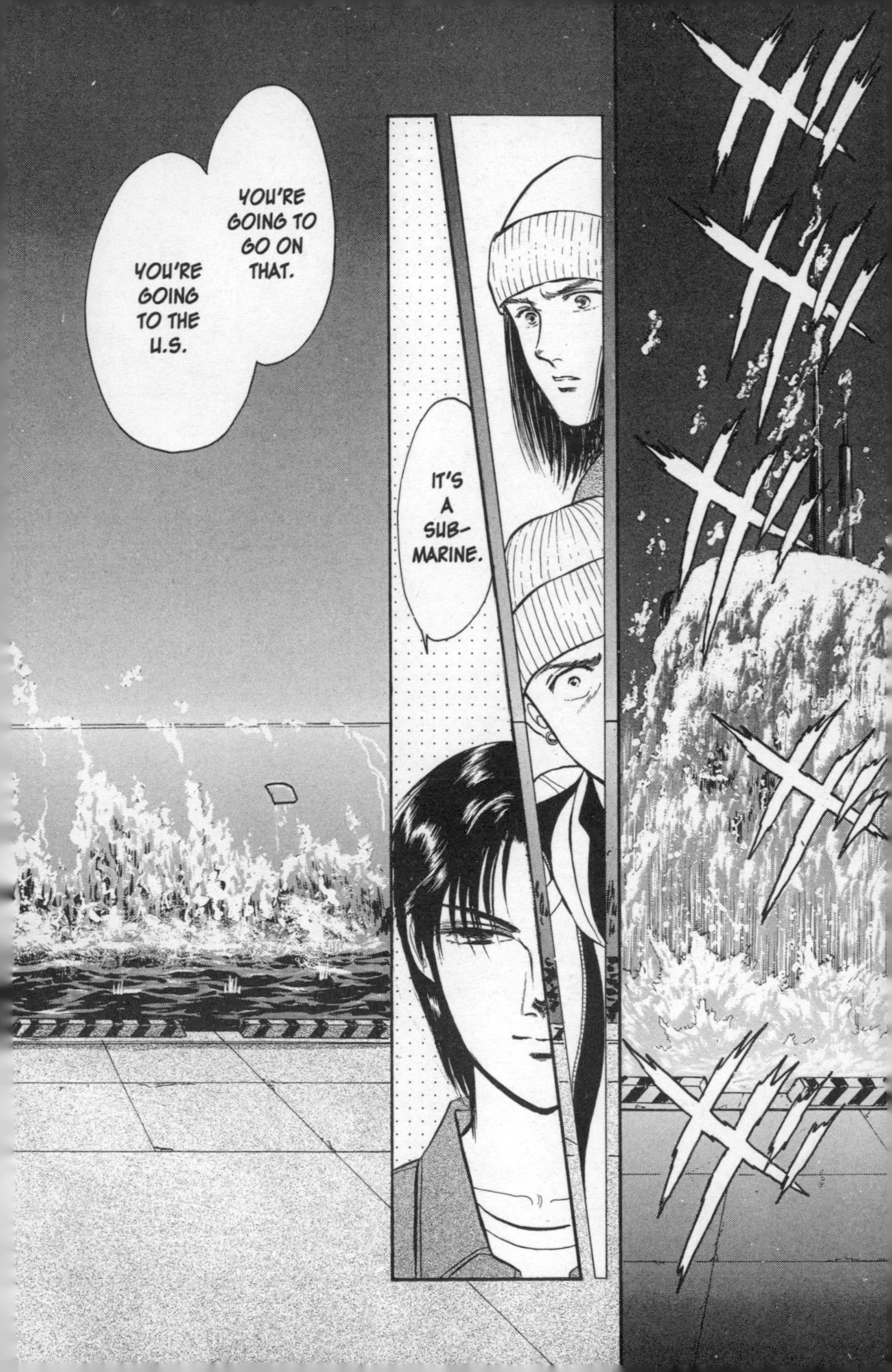
IT'S A SUB-MARINE.
YOU'RE GOING TO GO ON THAT.
YOU'RE GOING TO THE U.S.

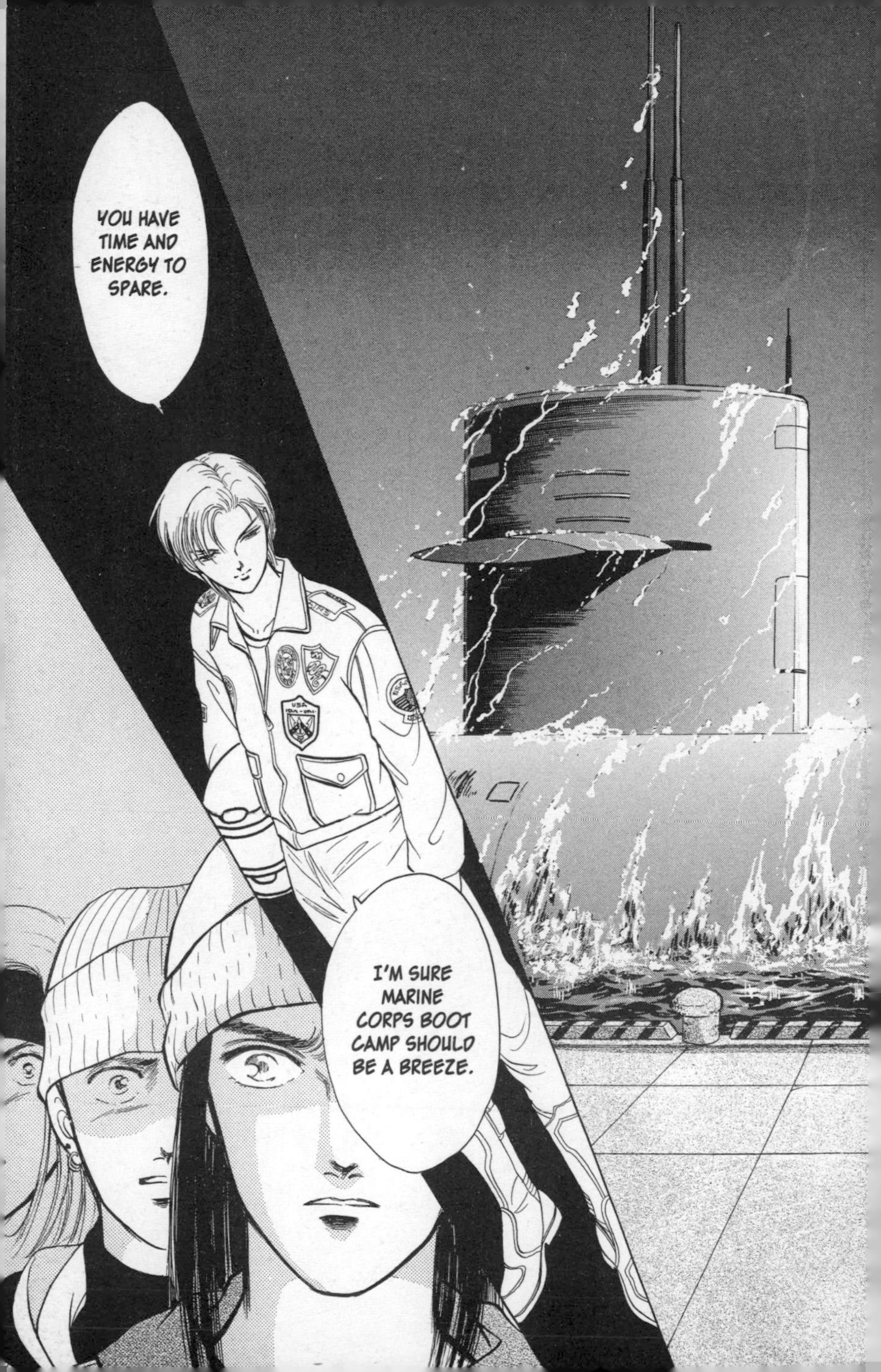
YOU HAVE TIME AND ENERGY TO SPARE.
I'M SURE MARINE CORPS BOOT CAMP SHOULD BE A BREEZE.

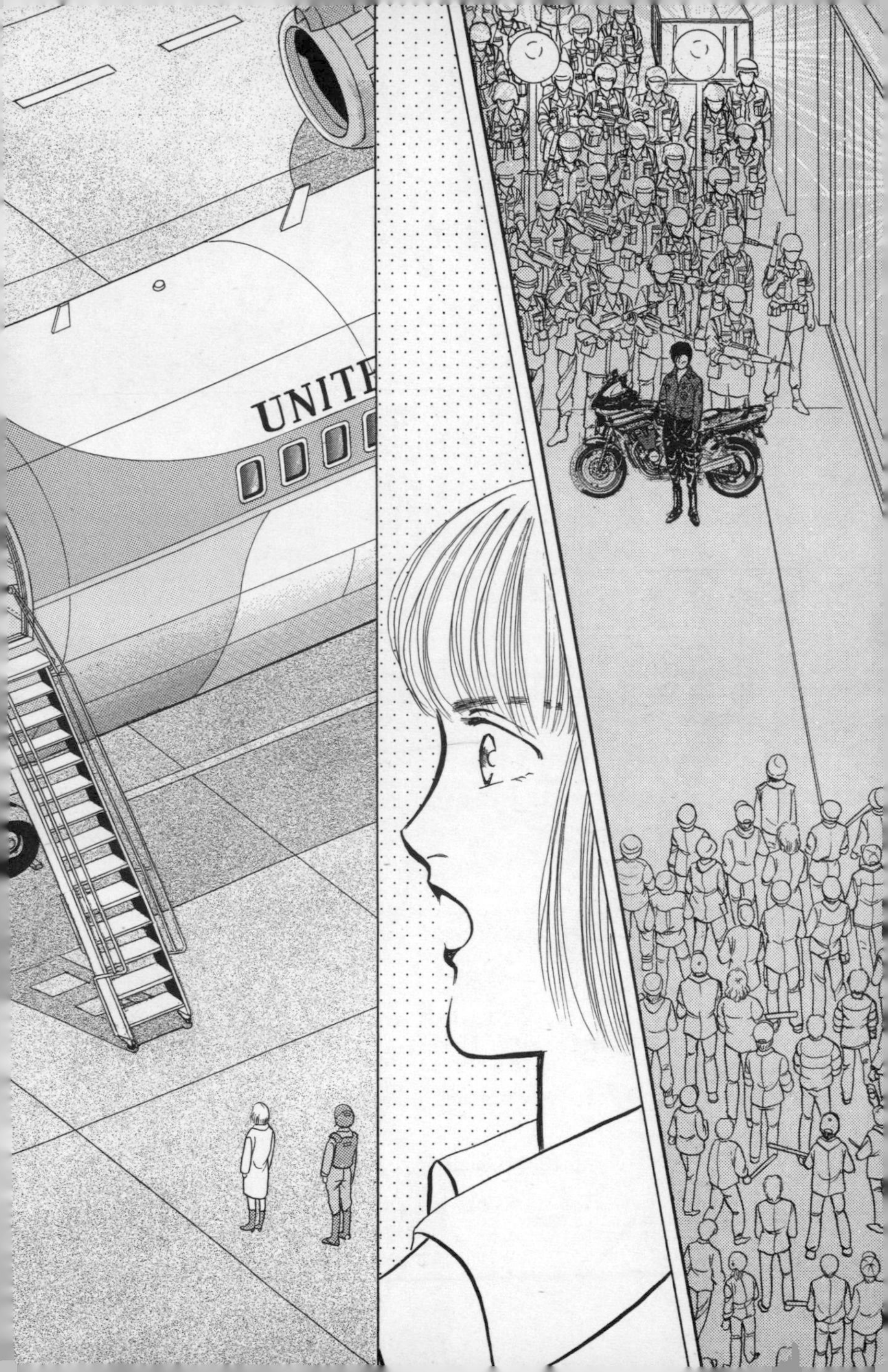
UNITE

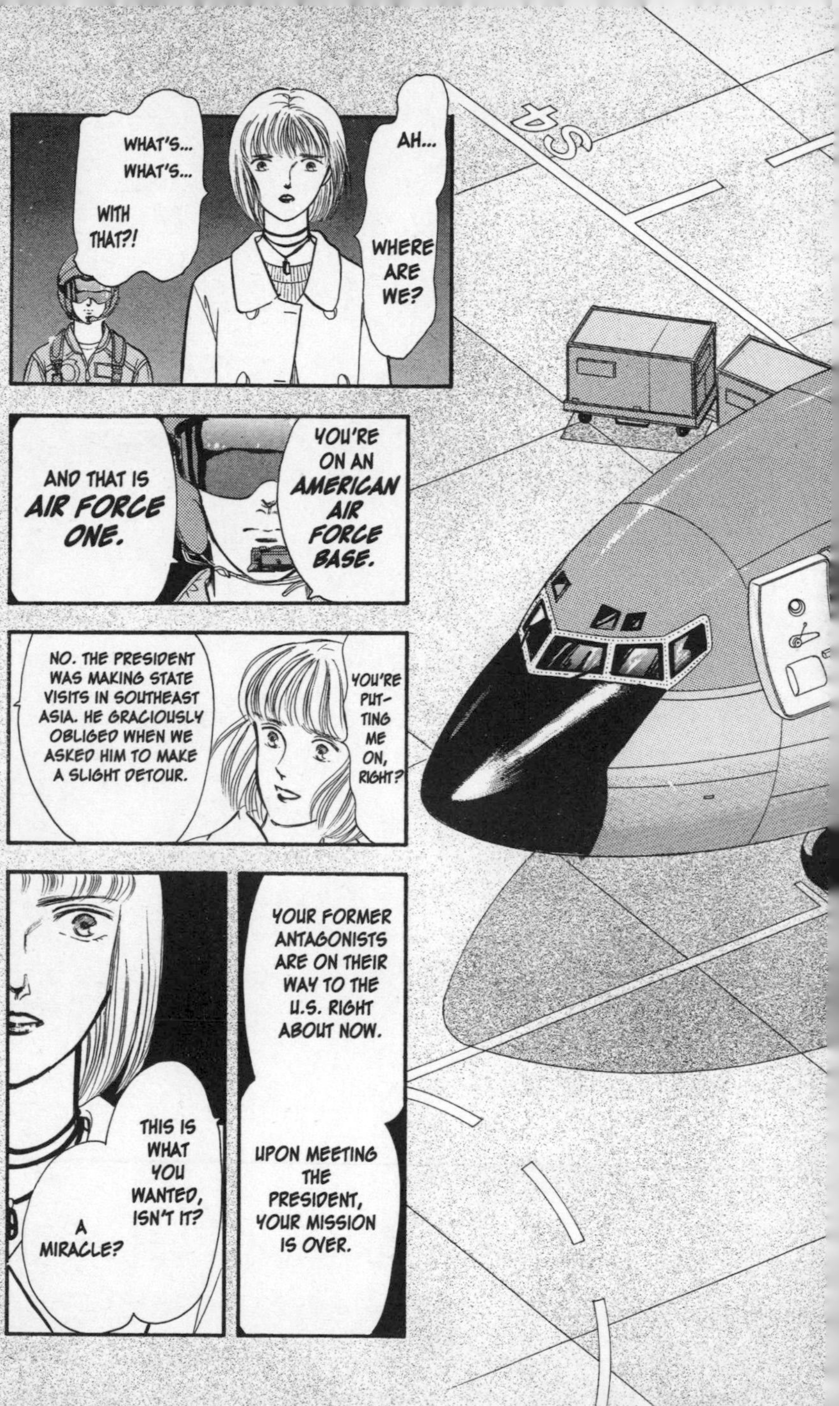
AH... WHERE ARE WE?
WHAT'S... WHAT'S... WITH THAT?!
YOU'RE ON AN AMERICAN AIR FORCE BASE.
AND THAT IS AIR FORCE ONE.
YOU'RE PUT-TING ME ON, RIGHT?
NO. THE PRESIDENT WAS MAKING STATE VISITS IN SOUTHEAST ASIA. HE GRACIOUSLY OBLIGED WHEN WE ASKED HIM TO MAKE A SLIGHT DETOUR.
YOUR FORMER ANTAGONISTS ARE ON THEIR WAY TO THE U.S. RIGHT ABOUT NOW.
UPON MEETING THE PRESIDENT, YOUR MISSION IS OVER.
THIS IS WHAT YOU WANTED, ISN'T IT?
A MIRACLE?

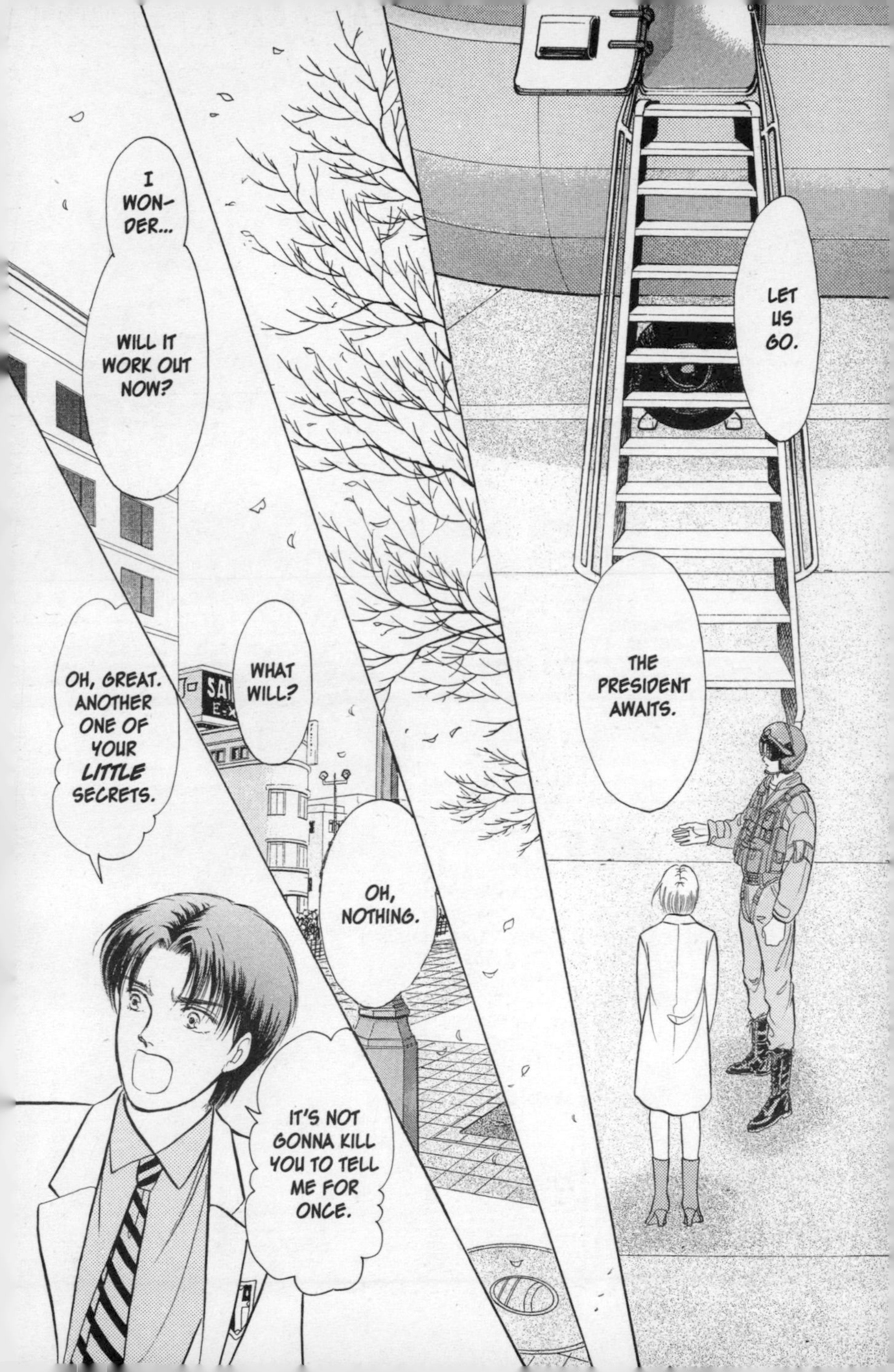

LET US GO.
THE PRESIDENT AWAITS.
I WON-DER...
WILL IT WORK OUT NOW?
WHAT WILL?
OH, NOTHING.
OH, GREAT. ANOTHER ONE OF YOUR *LITTLE* SECRETS.
IT'S NOT GONNA KILL YOU TO TELL ME FOR ONCE.

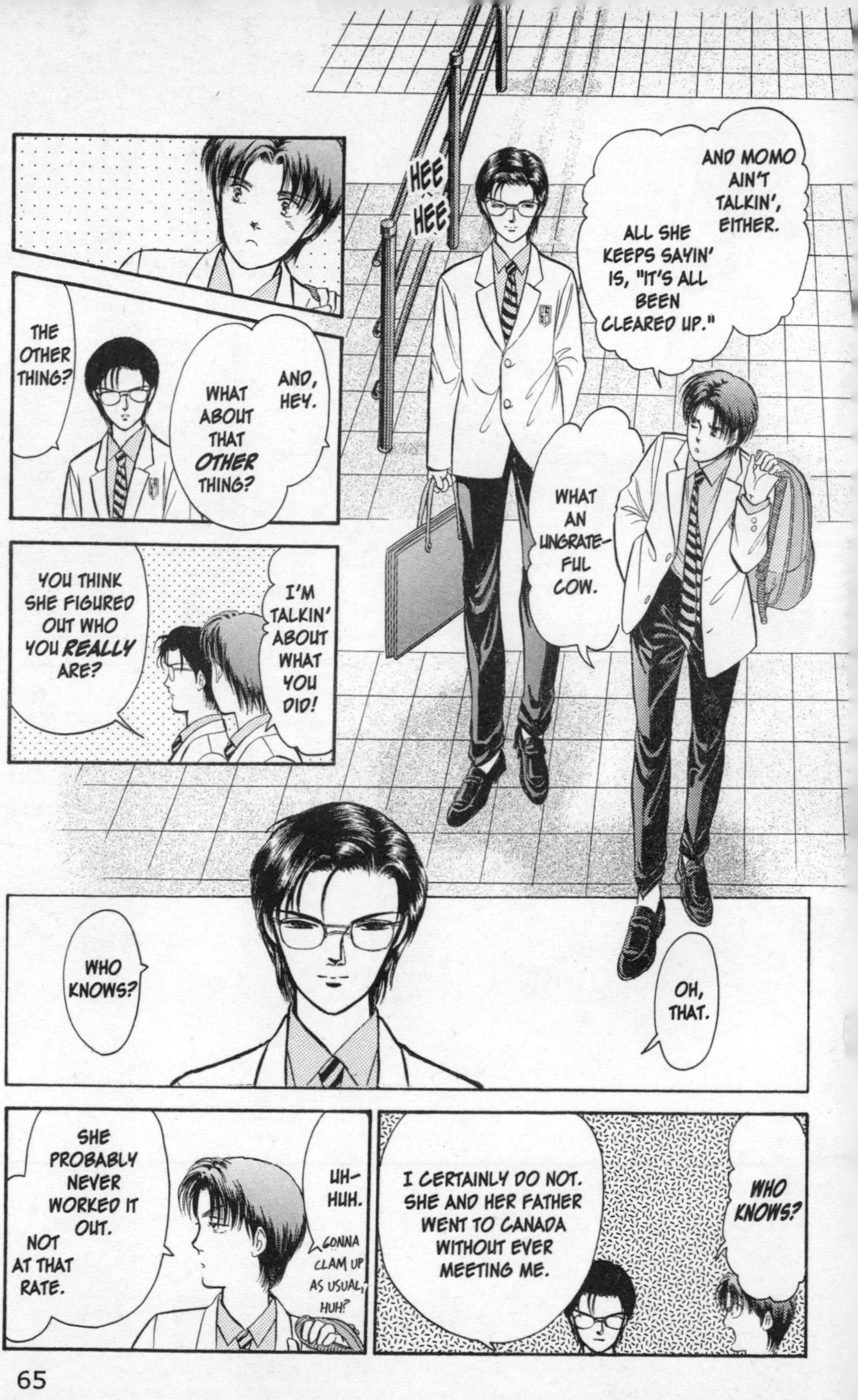
HEE HEE
AND MOMO AIN'T TALKIN', EITHER.
ALL SHE KEEPS SAYIN' IS, "IT'S ALL BEEN CLEARED UP."
WHAT AN UNGRATE-FUL COW.
AND, HEY.
WHAT ABOUT THAT *OTHER* THING?
THE OTHER THING?
I'M TALKIN' ABOUT WHAT YOU DID!
YOU THINK SHE FIGURED OUT WHO YOU *REALLY* ARE?
OH, THAT.
WHO KNOWS?
WHO KNOWS?
I CERTAINLY DO NOT. SHE AND HER FATHER WENT TO CANADA WITHOUT EVER MEETING ME.
UH-HUH.
SHE PROBABLY NEVER WORKED IT OUT.
NOT AT THAT RATE.
GONNA CLAM UP AS USUAL, HUH?

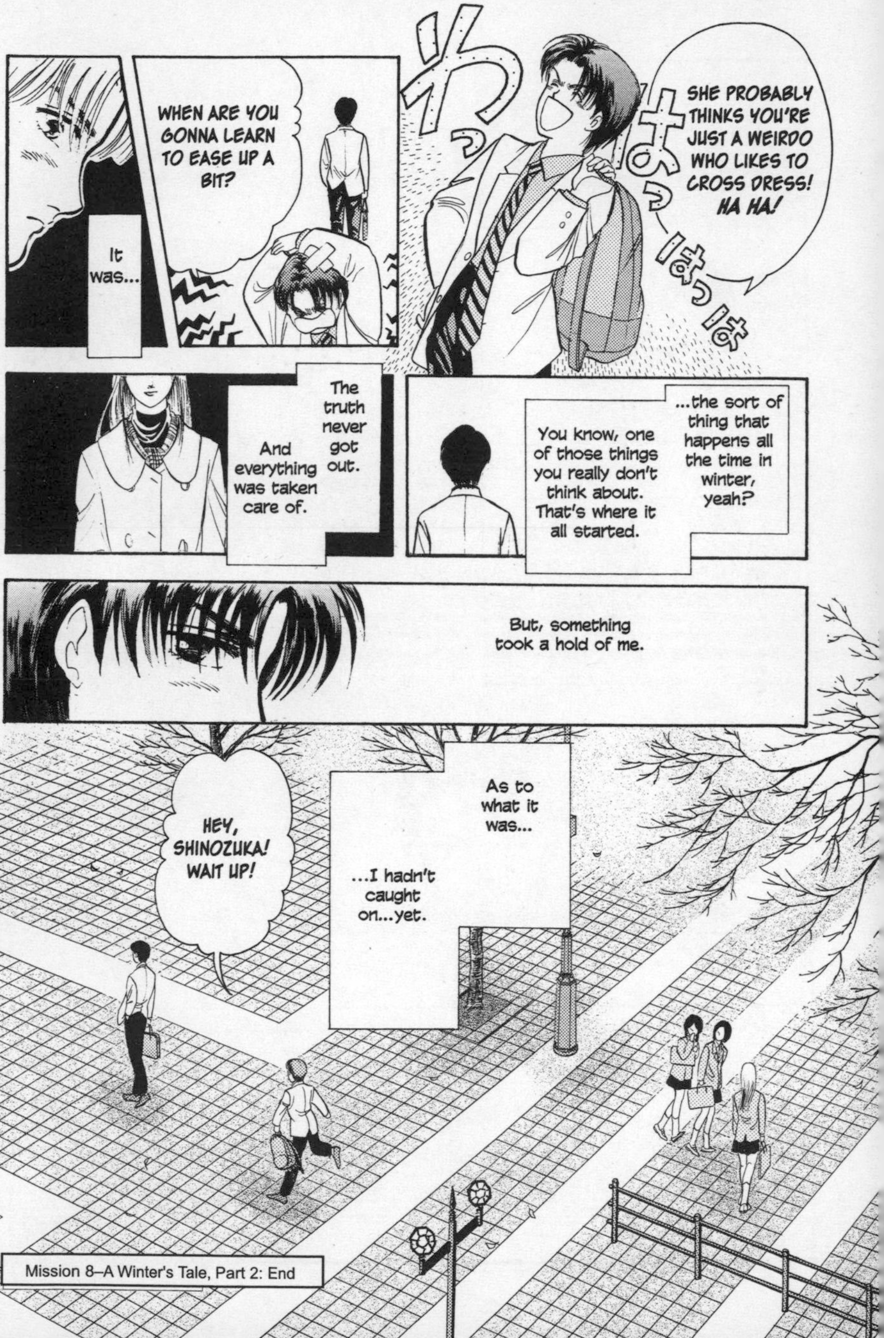
SHE PROBABLY THINKS YOU'RE JUST A WEIRDO WHO LIKES TO CROSS DRESS! HA HA!
わっはっ
はっは
WHEN ARE YOU GONNA LEARN TO EASE UP A BIT?
It was...
...the sort of thing that happens all the time in winter, yeah?
You know, one of those things you really don't think about. That's where it all started.
The truth never got out.
And everything was taken care of.
But, something took a hold of me.
As to what it was...
HEY, SHINOZUKA! WAIT UP!
...I hadn't caught on...yet.
Mission 8–A Winter's Tale, Part 2: End

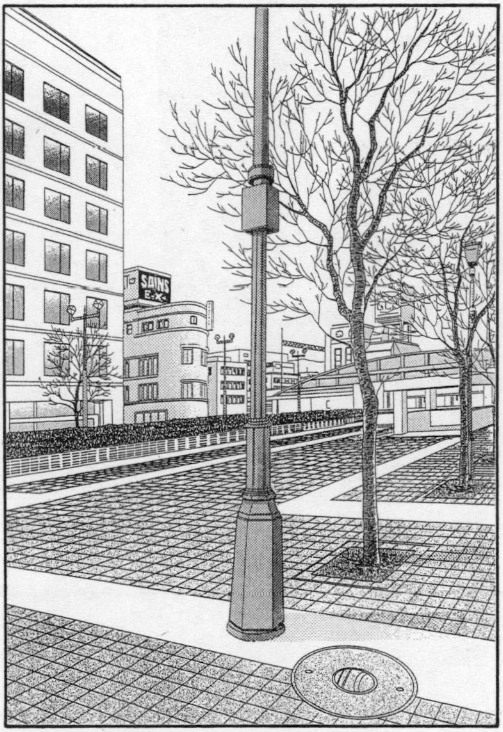
SAINS

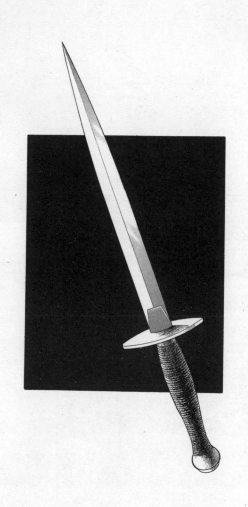

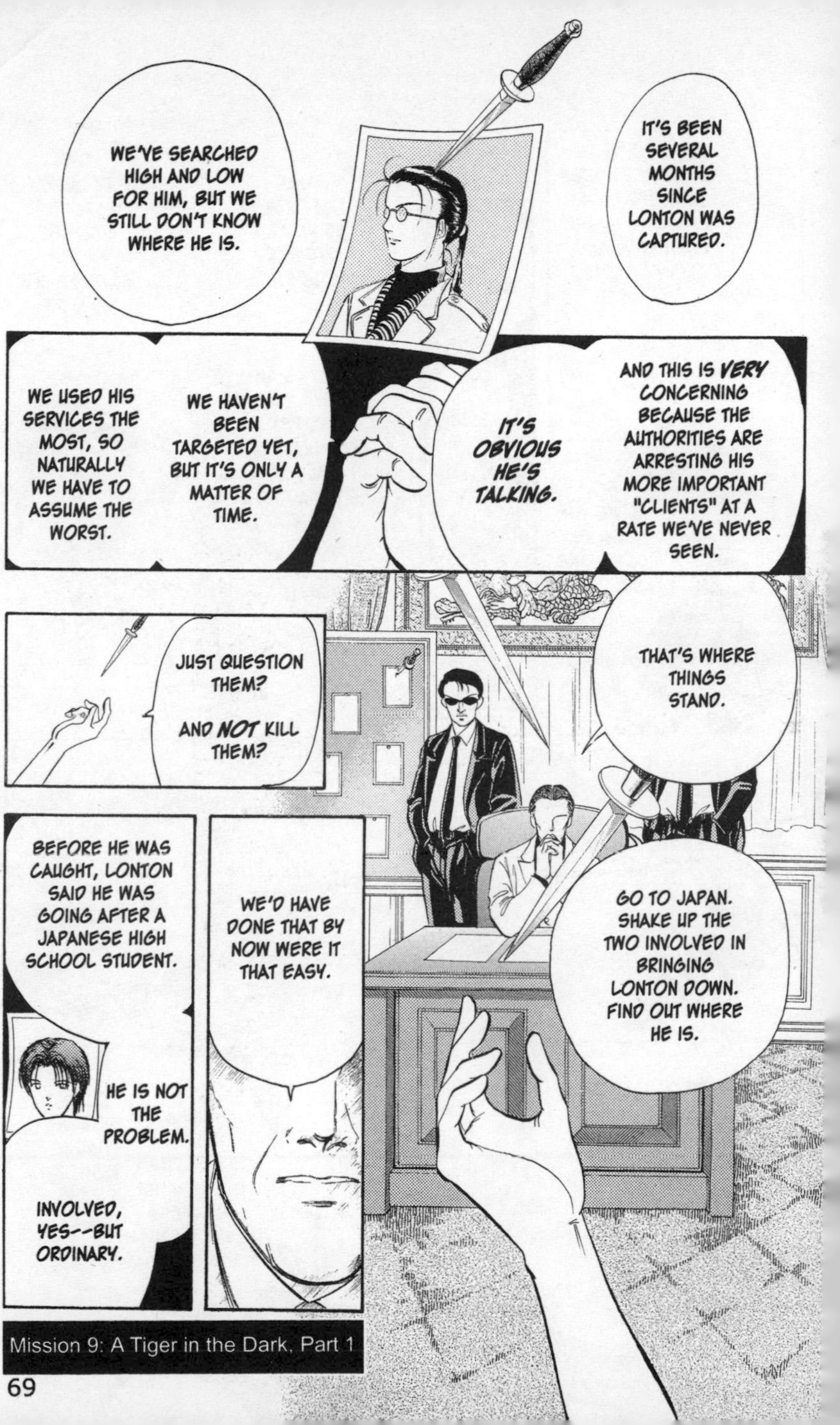
IT'S BEEN SEVERAL MONTHS SINCE LONTON WAS CAPTURED.
WE'VE SEARCHED HIGH AND LOW FOR HIM, BUT WE STILL DON'T KNOW WHERE HE IS.
AND THIS IS VERY CONCERNING BECAUSE THE AUTHORITIES ARE ARRESTING HIS MORE IMPORTANT "CLIENTS" AT A RATE WE'VE NEVER SEEN.
IT'S OBVIOUS HE'S TALKING.
WE HAVEN'T BEEN TARGETED YET, BUT IT'S ONLY A MATTER OF TIME.
WE USED HIS SERVICES THE MOST, SO NATURALLY WE HAVE TO ASSUME THE WORST.
THAT'S WHERE THINGS STAND.
GO TO JAPAN. SHAKE UP THE TWO INVOLVED IN BRINGING LONTON DOWN. FIND OUT WHERE HE IS.
JUST QUESTION THEM?
AND NOT KILL THEM?
WE'D HAVE DONE THAT BY NOW WERE IT THAT EASY.
BEFORE HE WAS CAUGHT, LONTON SAID HE WAS GOING AFTER A JAPANESE HIGH SCHOOL STUDENT.
HE IS NOT THE PROBLEM.
INVOLVED, YES--BUT ORDINARY.

Mission 9: A Tiger in the Dark, Part 1

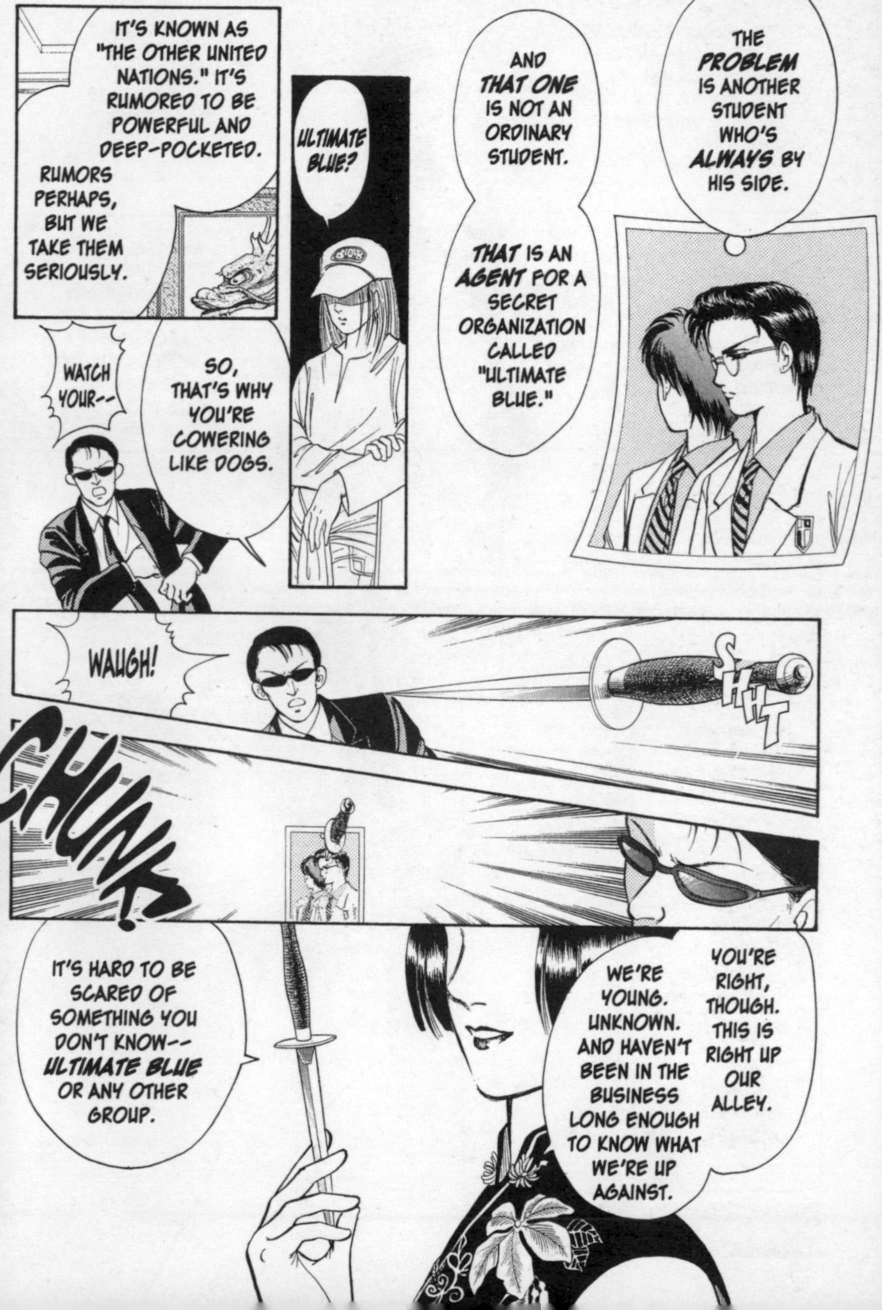
THE PROBLEM IS ANOTHER STUDENT WHO'S ALWAYS BY HIS SIDE.
AND THAT ONE IS NOT AN ORDINARY STUDENT.
THAT IS AN AGENT FOR A SECRET ORGANIZATION CALLED "ULTIMATE BLUE."
ULTIMATE BLUE?
IT'S KNOWN AS "THE OTHER UNITED NATIONS." IT'S RUMORED TO BE POWERFUL AND DEEP-POCKETED.
RUMORS PERHAPS, BUT WE TAKE THEM SERIOUSLY.
SO, THAT'S WHY YOU'RE COWERING LIKE DOGS.
WATCH YOUR--
SHHT
WAUGH!
CHUNK!
YOU'RE RIGHT, THOUGH. THIS IS RIGHT UP OUR ALLEY.
WE'RE YOUNG. UNKNOWN. AND HAVEN'T BEEN IN THE BUSINESS LONG ENOUGH TO KNOW WHAT WE'RE UP AGAINST.
IT'S HARD TO BE SCARED OF SOMETHING YOU DON'T KNOW-- ULTIMATE BLUE OR ANY OTHER GROUP.

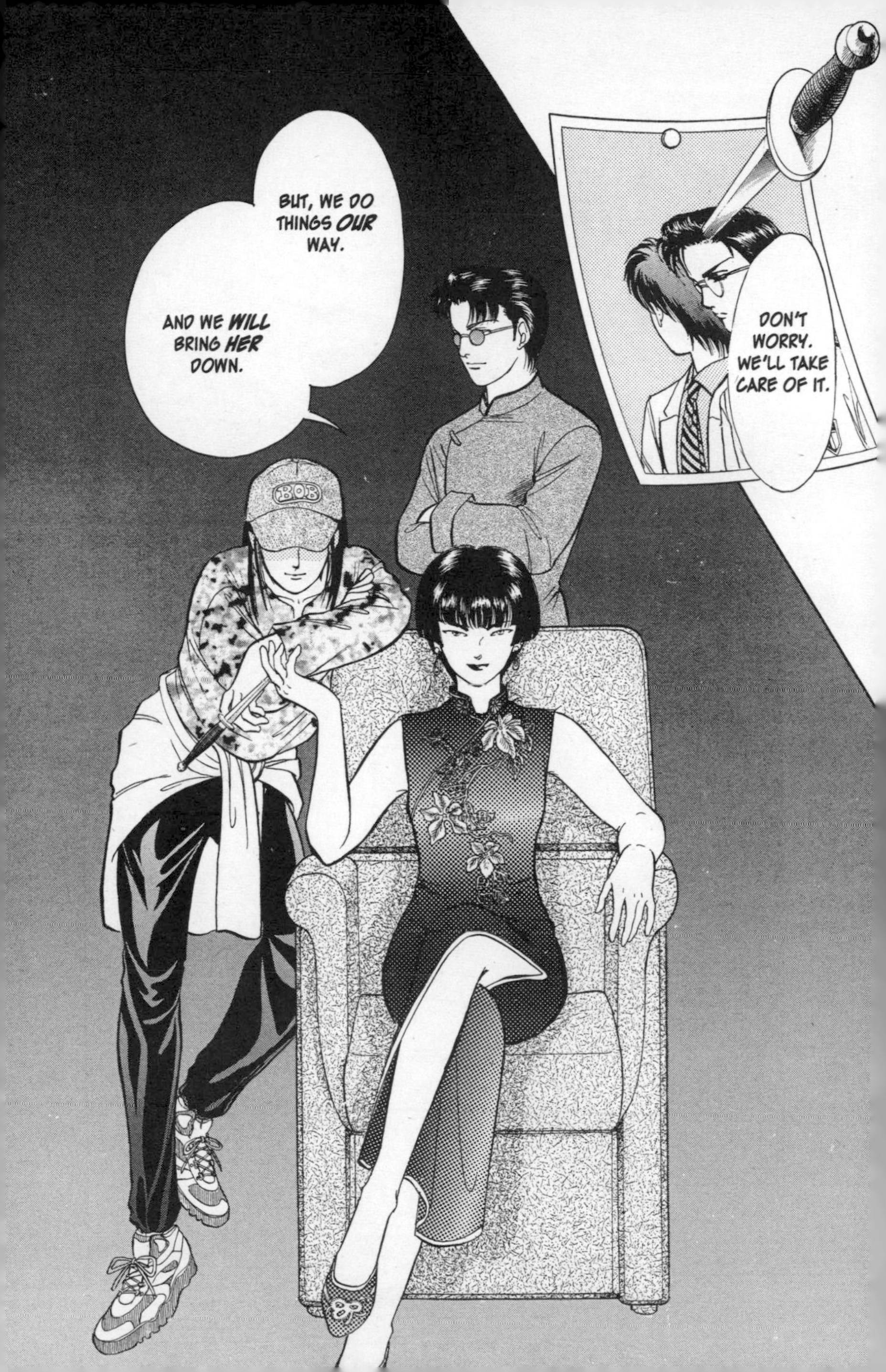
DON'T WORRY. WE'LL TAKE CARE OF IT.
BUT, WE DO THINGS *OUR* WAY.
AND WE *WILL* BRING *HER* DOWN.
BOB

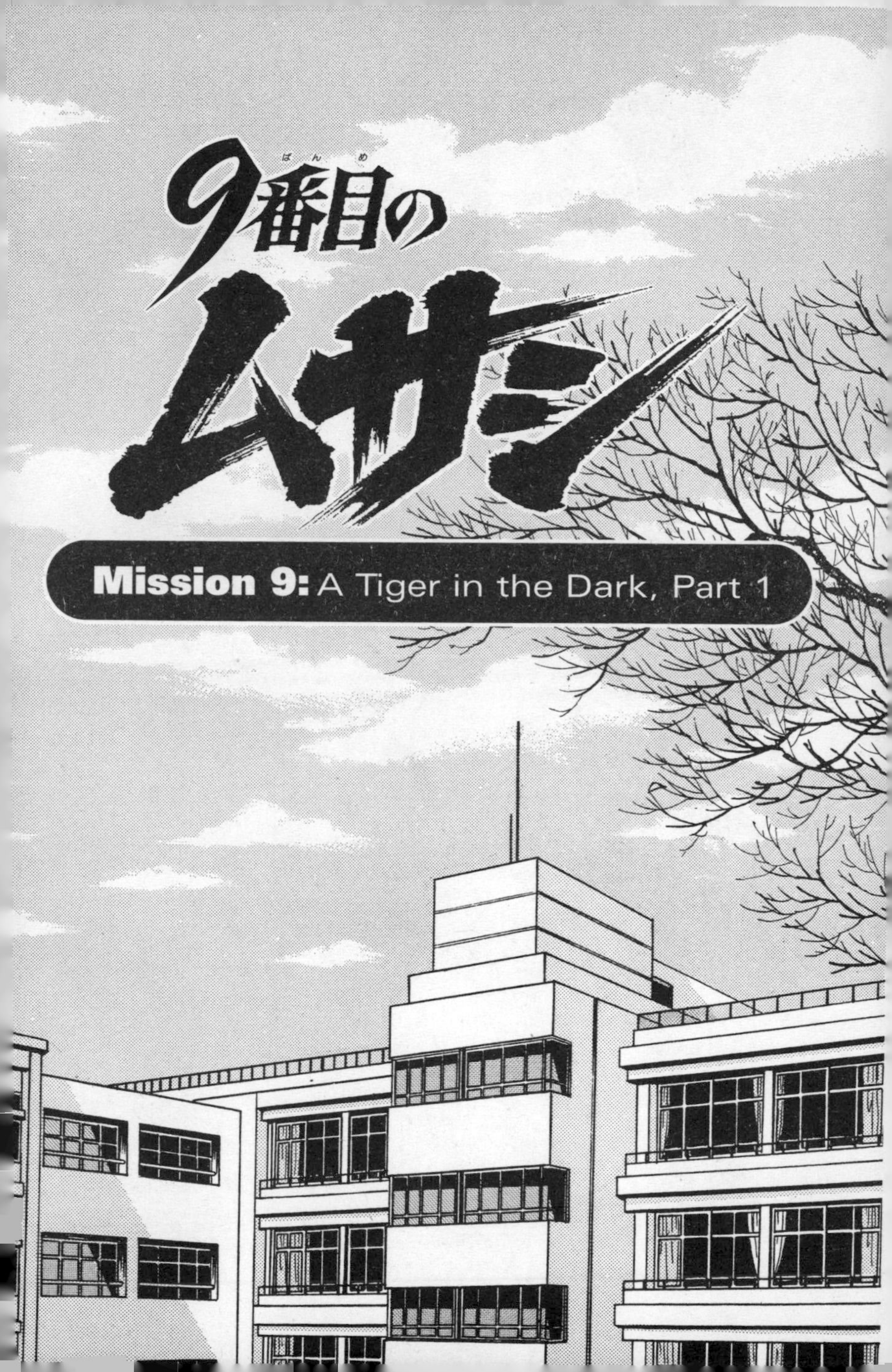
9番目のムサシ
Mission 9: A Tiger in the Dark, Part 1

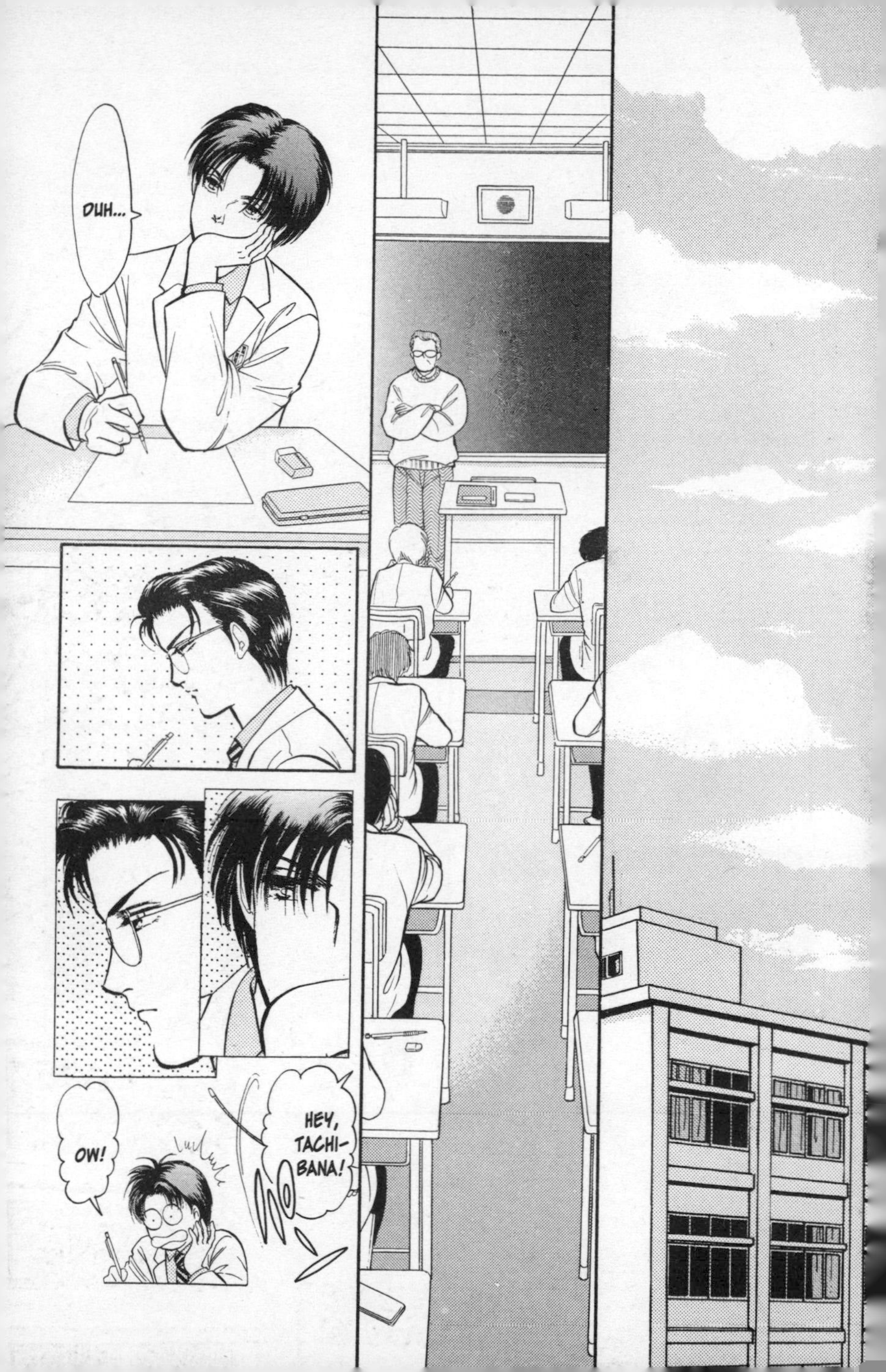
DUH...
HEY, TACHI-BANA!
OW!

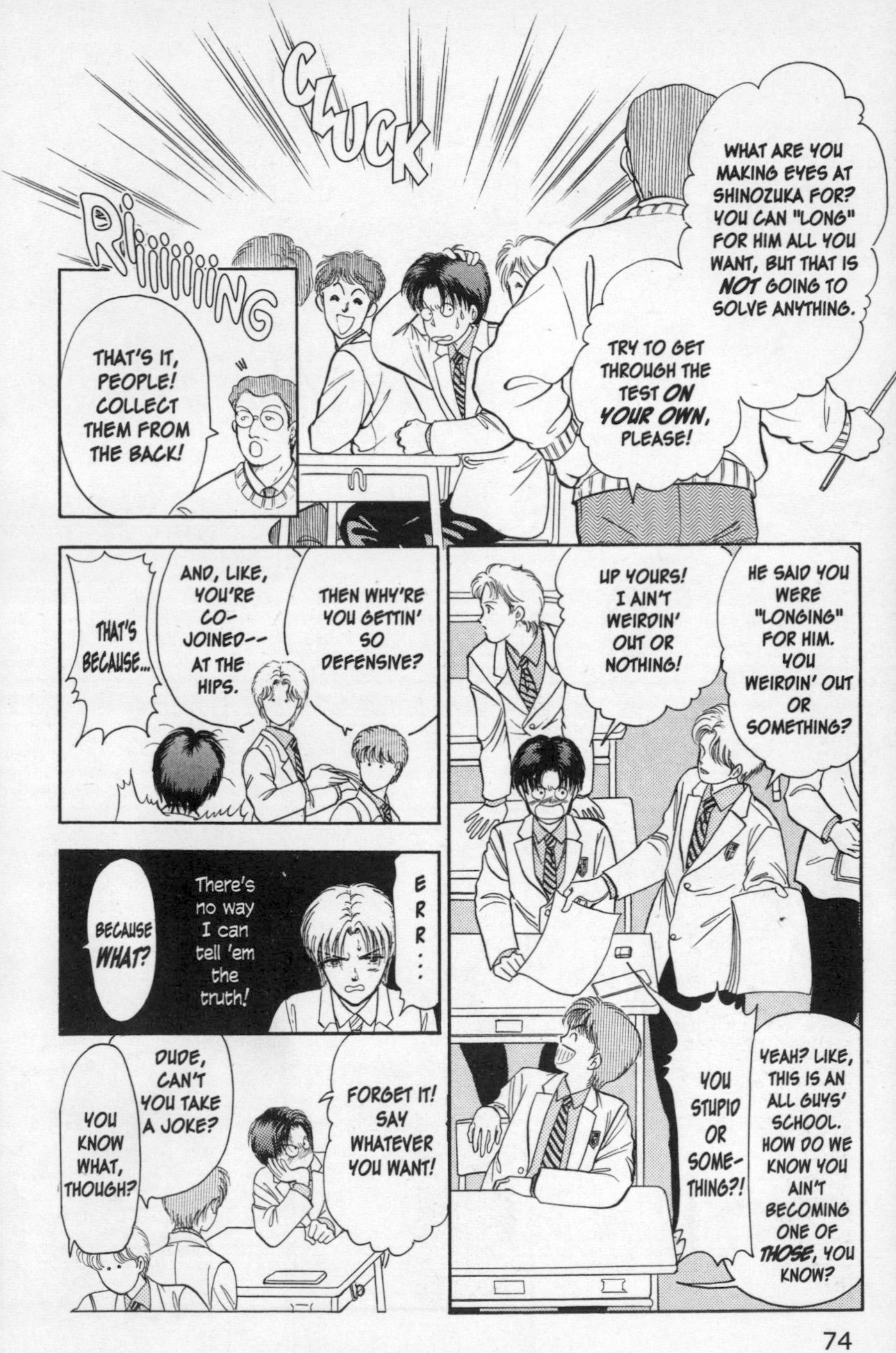
WHAT ARE YOU MAKING EYES AT SHINOZUKA FOR? YOU CAN "LONG" FOR HIM ALL YOU WANT, BUT THAT IS NOT GOING TO SOLVE ANYTHING.
TRY TO GET THROUGH THE TEST ON YOUR OWN, PLEASE!
CLUCK
RIIIIIIIING
THAT'S IT, PEOPLE! COLLECT THEM FROM THE BACK!
HE SAID YOU WERE "LONGING" FOR HIM. YOU WEIRDIN' OUT OR SOMETHING?
UP YOURS! I AIN'T WEIRDIN' OUT OR NOTHING!
THEN WHY'RE YOU GETTIN' SO DEFENSIVE?
AND, LIKE, YOU'RE CO-JOINED-- AT THE HIPS.
THAT'S BECAUSE...
ERR...
There's no way I can tell 'em the truth!
BECAUSE WHAT?
YEAH? LIKE, THIS IS AN ALL GUYS' SCHOOL. HOW DO WE KNOW YOU AIN'T BECOMING ONE OF THOSE, YOU KNOW?
YOU STUPID OR SOME-THING?!
FORGET IT! SAY WHATEVER YOU WANT!
DUDE, CAN'T YOU TAKE A JOKE?
YOU KNOW WHAT, THOUGH?

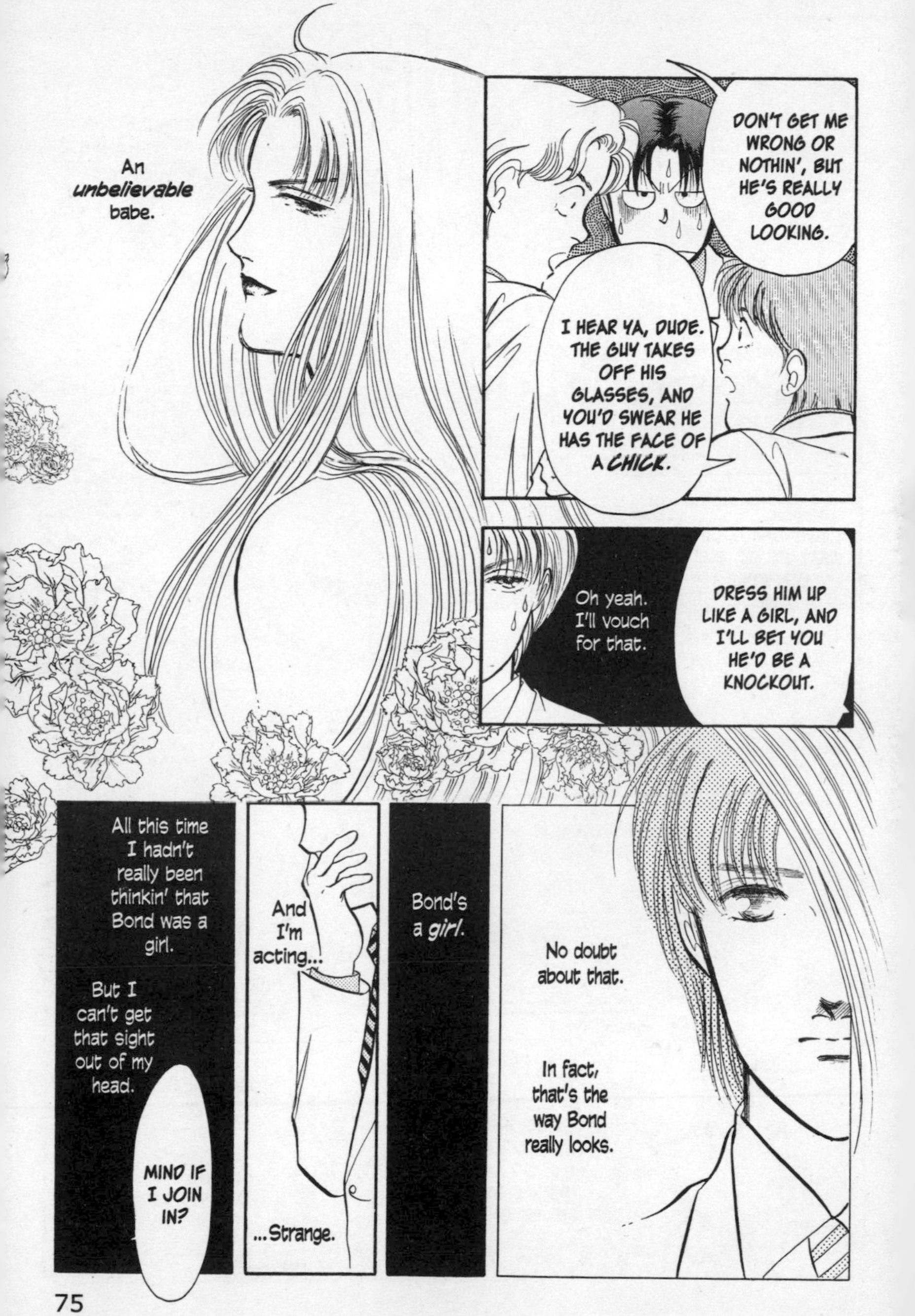
DON'T GET ME WRONG OR NOTHIN', BUT HE'S REALLY GOOD LOOKING.
I HEAR YA, DUDE. THE GUY TAKES OFF HIS GLASSES, AND YOU'D SWEAR HE HAS THE FACE OF A *CHICK*.
DRESS HIM UP LIKE A GIRL, AND I'LL BET YOU HE'D BE A KNOCKOUT.
Oh yeah. I'll vouch for that.
An *unbelievable* babe.
No doubt about that.
In fact, that's the way Bond really looks.
Bond's a *girl*.
And I'm acting...
...Strange.
All this time I hadn't really been thinkin' that Bond was a girl.
But I can't get that sight out of my head.
MIND IF I JOIN IN?

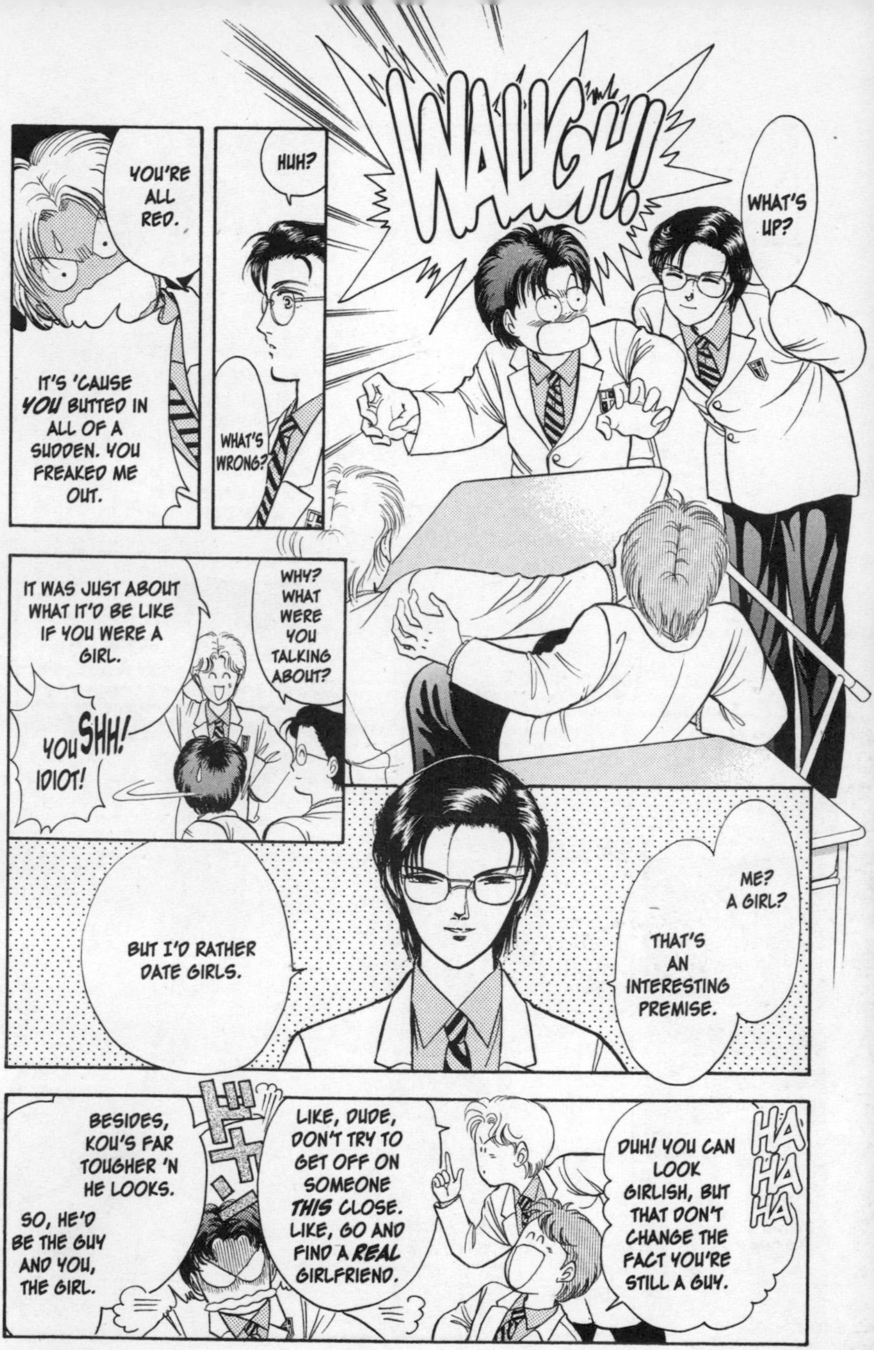
WHAT'S UP?
WAUGH!!
HUH?
WHAT'S WRONG?
YOU'RE ALL RED.
IT'S 'CAUSE YOU BUTTED IN ALL OF A SUDDEN. YOU FREAKED ME OUT.
WHY? WHAT WERE YOU TALKING ABOUT?
IT WAS JUST ABOUT WHAT IT'D BE LIKE IF YOU WERE A GIRL.
SHH!
YOU IDIOT!
ME? A GIRL?
THAT'S AN INTERESTING PREMISE.
BUT I'D RATHER DATE GIRLS.
HA HA HA
DUH! YOU CAN LOOK GIRLISH, BUT THAT DON'T CHANGE THE FACT YOU'RE STILL A GUY.
LIKE, DUDE, DON'T TRY TO GET OFF ON SOMEONE THIS CLOSE. LIKE, GO AND FIND A REAL GIRLFRIEND.
BESIDES, KOU'S FAR TOUGHER 'N HE LOOKS.
SO, HE'D BE THE GUY AND YOU, THE GIRL.

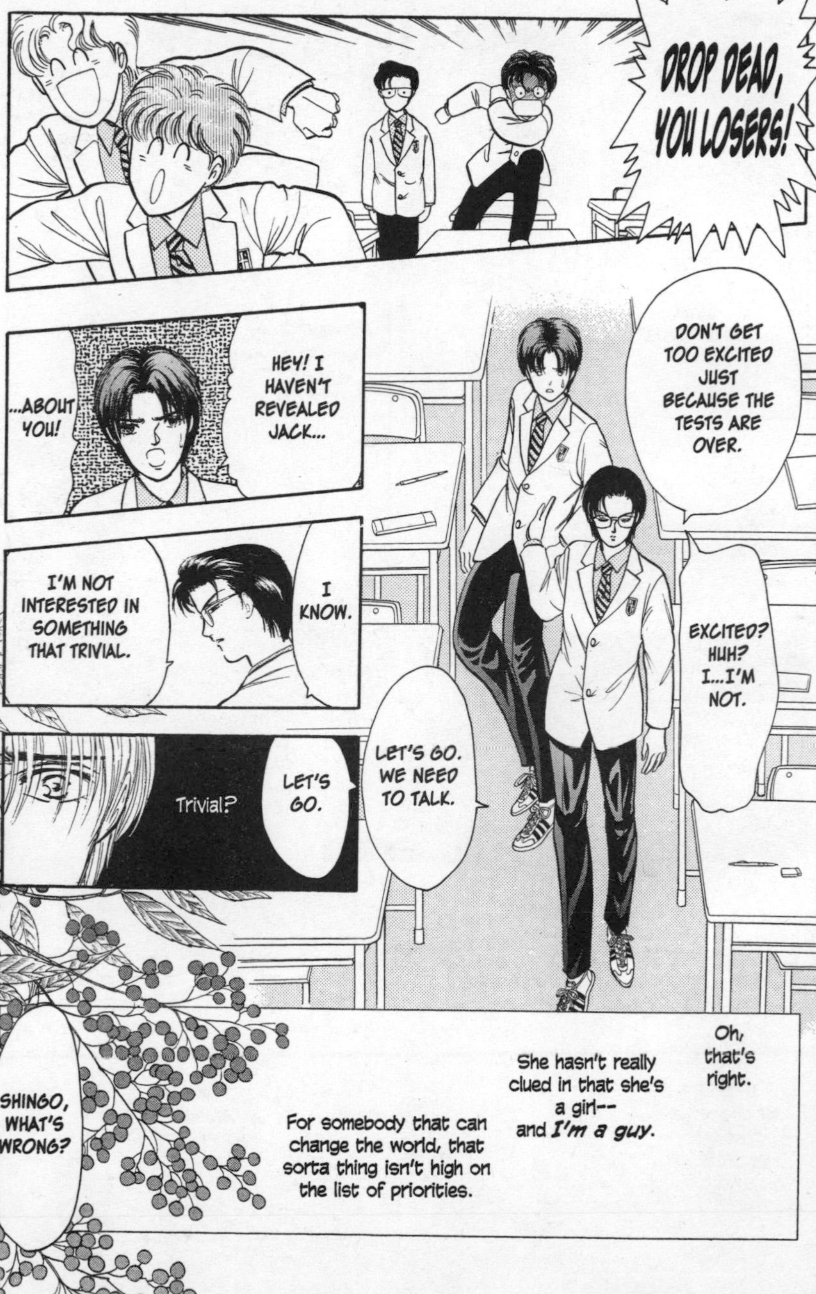
DROP DEAD, YOU LOSERS!
DON'T GET TOO EXCITED JUST BECAUSE THE TESTS ARE OVER.
EXCITED? HUH? I...I'M NOT.
LET'S GO. WE NEED TO TALK.
HEY! I HAVEN'T REVEALED JACK...
...ABOUT YOU!
I KNOW.
I'M NOT INTERESTED IN SOMETHING THAT TRIVIAL.
LET'S GO.
Trivial?
Oh, that's right.
She hasn't really clued in that she's a girl-- and *I'm a guy*.
For somebody that can change the world, that sorta thing isn't high on the list of priorities.
SHINGO, WHAT'S WRONG?

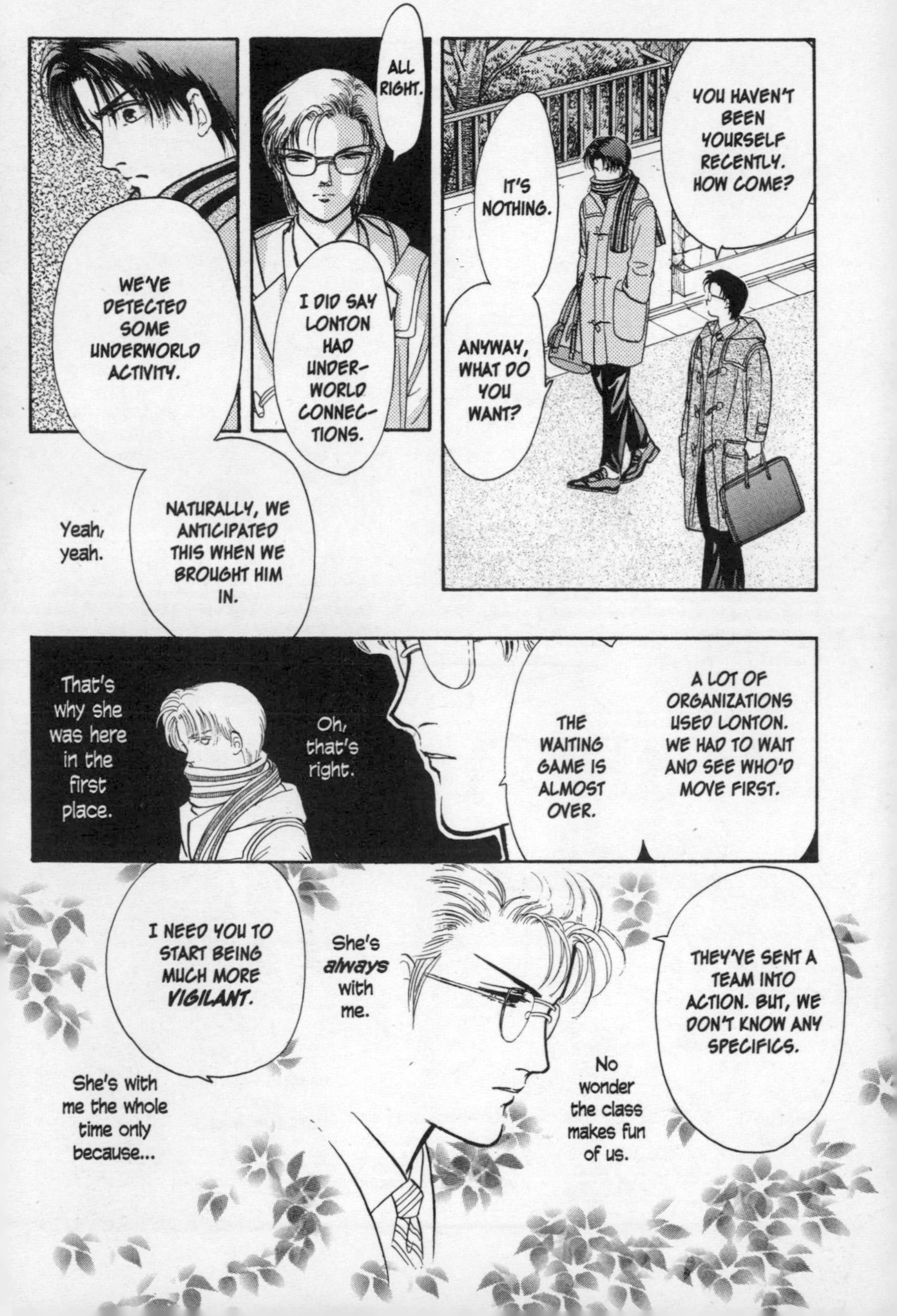
YOU HAVEN'T BEEN YOURSELF RECENTLY. HOW COME?
IT'S NOTHING.
ANYWAY, WHAT DO YOU WANT?
ALL RIGHT.
I DID SAY LONTON HAD UNDER-WORLD CONNECTIONS.
WE'VE DETECTED SOME UNDERWORLD ACTIVITY.
NATURALLY, WE ANTICIPATED THIS WHEN WE BROUGHT HIM IN.
Yeah, yeah.
A LOT OF ORGANIZATIONS USED LONTON. WE HAD TO WAIT AND SEE WHO'D MOVE FIRST.
THE WAITING GAME IS ALMOST OVER.
Oh, that's right.
That's why she was here in the first place.
THEY'VE SENT A TEAM INTO ACTION. BUT, WE DON'T KNOW ANY SPECIFICS.
No wonder the class makes fun of us.
She's *always* with me.
I NEED YOU TO START BEING MUCH MORE ***VIGILANT***.
She's with me the whole time only because...

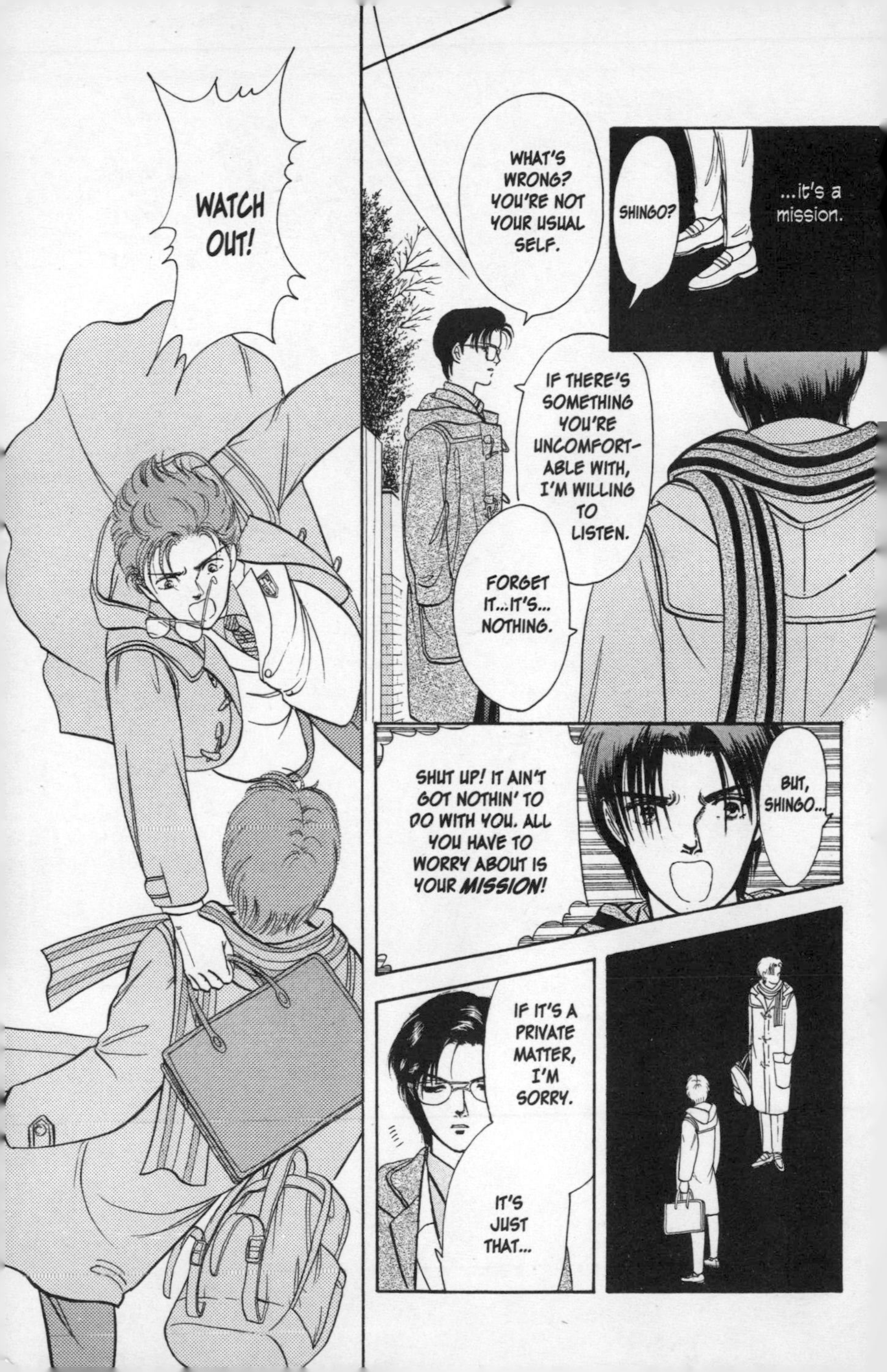
...it's a mission.
SHINGO?
WHAT'S WRONG? YOU'RE NOT YOUR USUAL SELF.
IF THERE'S SOMETHING YOU'RE UNCOMFORT-ABLE WITH, I'M WILLING TO LISTEN.
FORGET IT...IT'S... NOTHING.
BUT, SHINGO...
SHUT UP! IT AIN'T GOT NOTHIN' TO DO WITH YOU. ALL YOU HAVE TO WORRY ABOUT IS YOUR *MISSION*!
IF IT'S A PRIVATE MATTER, I'M SORRY.
IT'S JUST THAT...
WATCH OUT!

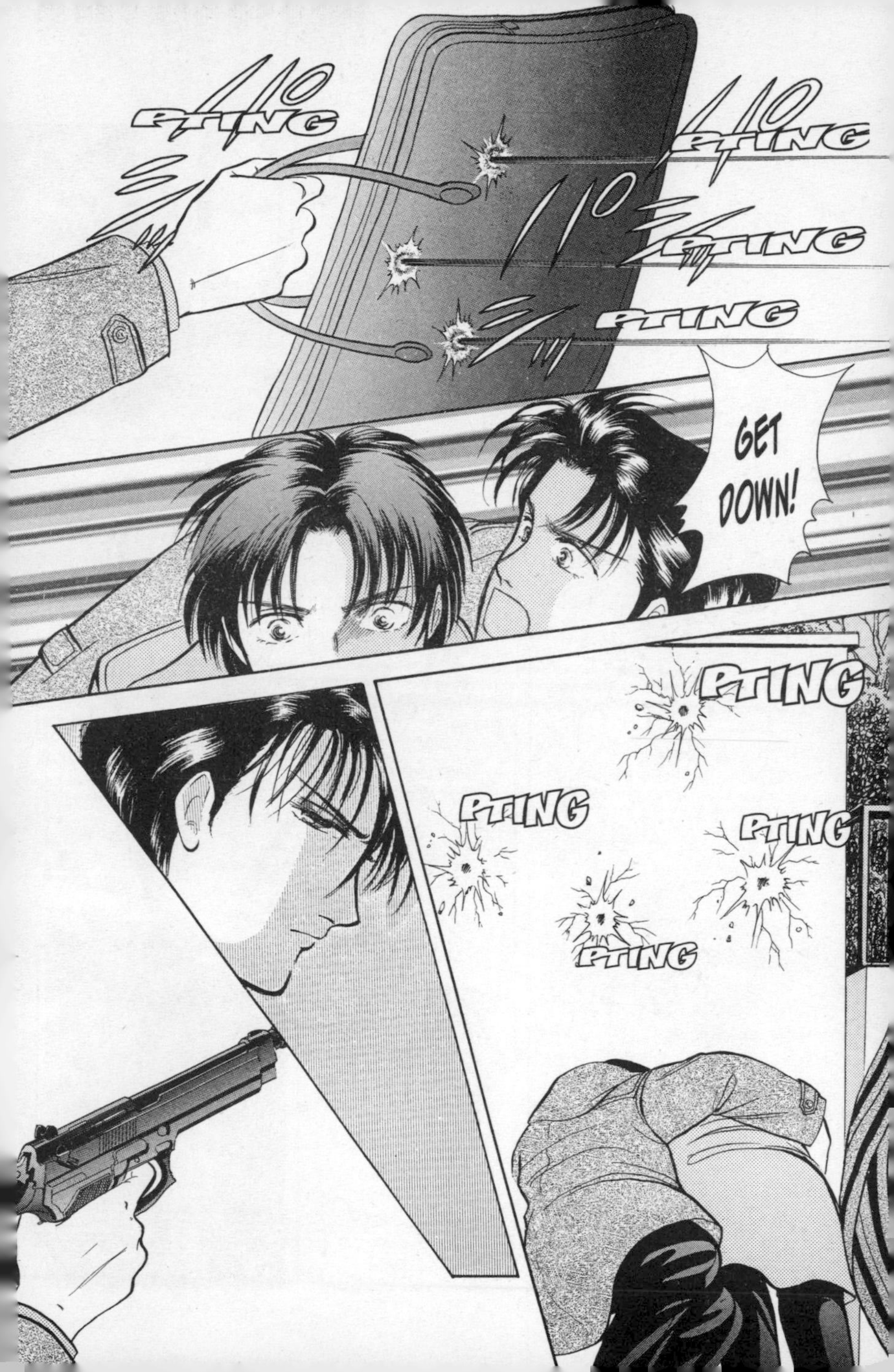
PTING
PTING
PTING
PTING
GET DOWN!
PTING
PTING
PTING
PTING

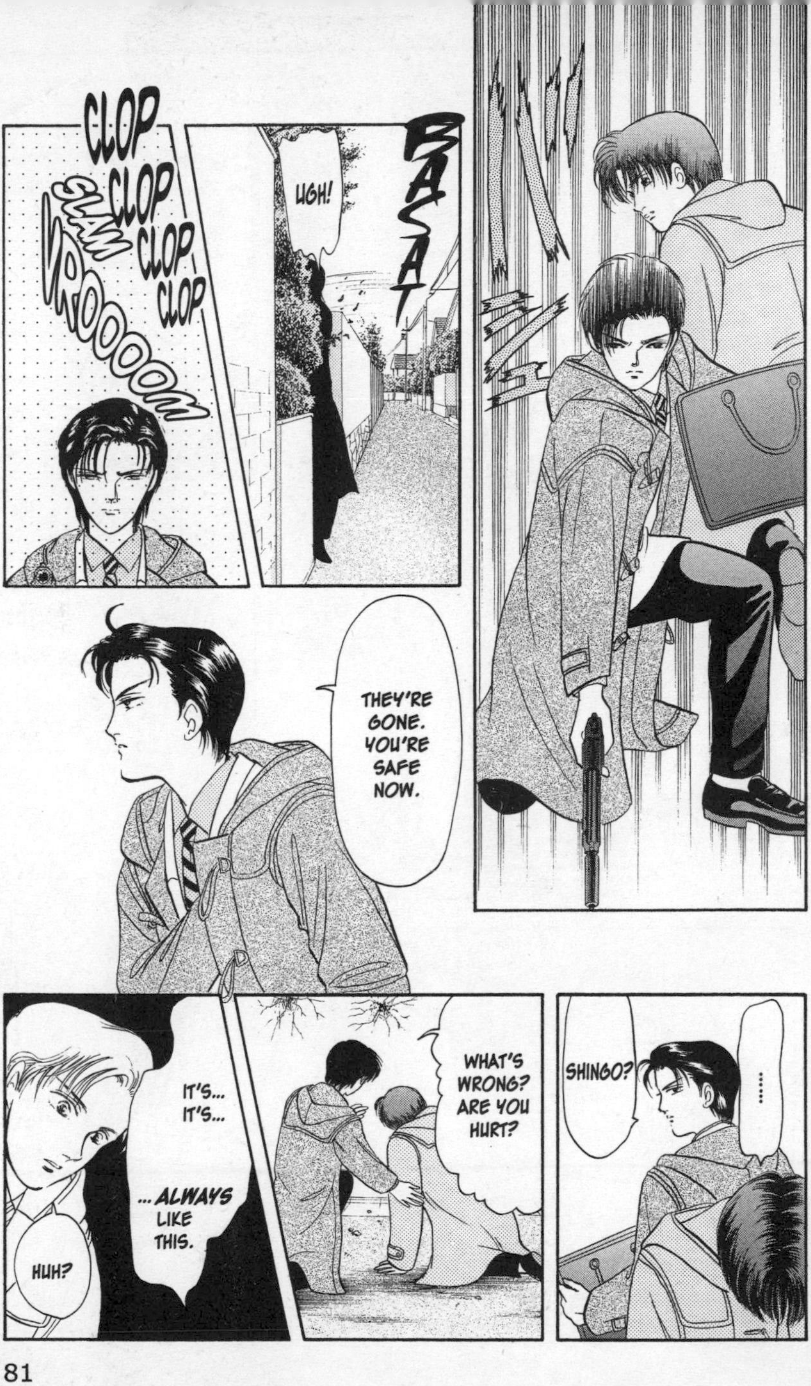
UGH!
BASAT
CLOP CLOP CLOP CLOP CLOP
SLAM
VROOOOOM
THEY'RE GONE. YOU'RE SAFE NOW.
......
SHINGO?
WHAT'S WRONG? ARE YOU HURT?
IT'S... IT'S...
...ALWAYS LIKE THIS.
HUH?

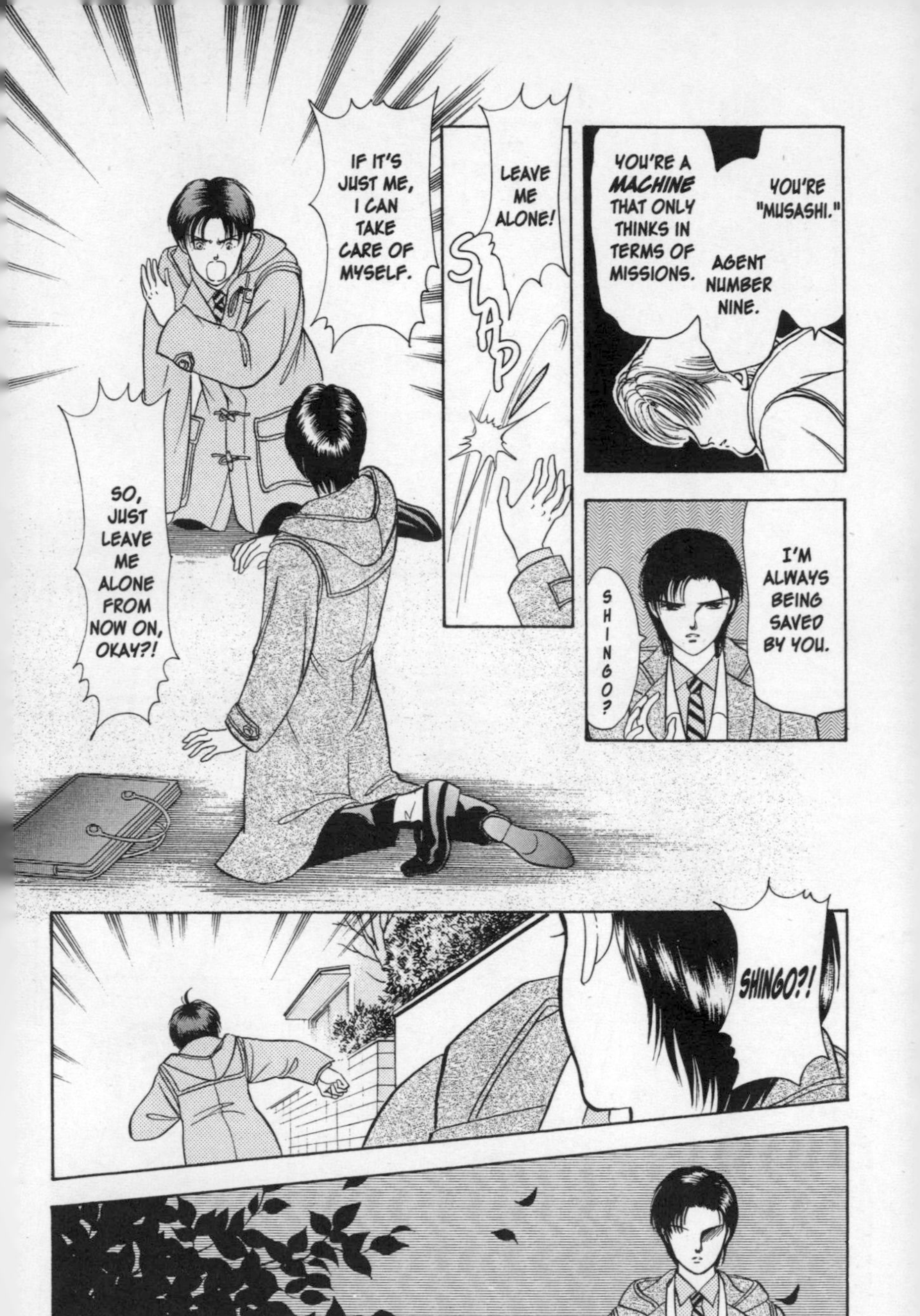
YOU'RE "MUSASHI."
AGENT NUMBER NINE.
YOU'RE A MACHINE THAT ONLY THINKS IN TERMS OF MISSIONS.
I'M ALWAYS BEING SAVED BY YOU.
SHINGO?
LEAVE ME ALONE!
SLAP
IF IT'S JUST ME, I CAN TAKE CARE OF MYSELF.
SO, JUST LEAVE ME ALONE FROM NOW ON, OKAY?!
SHINGO?!

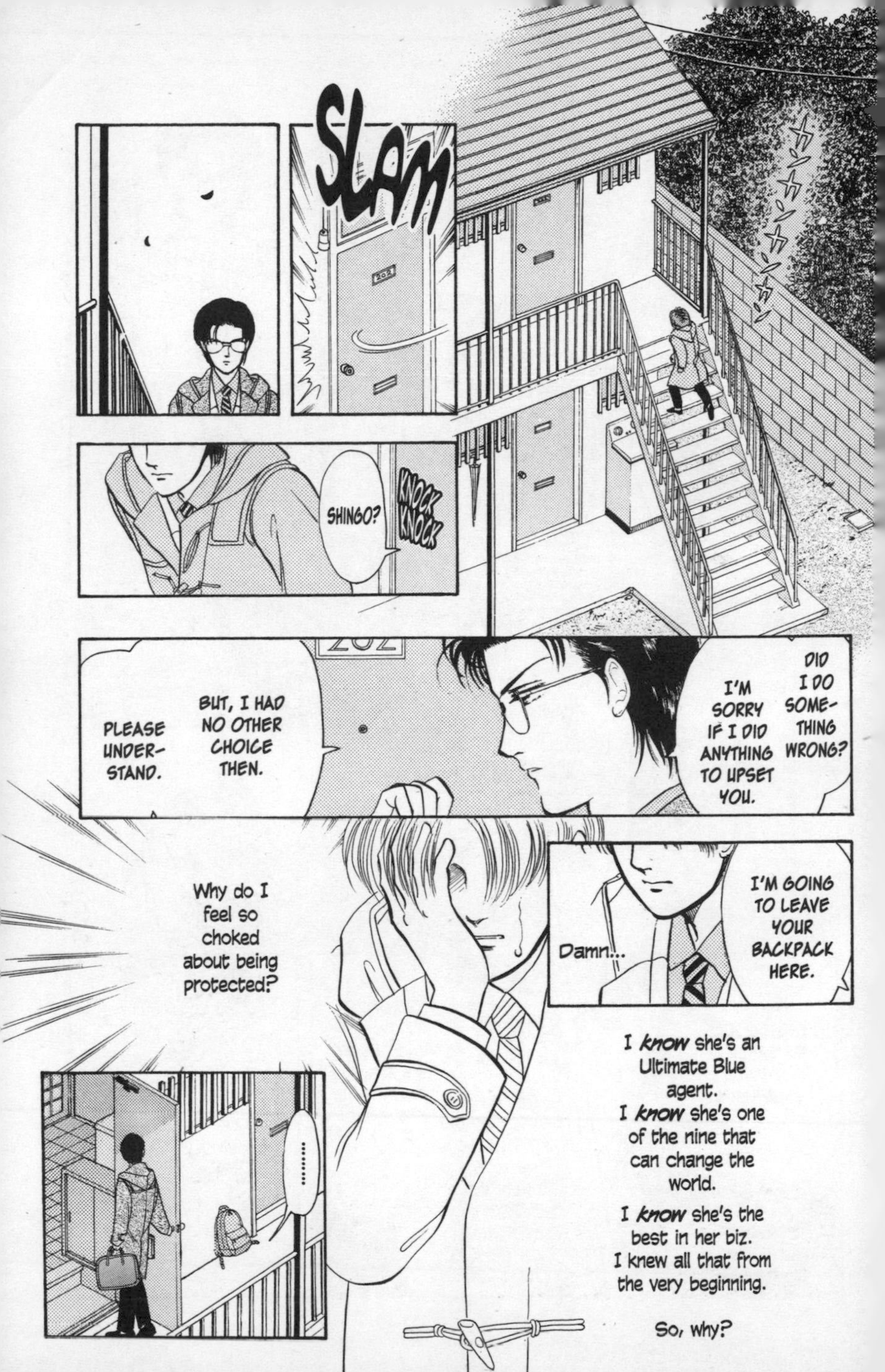
SLAM
SHINGO?
KNOCK KNOCK
DID I DO SOMETHING WRONG?
I'M SORRY IF I DID ANYTHING TO UPSET YOU.
BUT, I HAD NO OTHER CHOICE THEN.
PLEASE UNDERSTAND.
I'M GOING TO LEAVE YOUR BACKPACK HERE.
Damn...
Why do I feel so choked about being protected?
I *know* she's an Ultimate Blue agent.
I *know* she's one of the nine that can change the world.
I *know* she's the best in her biz.
I knew all that from the very beginning.
So, why?
......

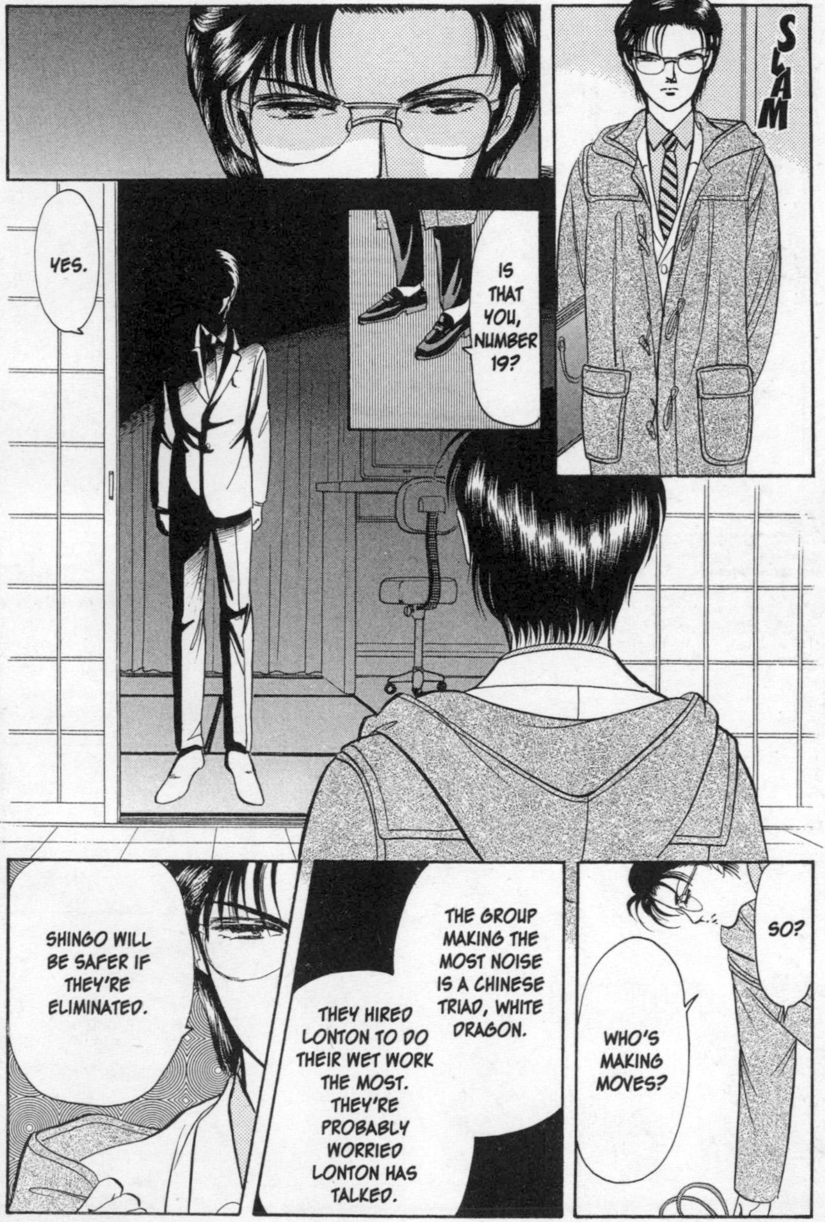
SLAM
IS THAT YOU, NUMBER 19?
YES.
SO?
WHO'S MAKING MOVES?
THE GROUP MAKING THE MOST NOISE IS A CHINESE TRIAD, WHITE DRAGON.
THEY HIRED LONTON TO DO THEIR WET WORK THE MOST. THEY'RE PROBABLY WORRIED LONTON HAS TALKED.
SHINGO WILL BE SAFER IF THEY'RE ELIMINATED.

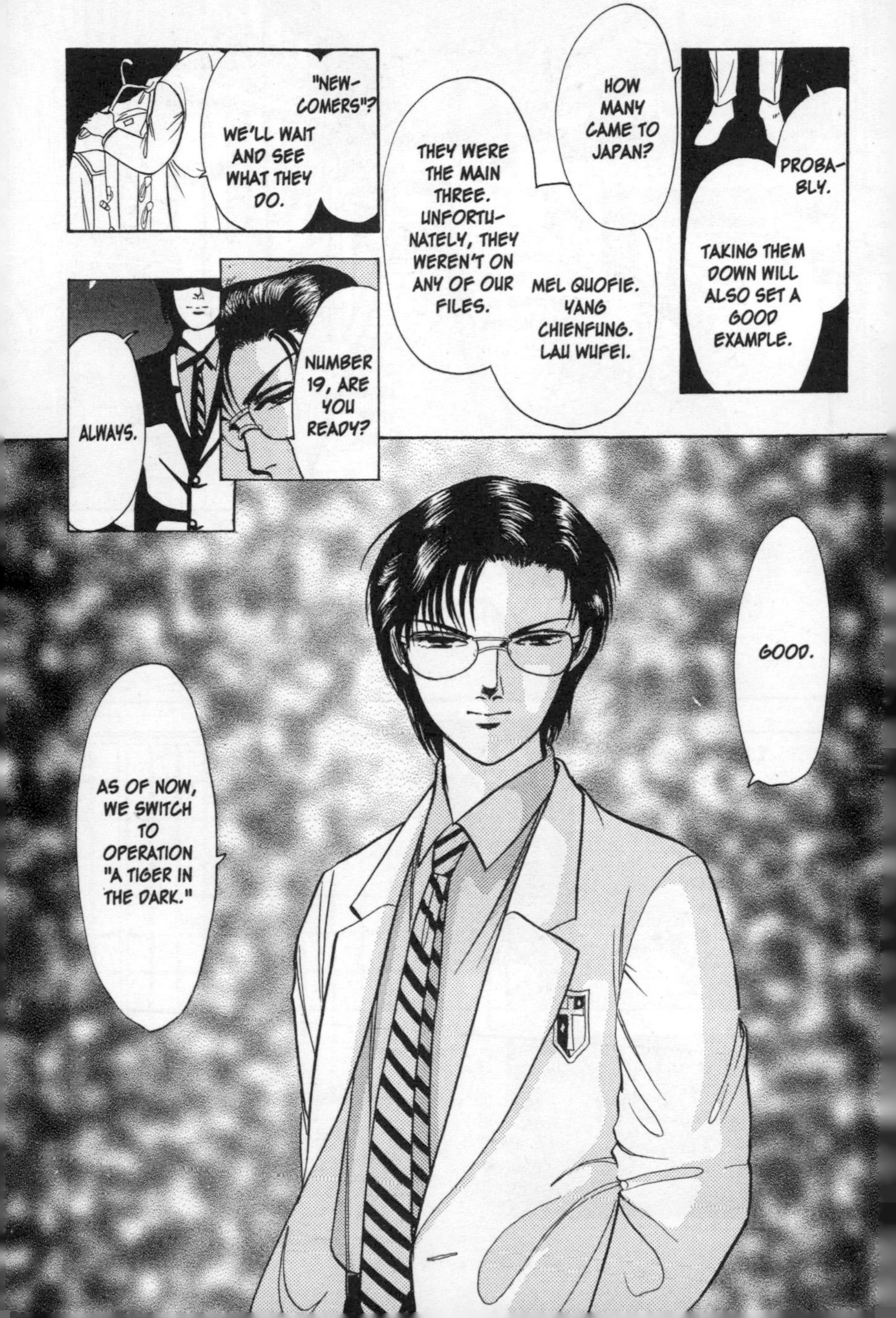
PROBA-BLY.
TAKING THEM DOWN WILL ALSO SET A GOOD EXAMPLE.
HOW MANY CAME TO JAPAN?
MEL QUOFIE. YANG CHIENFUNG. LAU WUFEI.
THEY WERE THE MAIN THREE. UNFORTU-NATELY, THEY WEREN'T ON ANY OF OUR FILES.
"NEW-COMERS"?
WE'LL WAIT AND SEE WHAT THEY DO.
NUMBER 19, ARE YOU READY?
ALWAYS.
GOOD.
AS OF NOW, WE SWITCH TO OPERATION "A TIGER IN THE DARK."

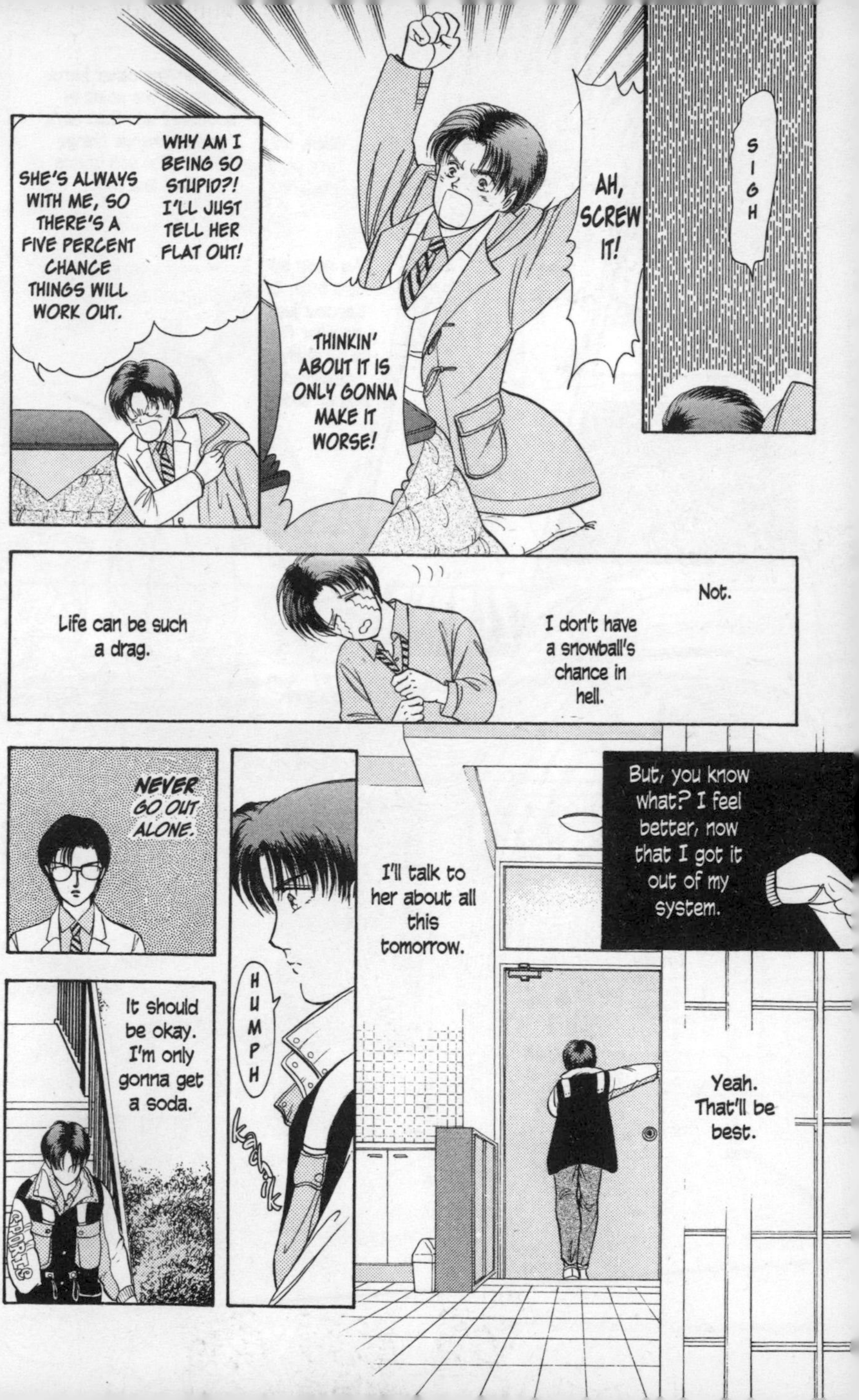
SIGH
AH, SCREW IT!
THINKIN' ABOUT IT IS ONLY GONNA MAKE IT WORSE!
WHY AM I BEING SO STUPID?! I'LL JUST TELL HER FLAT OUT!
SHE'S ALWAYS WITH ME, SO THERE'S A FIVE PERCENT CHANCE THINGS WILL WORK OUT.
Not.
I don't have a snowball's chance in hell.
Life can be such a drag.
But, you know what? I feel better, now that I got it out of my system.
I'll talk to her about all this tomorrow.
Yeah. That'll be best.
HUMPH
NEVER GO OUT ALONE.
It should be okay. I'm only gonna get a soda.

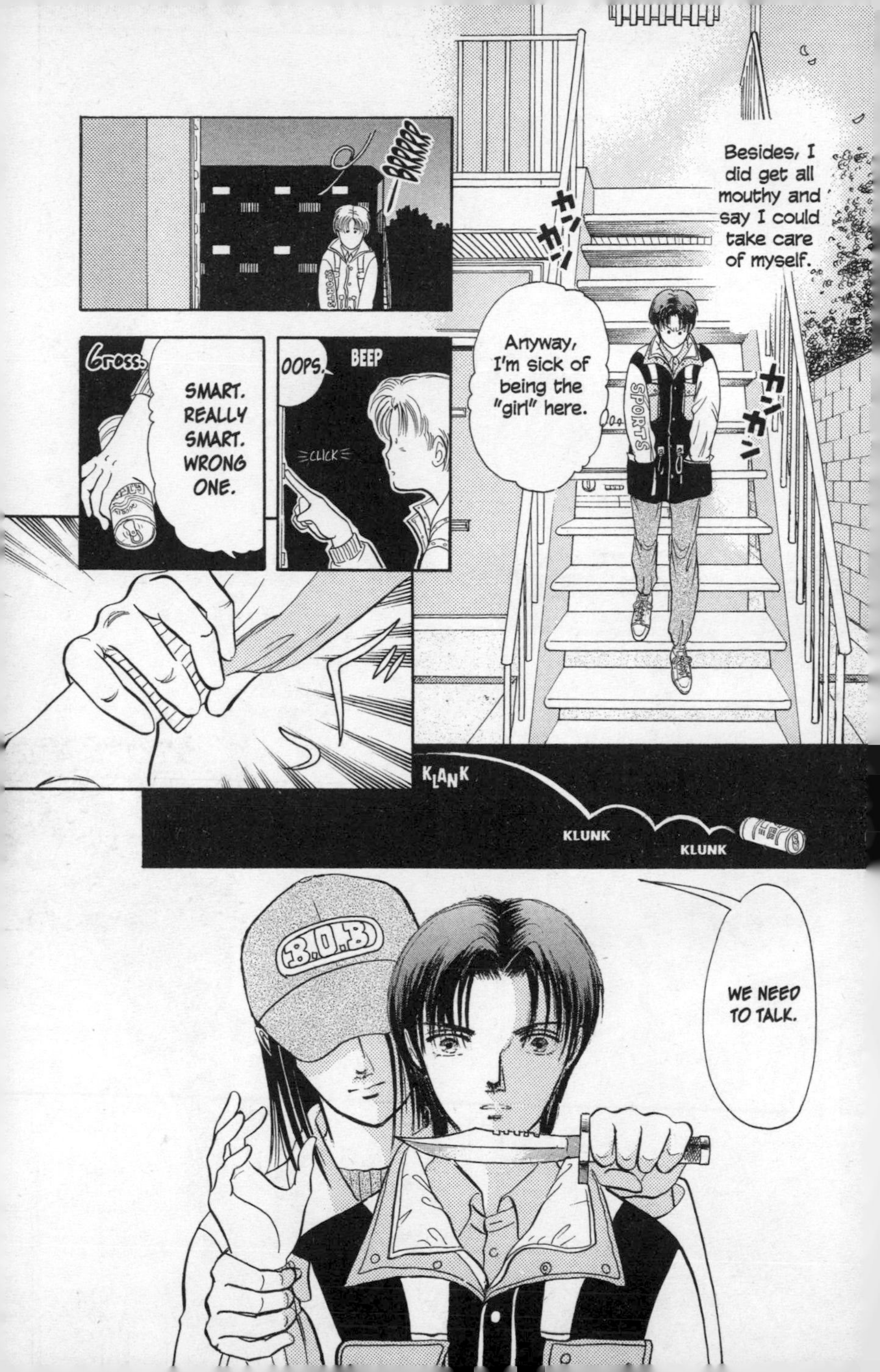
Besides, I did get all mouthy and say I could take care of myself.
カンカン
カンカン
Anyway, I'm sick of being the "girl" here.
BRRRRR
OOPS.
BEEP
CLICK
Gross.
SMART. REALLY SMART. WRONG ONE.
KLANK
KLUNK
KLUNK
WE NEED TO TALK.

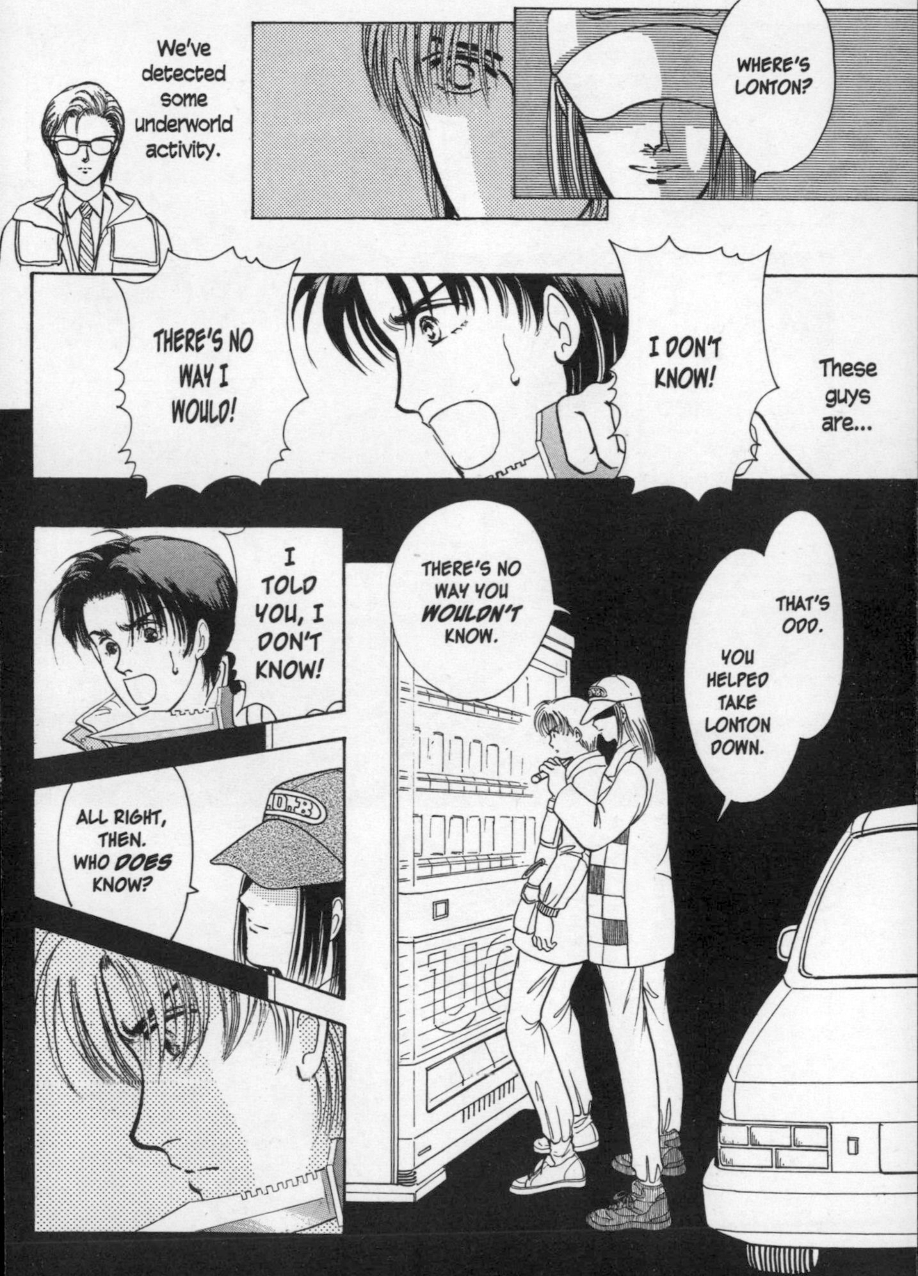
WHERE'S LONTON?
We've detected some underworld activity.
These guys are...
I DON'T KNOW!
THERE'S NO WAY I WOULD!
THAT'S ODD. YOU HELPED TAKE LONTON DOWN.
THERE'S NO WAY YOU *WOULDN'T* KNOW.
I TOLD YOU, I DON'T KNOW!
ALL RIGHT, THEN. WHO *DOES* KNOW?

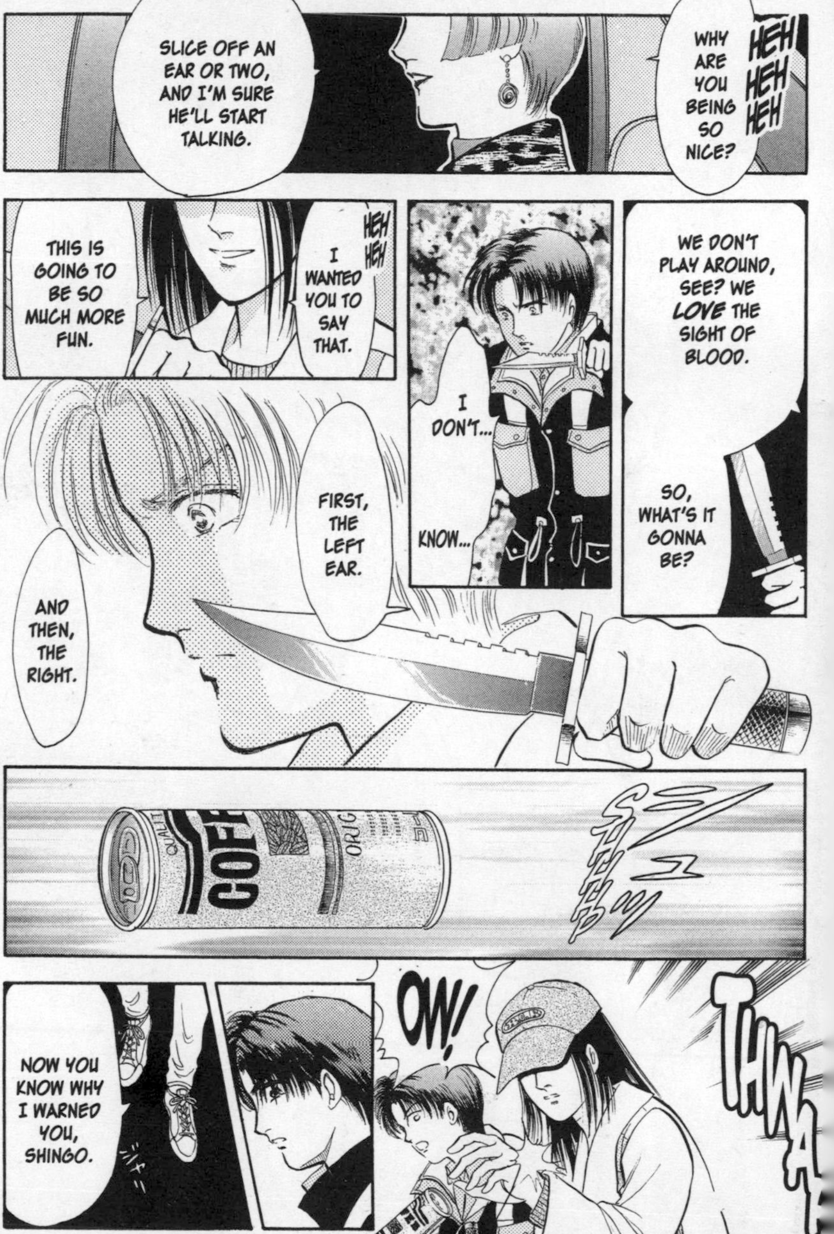
WHY ARE YOU BEING SO NICE?
HEH HEH HEH
SLICE OFF AN EAR OR TWO, AND I'M SURE HE'LL START TALKING.
WE DON'T PLAY AROUND, SEE? WE LOVE THE SIGHT OF BLOOD.
SO, WHAT'S IT GONNA BE?
I DON'T...
KNOW...
HEH HEH
I WANTED YOU TO SAY THAT.
THIS IS GOING TO BE SO MUCH MORE FUN.
FIRST, THE LEFT EAR.
AND THEN, THE RIGHT.
THWA
OW!
NOW YOU KNOW WHY I WARNED YOU, SHINGO.

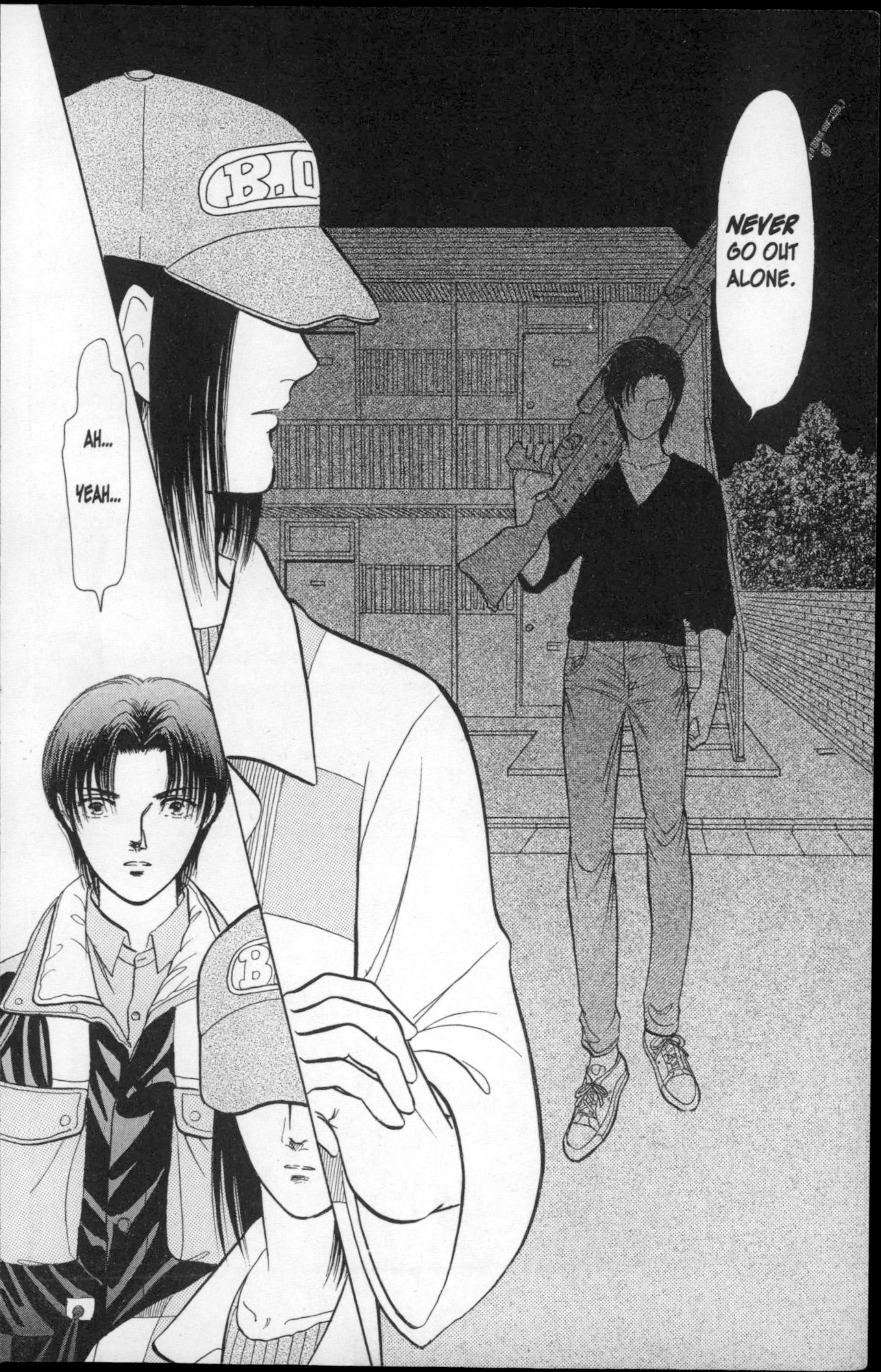
NEVER GO OUT ALONE.
AH... YEAH...

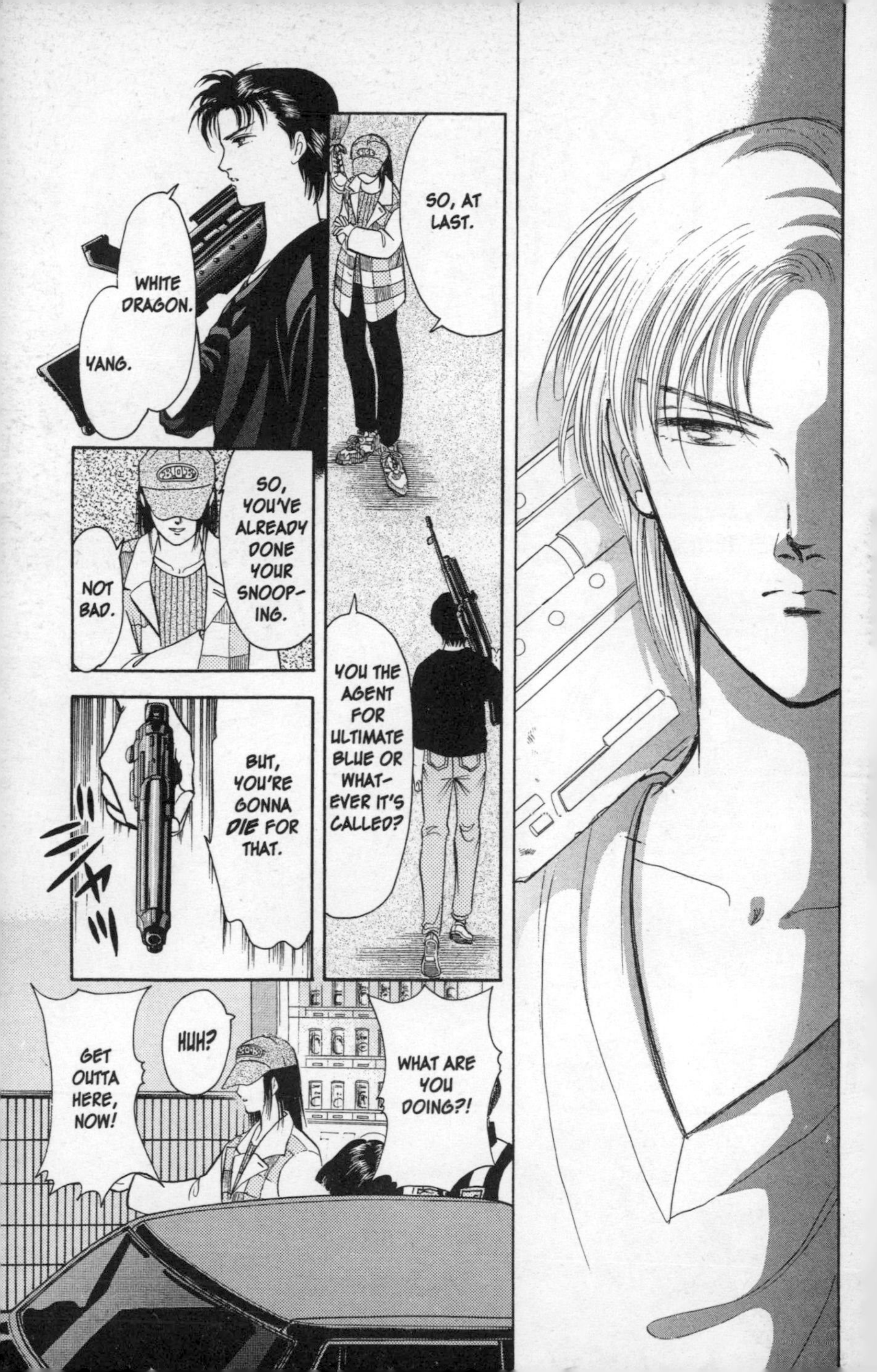
SO, AT LAST.
WHITE DRAGON.
YANG.
YOU THE AGENT FOR ULTIMATE BLUE OR WHAT-EVER IT'S CALLED?
SO, YOU'VE ALREADY DONE YOUR SNOOP-ING.
NOT BAD.
BUT, YOU'RE GONNA DIE FOR THAT.
WHAT ARE YOU DOING?!
HUH?
GET OUTTA HERE, NOW!

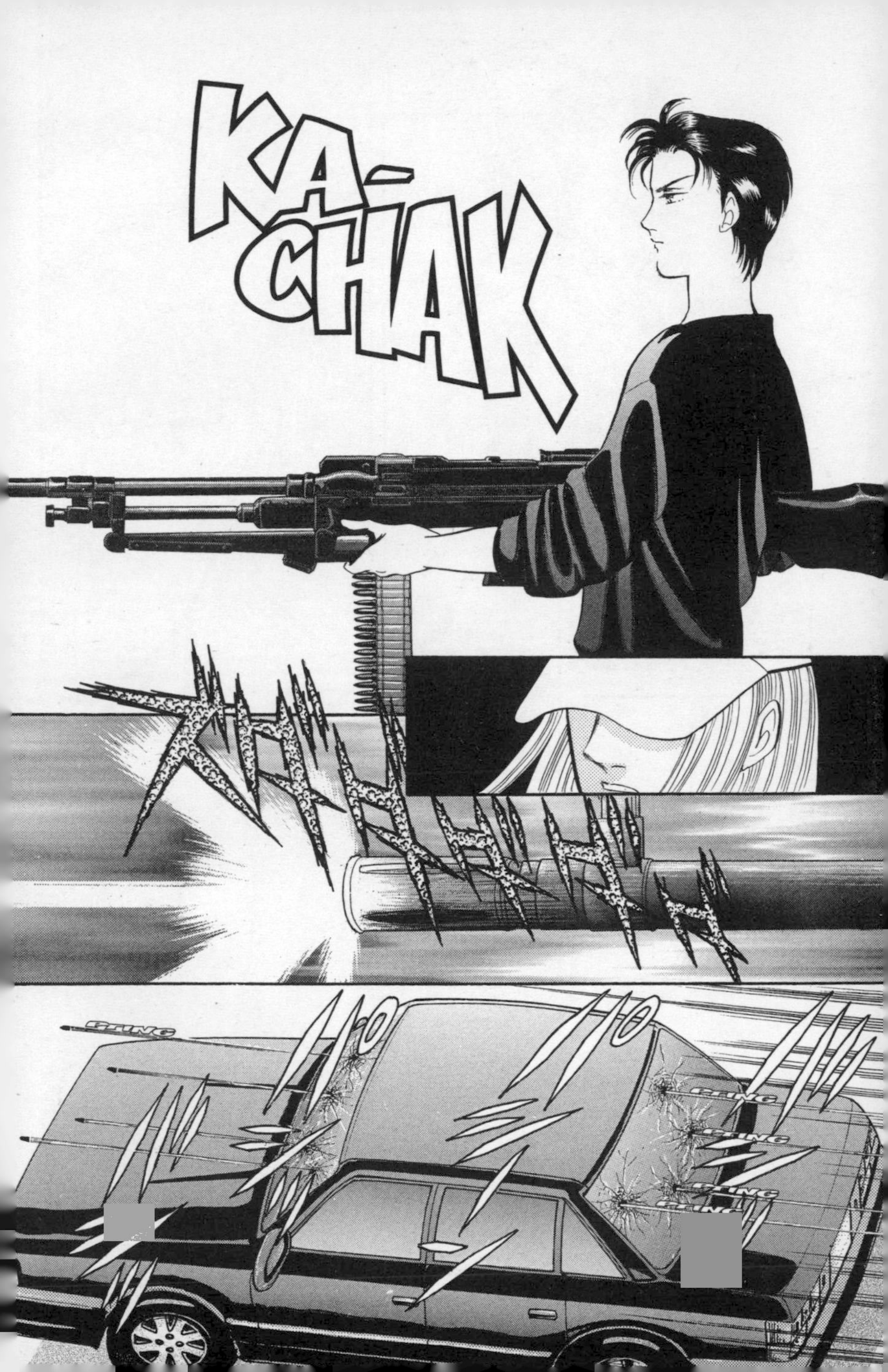
KA-CHAK
PTING
PTING
PTING
PTING
PTING

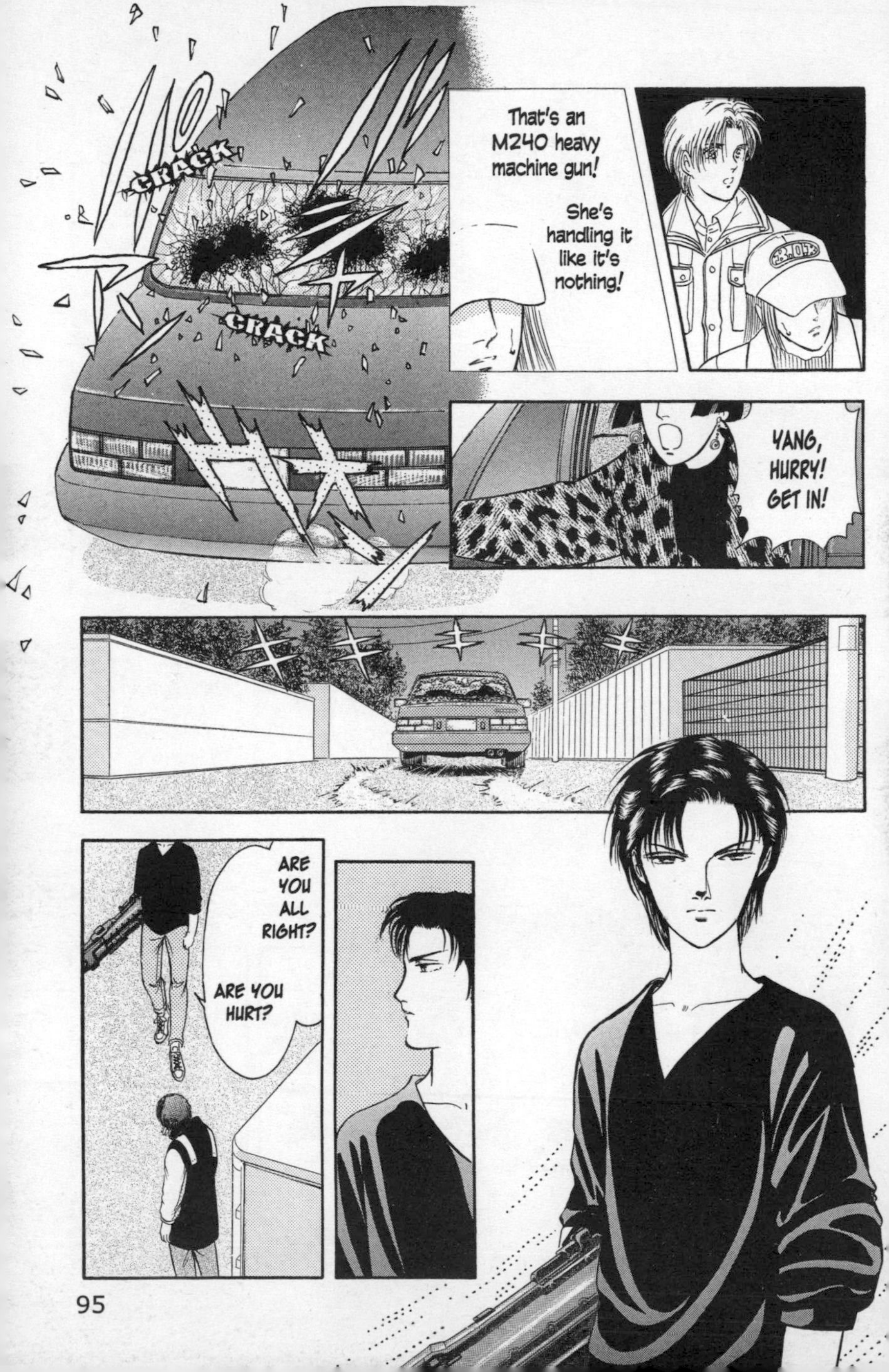
That's an M240 heavy machine gun!
She's handling it like it's nothing!
YANG, HURRY! GET IN!
CRACK
CRACK
ARE YOU ALL RIGHT?
ARE YOU HURT?

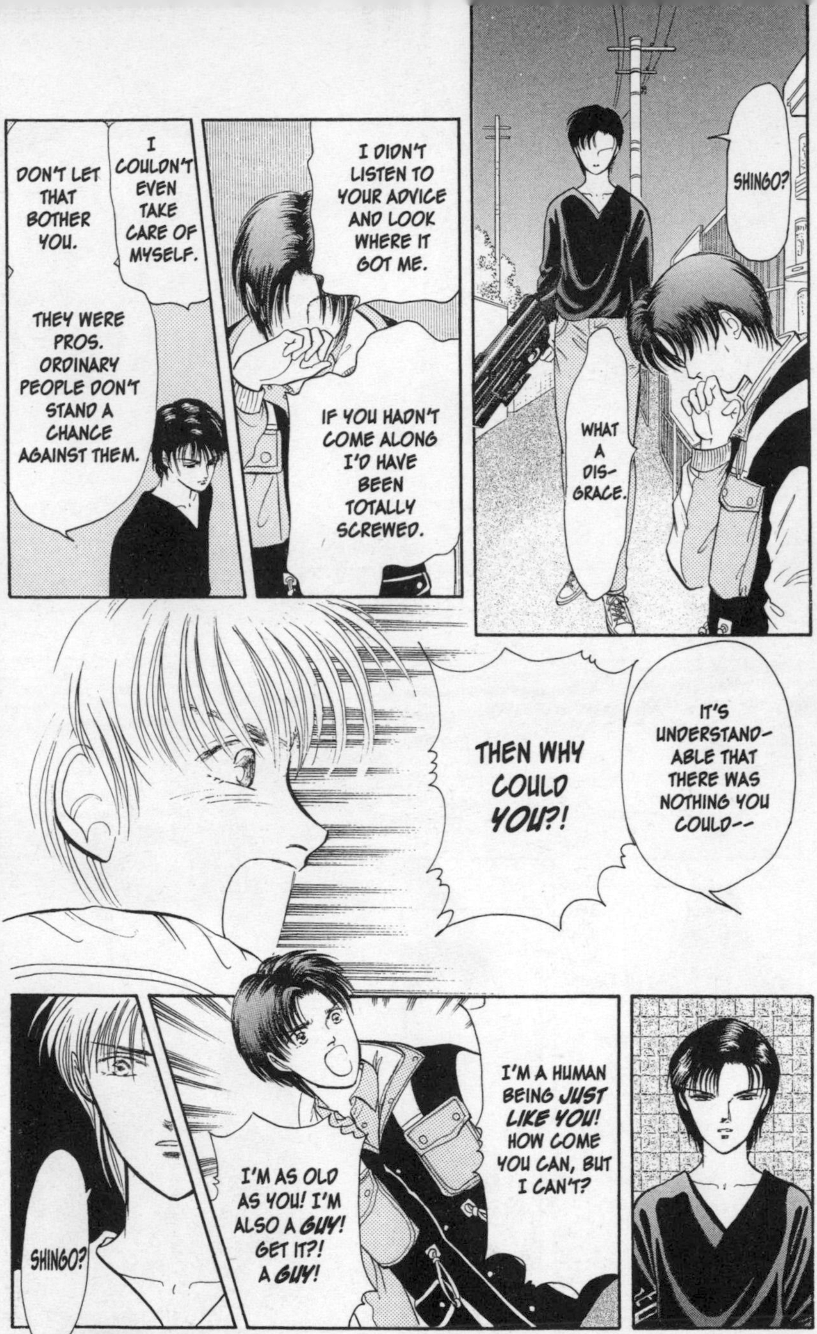
SHINGO?
WHAT A DIS-GRACE.
I DIDN'T LISTEN TO YOUR ADVICE AND LOOK WHERE IT GOT ME.
IF YOU HADN'T COME ALONG I'D HAVE BEEN TOTALLY SCREWED.
I COULDN'T EVEN TAKE CARE OF MYSELF.
DON'T LET THAT BOTHER YOU.
THEY WERE PROS. ORDINARY PEOPLE DON'T STAND A CHANCE AGAINST THEM.
IT'S UNDERSTAND-ABLE THAT THERE WAS NOTHING YOU COULD--
THEN WHY COULD *YOU*?!
I'M A HUMAN BEING *JUST LIKE YOU*! HOW COME YOU CAN, BUT I CAN'T?
I'M AS OLD AS YOU! I'M ALSO A *GUY*! GET IT?! A *GUY*!
SHINGO?

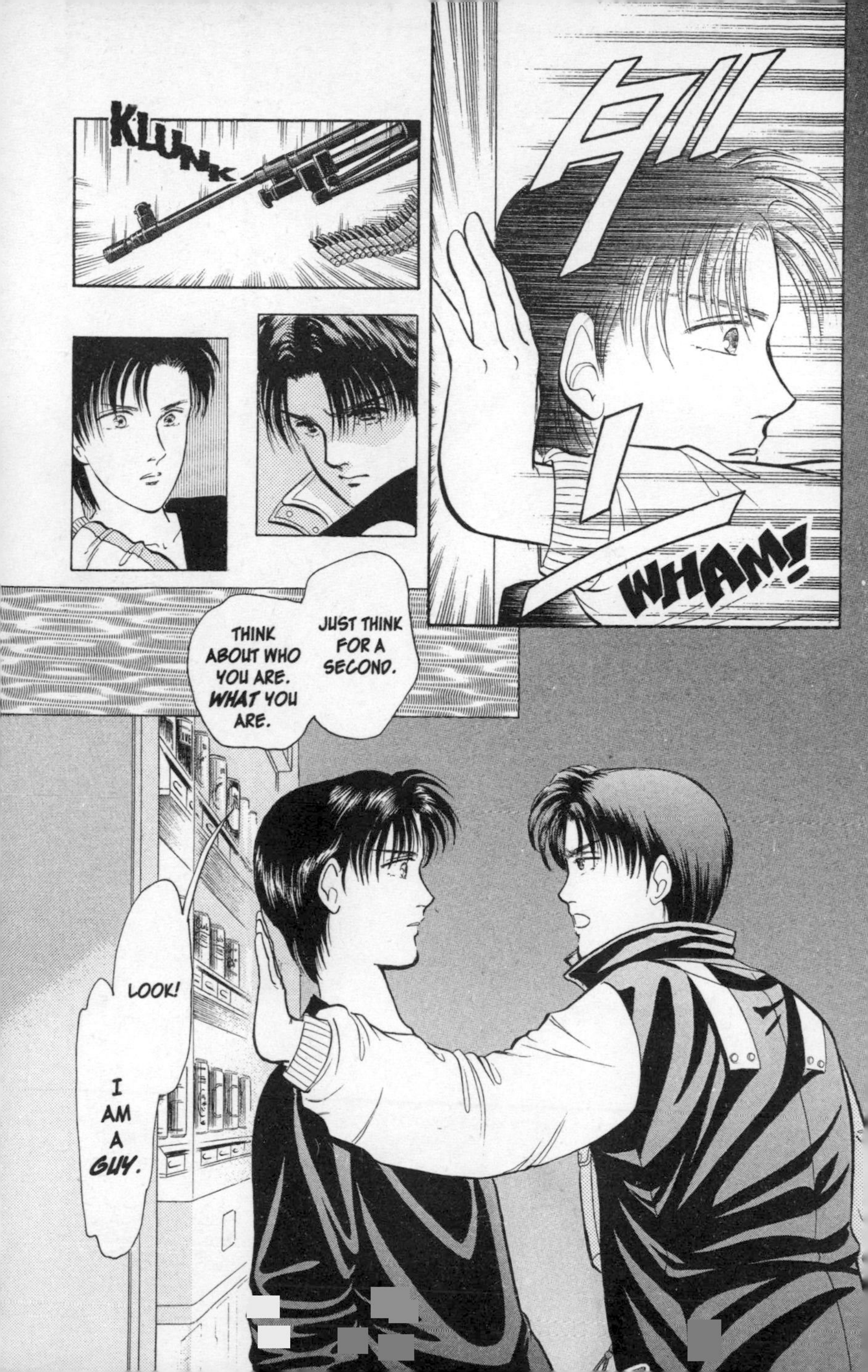
WHAM!
KLUNK
JUST THINK FOR A SECOND.
THINK ABOUT WHO YOU ARE. WHAT YOU ARE.
LOOK!
I AM A GUY.

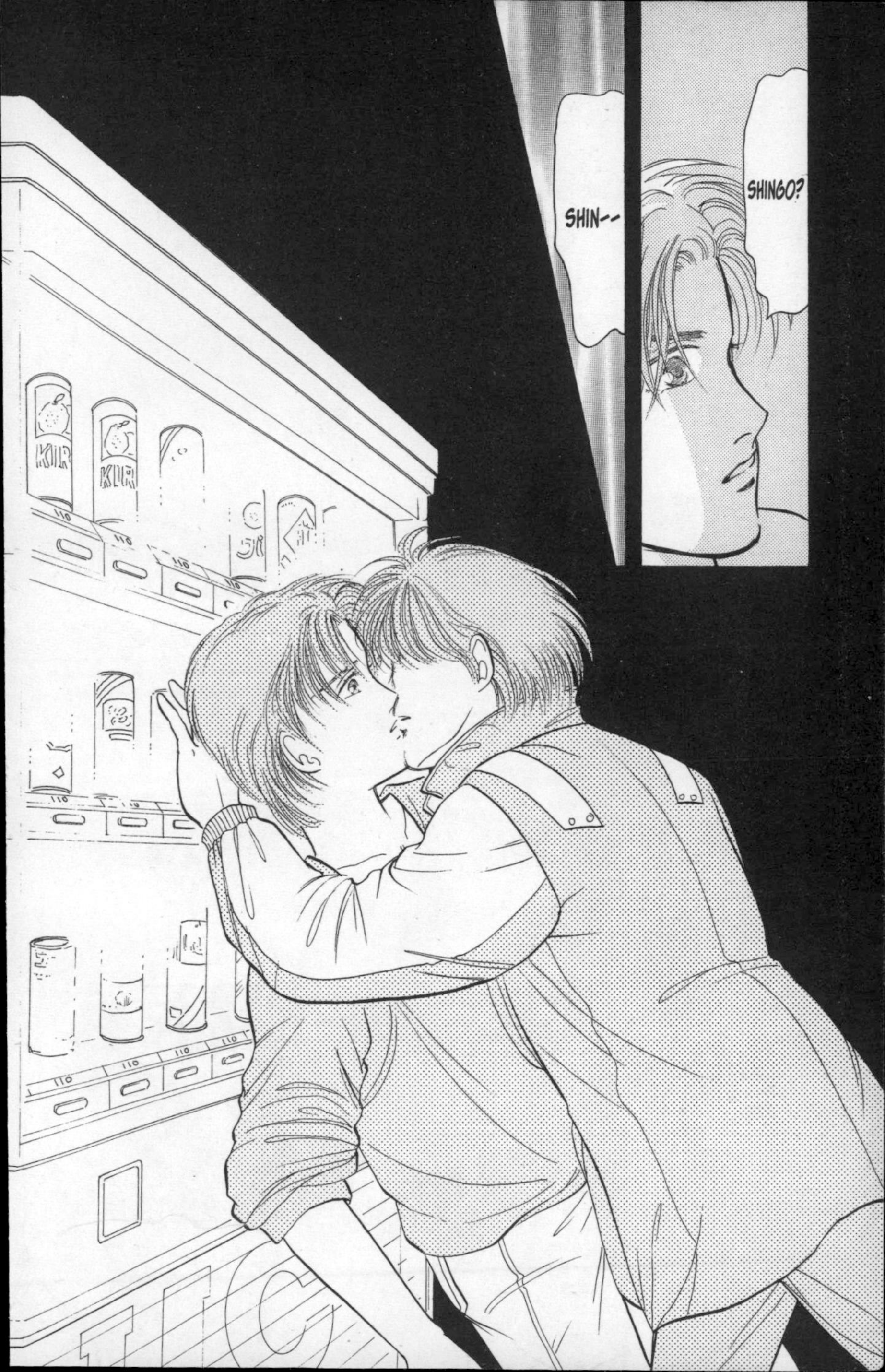
SHINGO?
SHIN--

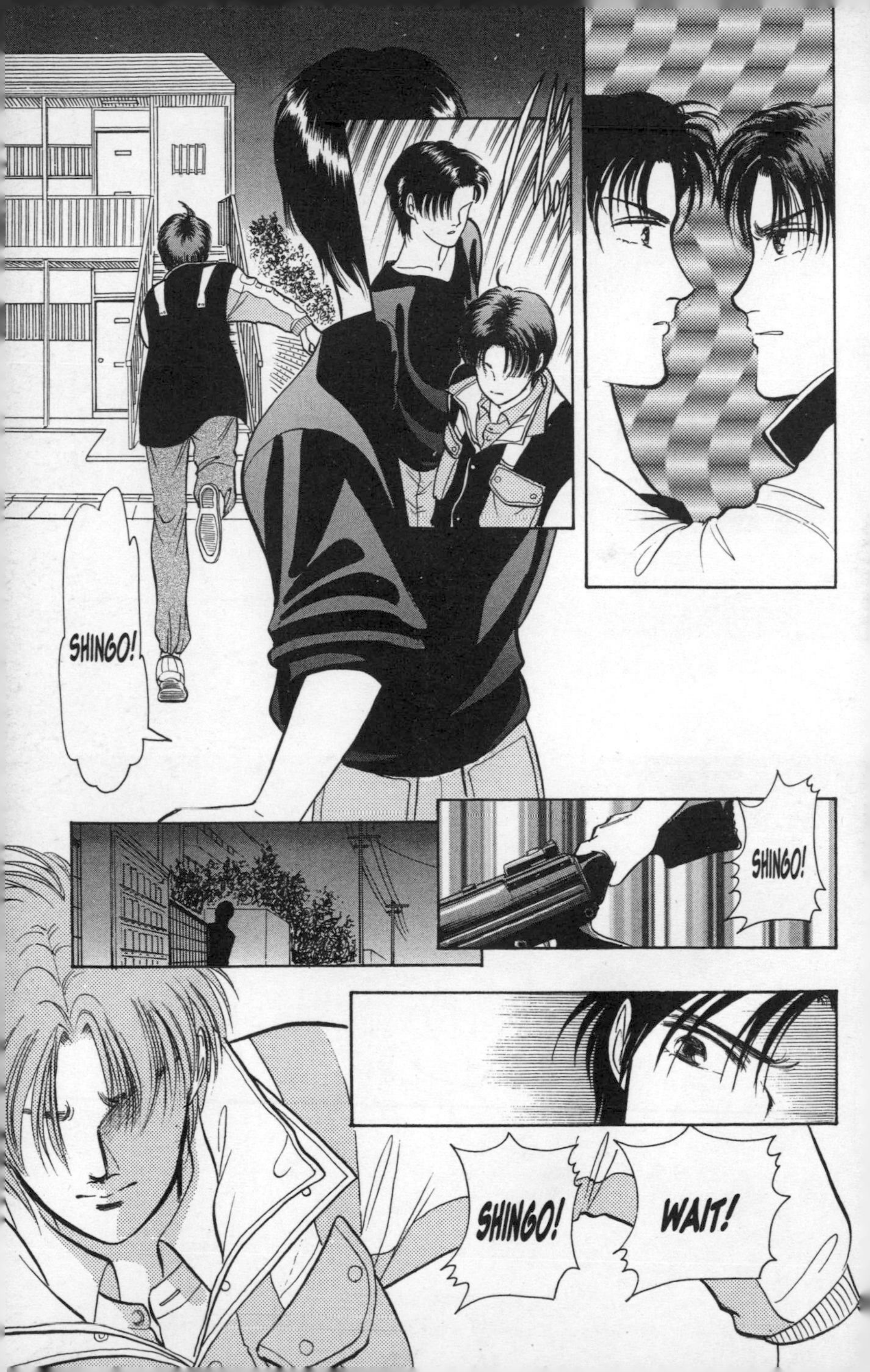
SHINGO!
SHINGO!
WAIT!
SHINGO!

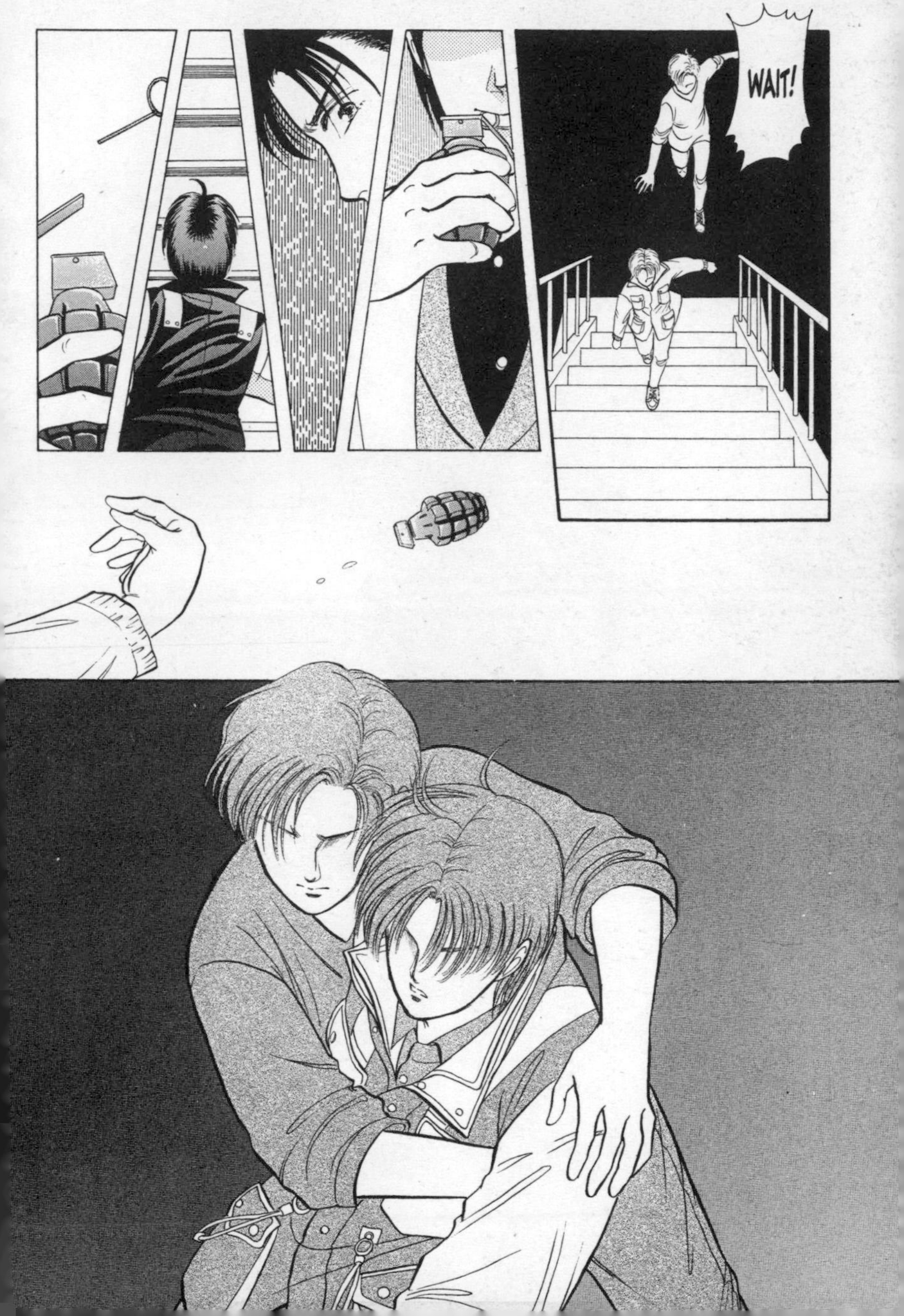
WAIT!

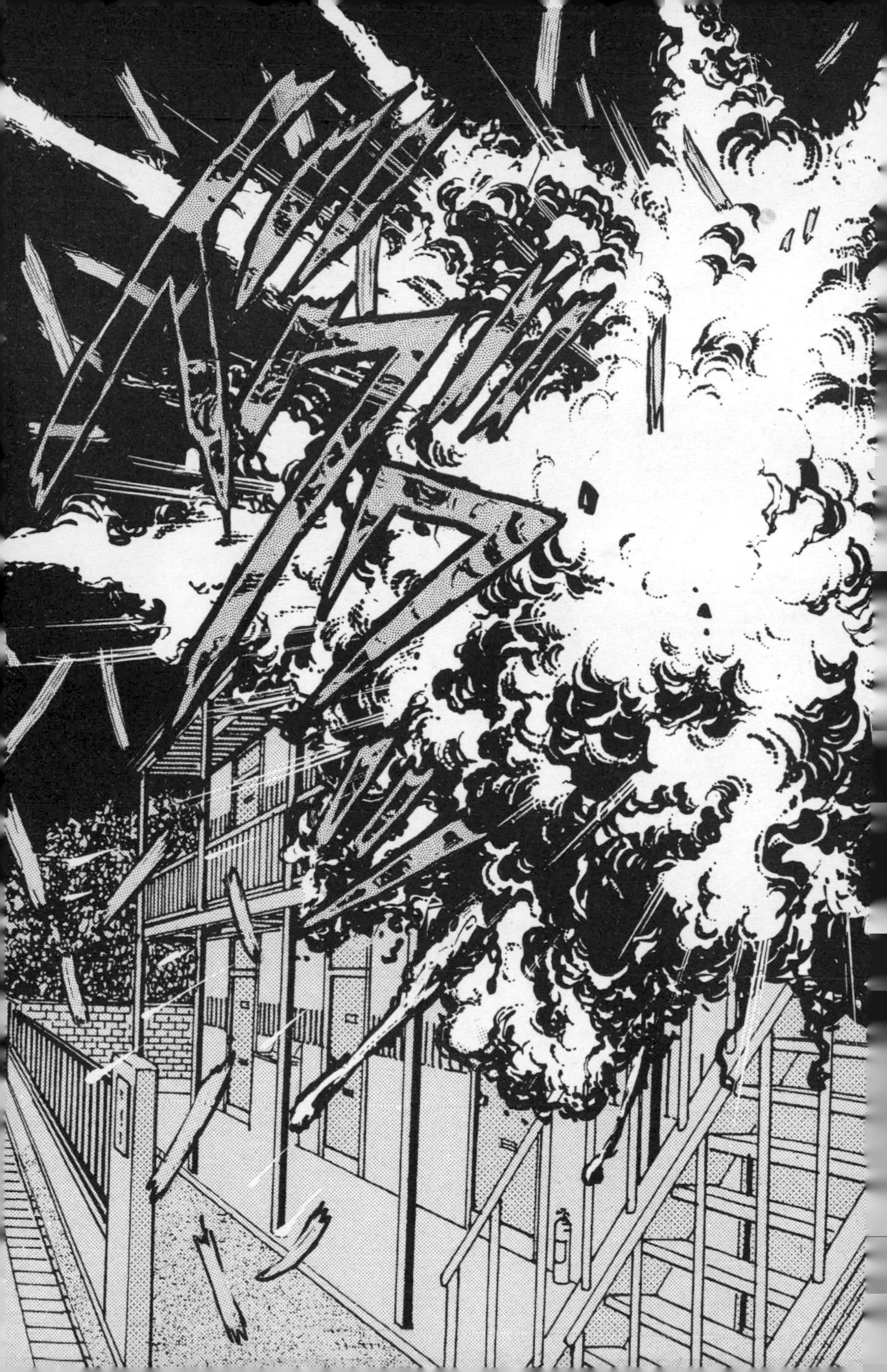

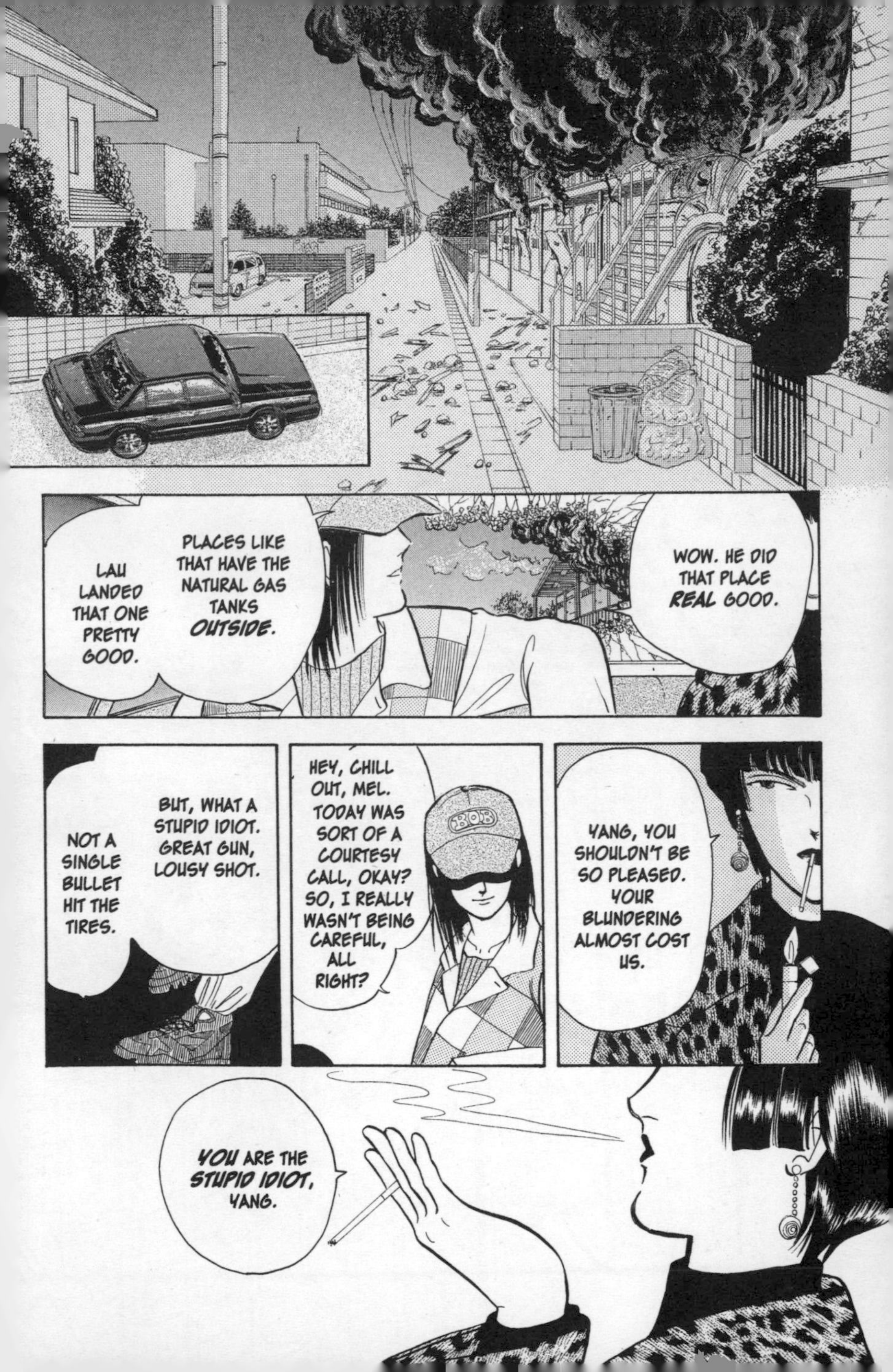
WOW. HE DID THAT PLACE REAL GOOD.
PLACES LIKE THAT HAVE THE NATURAL GAS TANKS OUTSIDE.
LAU LANDED THAT ONE PRETTY GOOD.
YANG, YOU SHOULDN'T BE SO PLEASED. YOUR BLUNDERING ALMOST COST US.
HEY, CHILL OUT, MEL. TODAY WAS SORT OF A COURTESY CALL, OKAY? SO, I REALLY WASN'T BEING CAREFUL, ALL RIGHT?
BUT, WHAT A STUPID IDIOT. GREAT GUN, LOUSY SHOT.
NOT A SINGLE BULLET HIT THE TIRES.
YOU ARE THE STUPID IDIOT, YANG.

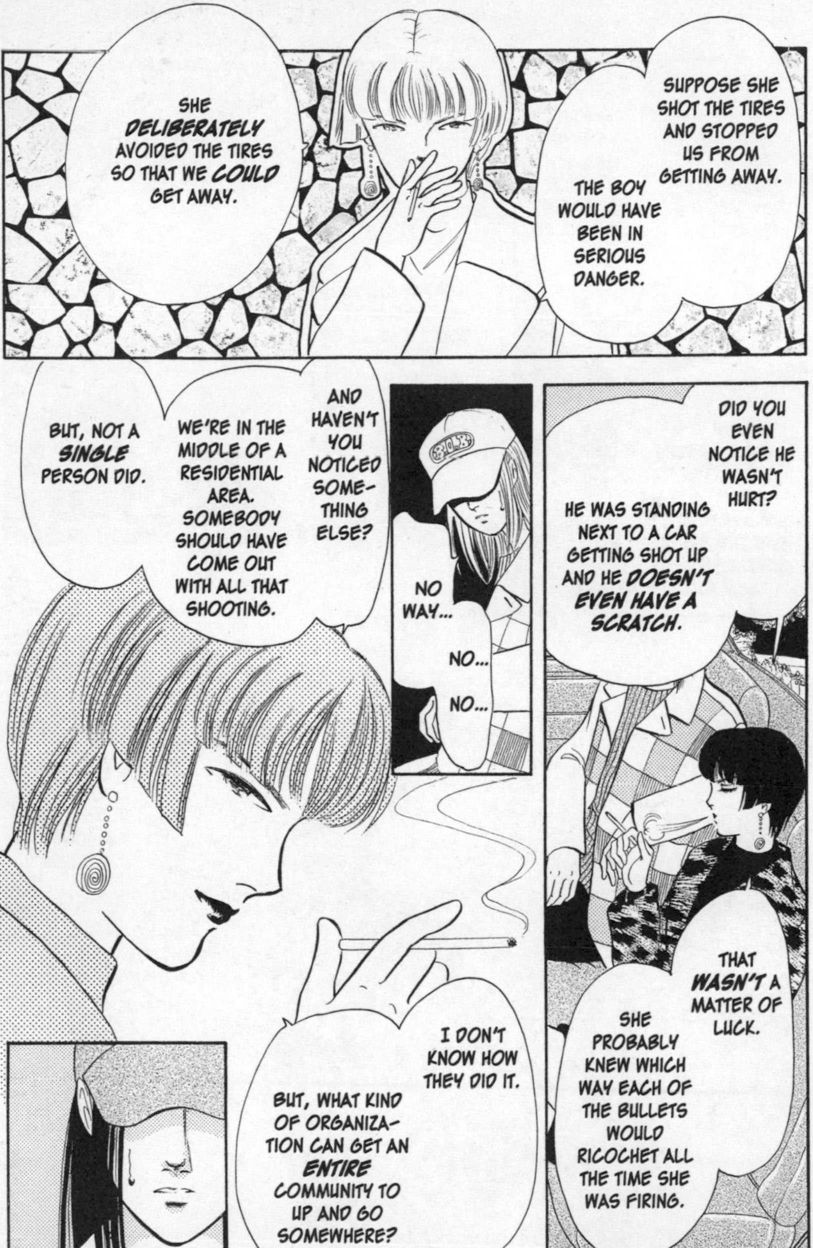
SUPPOSE SHE SHOT THE TIRES AND STOPPED US FROM GETTING AWAY.
THE BOY WOULD HAVE BEEN IN SERIOUS DANGER.
SHE DELIBERATELY AVOIDED THE TIRES SO THAT WE COULD GET AWAY.
DID YOU EVEN NOTICE HE WASN'T HURT?
HE WAS STANDING NEXT TO A CAR GETTING SHOT UP AND HE DOESN'T EVEN HAVE A SCRATCH.
THAT WASN'T A MATTER OF LUCK.
SHE PROBABLY KNEW WHICH WAY EACH OF THE BULLETS WOULD RICOCHET ALL THE TIME SHE WAS FIRING.
NO WAY...
NO...
NO...
AND HAVEN'T YOU NOTICED SOME-THING ELSE?
WE'RE IN THE MIDDLE OF A RESIDENTIAL AREA. SOMEBODY SHOULD HAVE COME OUT WITH ALL THAT SHOOTING.
BUT, NOT A SINGLE PERSON DID.
I DON'T KNOW HOW THEY DID IT.
BUT, WHAT KIND OF ORGANIZA-TION CAN GET AN ENTIRE COMMUNITY TO UP AND GO SOMEWHERE?

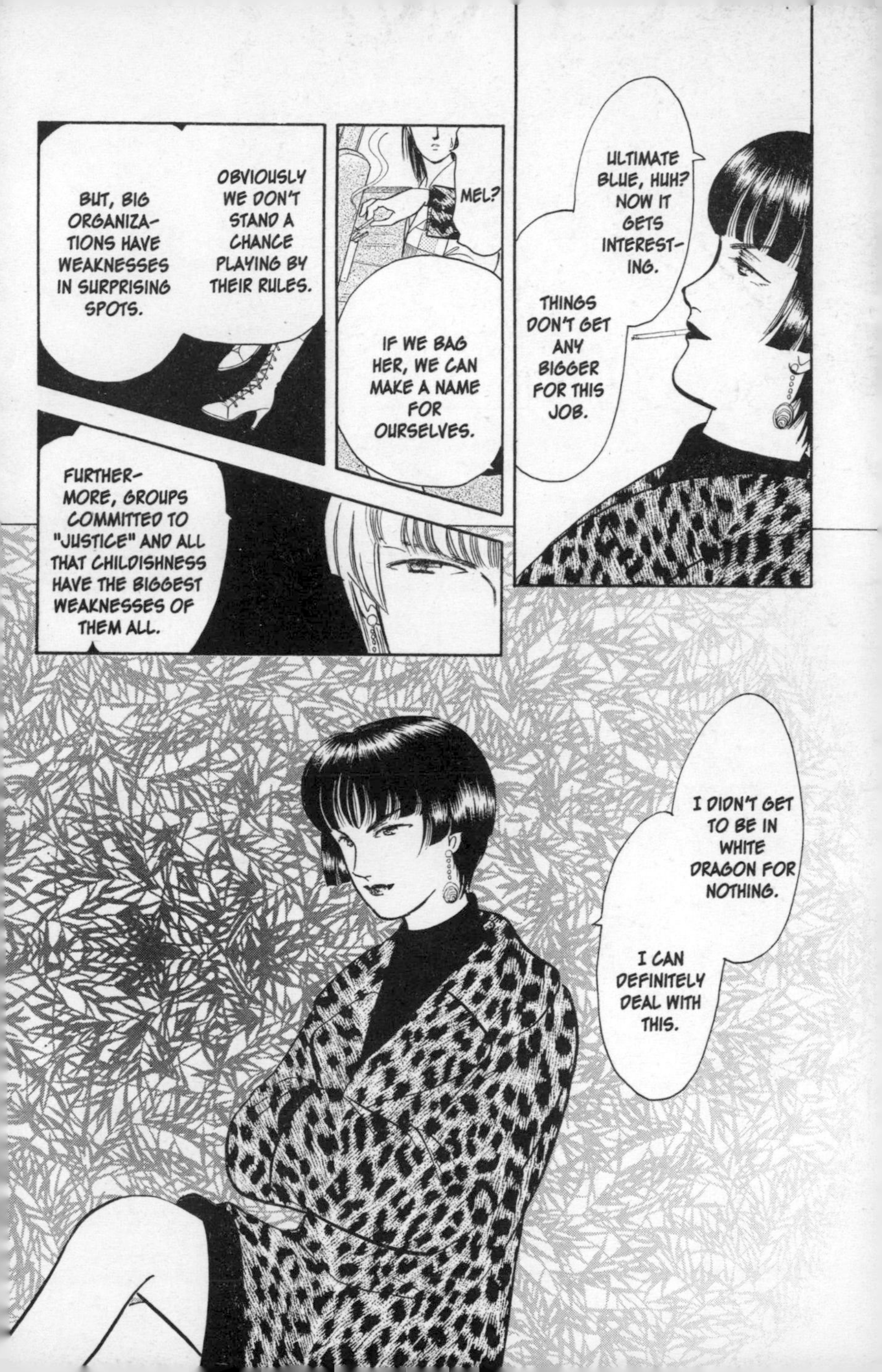
ULTIMATE BLUE, HUH? NOW IT GETS INTEREST-ING.
THINGS DON'T GET ANY BIGGER FOR THIS JOB.
MEL?
IF WE BAG HER, WE CAN MAKE A NAME FOR OURSELVES.
OBVIOUSLY WE DON'T STAND A CHANCE PLAYING BY THEIR RULES.
BUT, BIG ORGANIZA-TIONS HAVE WEAKNESSES IN SURPRISING SPOTS.
FURTHER-MORE, GROUPS COMMITTED TO "JUSTICE" AND ALL THAT CHILDISHNESS HAVE THE BIGGEST WEAKNESSES OF THEM ALL.
I DIDN'T GET TO BE IN WHITE DRAGON FOR NOTHING.
I CAN DEFINITELY DEAL WITH THIS.

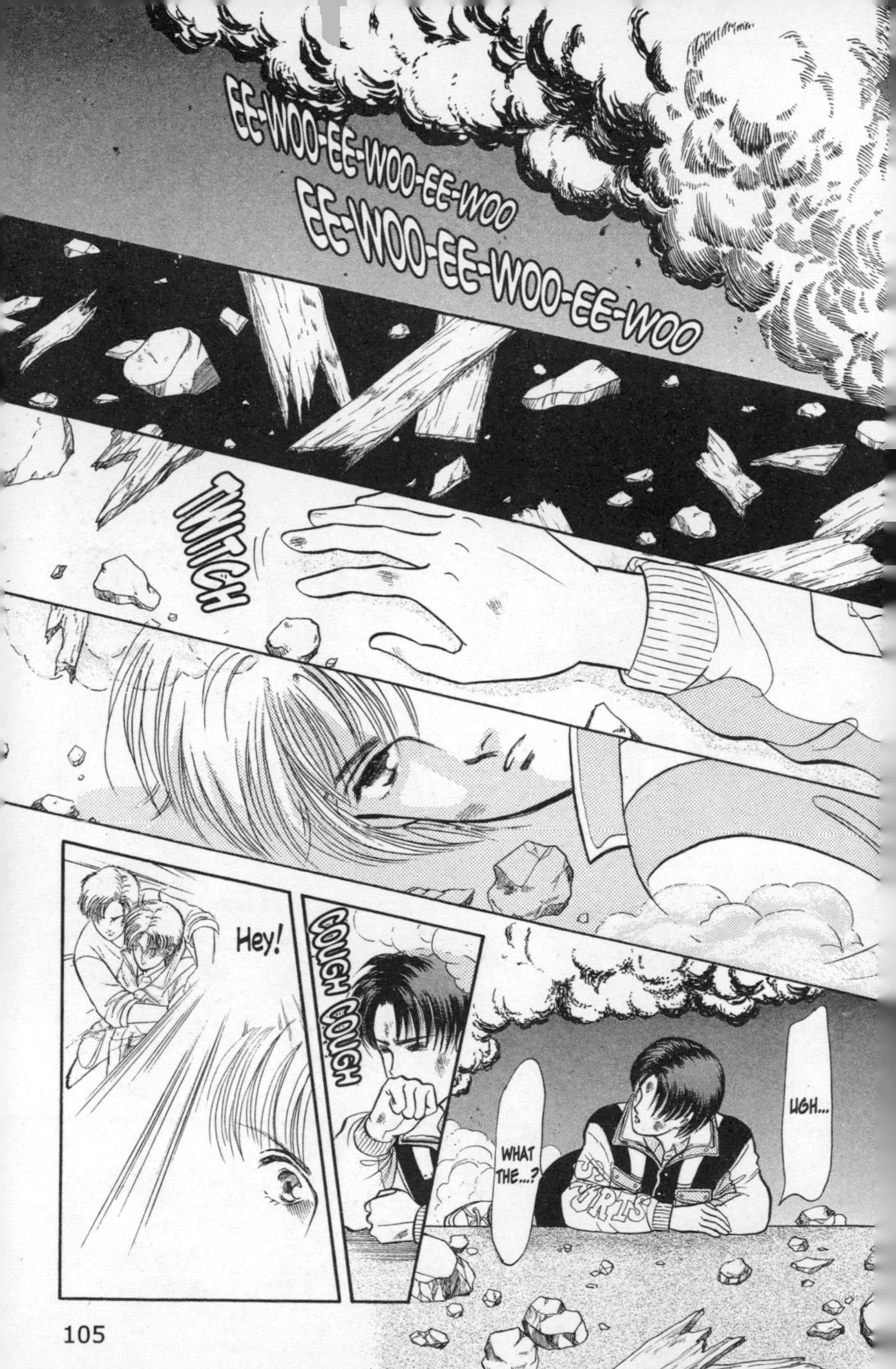
EE-WOO-EE-WOO-EE-WOO
EE-WOO-EE-WOO-EE-WOO
TWITCH
UGH...
WHAT THE...?
COUGH COUGH
Hey!

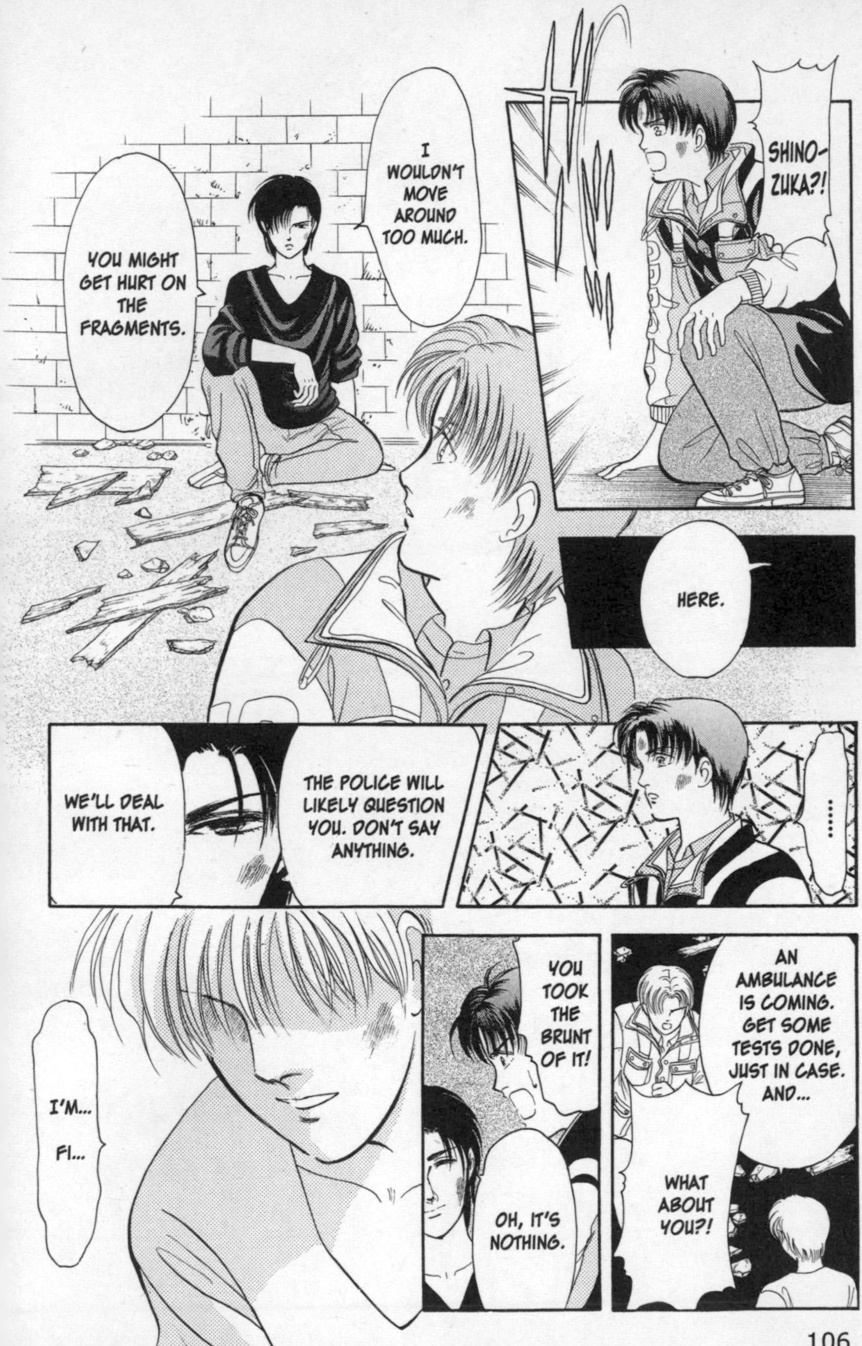
SHINO-ZUKA?!
HERE.
I WOULDN'T MOVE AROUND TOO MUCH.
YOU MIGHT GET HURT ON THE FRAGMENTS.
......
THE POLICE WILL LIKELY QUESTION YOU. DON'T SAY ANYTHING.
WE'LL DEAL WITH THAT.
AN AMBULANCE IS COMING. GET SOME TESTS DONE, JUST IN CASE. AND...
WHAT ABOUT YOU?!
YOU TOOK THE BRUNT OF IT!
OH, IT'S NOTHING.
I'M...
FI...

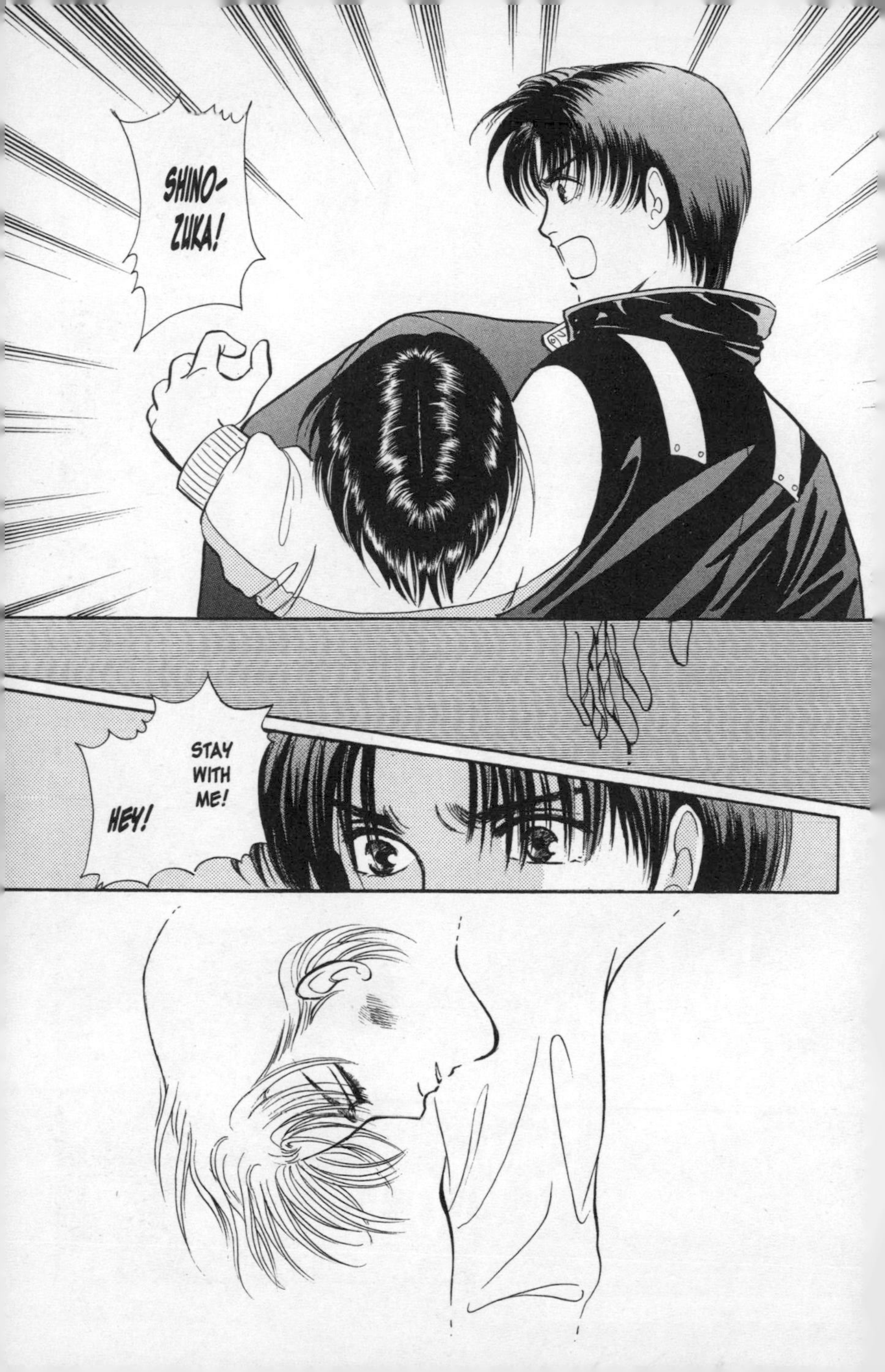
SHINO-ZUKA!
STAY WITH ME!
HEY!

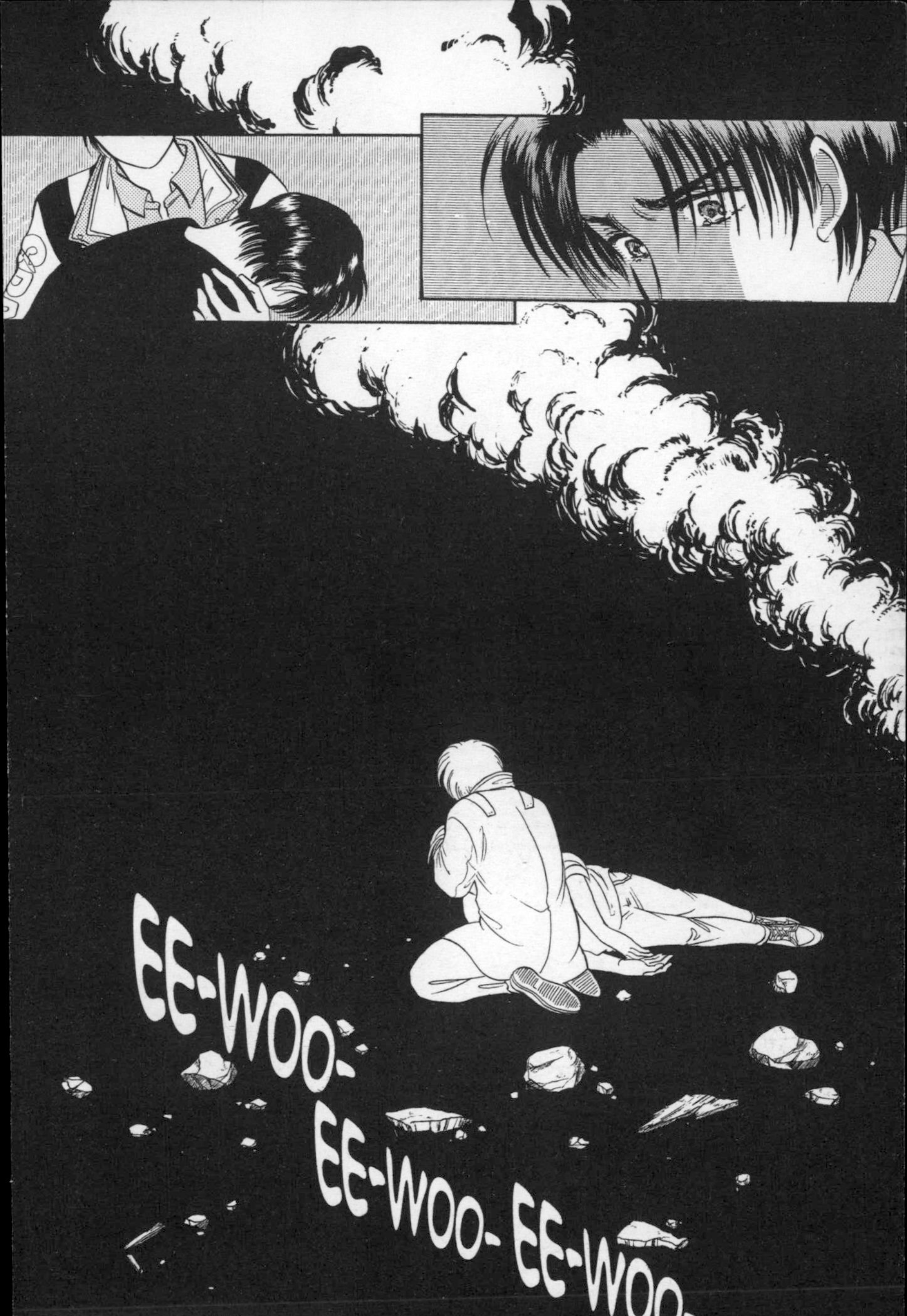
EE-WOO-
EE-WOO- EE-WOO-

Mission 9: A Tiger in the Dark 1—End

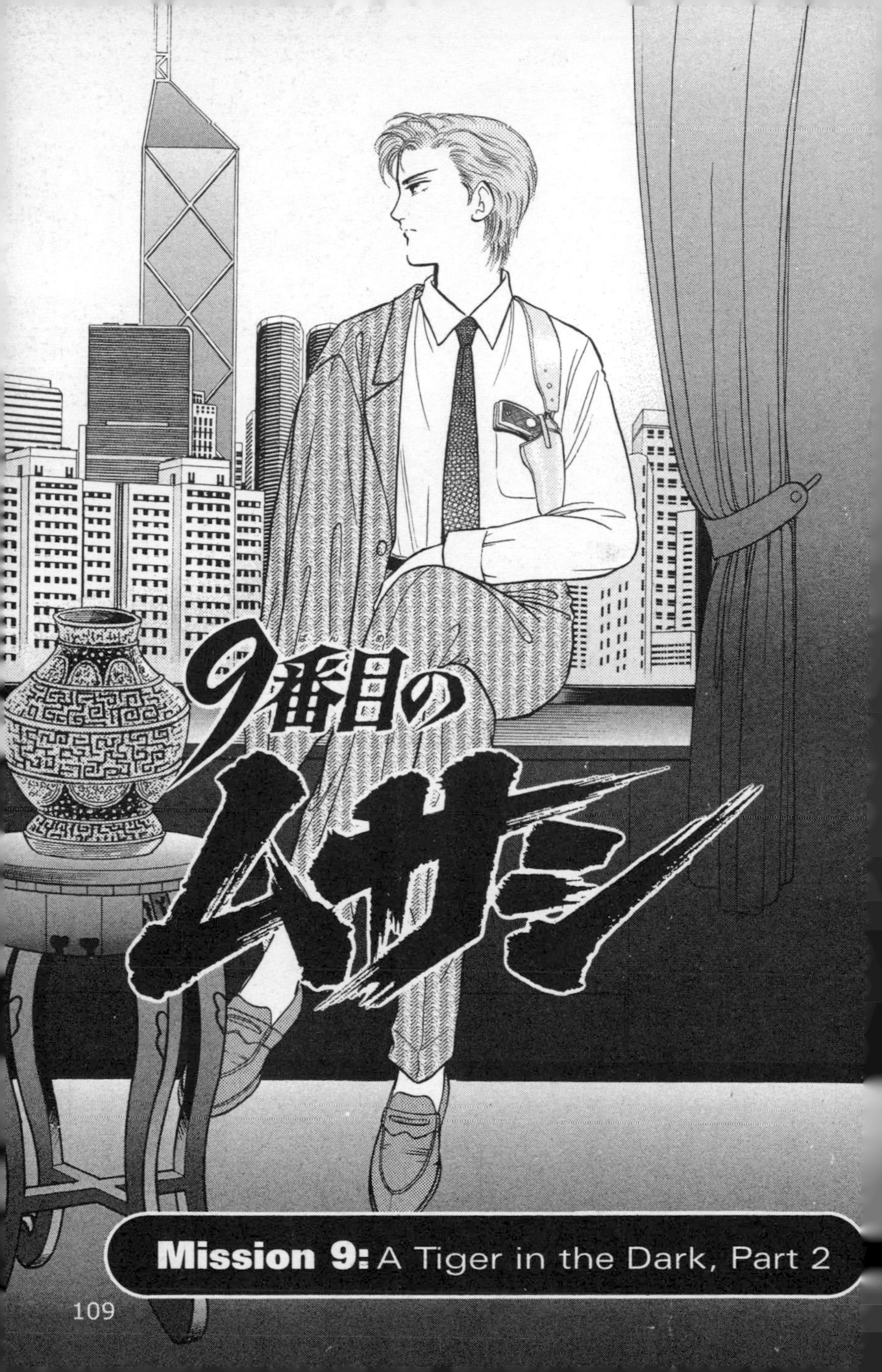
9番目のムサシ
Mission 9: A Tiger in the Dark, Part 2

Shinozuka shielded me from the blast, so she was hurt pretty bad.
I felt like dirt. Here it was, all my fault. All because I couldn't hack being protected. All because I couldn't keep my feelings for her in check.
All that stuff was going through my head, but I only had one clear thought. "Gee, her blood is red--just like mine."
It was something ridiculously obvious.

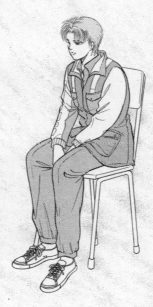

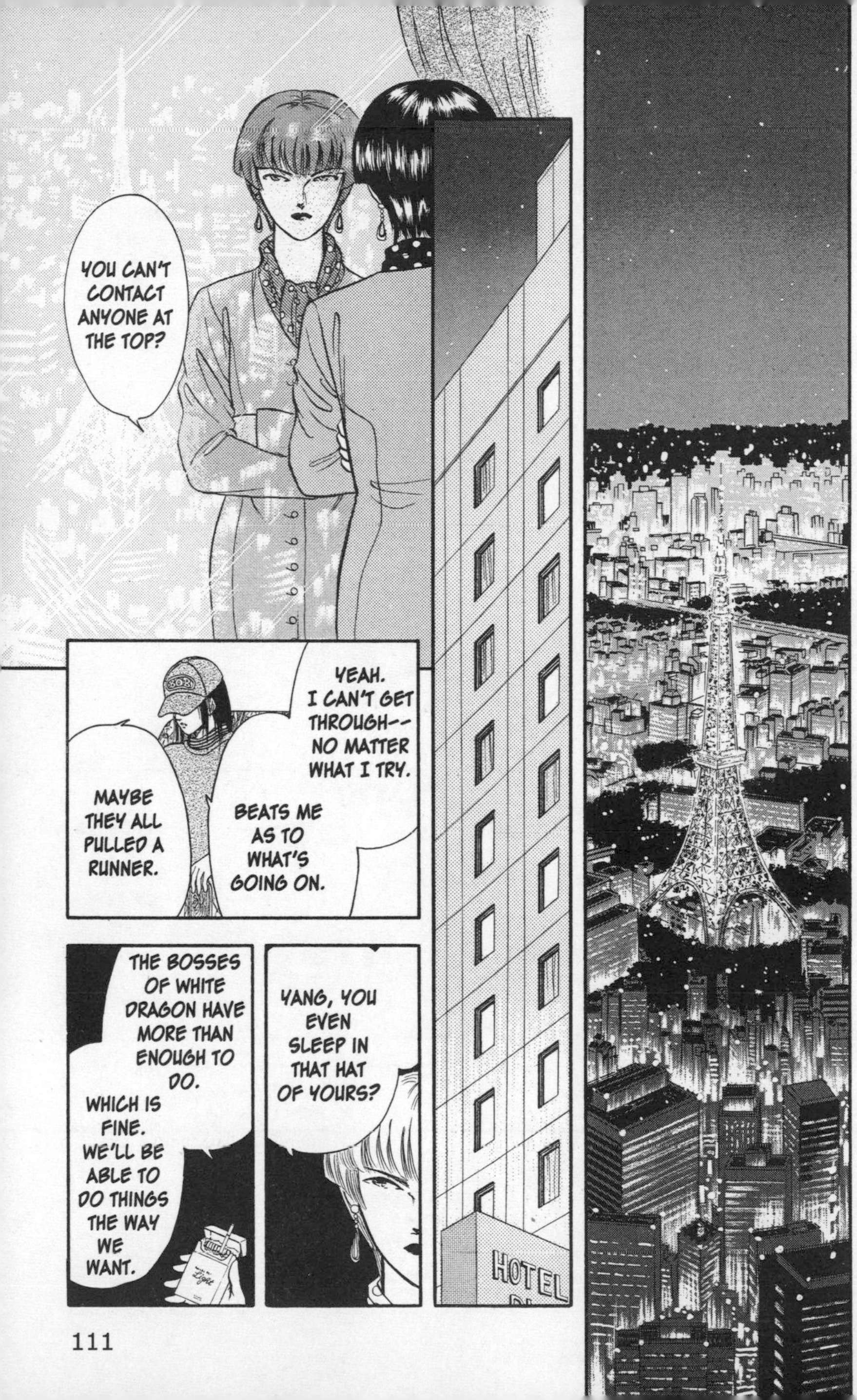
HOTEL
YOU CAN'T CONTACT ANYONE AT THE TOP?
YEAH. I CAN'T GET THROUGH-- NO MATTER WHAT I TRY.
BEATS ME AS TO WHAT'S GOING ON.
MAYBE THEY ALL PULLED A RUNNER.
YANG, YOU EVEN SLEEP IN THAT HAT OF YOURS?
THE BOSSES OF WHITE DRAGON HAVE MORE THAN ENOUGH TO DO.
WHICH IS FINE. WE'LL BE ABLE TO DO THINGS THE WAY WE WANT.
Light

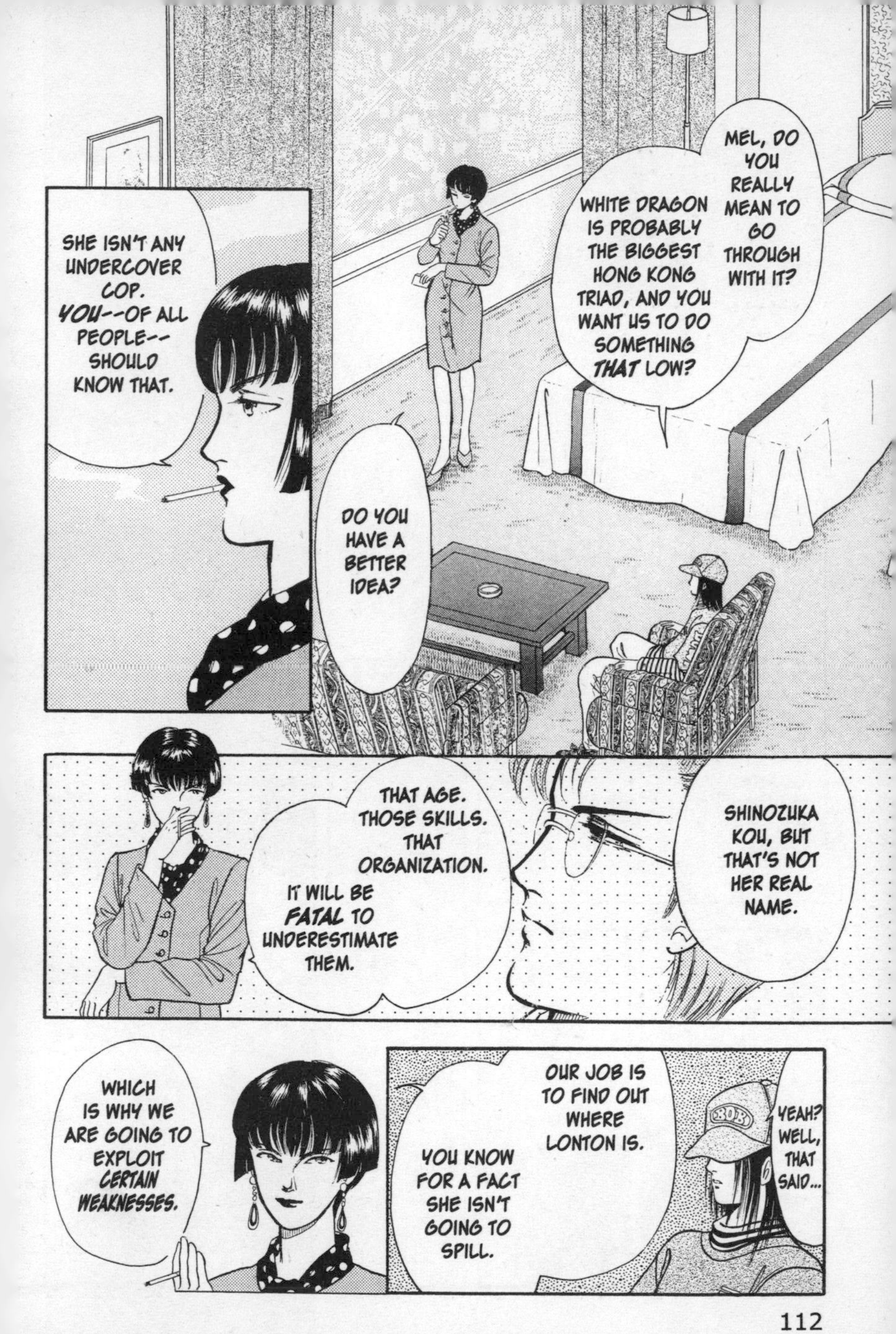
MEL, DO YOU REALLY MEAN TO GO THROUGH WITH IT?
WHITE DRAGON IS PROBABLY THE BIGGEST HONG KONG TRIAD, AND YOU WANT US TO DO SOMETHING *THAT* LOW?
DO YOU HAVE A BETTER IDEA?
SHE ISN'T ANY UNDERCOVER COP. *YOU*--OF ALL PEOPLE--SHOULD KNOW THAT.
SHINOZUKA KOU, BUT THAT'S NOT HER REAL NAME.
THAT AGE. THOSE SKILLS. THAT ORGANIZATION.
IT WILL BE *FATAL* TO UNDERESTIMATE THEM.
YEAH? WELL, THAT SAID...
OUR JOB IS TO FIND OUT WHERE LONTON IS.
YOU KNOW FOR A FACT SHE ISN'T GOING TO SPILL.
WHICH IS WHY WE ARE GOING TO EXPLOIT *CERTAIN WEAKNESSES.*

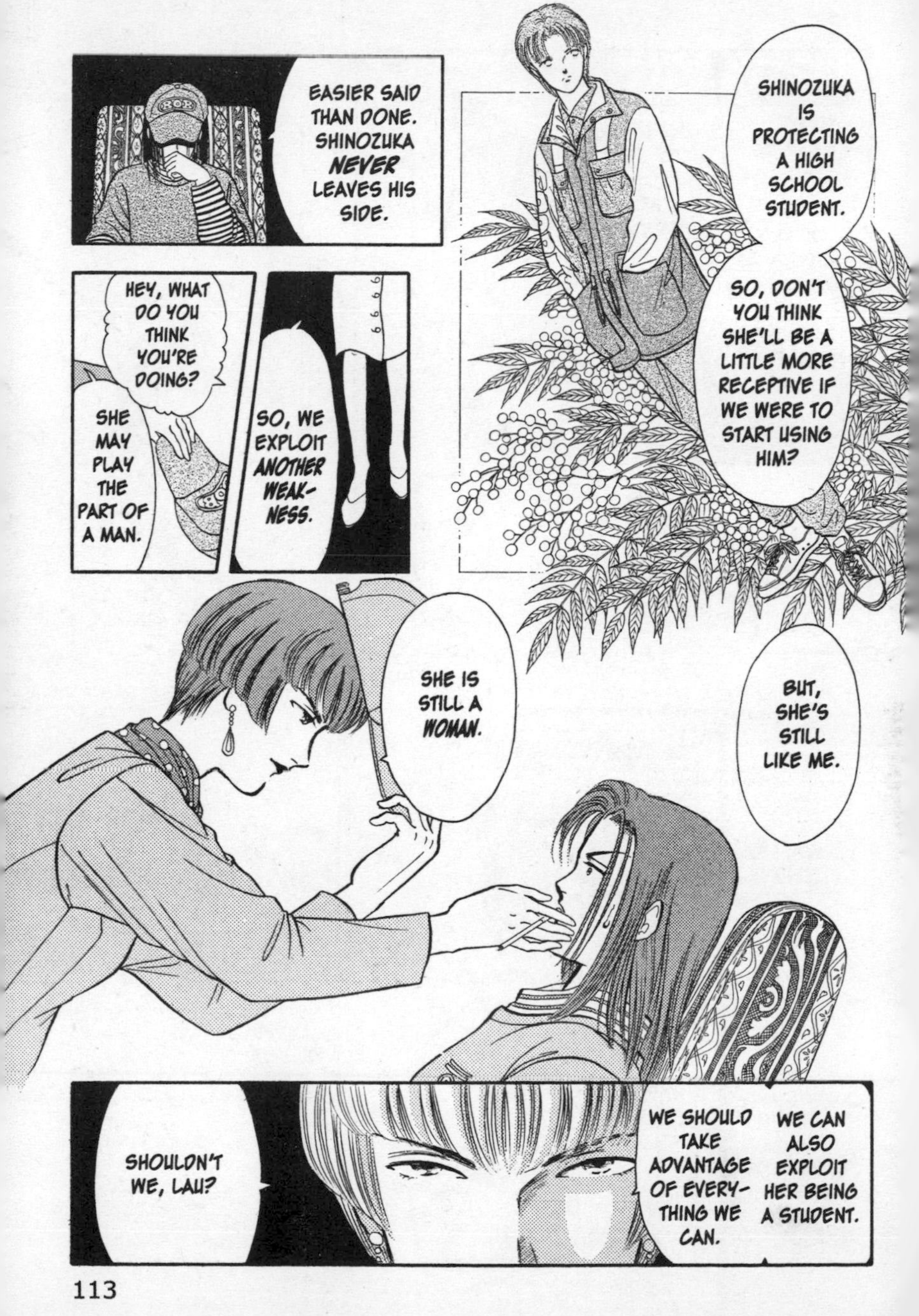
SHINOZUKA IS PROTECTING A HIGH SCHOOL STUDENT.
SO, DON'T YOU THINK SHE'LL BE A LITTLE MORE RECEPTIVE IF WE WERE TO START USING HIM?
EASIER SAID THAN DONE. SHINOZUKA NEVER LEAVES HIS SIDE.
SO, WE EXPLOIT ANOTHER WEAK-NESS.
HEY, WHAT DO YOU THINK YOU'RE DOING?
SHE MAY PLAY THE PART OF A MAN.
SHE IS STILL A WOMAN.
BUT, SHE'S STILL LIKE ME.
WE CAN ALSO EXPLOIT HER BEING A STUDENT.
WE SHOULD TAKE ADVANTAGE OF EVERY-THING WE CAN.
SHOULDN'T WE, LAU?

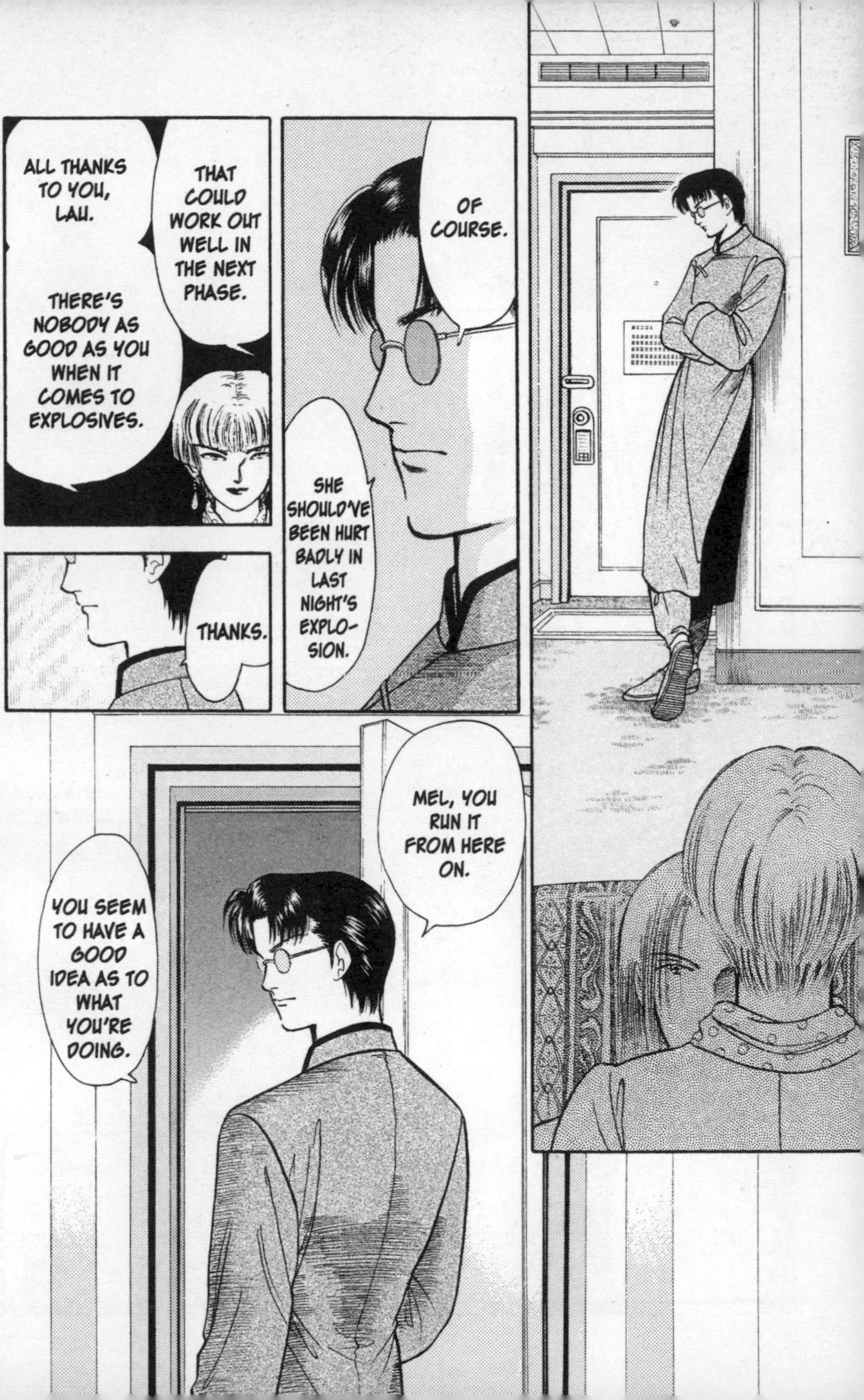
OF COURSE.
SHE SHOULD'VE BEEN HURT BADLY IN LAST NIGHT'S EXPLO-SION.
THAT COULD WORK OUT WELL IN THE NEXT PHASE.
ALL THANKS TO YOU, LAU.
THERE'S NOBODY AS GOOD AS YOU WHEN IT COMES TO EXPLOSIVES.
THANKS.
MEL, YOU RUN IT FROM HERE ON.
YOU SEEM TO HAVE A GOOD IDEA AS TO WHAT YOU'RE DOING.

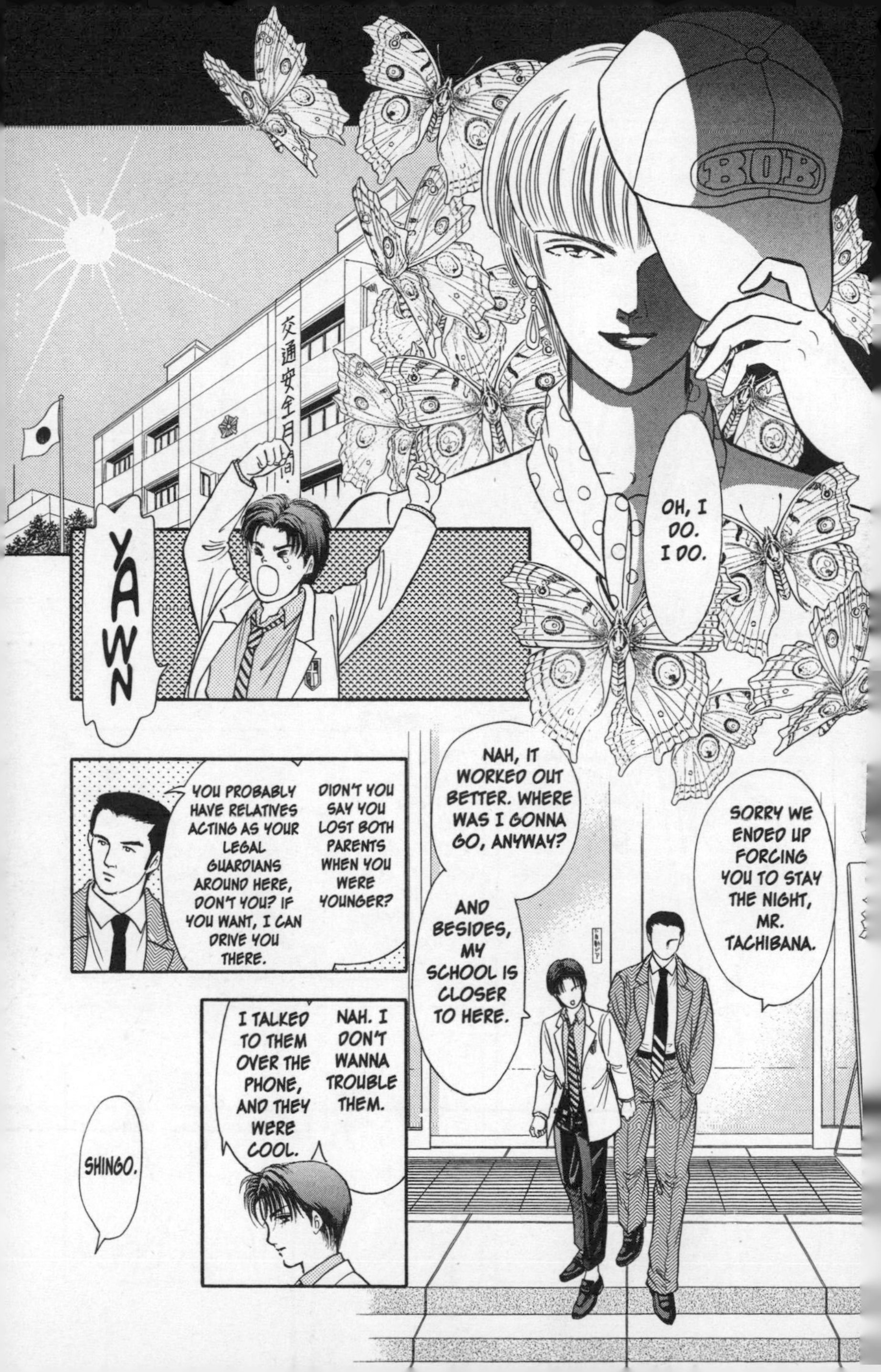
OH, I DO. I DO.
交通安全月間
YAWN
SORRY WE ENDED UP FORCING YOU TO STAY THE NIGHT, MR. TACHIBANA.
NAH, IT WORKED OUT BETTER. WHERE WAS I GONNA GO, ANYWAY?
AND BESIDES, MY SCHOOL IS CLOSER TO HERE.
DIDN'T YOU SAY YOU LOST BOTH PARENTS WHEN YOU WERE YOUNGER?
YOU PROBABLY HAVE RELATIVES ACTING AS YOUR LEGAL GUARDIANS AROUND HERE, DON'T YOU? IF YOU WANT, I CAN DRIVE YOU THERE.
NAH. I DON'T WANNA TROUBLE THEM.
I TALKED TO THEM OVER THE PHONE, AND THEY WERE COOL.
SHINGO.

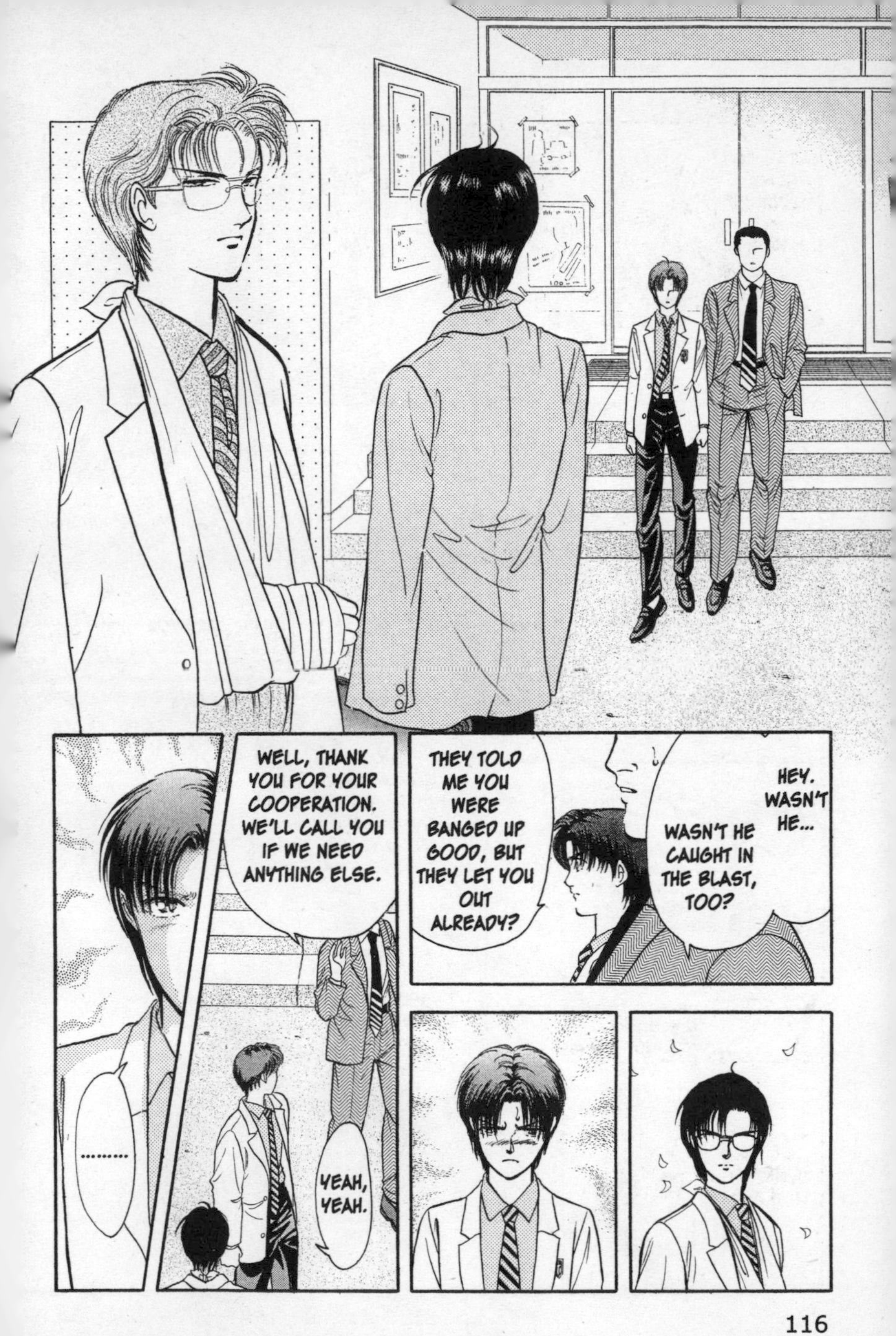
HEY. WASN'T HE...
WASN'T HE CAUGHT IN THE BLAST, TOO?
THEY TOLD ME YOU WERE BANGED UP GOOD, BUT THEY LET YOU OUT ALREADY?
WELL, THANK YOU FOR YOUR COOPERATION. WE'LL CALL YOU IF WE NEED ANYTHING ELSE.
YEAH, YEAH.
....

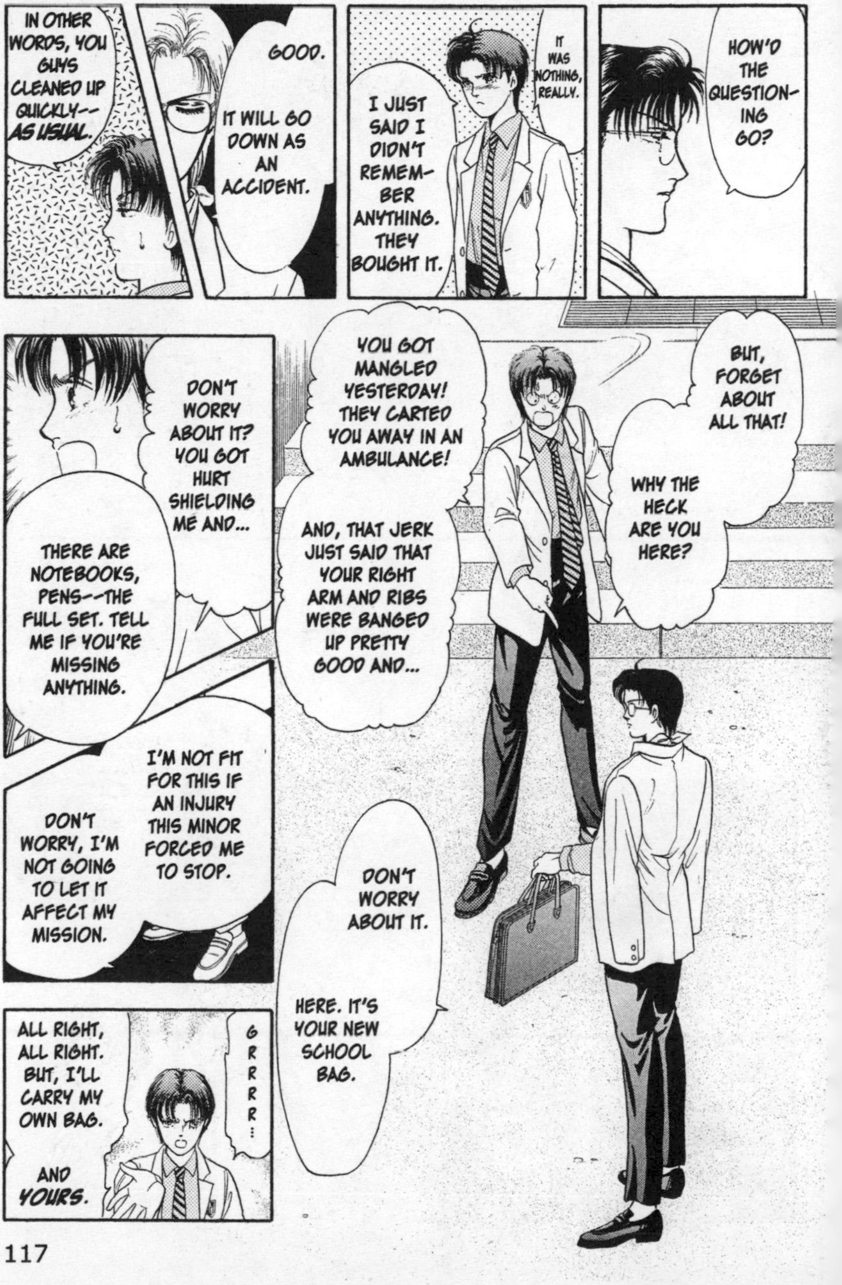
HOW'D THE QUESTIONING GO?
IT WAS NOTHING, REALLY.
I JUST SAID I DIDN'T REMEMBER ANYTHING. THEY BOUGHT IT.
GOOD.
IT WILL GO DOWN AS AN ACCIDENT.
IN OTHER WORDS, YOU GUYS CLEANED UP QUICKLY-- AS USUAL.
BUT, FORGET ABOUT ALL THAT!
WHY THE HECK ARE YOU HERE?
YOU GOT MANGLED YESTERDAY! THEY CARTED YOU AWAY IN AN AMBULANCE!
AND, THAT JERK JUST SAID THAT YOUR RIGHT ARM AND RIBS WERE BANGED UP PRETTY GOOD AND...
DON'T WORRY ABOUT IT.
HERE. IT'S YOUR NEW SCHOOL BAG.
DON'T WORRY ABOUT IT? YOU GOT HURT SHIELDING ME AND...
THERE ARE NOTEBOOKS, PENS--THE FULL SET. TELL ME IF YOU'RE MISSING ANYTHING.
I'M NOT FIT FOR THIS IF AN INJURY THIS MINOR FORCED ME TO STOP.
DON'T WORRY, I'M NOT GOING TO LET IT AFFECT MY MISSION.
GRRRR...
ALL RIGHT, ALL RIGHT. BUT, I'LL CARRY MY OWN BAG.
AND YOURS.

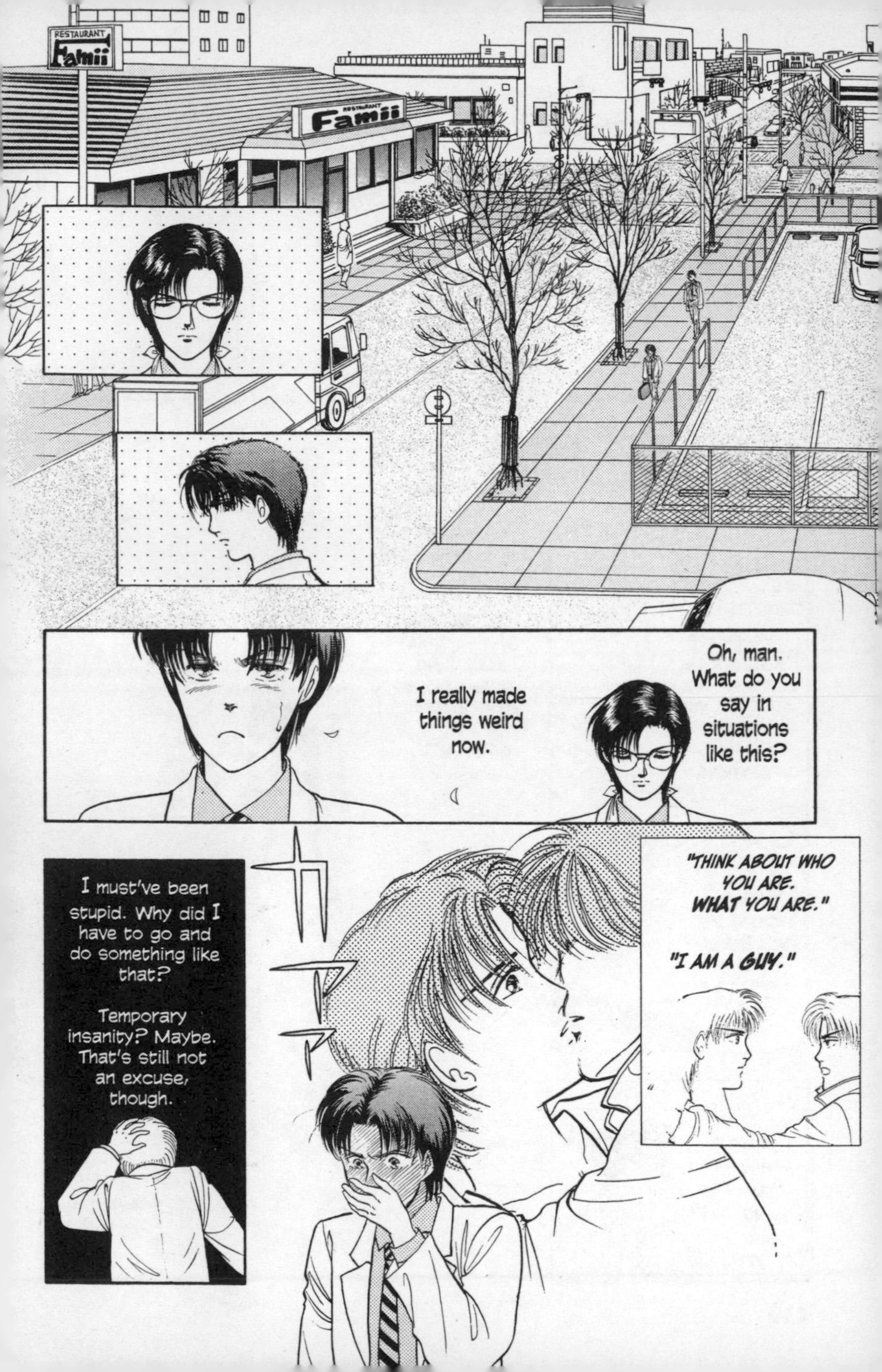
RESTAURANT
Famii
RESTAURANT
Famii
Oh, man. What do you say in situations like this?
I really made things weird now.
"THINK ABOUT WHO YOU ARE. WHAT YOU ARE."
"I AM A GUY."
I must've been stupid. Why did I have to go and do something like that?
Temporary insanity? Maybe. That's still not an excuse, though.

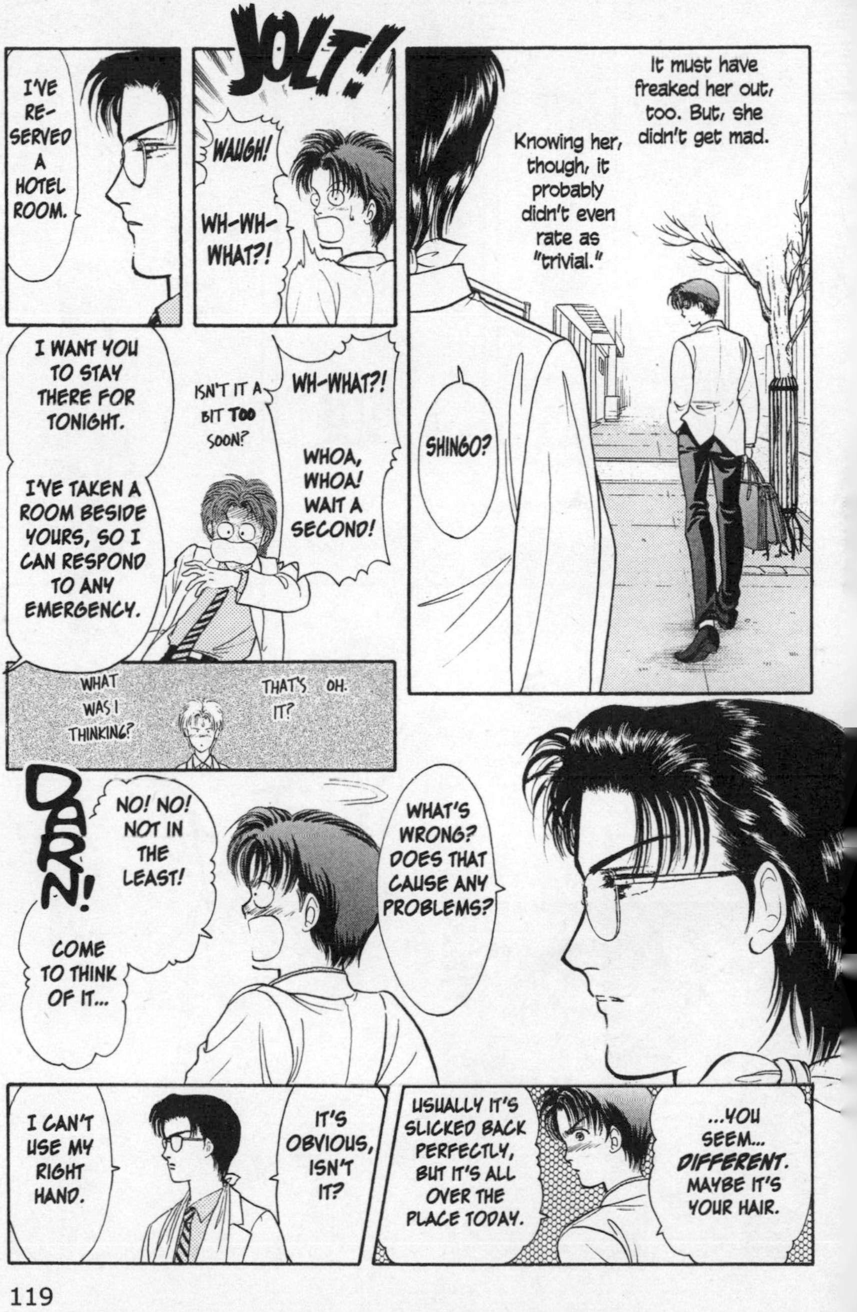
It must have freaked her out, too. But, she didn't get mad.
Knowing her, though, it probably didn't even rate as "trivial."
SHINGO?
JOLT!
WAUGH!
WH-WH-WHAT?!
I'VE RE-SERVED A HOTEL ROOM.
WH-WHAT?!
ISN'T IT A BIT TOO SOON?
I WANT YOU TO STAY THERE FOR TONIGHT.
WHOA, WHOA! WAIT A SECOND!
I'VE TAKEN A ROOM BESIDE YOURS, SO I CAN RESPOND TO ANY EMERGENCY.
OH.
THAT'S IT?
WHAT WAS I THINKING?
WHAT'S WRONG? DOES THAT CAUSE ANY PROBLEMS?
NO! NO! NOT IN THE LEAST!
DARN!
COME TO THINK OF IT...
...YOU SEEM... DIFFERENT. MAYBE IT'S YOUR HAIR.
USUALLY IT'S SLICKED BACK PERFECTLY, BUT IT'S ALL OVER THE PLACE TODAY.
IT'S OBVIOUS, ISN'T IT?
I CAN'T USE MY RIGHT HAND.

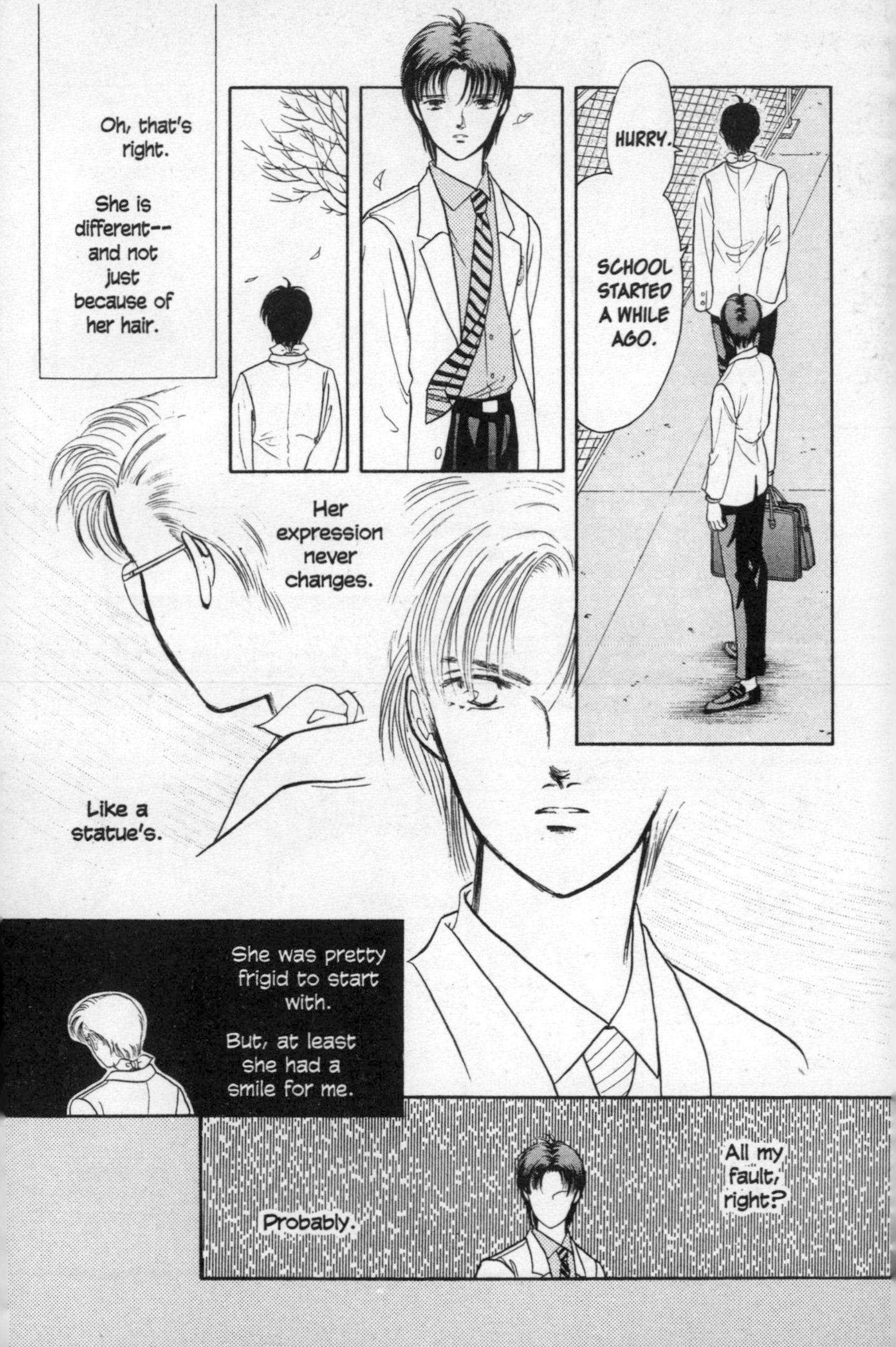
HURRY.
SCHOOL STARTED A WHILE AGO.
Oh, that's right.
She is different-- and not just because of her hair.
Her expression never changes.
Like a statue's.
She was pretty frigid to start with.
But, at least she had a smile for me.
All my fault, right?
Probably.

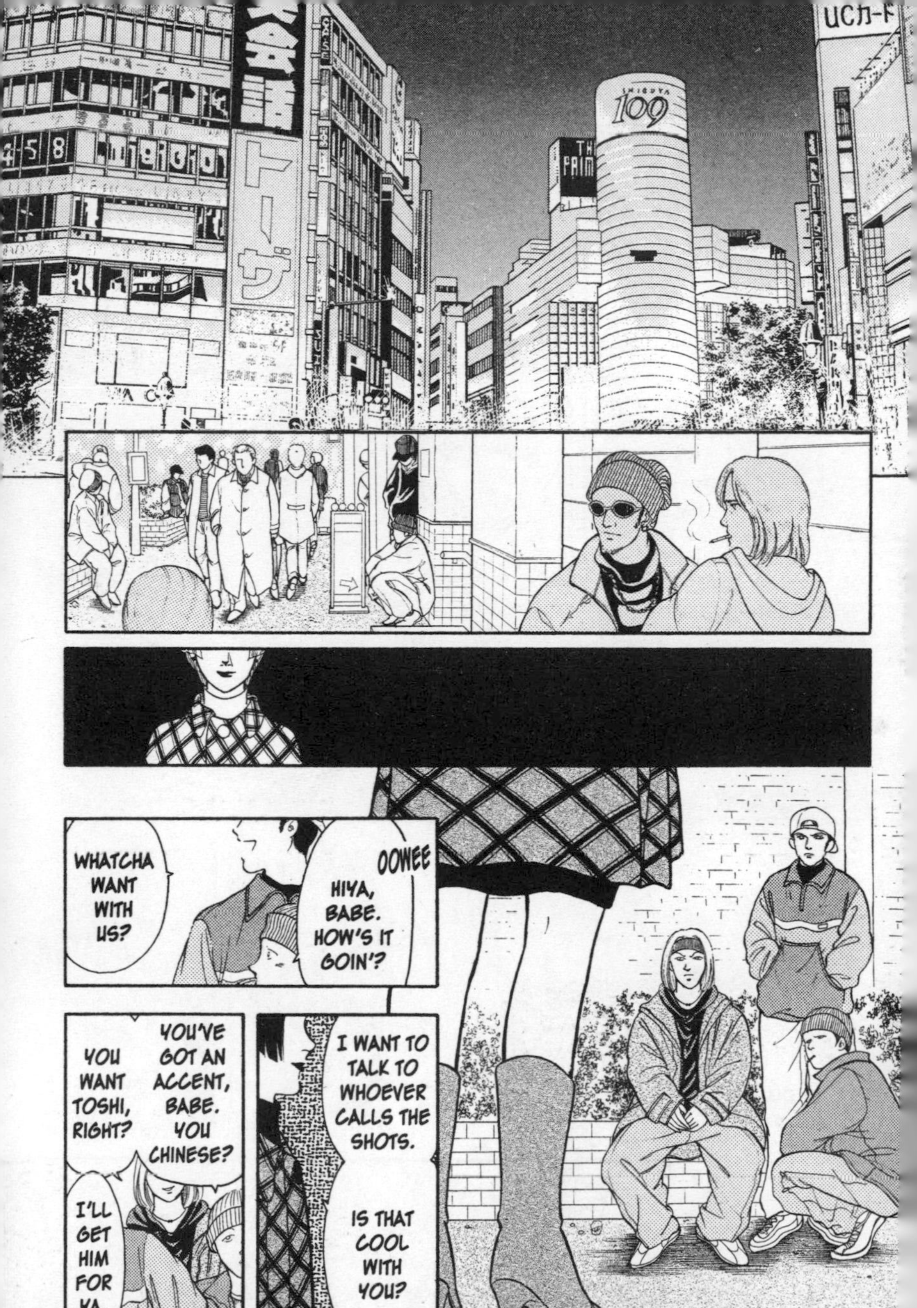
UCカード
109
OOWEE
HIYA, BABE. HOW'S IT GOIN'?
WHATCHA WANT WITH US?
I WANT TO TALK TO WHOEVER CALLS THE SHOTS.
IS THAT COOL WITH YOU?
YOU'VE GOT AN ACCENT, BABE. YOU CHINESE?
YOU WANT TOSHI, RIGHT?
I'LL GET HIM FOR YA.

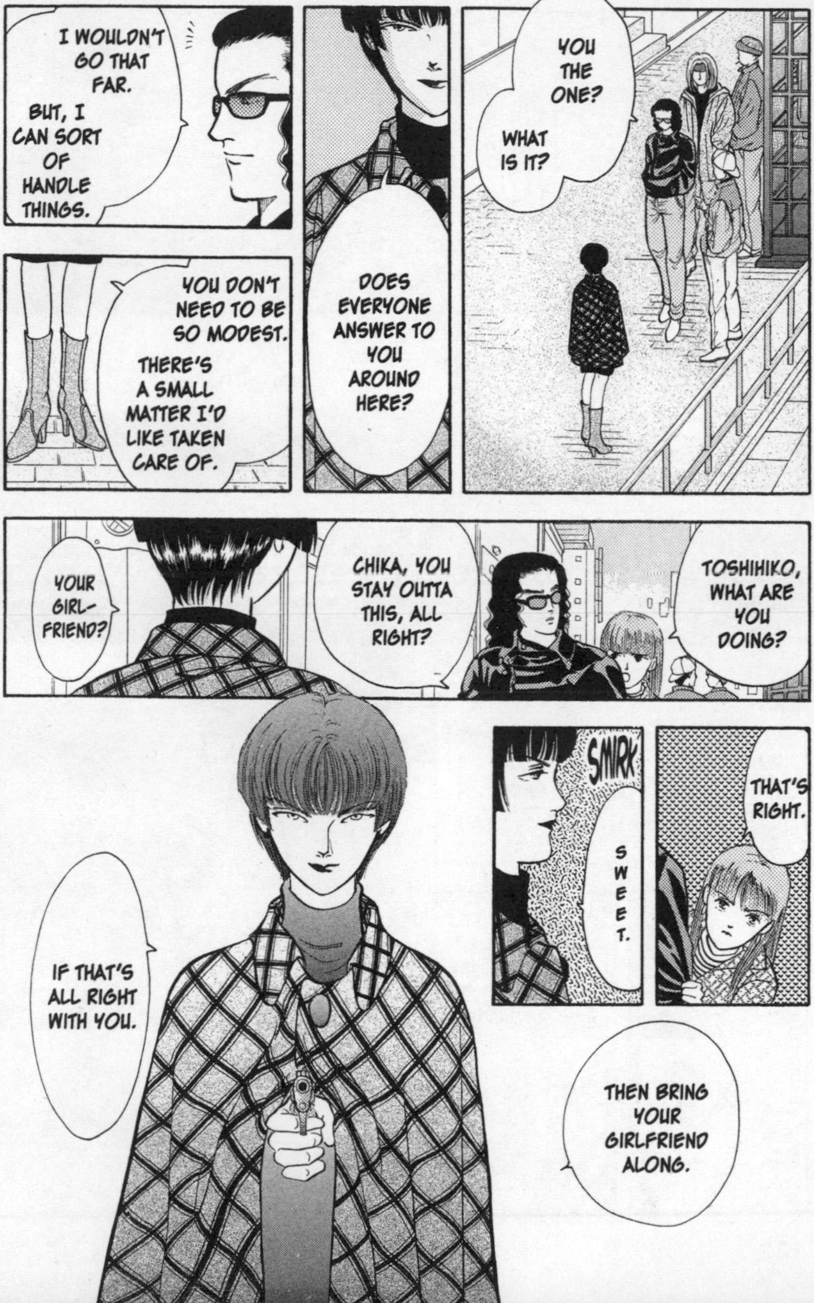
YOU THE ONE?
WHAT IS IT?
DOES EVERYONE ANSWER TO YOU AROUND HERE?
I WOULDN'T GO THAT FAR.
BUT, I CAN SORT OF HANDLE THINGS.
YOU DON'T NEED TO BE SO MODEST.
THERE'S A SMALL MATTER I'D LIKE TAKEN CARE OF.
TOSHIHIKO, WHAT ARE YOU DOING?
CHIKA, YOU STAY OUTTA THIS, ALL RIGHT?
YOUR GIRL-FRIEND?
THAT'S RIGHT.
SMIRK
SWEET.
THEN BRING YOUR GIRLFRIEND ALONG.
IF THAT'S ALL RIGHT WITH YOU.

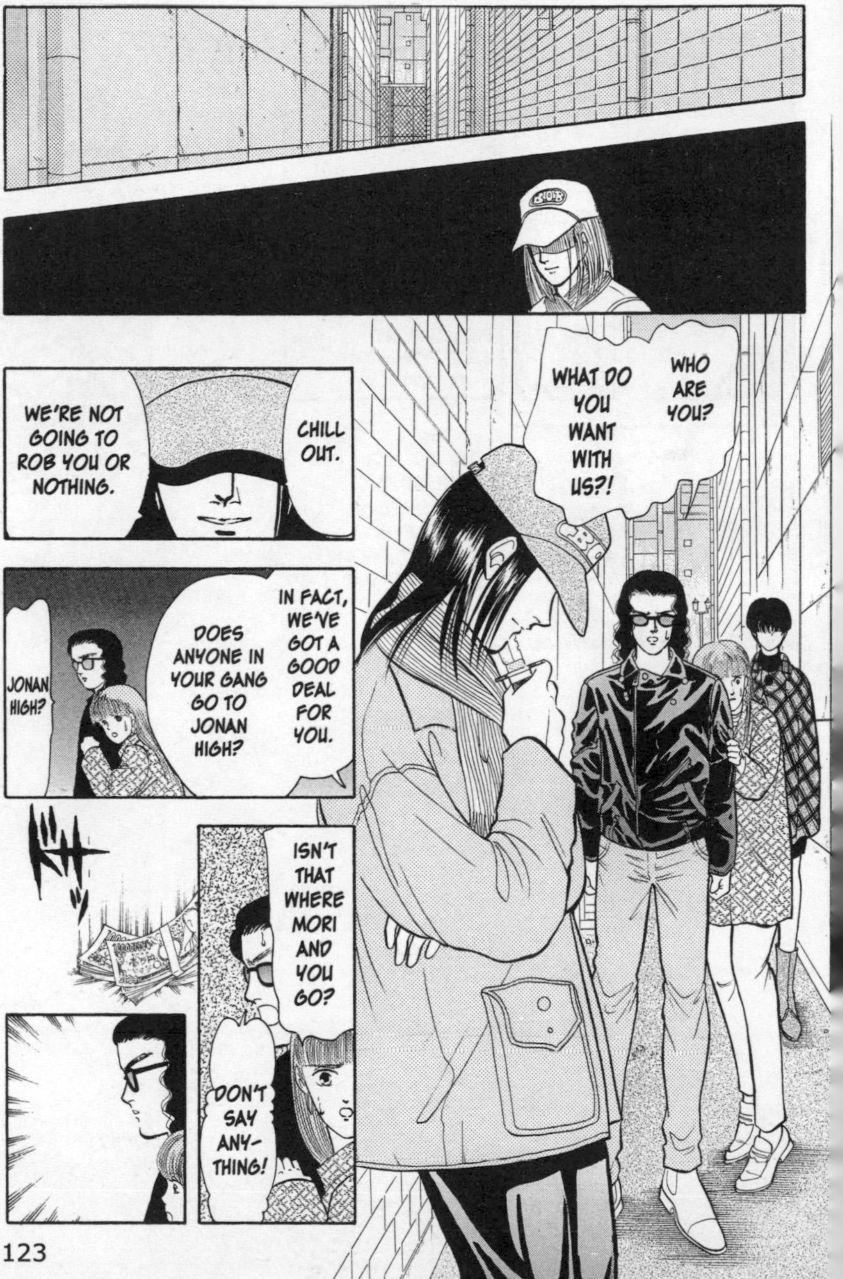
WHO ARE YOU?
WHAT DO YOU WANT WITH US?!
CHILL OUT.
WE'RE NOT GOING TO ROB YOU OR NOTHING.
IN FACT, WE'VE GOT A GOOD DEAL FOR YOU.
DOES ANYONE IN YOUR GANG GO TO JONAN HIGH?
JONAN HIGH?
ISN'T THAT WHERE MORI AND YOU GO?
DON'T SAY ANY-THING!

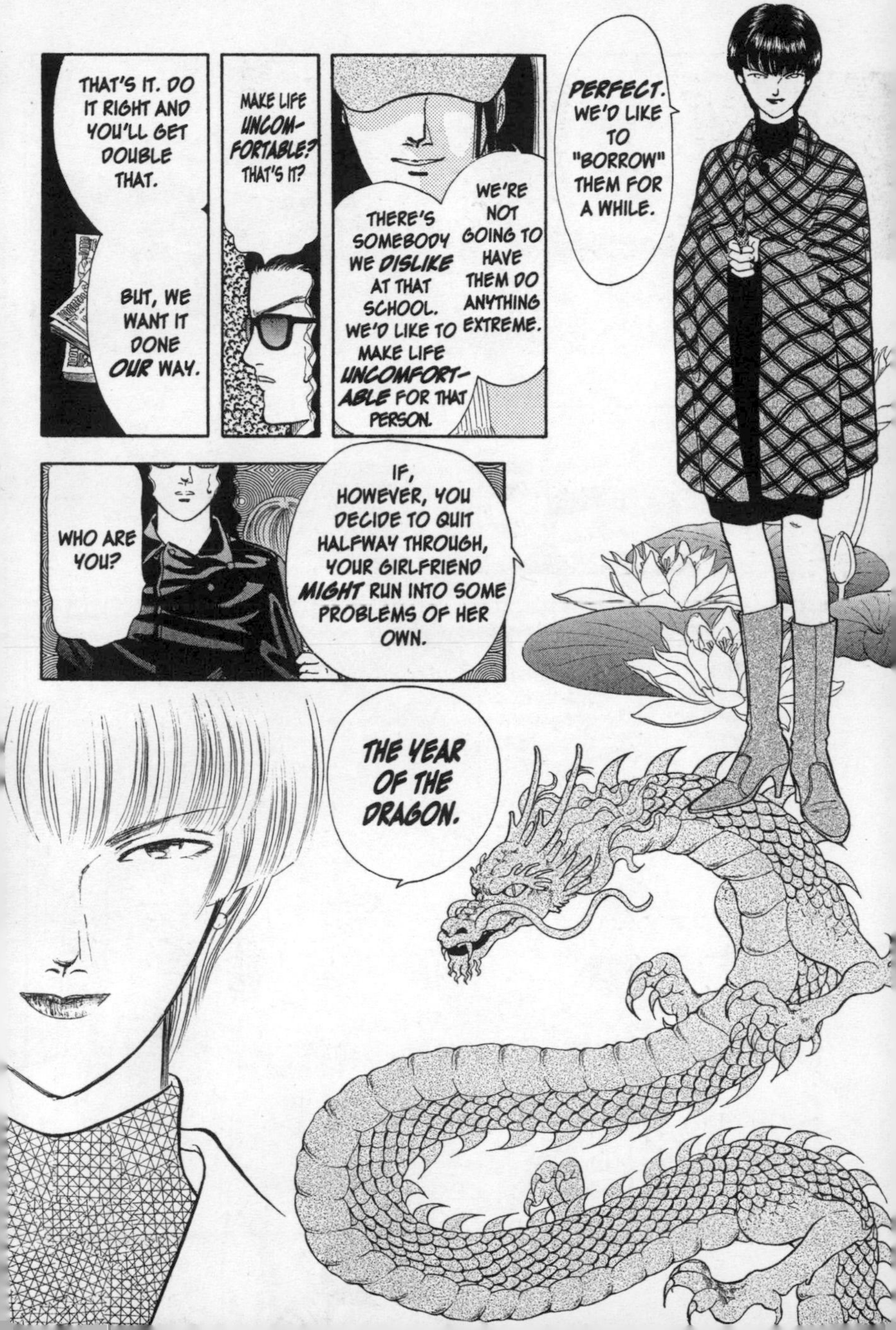
PERFECT. WE'D LIKE TO "BORROW" THEM FOR A WHILE.
THERE'S SOMEBODY WE DISLIKE AT THAT SCHOOL. WE'D LIKE TO MAKE LIFE UNCOMFORTABLE FOR THAT PERSON.
WE'RE NOT GOING TO HAVE THEM DO ANYTHING EXTREME.
MAKE LIFE UNCOMFORTABLE? THAT'S IT?
THAT'S IT. DO IT RIGHT AND YOU'LL GET DOUBLE THAT.
BUT, WE WANT IT DONE OUR WAY.
IF, HOWEVER, YOU DECIDE TO QUIT HALFWAY THROUGH, YOUR GIRLFRIEND MIGHT RUN INTO SOME PROBLEMS OF HER OWN.
WHO ARE YOU?
THE YEAR OF THE DRAGON.

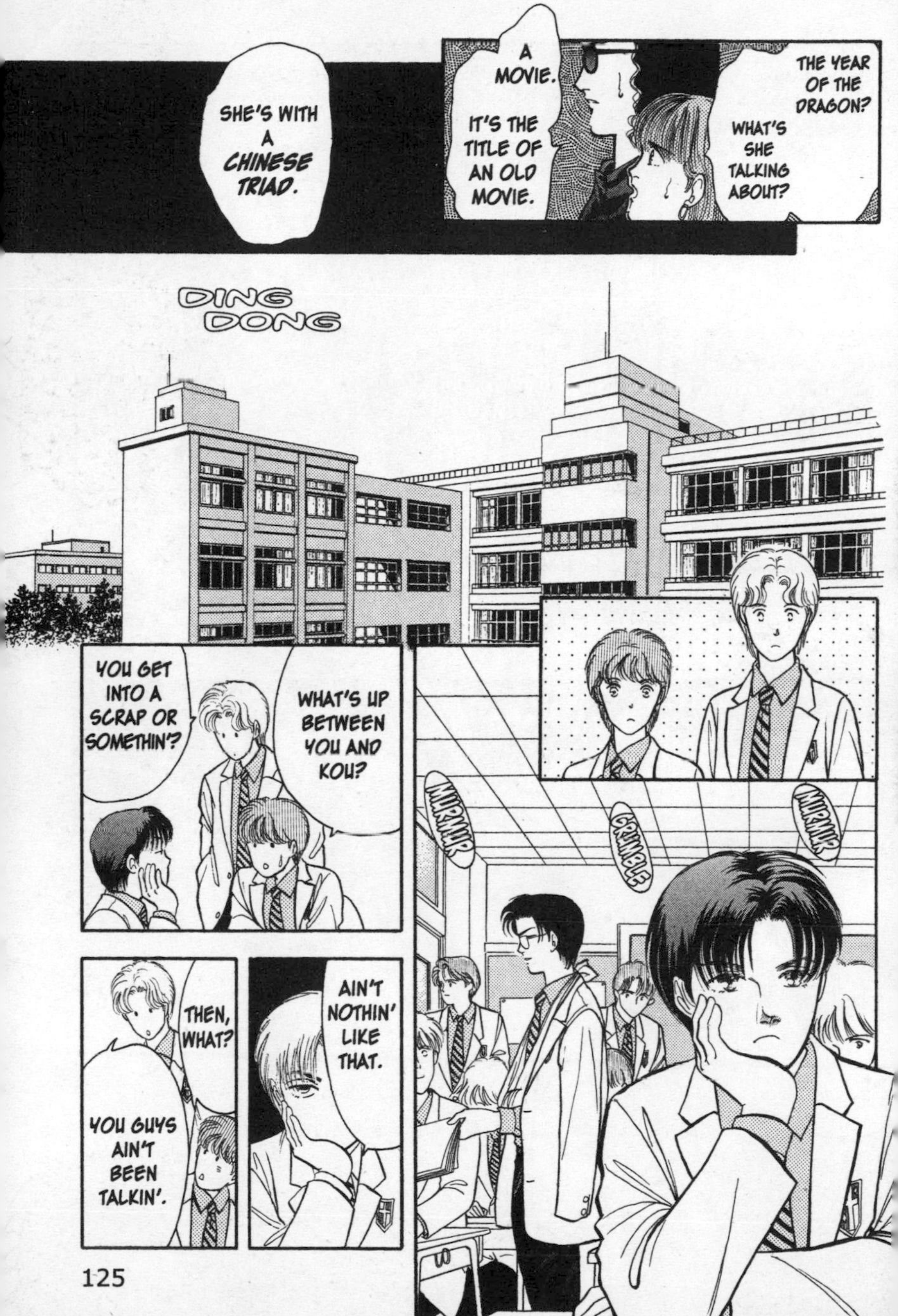
THE YEAR OF THE DRAGON?
WHAT'S SHE TALKING ABOUT?
A MOVIE.
IT'S THE TITLE OF AN OLD MOVIE.
SHE'S WITH A CHINESE TRIAD.
DING DONG
MURMUR
GRUMBLE
MURMUR
WHAT'S UP BETWEEN YOU AND KOU?
YOU GET INTO A SCRAP OR SOMETHIN'?
AIN'T NOTHIN' LIKE THAT.
THEN, WHAT?
YOU GUYS AIN'T BEEN TALKIN'.

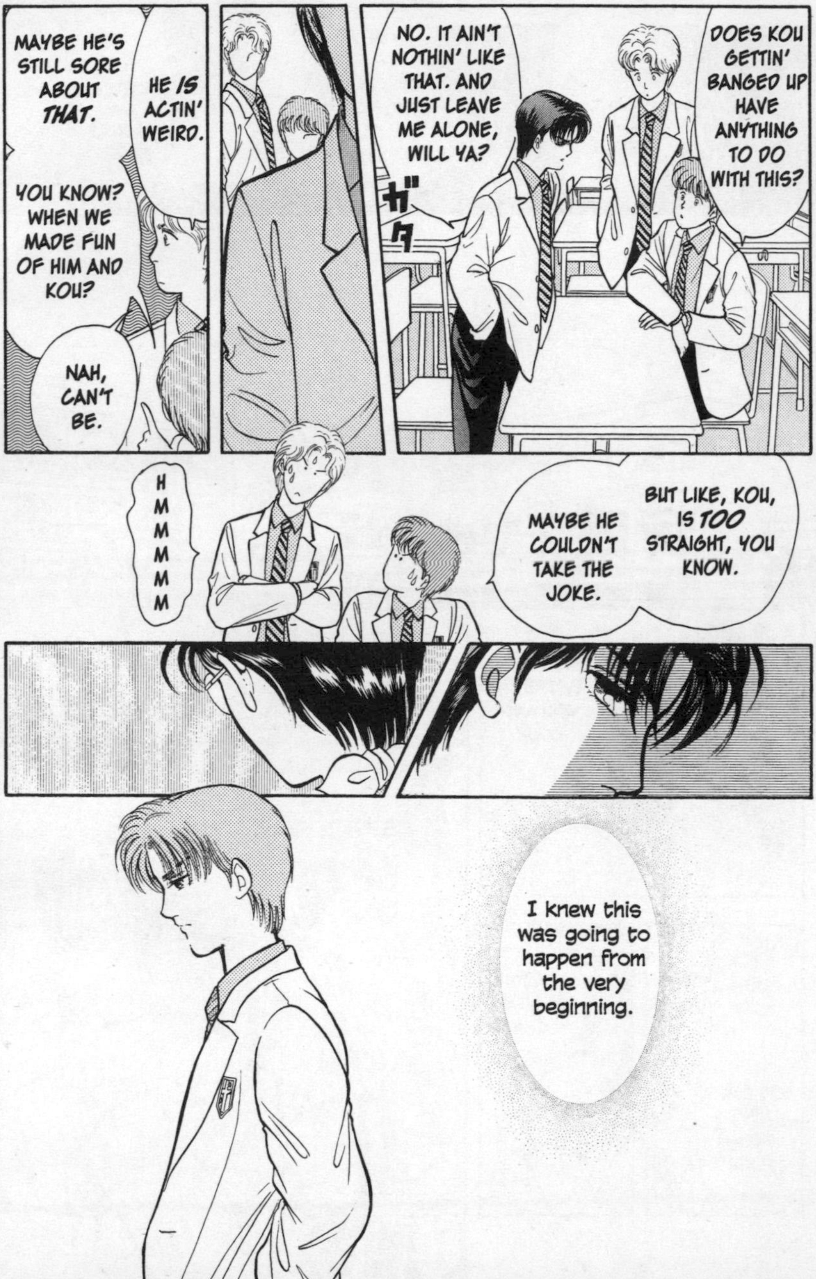
DOES KOU GETTIN' BANGED UP HAVE ANYTHING TO DO WITH THIS?
NO. IT AIN'T NOTHIN' LIKE THAT. AND JUST LEAVE ME ALONE, WILL YA?
ガタ
HE *IS* ACTIN' WEIRD.
MAYBE HE'S STILL SORE ABOUT *THAT*.
YOU KNOW? WHEN WE MADE FUN OF HIM AND KOU?
NAH, CAN'T BE.
BUT LIKE, KOU, IS *TOO* STRAIGHT, YOU KNOW.
MAYBE HE COULDN'T TAKE THE JOKE.
HMMMMMM
I knew this was going to happen from the very beginning.

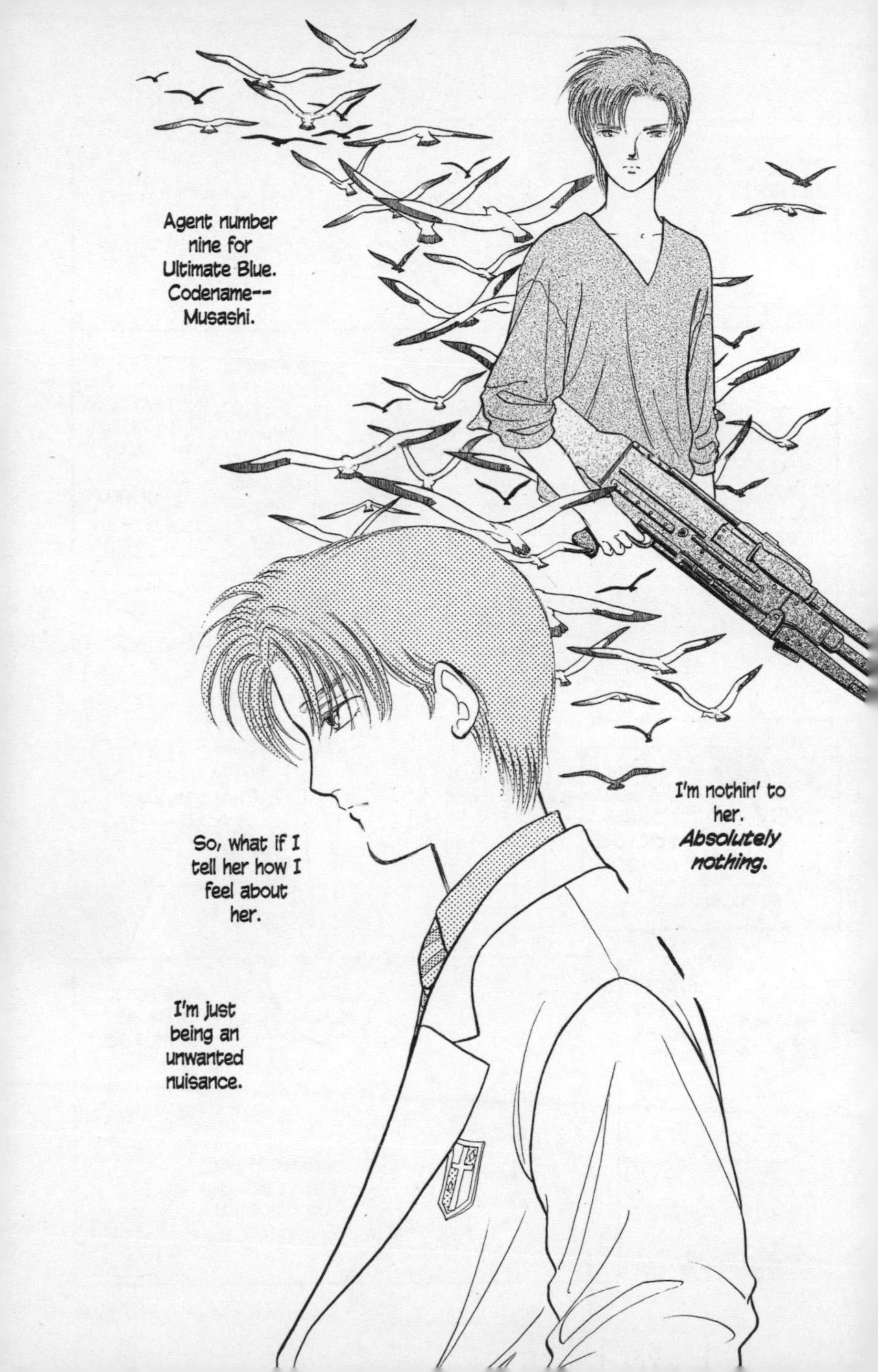
Agent number nine for Ultimate Blue. Codename-- Musashi.
I'm nothin' to her. *Absolutely nothing.*
So, what if I tell her how I feel about her.
I'm just being an unwanted nuisance.

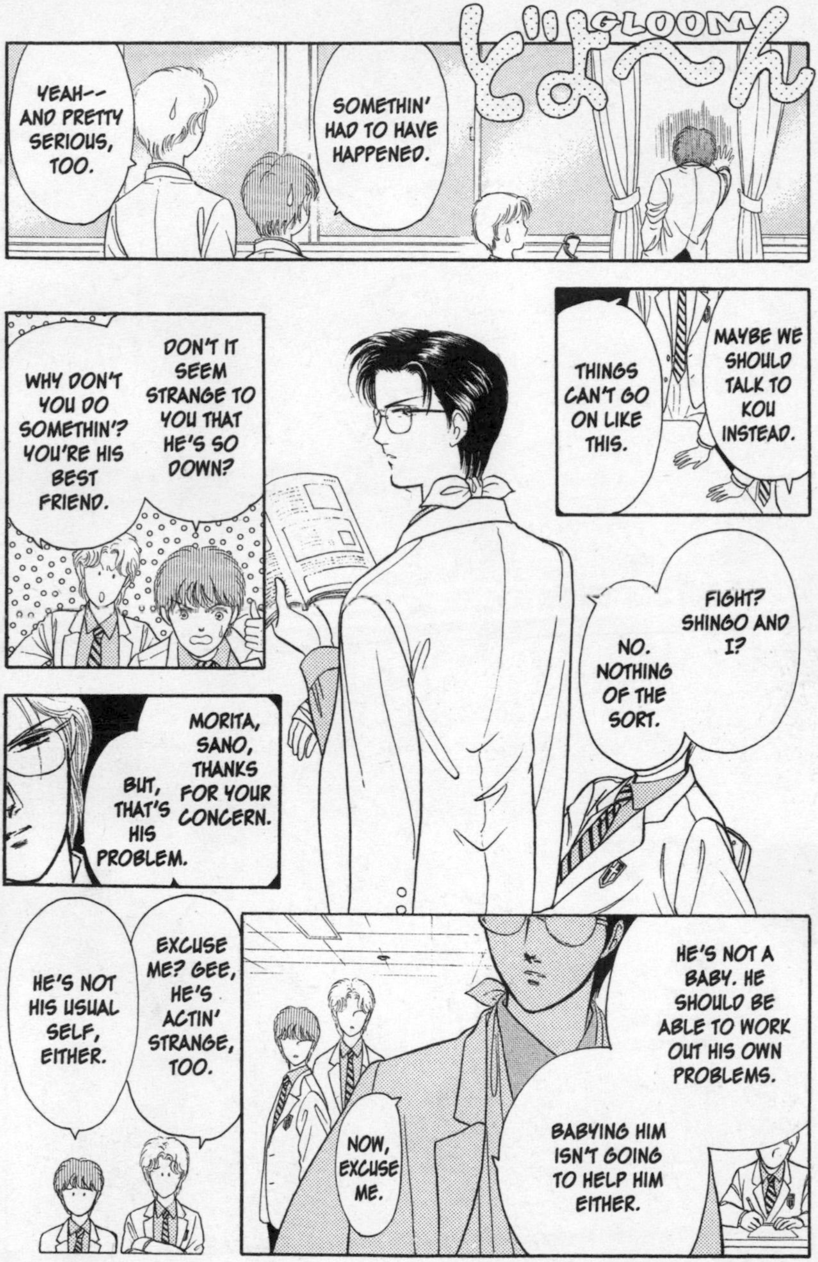
どよ〜ん
GLOOM
SOMETHIN' HAD TO HAVE HAPPENED.
YEAH-- AND PRETTY SERIOUS, TOO.
MAYBE WE SHOULD TALK TO KOU INSTEAD.
THINGS CAN'T GO ON LIKE THIS.
FIGHT? SHINGO AND I?
NO. NOTHING OF THE SORT.
DON'T IT SEEM STRANGE TO YOU THAT HE'S SO DOWN?
WHY DON'T YOU DO SOMETHIN'? YOU'RE HIS BEST FRIEND.
MORITA, SANO, THANKS FOR YOUR CONCERN.
BUT, THAT'S HIS PROBLEM.
HE'S NOT A BABY. HE SHOULD BE ABLE TO WORK OUT HIS OWN PROBLEMS.
BABYING HIM ISN'T GOING TO HELP HIM EITHER.
NOW, EXCUSE ME.
EXCUSE ME? GEE, HE'S ACTIN' STRANGE, TOO.
HE'S NOT HIS USUAL SELF, EITHER.

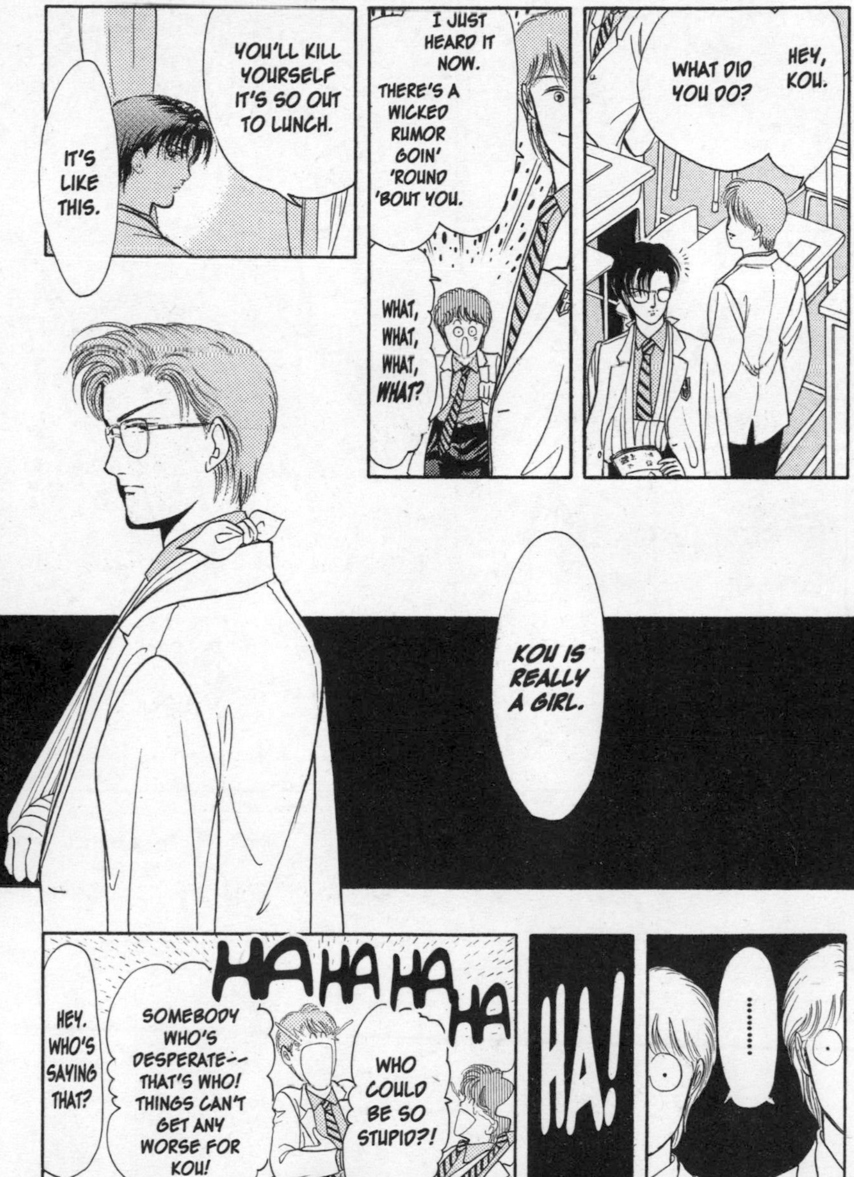
HEY, KOU.
WHAT DID YOU DO?
I JUST HEARD IT NOW. THERE'S A WICKED RUMOR GOIN' 'ROUND 'BOUT YOU.
WHAT, WHAT, WHAT, WHAT?
YOU'LL KILL YOURSELF IT'S SO OUT TO LUNCH.
IT'S LIKE THIS.
KOU IS REALLY A GIRL.
......
HA!
HAHAHAHAHA
WHO COULD BE SO STUPID?!
SOMEBODY WHO'S DESPERATE-- THAT'S WHO! THINGS CAN'T GET ANY WORSE FOR KOU!
HEY. WHO'S SAYING THAT?

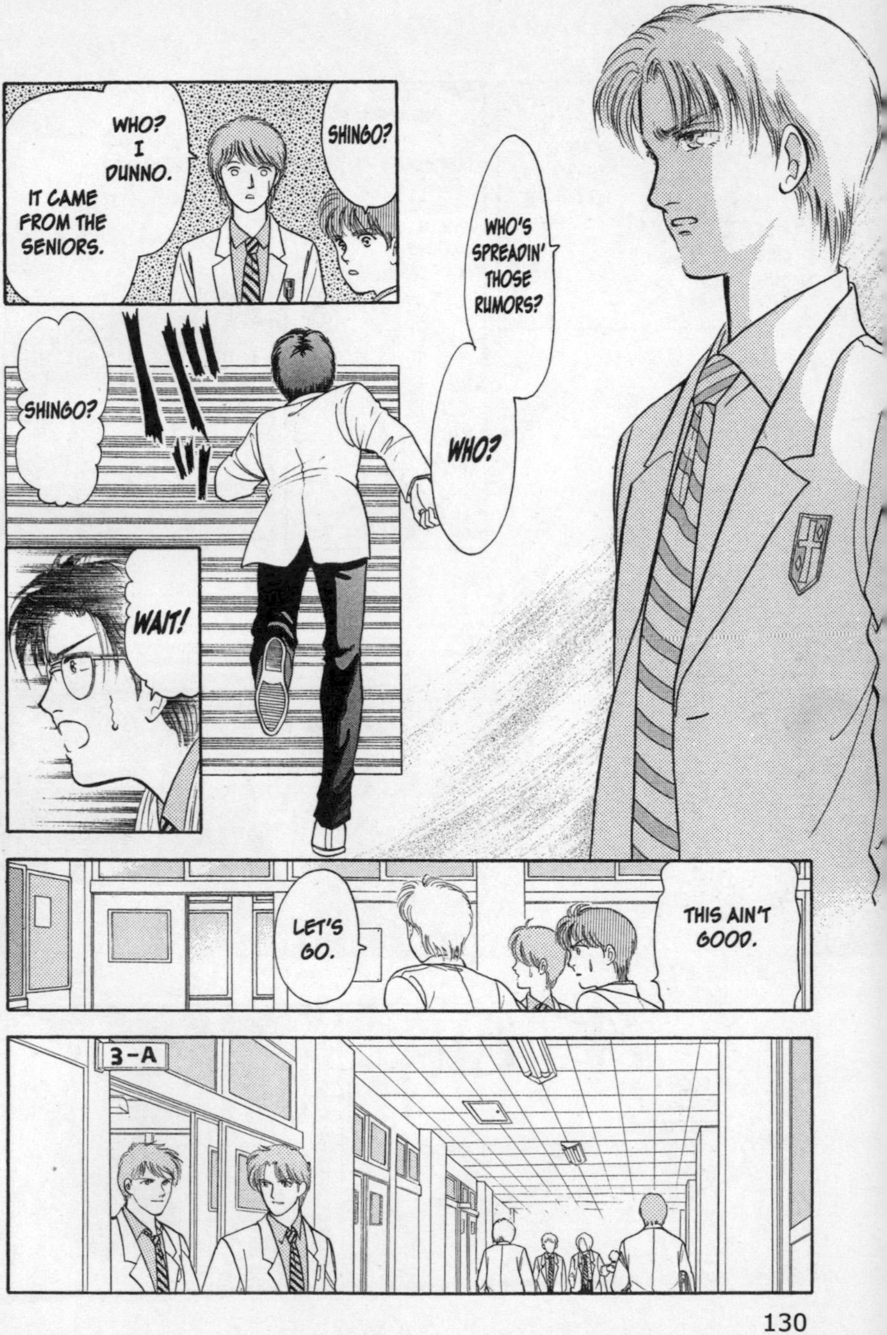
WHO'S SPREADIN' THOSE RUMORS?
WHO?
SHINGO?
WHO? I DUNNO.
IT CAME FROM THE SENIORS.
SHINGO?
WAIT!
THIS AIN'T GOOD.
LET'S GO.
3-A

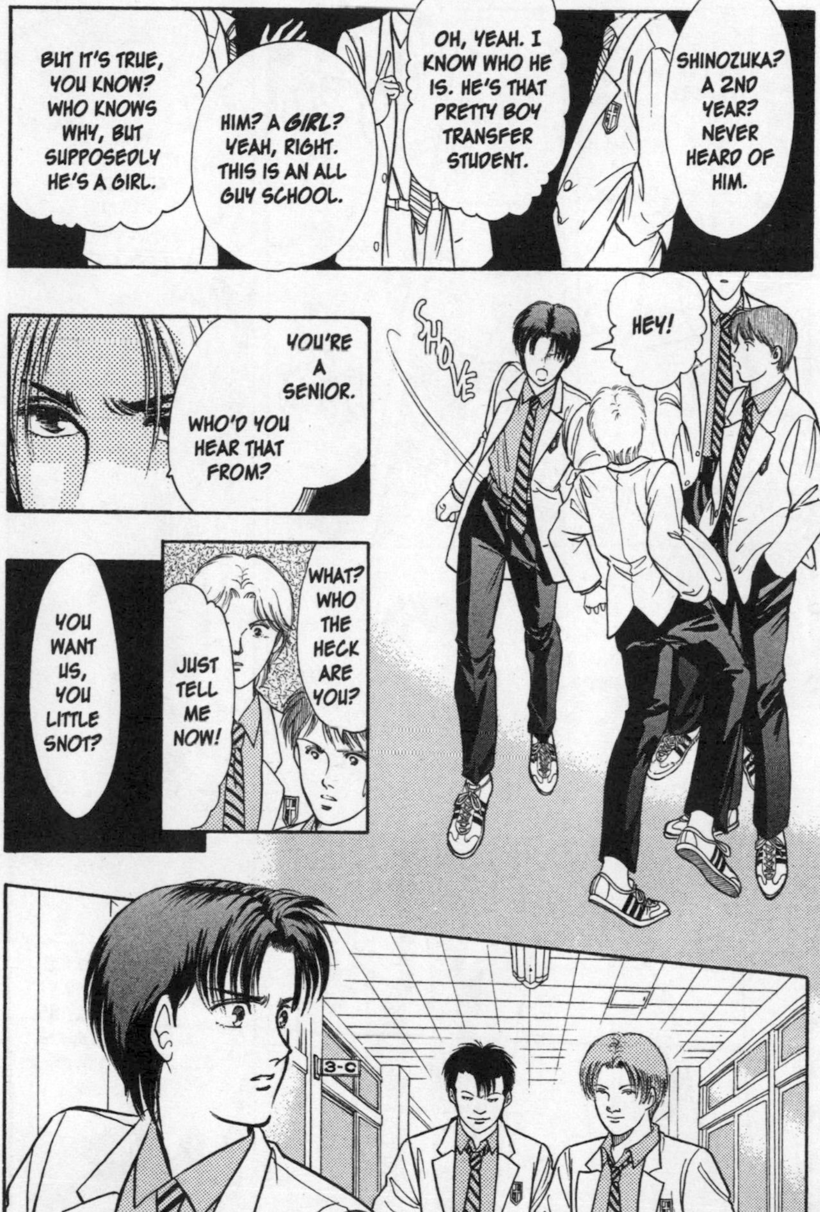
SHINOZUKA? A 2ND YEAR? NEVER HEARD OF HIM.
OH, YEAH. I KNOW WHO HE IS. HE'S THAT PRETTY BOY TRANSFER STUDENT.
HIM? A *GIRL*? YEAH, RIGHT. THIS IS AN ALL GUY SCHOOL.
BUT IT'S TRUE, YOU KNOW? WHO KNOWS WHY, BUT SUPPOSEDLY HE'S A GIRL.
SHOVE
HEY!
YOU'RE A SENIOR.
WHO'D YOU HEAR THAT FROM?
WHAT? WHO THE HECK ARE YOU?
JUST TELL ME NOW!
YOU WANT US, YOU LITTLE SNOT?
3-C

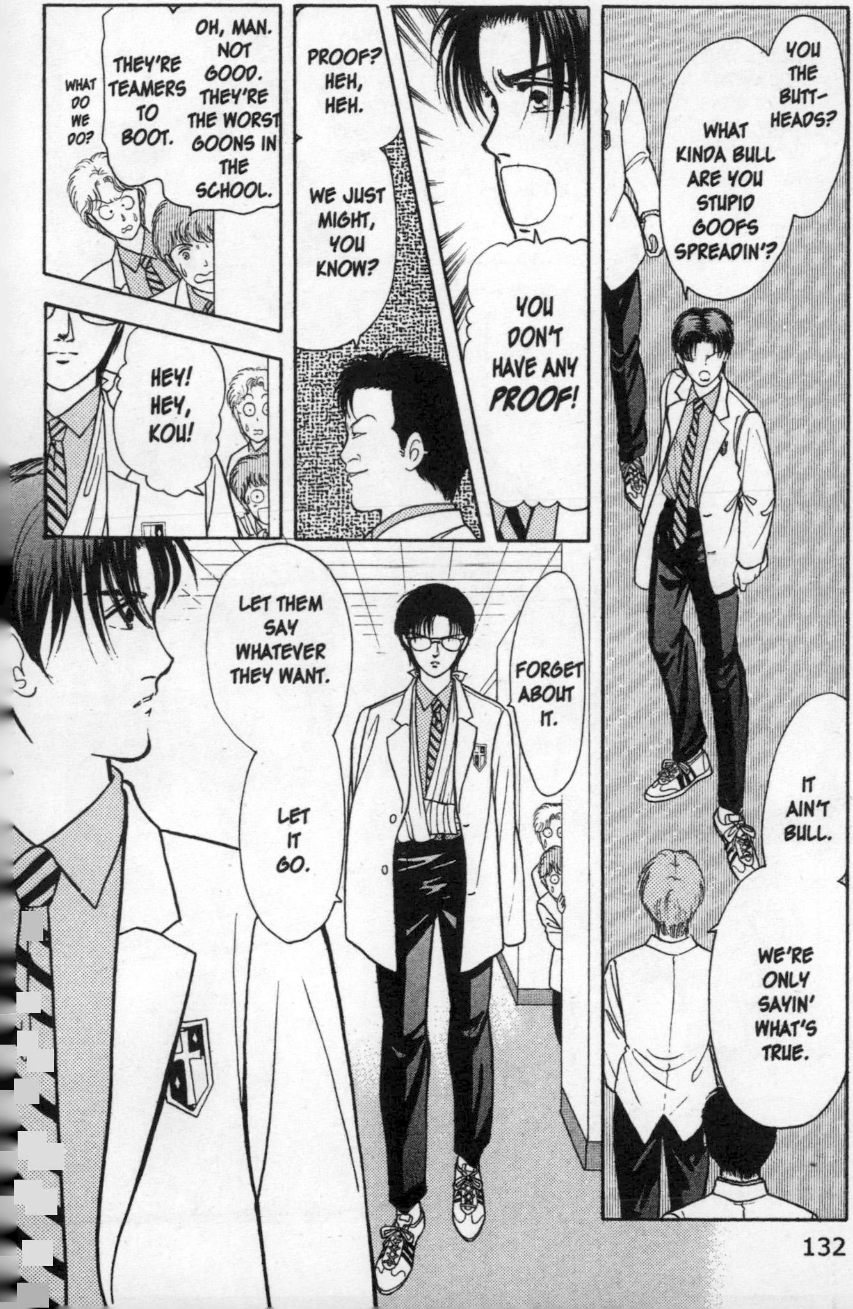
YOU THE BUTT-HEADS?
WHAT KINDA BULL ARE YOU STUPID GOOFS SPREADIN'?
IT AIN'T BULL.
WE'RE ONLY SAYIN' WHAT'S TRUE.
YOU DON'T HAVE ANY PROOF!
PROOF? HEH, HEH.
WE JUST MIGHT, YOU KNOW?
OH, MAN. NOT GOOD. THEY'RE THE WORST GOONS IN THE SCHOOL.
THEY'RE TEAMERS TO BOOT.
WHAT DO WE DO?
HEY! HEY, KOU!
FORGET ABOUT IT.
LET THEM SAY WHATEVER THEY WANT.
LET IT GO.

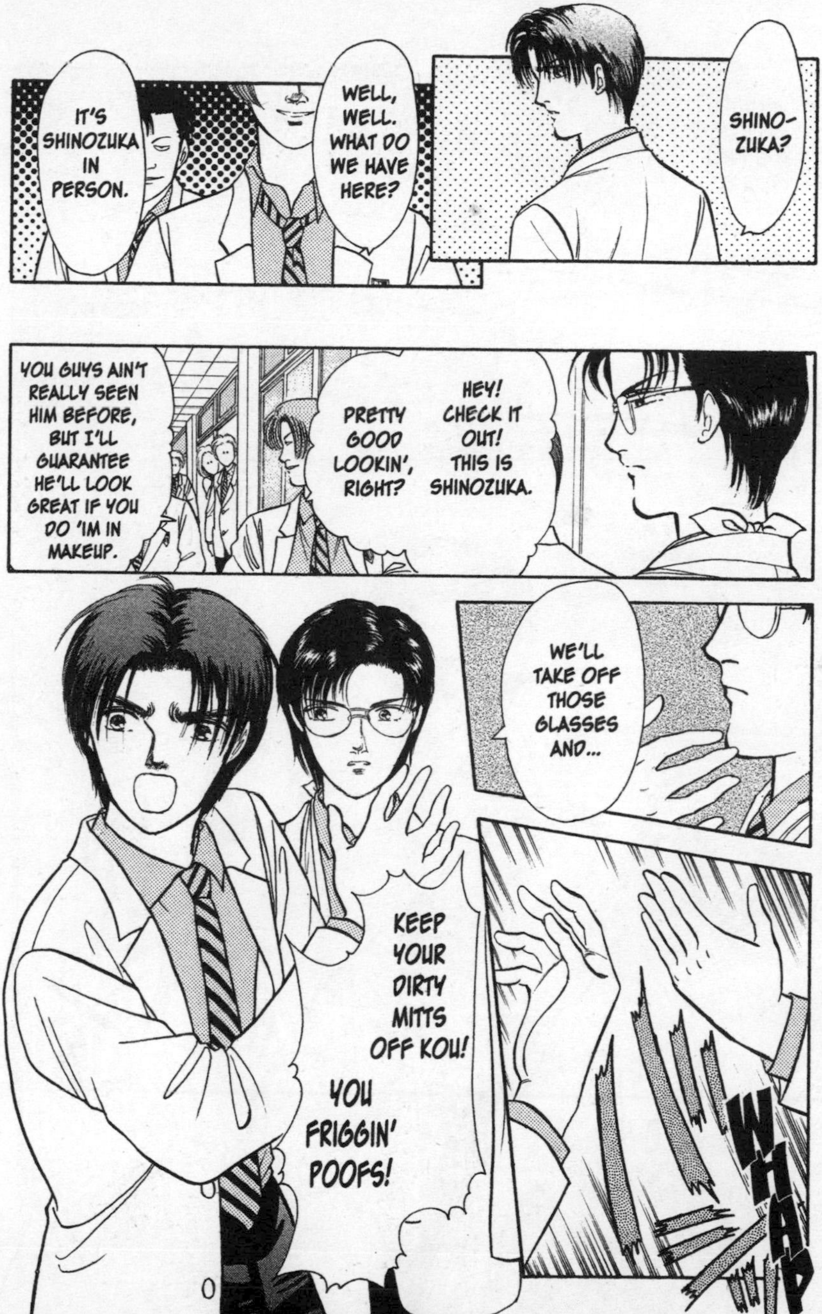
SHINO-ZUKA?
WELL, WELL. WHAT DO WE HAVE HERE?
IT'S SHINOZUKA IN PERSON.
HEY! CHECK IT OUT! THIS IS SHINOZUKA.
PRETTY GOOD LOOKIN', RIGHT?
YOU GUYS AIN'T REALLY SEEN HIM BEFORE, BUT I'LL GUARANTEE HE'LL LOOK GREAT IF YOU DO 'IM IN MAKEUP.
WE'LL TAKE OFF THOSE GLASSES AND...
WHAP
KEEP YOUR DIRTY MITTS OFF KOU!
YOU FRIGGIN' POOFS!

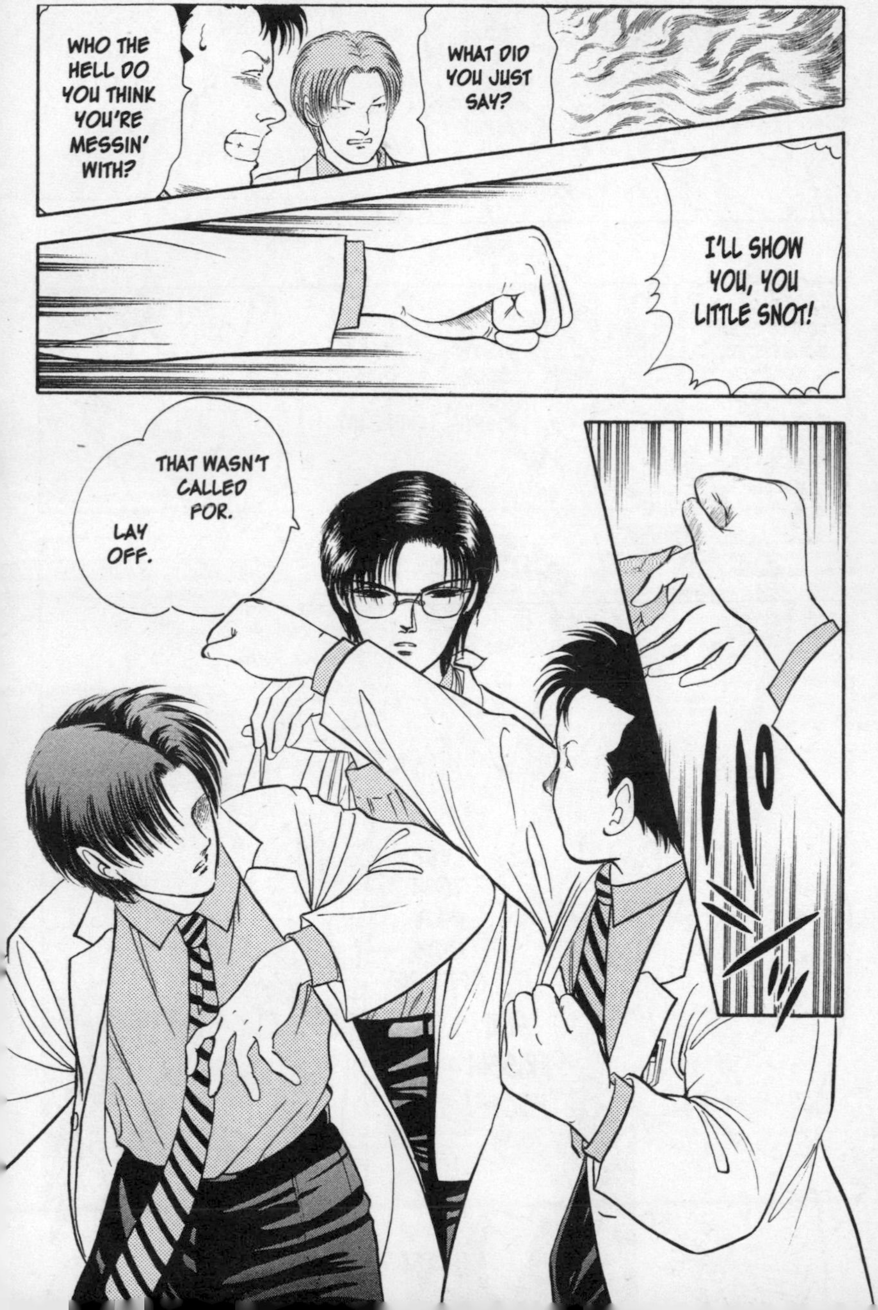
WHAT DID YOU JUST SAY?
WHO THE HELL DO YOU THINK YOU'RE MESSIN' WITH?
I'LL SHOW YOU, YOU LITTLE SNOT!
THAT WASN'T CALLED FOR.
LAY OFF.

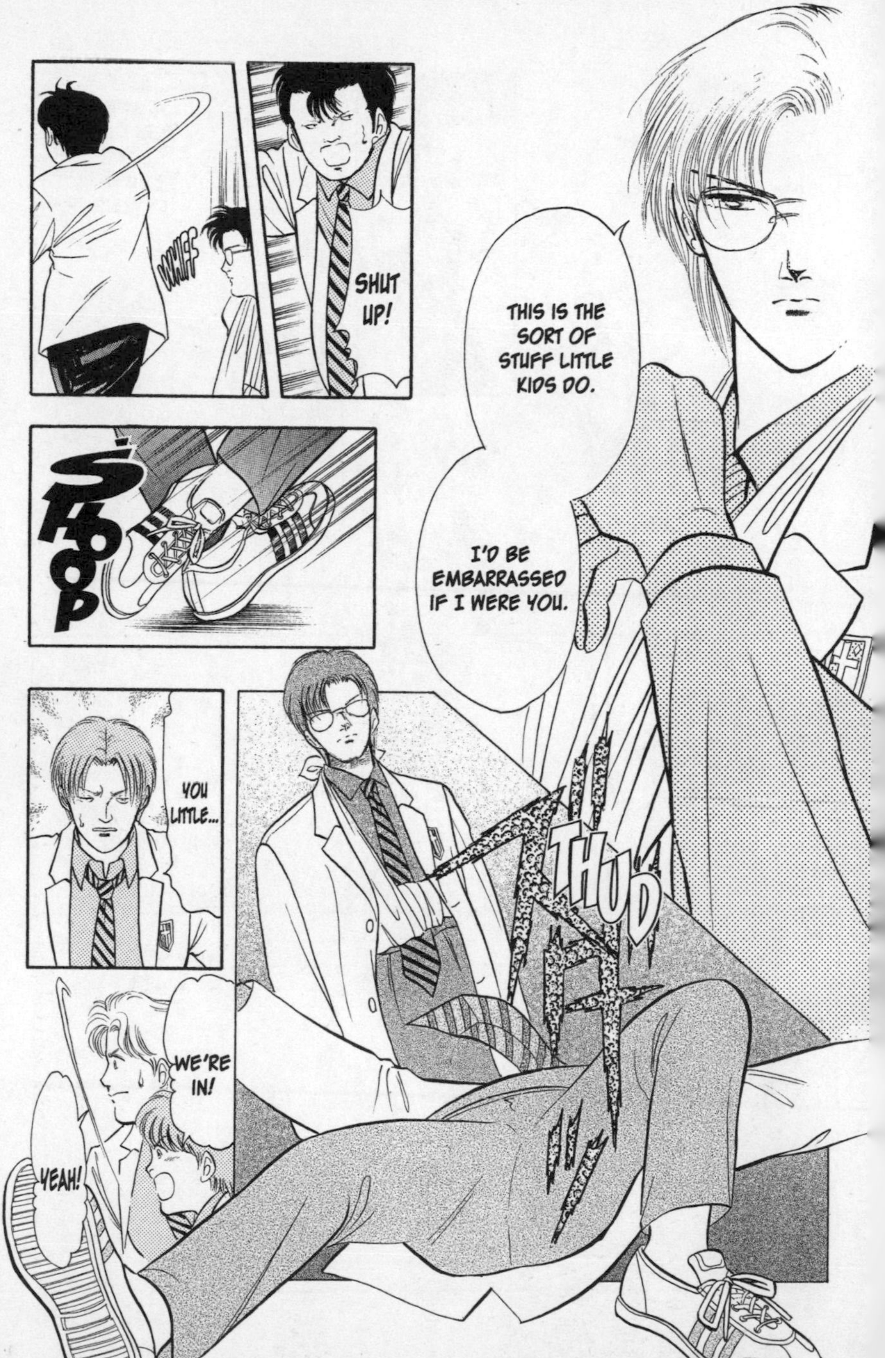
THIS IS THE SORT OF STUFF LITTLE KIDS DO.
I'D BE EMBARRASSED IF I WERE YOU.
SHUT UP!
WHIFF
SHOOP
THUD
YOU LITTLE...
WE'RE IN!
YEAH!

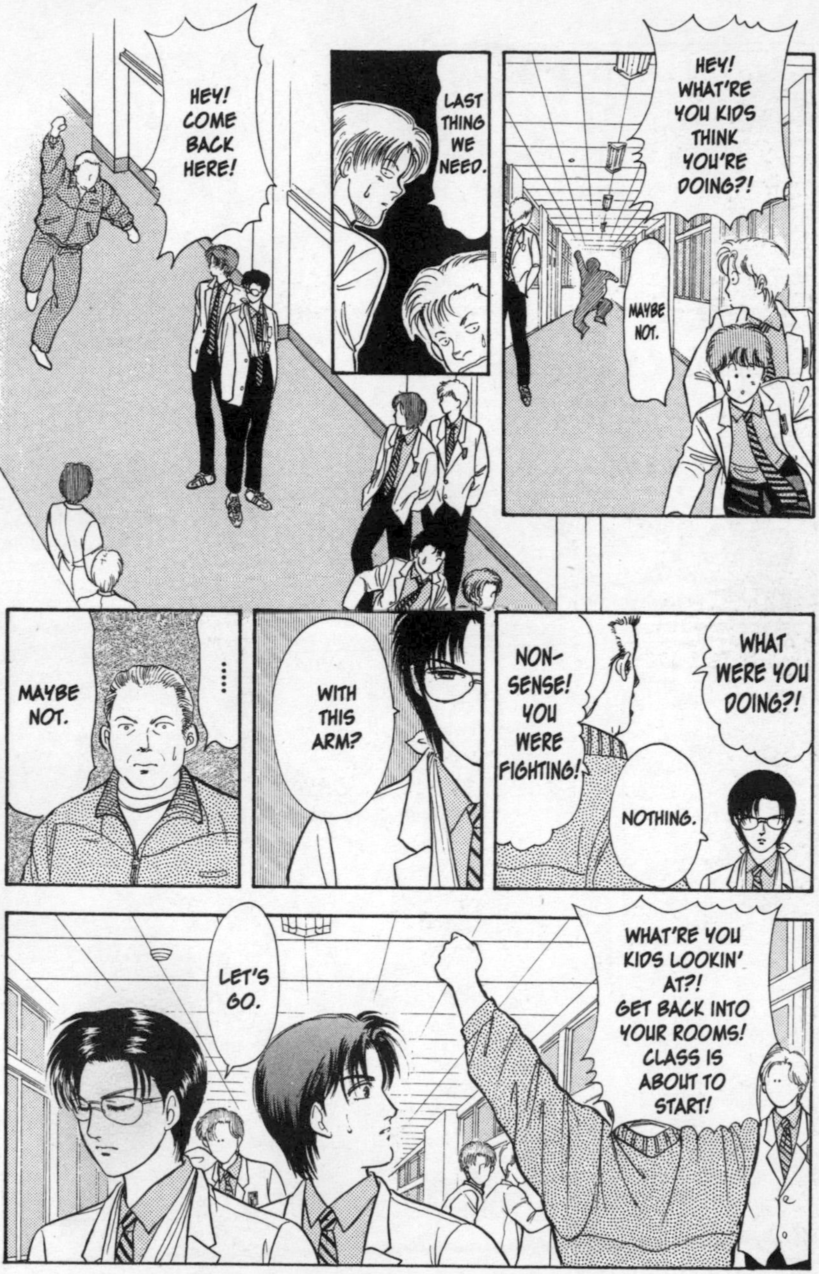
HEY! WHAT'RE YOU KIDS THINK YOU'RE DOING?!
MAYBE NOT.
LAST THING WE NEED.
HEY! COME BACK HERE!
WHAT WERE YOU DOING?!
NOTHING.
NON-SENSE! YOU WERE FIGHTING!
WITH THIS ARM?
....
MAYBE NOT.
WHAT'RE YOU KIDS LOOKIN' AT?! GET BACK INTO YOUR ROOMS! CLASS IS ABOUT TO START!
LET'S GO.

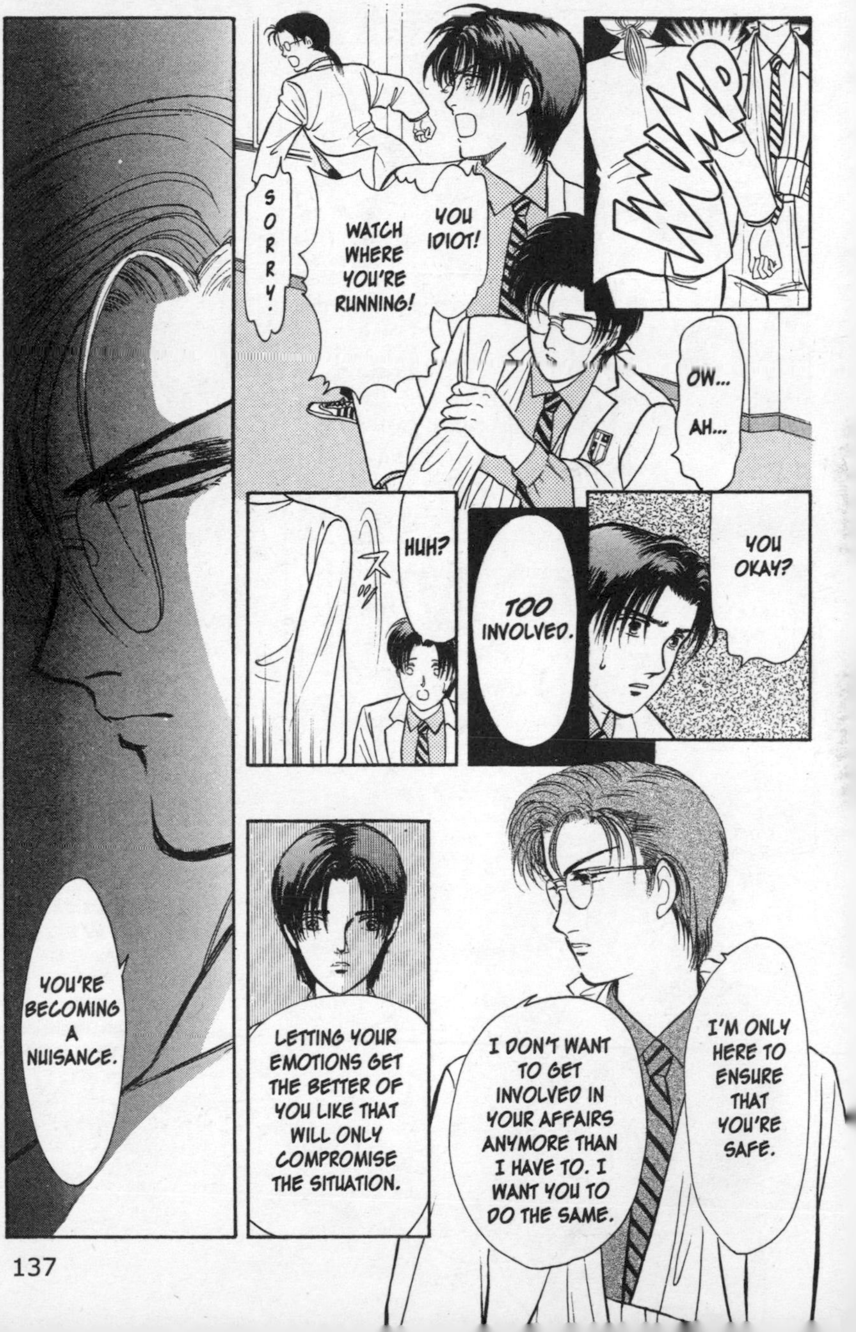
WMMP
YOU IDIOT!
WATCH WHERE YOU'RE RUNNING!
SORRY.
OW... AH...
YOU OKAY?
TOO INVOLVED.
HUH?
I'M ONLY HERE TO ENSURE THAT YOU'RE SAFE.
I DON'T WANT TO GET INVOLVED IN YOUR AFFAIRS ANYMORE THAN I HAVE TO. I WANT YOU TO DO THE SAME.
LETTING YOUR EMOTIONS GET THE BETTER OF YOU LIKE THAT WILL ONLY COMPROMISE THE SITUATION.
YOU'RE BECOMING A NUISANCE.

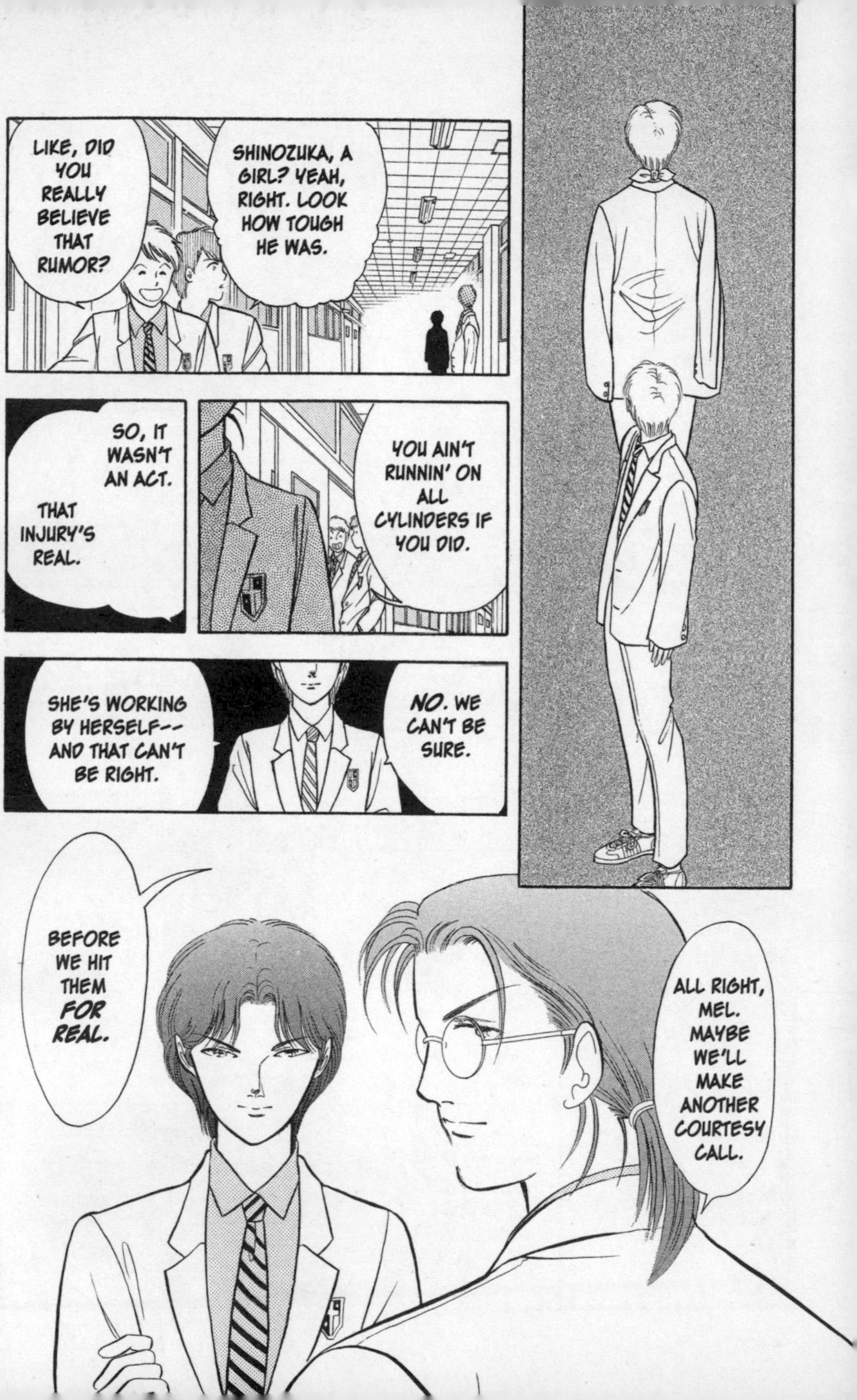
SHINOZUKA, A GIRL? YEAH, RIGHT. LOOK HOW TOUGH HE WAS.
LIKE, DID YOU REALLY BELIEVE THAT RUMOR?
YOU AIN'T RUNNIN' ON ALL CYLINDERS IF YOU DID.
SO, IT WASN'T AN ACT.
THAT INJURY'S REAL.
NO. WE CAN'T BE SURE.
SHE'S WORKING BY HERSELF-- AND THAT CAN'T BE RIGHT.
ALL RIGHT, MEL. MAYBE WE'LL MAKE ANOTHER COURTESY CALL.
BEFORE WE HIT THEM *FOR REAL*.

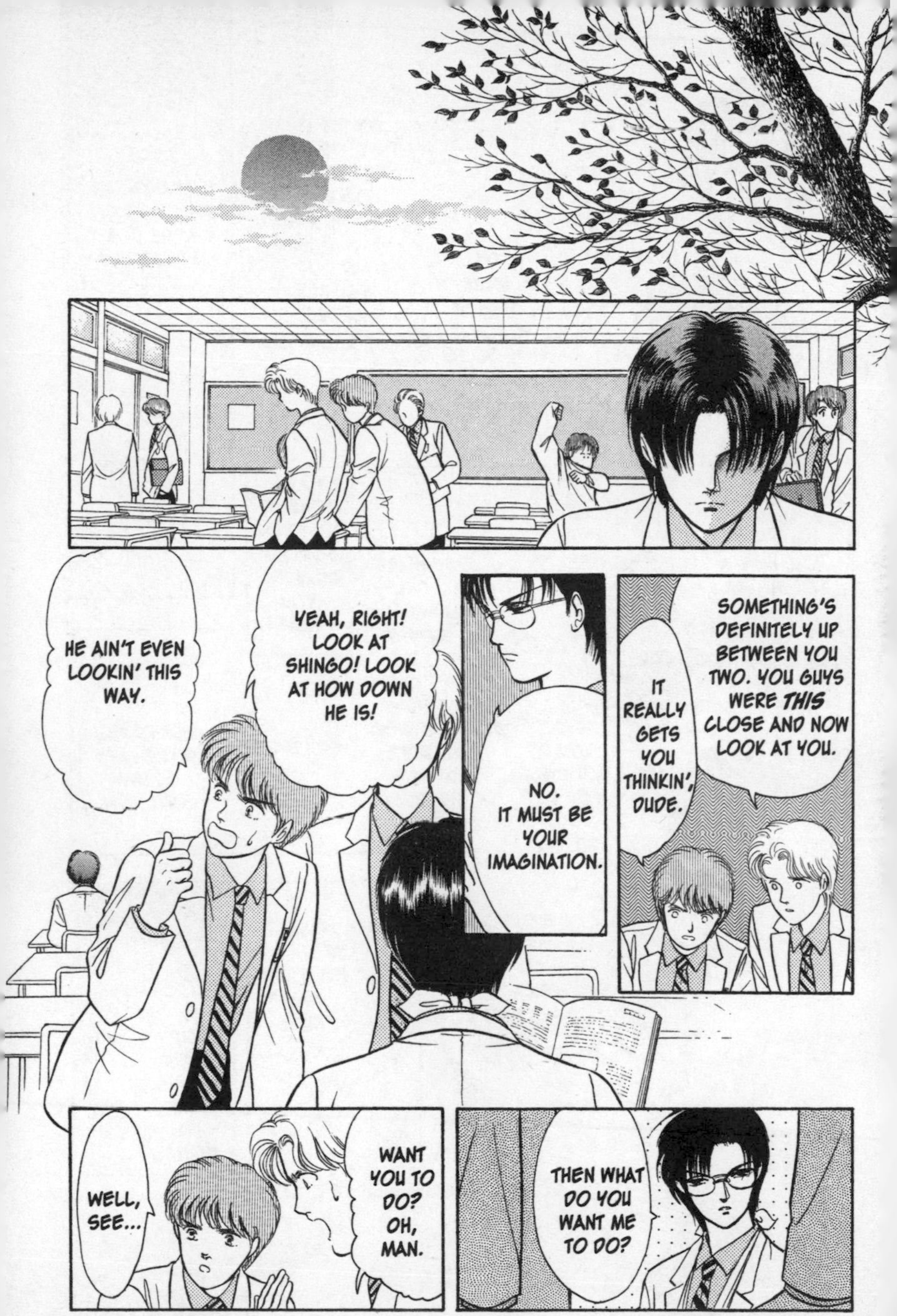
SOMETHING'S DEFINITELY UP BETWEEN YOU TWO. YOU GUYS WERE *THIS* CLOSE AND NOW LOOK AT YOU.
IT REALLY GETS YOU THINKIN', DUDE.
NO. IT MUST BE YOUR IMAGINATION.
YEAH, RIGHT! LOOK AT SHINGO! LOOK AT HOW DOWN HE IS!
HE AIN'T EVEN LOOKIN' THIS WAY.
THEN WHAT DO YOU WANT ME TO DO?
WANT YOU TO DO? OH, MAN.
WELL, SEE...

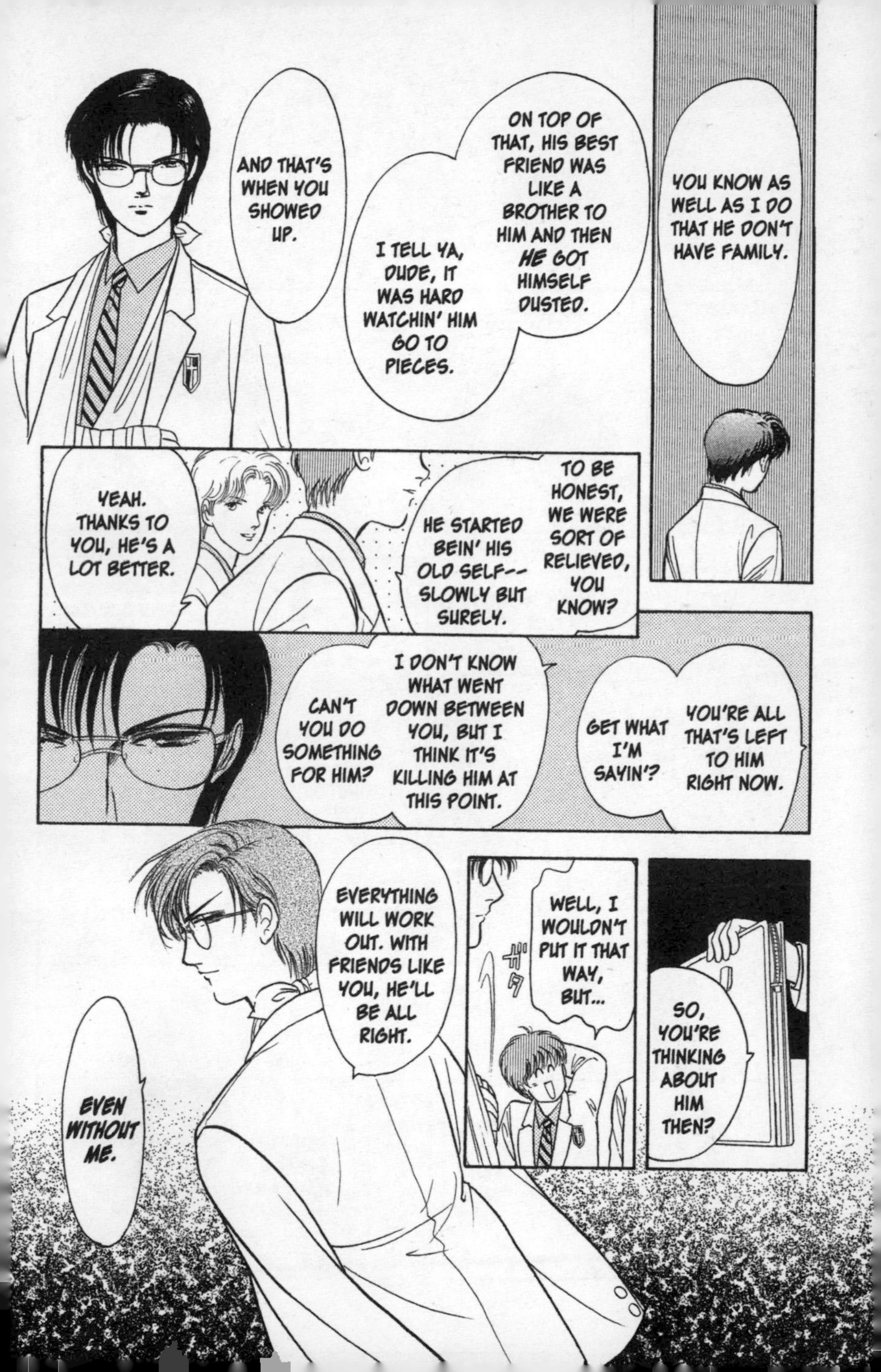
YOU KNOW AS WELL AS I DO THAT HE DON'T HAVE FAMILY.
ON TOP OF THAT, HIS BEST FRIEND WAS LIKE A BROTHER TO HIM AND THEN *HE* GOT HIMSELF DUSTED.
I TELL YA, DUDE, IT WAS HARD WATCHIN' HIM GO TO PIECES.
AND THAT'S WHEN YOU SHOWED UP.
TO BE HONEST, WE WERE SORT OF RELIEVED, YOU KNOW?
HE STARTED BEIN' HIS OLD SELF-- SLOWLY BUT SURELY.
YEAH. THANKS TO YOU, HE'S A LOT BETTER.
YOU'RE ALL THAT'S LEFT TO HIM RIGHT NOW.
GET WHAT I'M SAYIN'?
I DON'T KNOW WHAT WENT DOWN BETWEEN YOU, BUT I THINK IT'S KILLING HIM AT THIS POINT.
CAN'T YOU DO SOMETHING FOR HIM?
SO, YOU'RE THINKING ABOUT HIM THEN?
WELL, I WOULDN'T PUT IT THAT WAY, BUT...
ガタ
EVERYTHING WILL WORK OUT. WITH FRIENDS LIKE YOU, HE'LL BE ALL RIGHT.
EVEN WITHOUT ME.

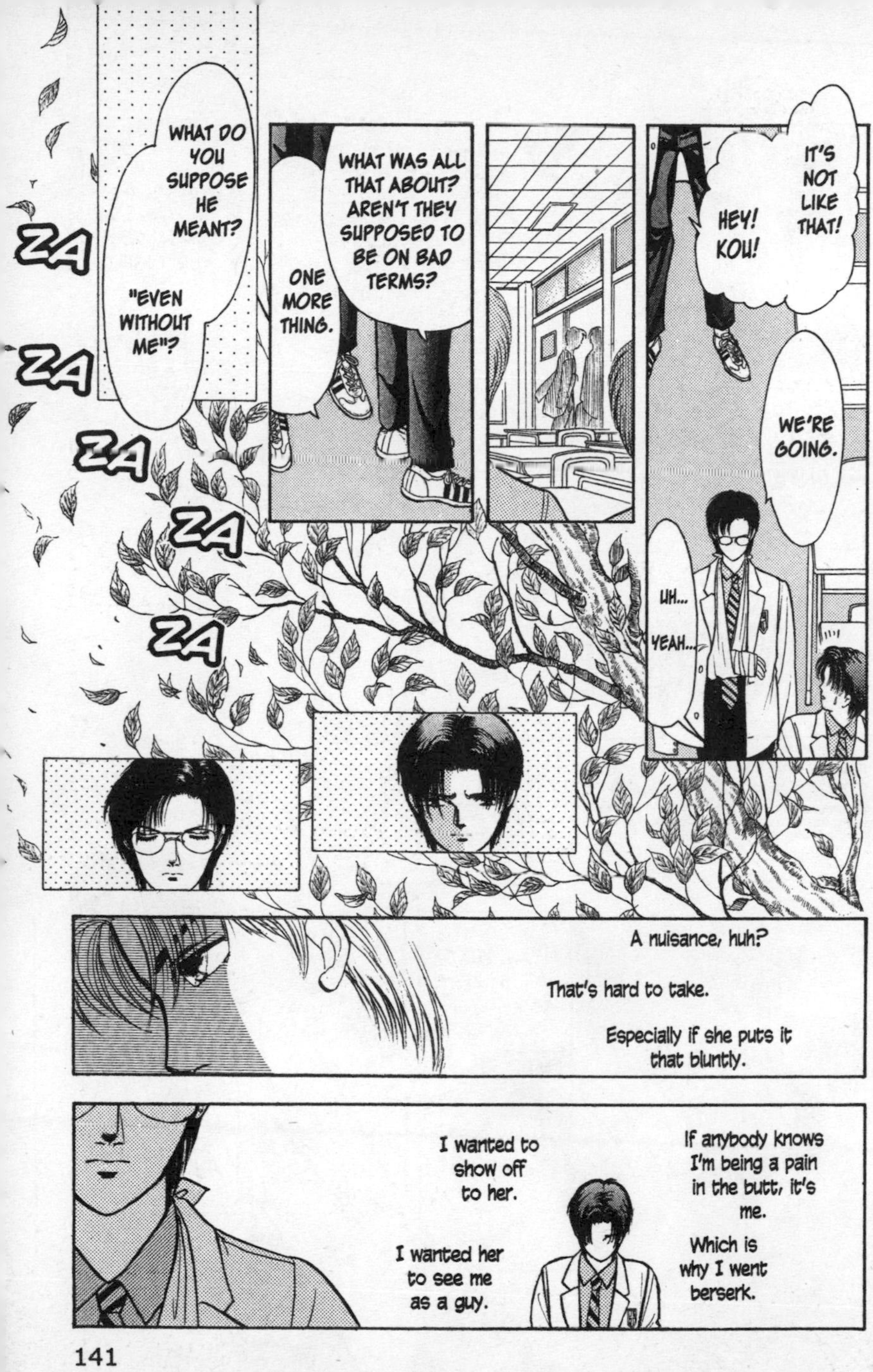
IT'S NOT LIKE THAT!
HEY! KOU!
WE'RE GOING.
UH... YEAH...
WHAT WAS ALL THAT ABOUT? AREN'T THEY SUPPOSED TO BE ON BAD TERMS?
ONE MORE THING.
WHAT DO YOU SUPPOSE HE MEANT?
"EVEN WITHOUT ME"?
ZA
ZA
ZA
ZA
ZA
A nuisance, huh?
That's hard to take.
Especially if she puts it that bluntly.
If anybody knows I'm being a pain in the butt, it's me.
Which is why I went berserk.
I wanted to show off to her.
I wanted her to see me as a guy.

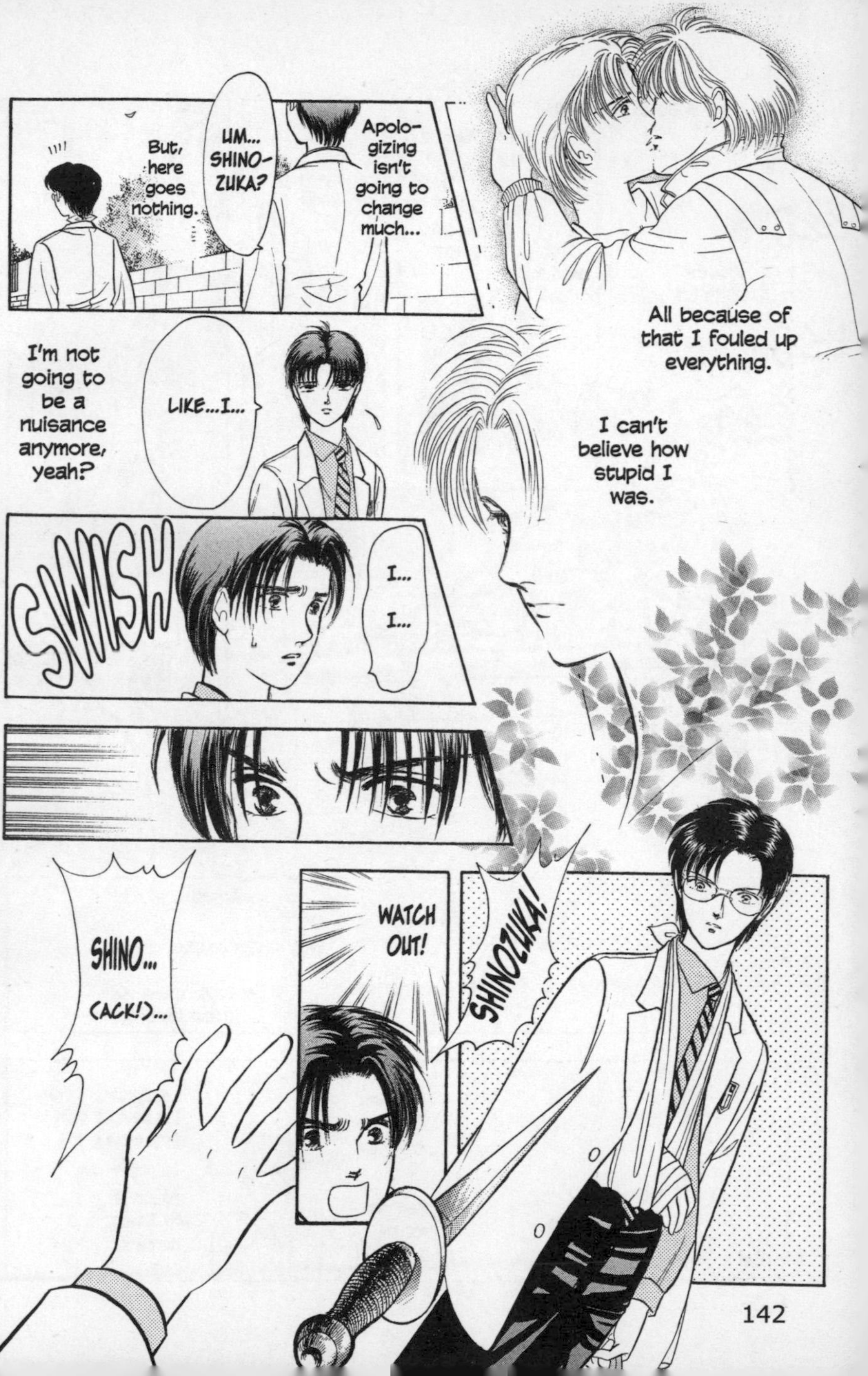
All because of that I fouled up everything.
I can't believe how stupid I was.
Apolo-gizing isn't going to change much...
UM... SHINO-ZUKA?
But, here goes nothing.
LIKE...I...
I'm not going to be a nuisance anymore, yeah?
I... I...
SWISH
SHINOZUKA!
WATCH OUT!
SHINO... (ACK!)...

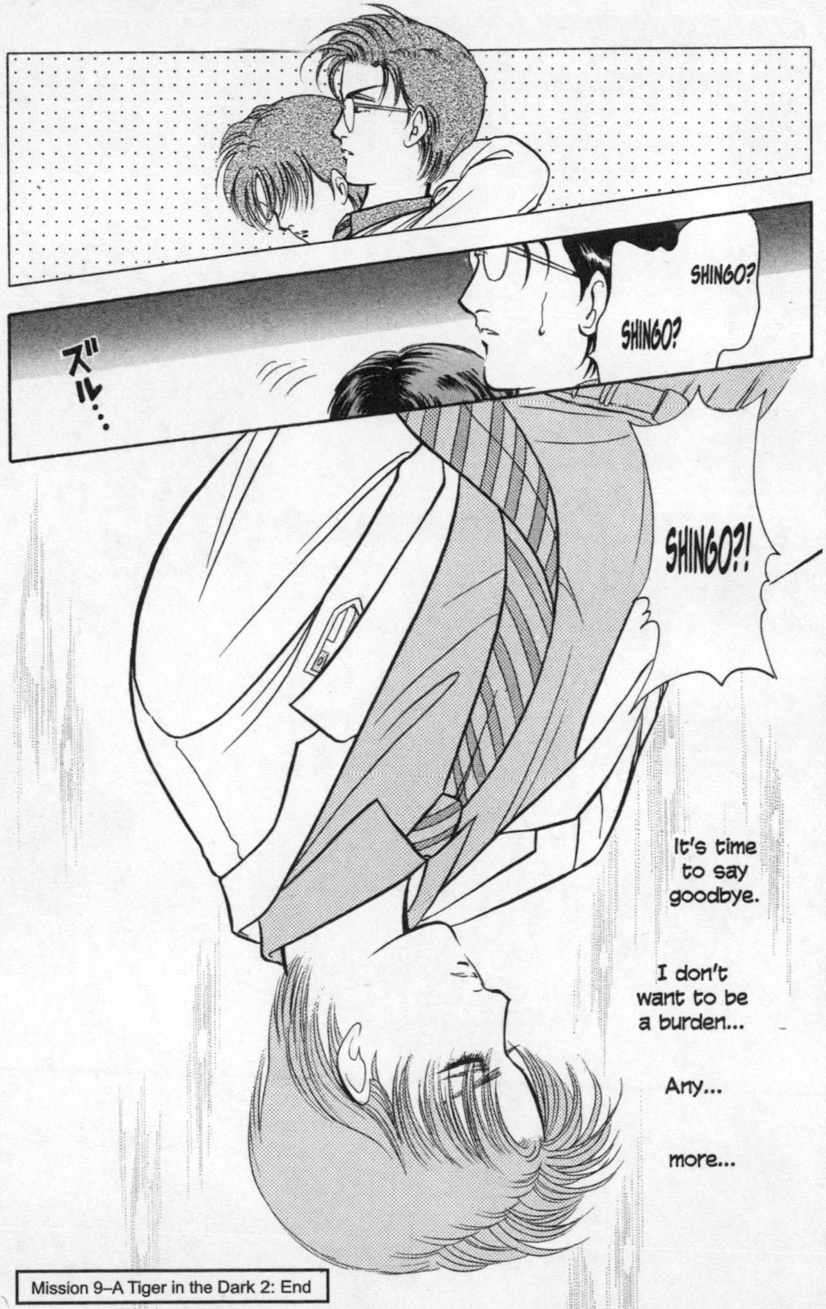
SHINGO?
SHINGO?
ズル…
SHINGO?!
It's time to say goodbye.
I don't want to be a burden...
Any...
more...
Mission 9–A Tiger in the Dark 2: End

Mission 9: A Tiger in the Dark, Part 3

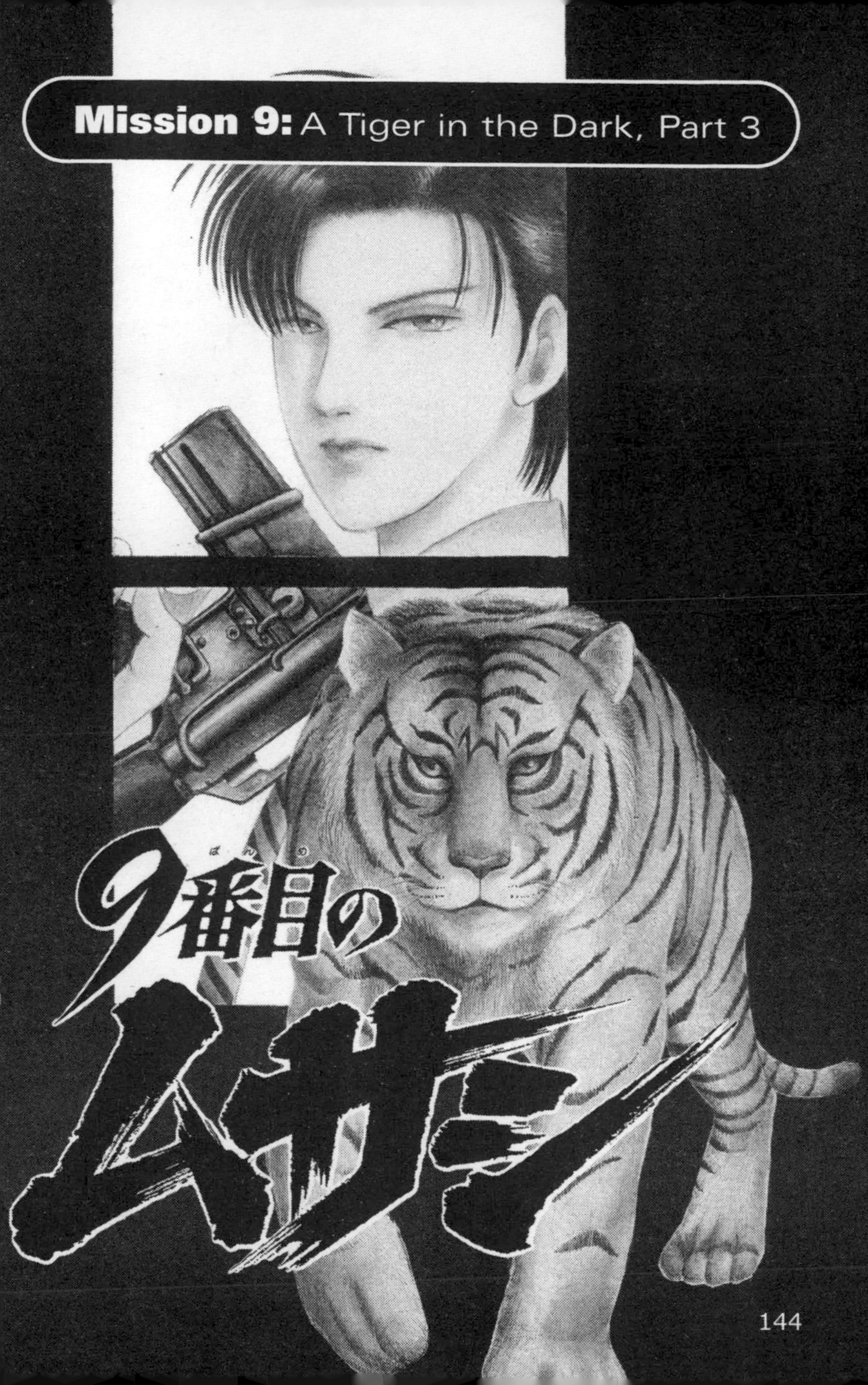
9番目のムサシ

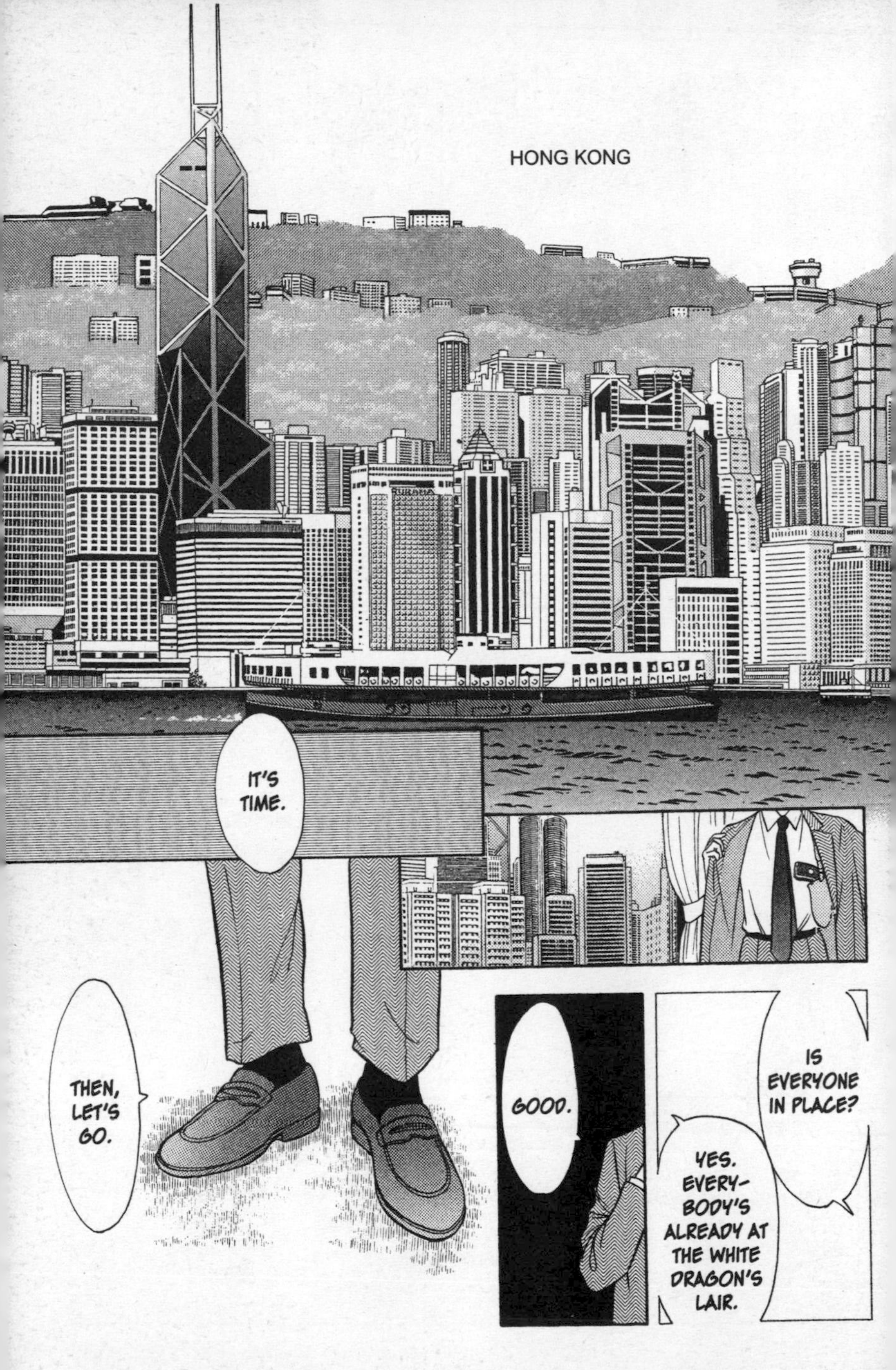
HONG KONG
IS EVERYONE IN PLACE?
YES. EVERYBODY'S ALREADY AT THE WHITE DRAGON'S LAIR.
GOOD.
IT'S TIME.
THEN, LET'S GO.

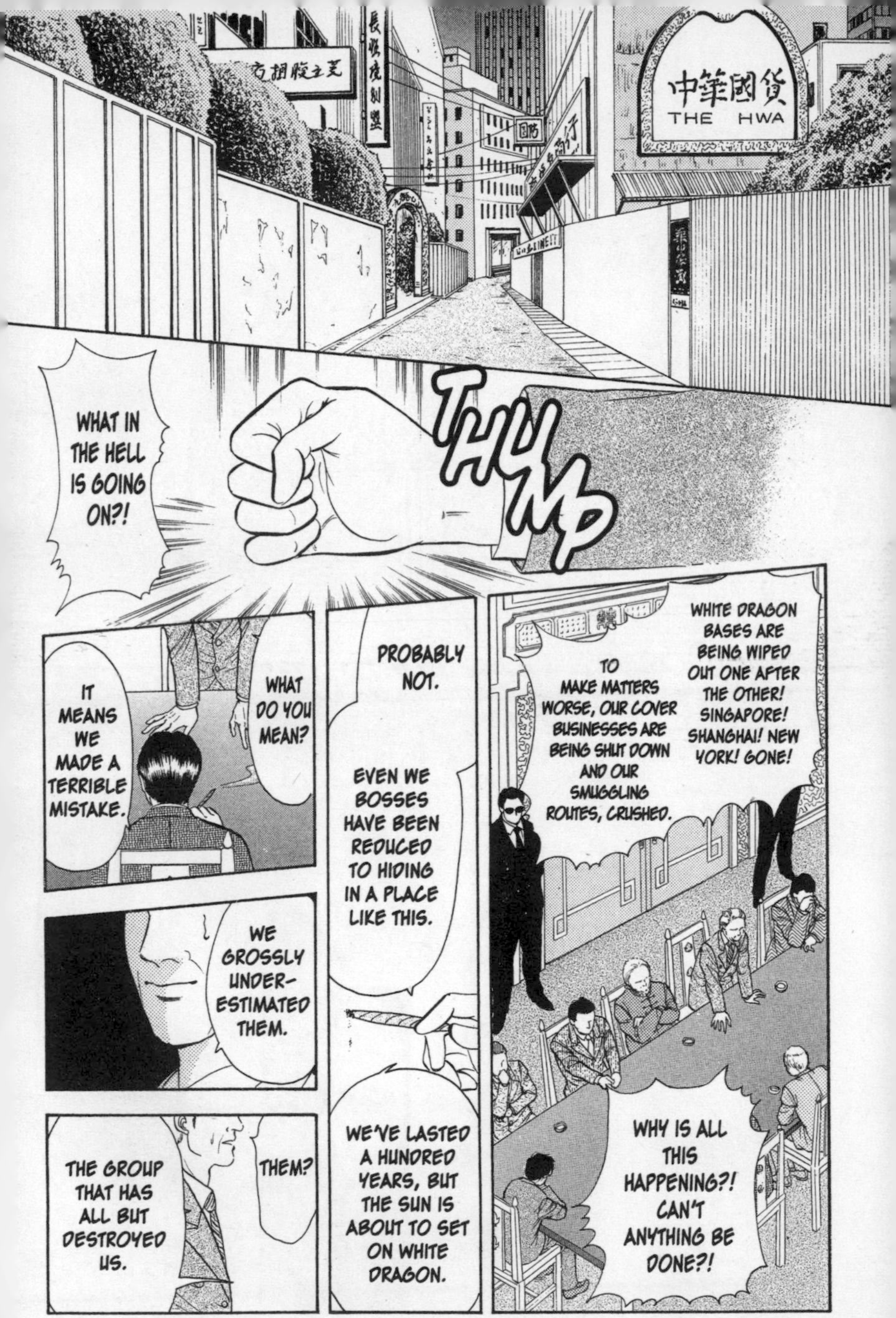
中華國貨
THE HWA
WHAT IN THE HELL IS GOING ON?!
THUMP
WHITE DRAGON BASES ARE BEING WIPED OUT ONE AFTER THE OTHER! SINGAPORE! SHANGHAI! NEW YORK! GONE!
TO MAKE MATTERS WORSE, OUR COVER BUSINESSES ARE BEING SHUT DOWN AND OUR SMUGGLING ROUTES, CRUSHED.
WHY IS ALL THIS HAPPENING?! CAN'T ANYTHING BE DONE?!
PROBABLY NOT.
EVEN WE BOSSES HAVE BEEN REDUCED TO HIDING IN A PLACE LIKE THIS.
WE'VE LASTED A HUNDRED YEARS, BUT THE SUN IS ABOUT TO SET ON WHITE DRAGON.
WHAT DO YOU MEAN?
IT MEANS WE MADE A TERRIBLE MISTAKE.
WE GROSSLY UNDER-ESTIMATED THEM.
THEM?
THE GROUP THAT HAS ALL BUT DESTROYED US.

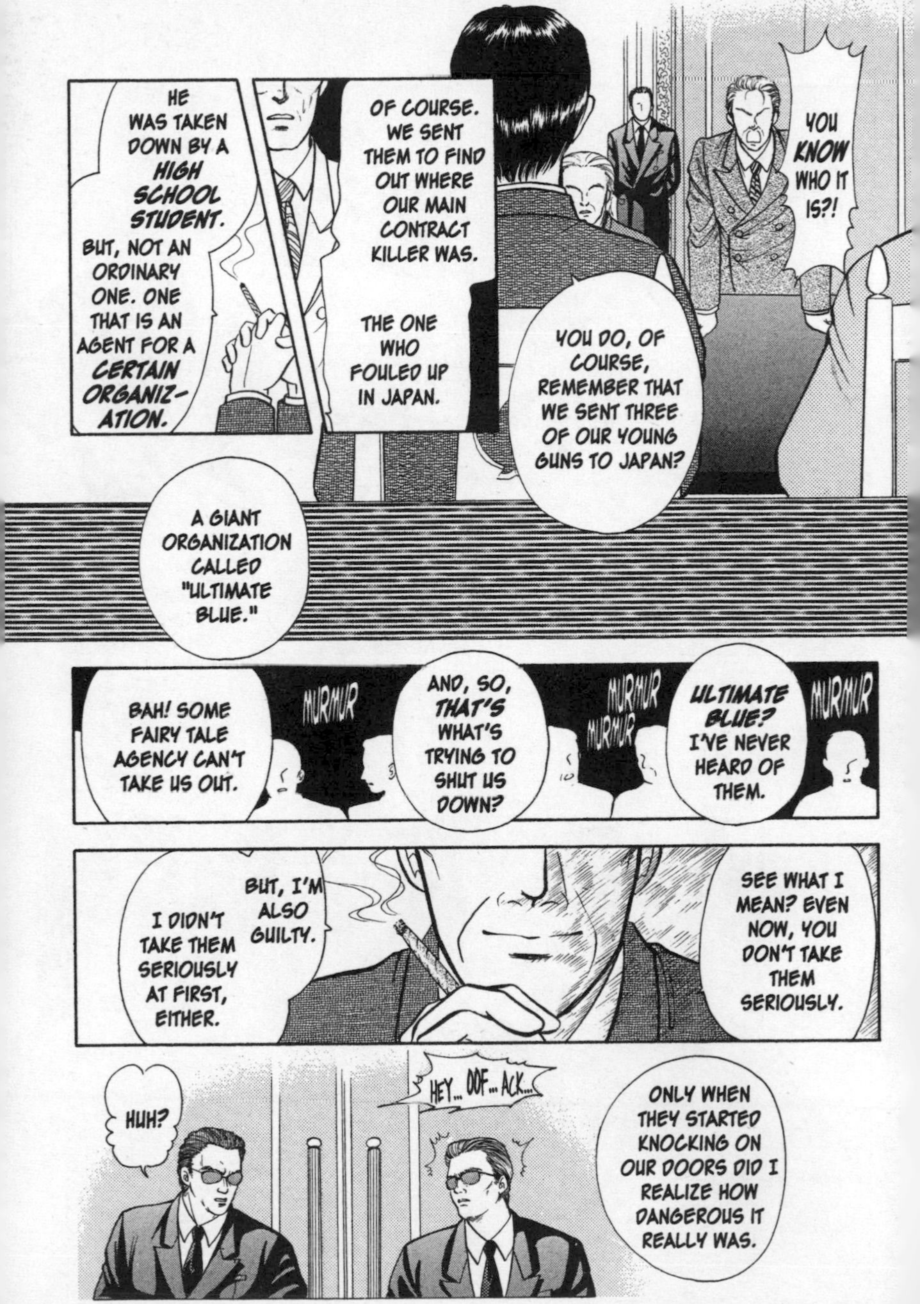
YOU KNOW WHO IT IS?!
YOU DO, OF COURSE, REMEMBER THAT WE SENT THREE OF OUR YOUNG GUNS TO JAPAN?
OF COURSE. WE SENT THEM TO FIND OUT WHERE OUR MAIN CONTRACT KILLER WAS.
THE ONE WHO FOULED UP IN JAPAN.
HE WAS TAKEN DOWN BY A HIGH SCHOOL STUDENT.
BUT, NOT AN ORDINARY ONE. ONE THAT IS AN AGENT FOR A CERTAIN ORGANIZATION.
A GIANT ORGANIZATION CALLED "ULTIMATE BLUE."
MURMUR
ULTIMATE BLUE? I'VE NEVER HEARD OF THEM.
MURMUR MURMUR
AND, SO, THAT'S WHAT'S TRYING TO SHUT US DOWN?
MURMUR
BAH! SOME FAIRY TALE AGENCY CAN'T TAKE US OUT.
SEE WHAT I MEAN? EVEN NOW, YOU DON'T TAKE THEM SERIOUSLY.
BUT, I'M ALSO GUILTY.
I DIDN'T TAKE THEM SERIOUSLY AT FIRST, EITHER.
ONLY WHEN THEY STARTED KNOCKING ON OUR DOORS DID I REALIZE HOW DANGEROUS IT REALLY WAS.
HEY... OOF... ACK...
HUH?

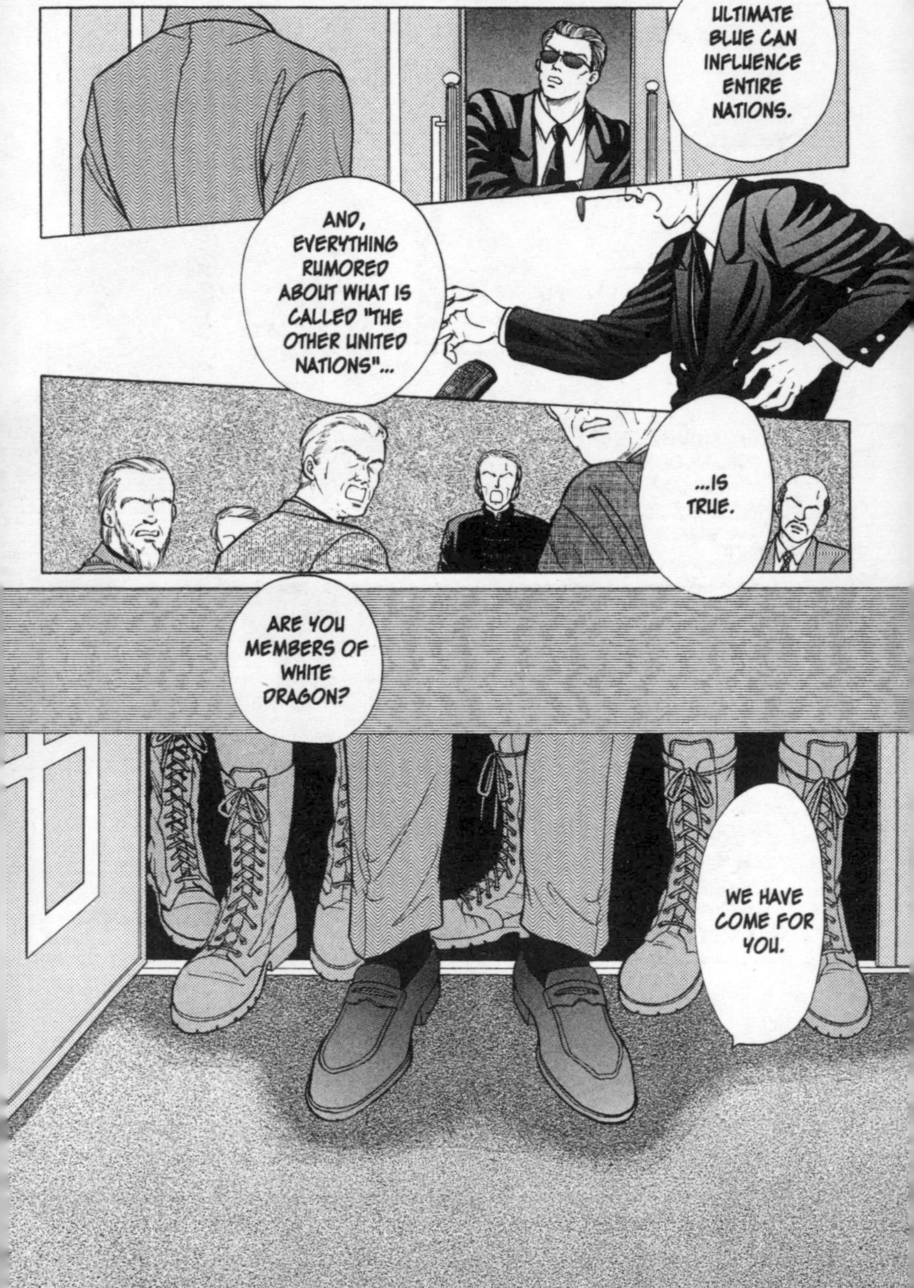
ULTIMATE BLUE CAN INFLUENCE ENTIRE NATIONS.
AND, EVERYTHING RUMORED ABOUT WHAT IS CALLED "THE OTHER UNITED NATIONS"...
...IS TRUE.
ARE YOU MEMBERS OF WHITE DRAGON?
WE HAVE COME FOR YOU.

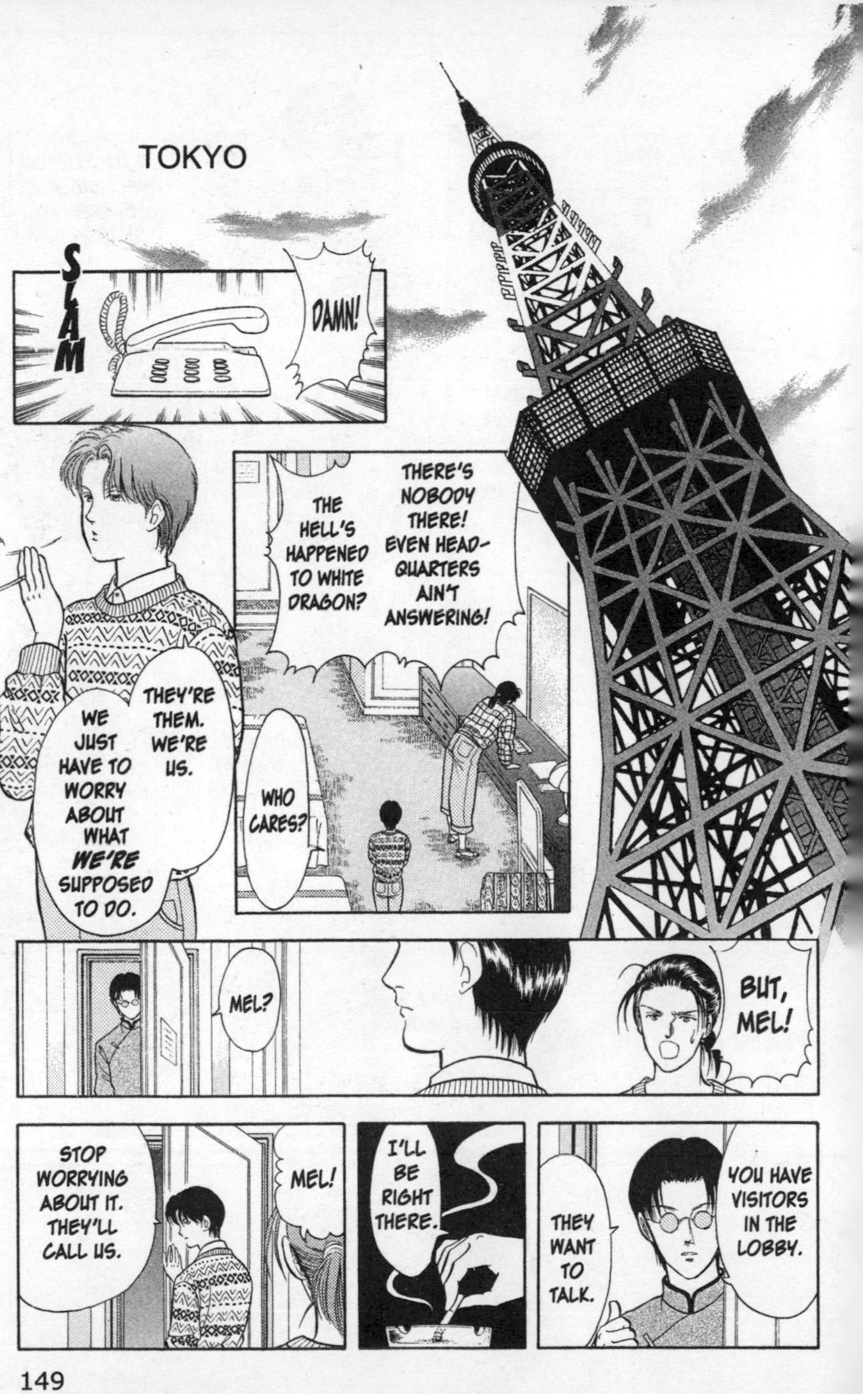
TOKYO
DAMN!
SLAM
THERE'S NOBODY THERE! EVEN HEAD-QUARTERS AIN'T ANSWERING!
THE HELL'S HAPPENED TO WHITE DRAGON?
WHO CARES?
THEY'RE THEM. WE'RE US.
WE JUST HAVE TO WORRY ABOUT WHAT *WE'RE* SUPPOSED TO DO.
BUT, MEL!
MEL?
YOU HAVE VISITORS IN THE LOBBY.
THEY WANT TO TALK.
I'LL BE RIGHT THERE.
MEL!
STOP WORRYING ABOUT IT. THEY'LL CALL US.

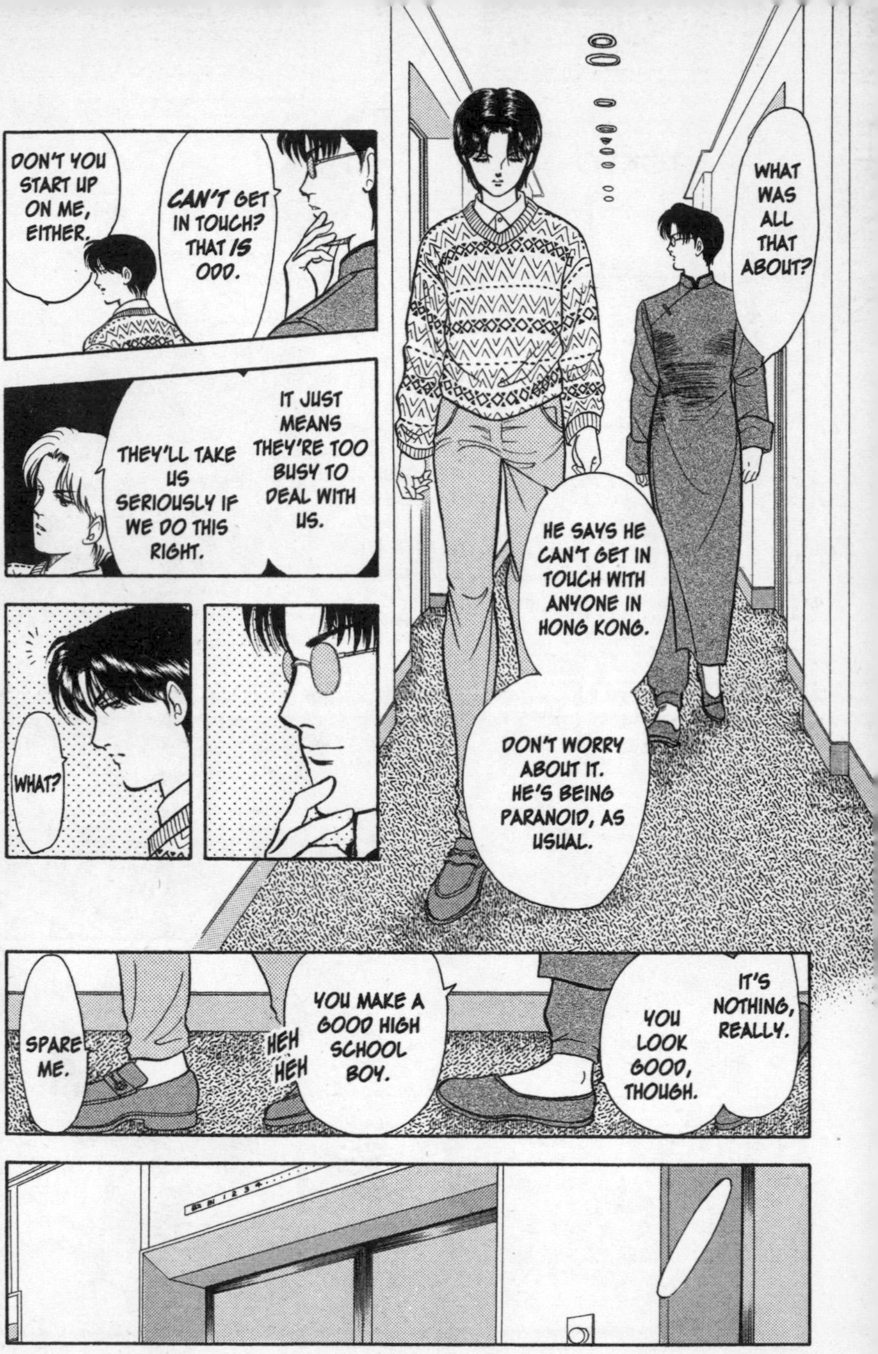
WHAT WAS ALL THAT ABOUT?
HE SAYS HE CAN'T GET IN TOUCH WITH ANYONE IN HONG KONG.
DON'T WORRY ABOUT IT. HE'S BEING PARANOID, AS USUAL.
CAN'T GET IN TOUCH? THAT IS ODD.
DON'T YOU START UP ON ME, EITHER.
IT JUST MEANS THEY'RE TOO BUSY TO DEAL WITH US.
THEY'LL TAKE US SERIOUSLY IF WE DO THIS RIGHT.
WHAT?
IT'S NOTHING, REALLY.
YOU LOOK GOOD, THOUGH.
YOU MAKE A GOOD HIGH SCHOOL BOY.
HEH HEH
SPARE ME.

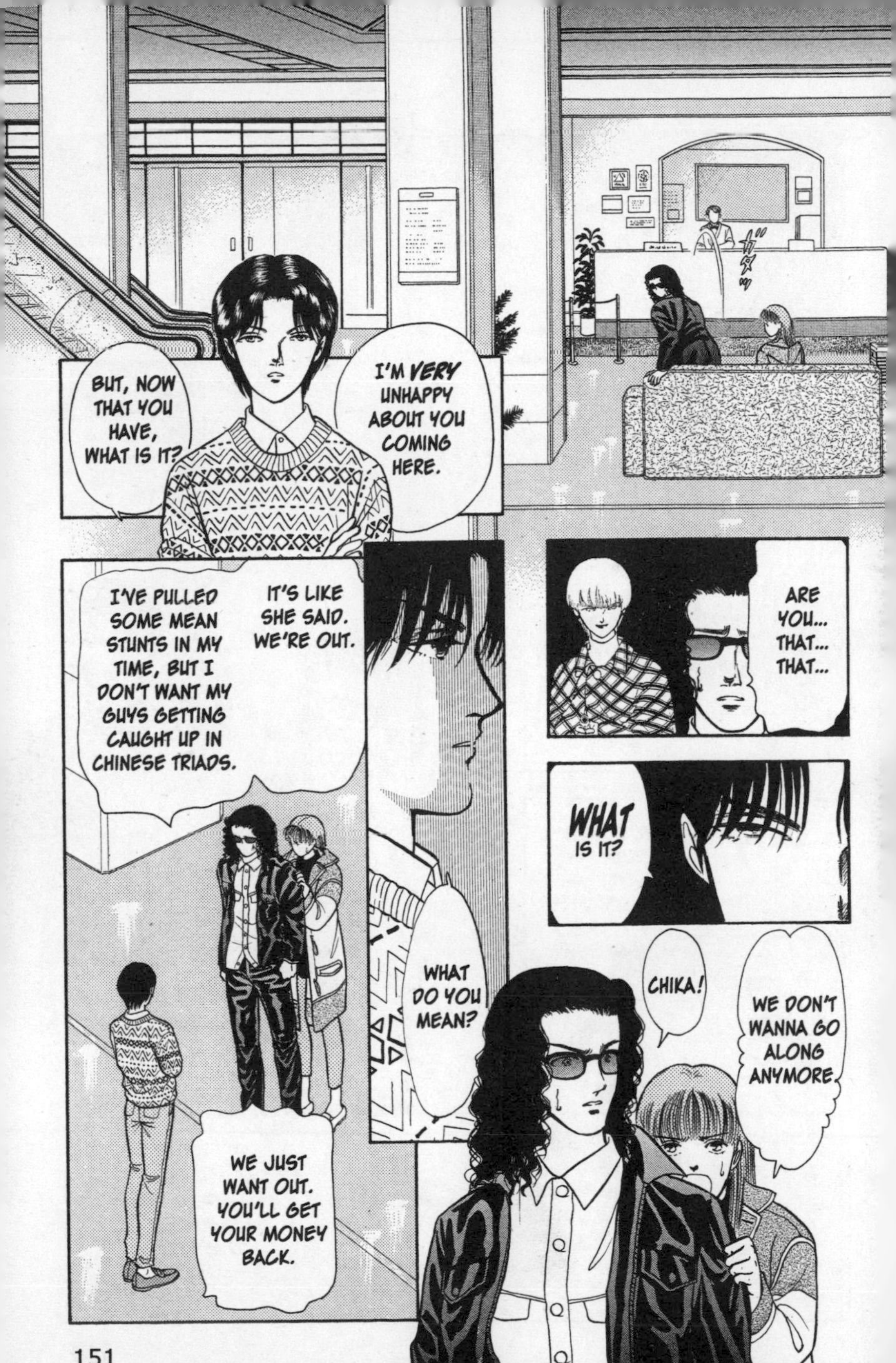
I'M VERY UNHAPPY ABOUT YOU COMING HERE.
BUT, NOW THAT YOU HAVE, WHAT IS IT?
ARE YOU... THAT... THAT...
WHAT IS IT?
WE DON'T WANNA GO ALONG ANYMORE.
CHIKA!
WHAT DO YOU MEAN?
IT'S LIKE SHE SAID. WE'RE OUT.
I'VE PULLED SOME MEAN STUNTS IN MY TIME, BUT I DON'T WANT MY GUYS GETTING CAUGHT UP IN CHINESE TRIADS.
WE JUST WANT OUT. YOU'LL GET YOUR MONEY BACK.

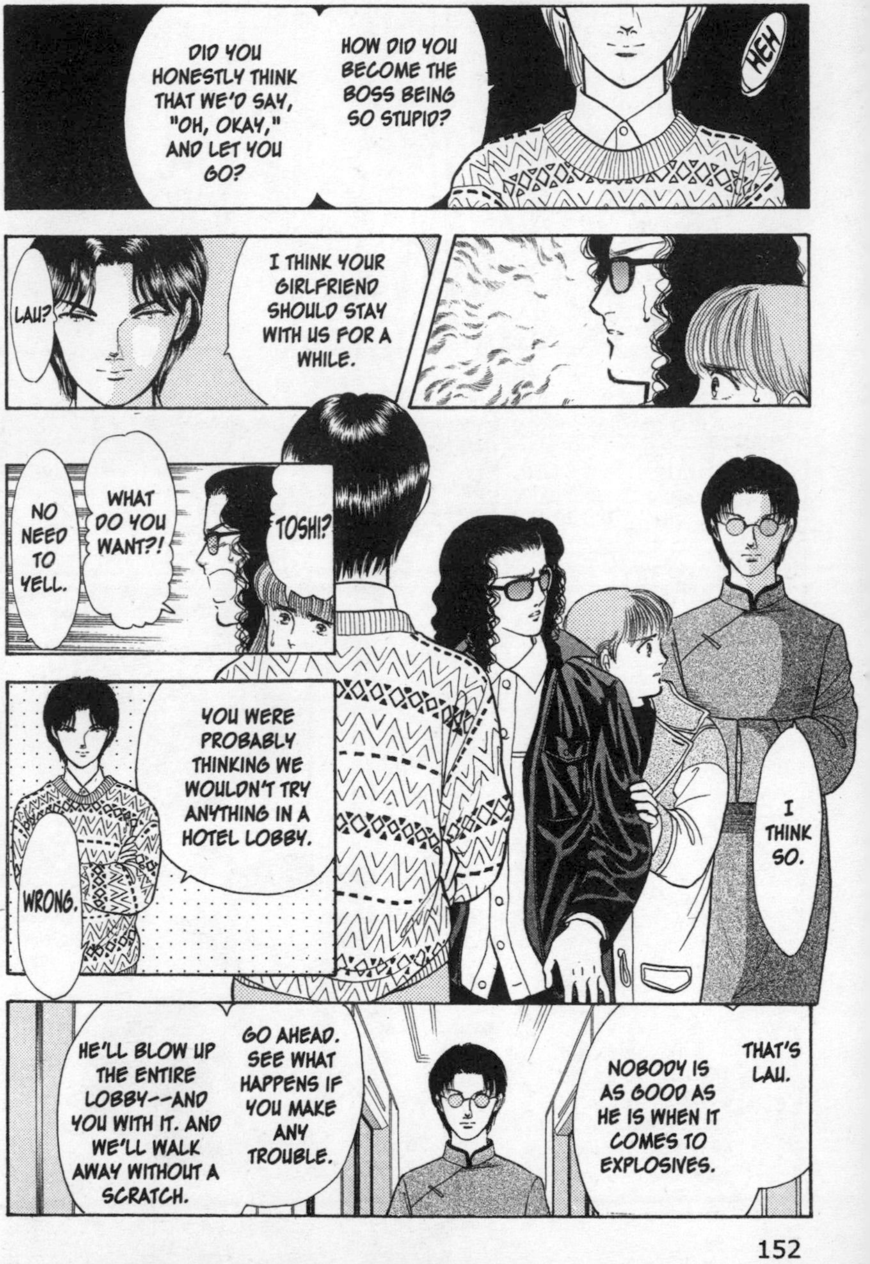

HEH
HOW DID YOU BECOME THE BOSS BEING SO STUPID?
DID YOU HONESTLY THINK THAT WE'D SAY, "OH, OKAY," AND LET YOU GO?
I THINK YOUR GIRLFRIEND SHOULD STAY WITH US FOR A WHILE.
LAU?
I THINK SO.
TOSHI?
WHAT DO YOU WANT?!
NO NEED TO YELL.
YOU WERE PROBABLY THINKING WE WOULDN'T TRY ANYTHING IN A HOTEL LOBBY.
WRONG.
THAT'S LAU.
NOBODY IS AS GOOD AS HE IS WHEN IT COMES TO EXPLOSIVES.
GO AHEAD. SEE WHAT HAPPENS IF YOU MAKE ANY TROUBLE.
HE'LL BLOW UP THE ENTIRE LOBBY--AND YOU WITH IT. AND WE'LL WALK AWAY WITHOUT A SCRATCH.

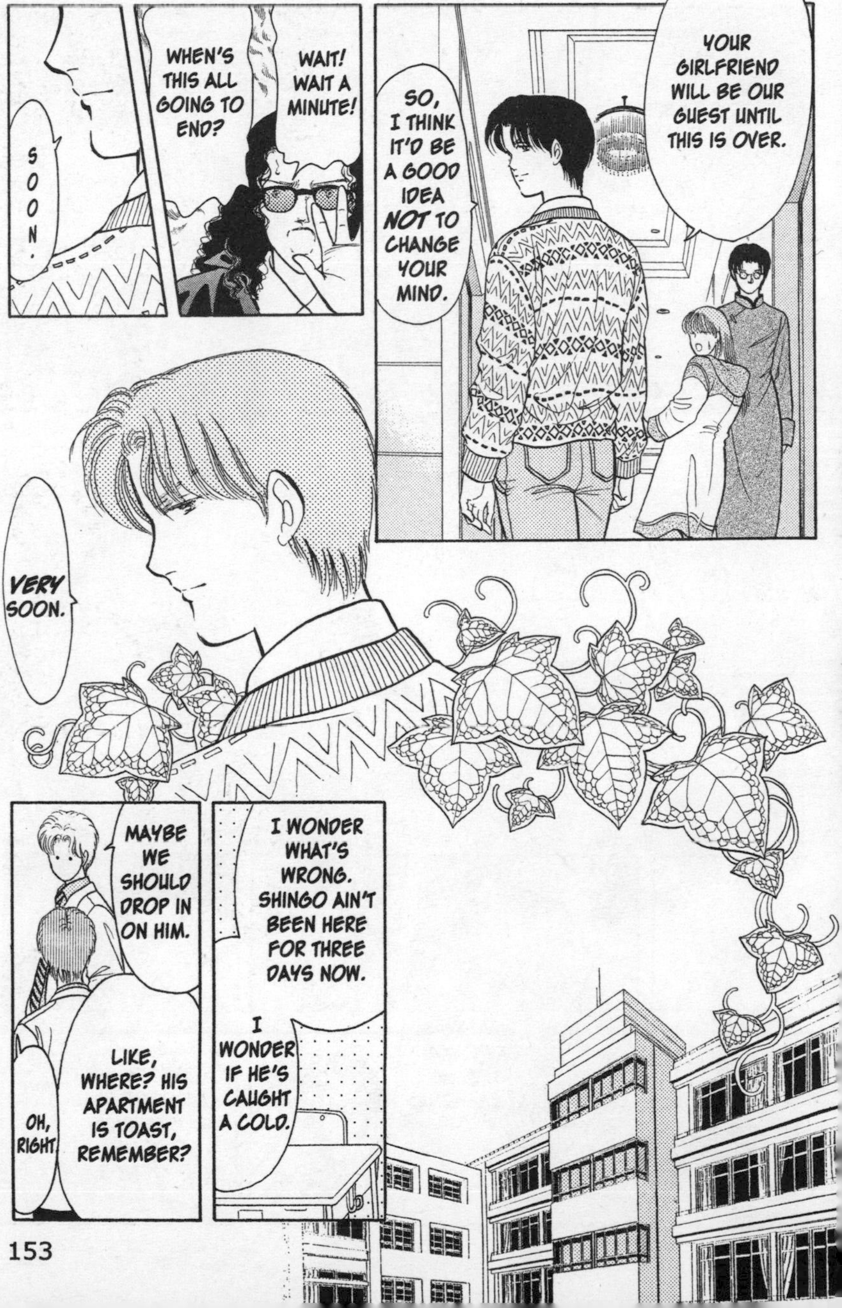
YOUR GIRLFRIEND WILL BE OUR GUEST UNTIL THIS IS OVER.
SO, I THINK IT'D BE A GOOD IDEA NOT TO CHANGE YOUR MIND.
WAIT! WAIT A MINUTE!
WHEN'S THIS ALL GOING TO END?
SOON.
VERY SOON.
I WONDER WHAT'S WRONG. SHINGO AIN'T BEEN HERE FOR THREE DAYS NOW.
I WONDER IF HE'S CAUGHT A COLD.
MAYBE WE SHOULD DROP IN ON HIM.
LIKE, WHERE? HIS APARTMENT IS TOAST, REMEMBER?
OH, RIGHT.

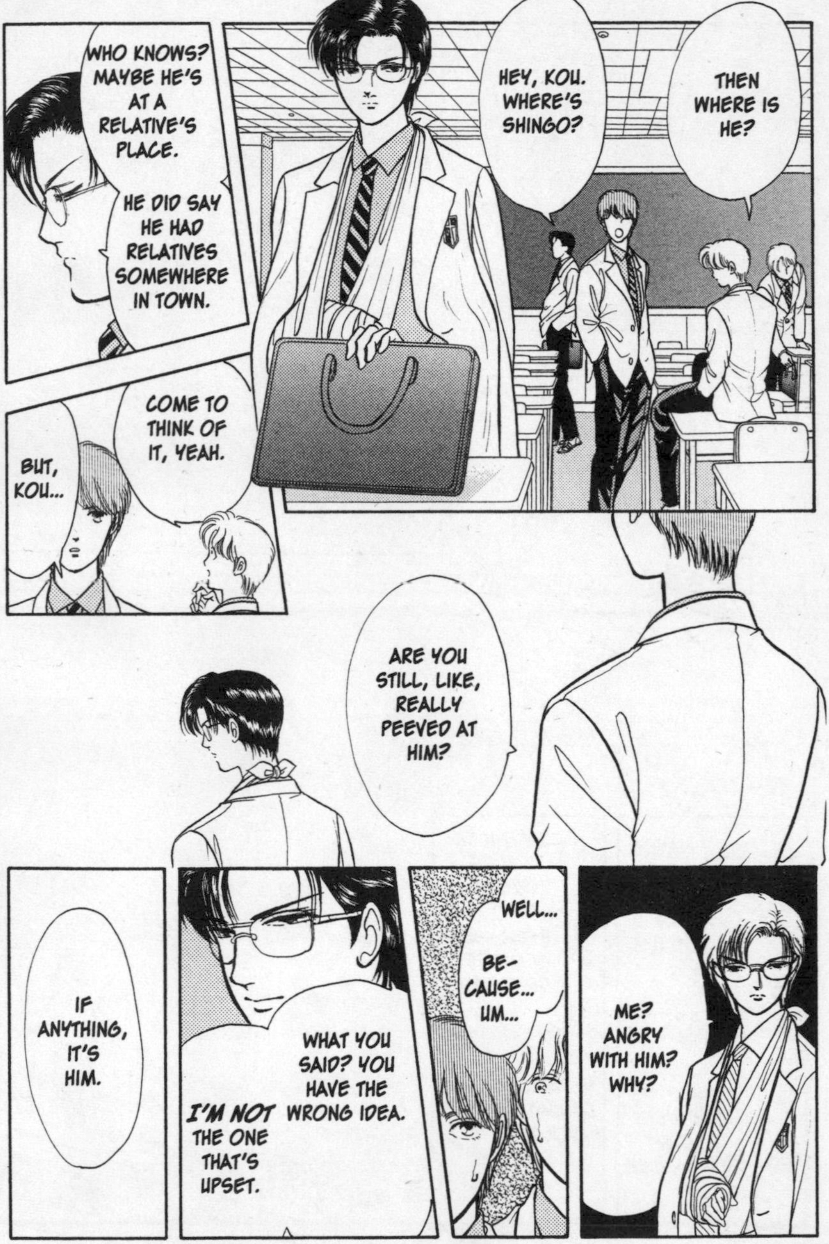
THEN WHERE IS HE?
HEY, KOU. WHERE'S SHINGO?
WHO KNOWS? MAYBE HE'S AT A RELATIVE'S PLACE.
HE DID SAY HE HAD RELATIVES SOMEWHERE IN TOWN.
COME TO THINK OF IT, YEAH.
BUT, KOU...
ARE YOU STILL, LIKE, REALLY PEEVED AT HIM?
ME? ANGRY WITH HIM? WHY?
WELL...
BE-CAUSE... UM...
WHAT YOU SAID? YOU HAVE THE WRONG IDEA.
I'M NOT THE ONE THAT'S UPSET.
IF ANYTHING, IT'S HIM.

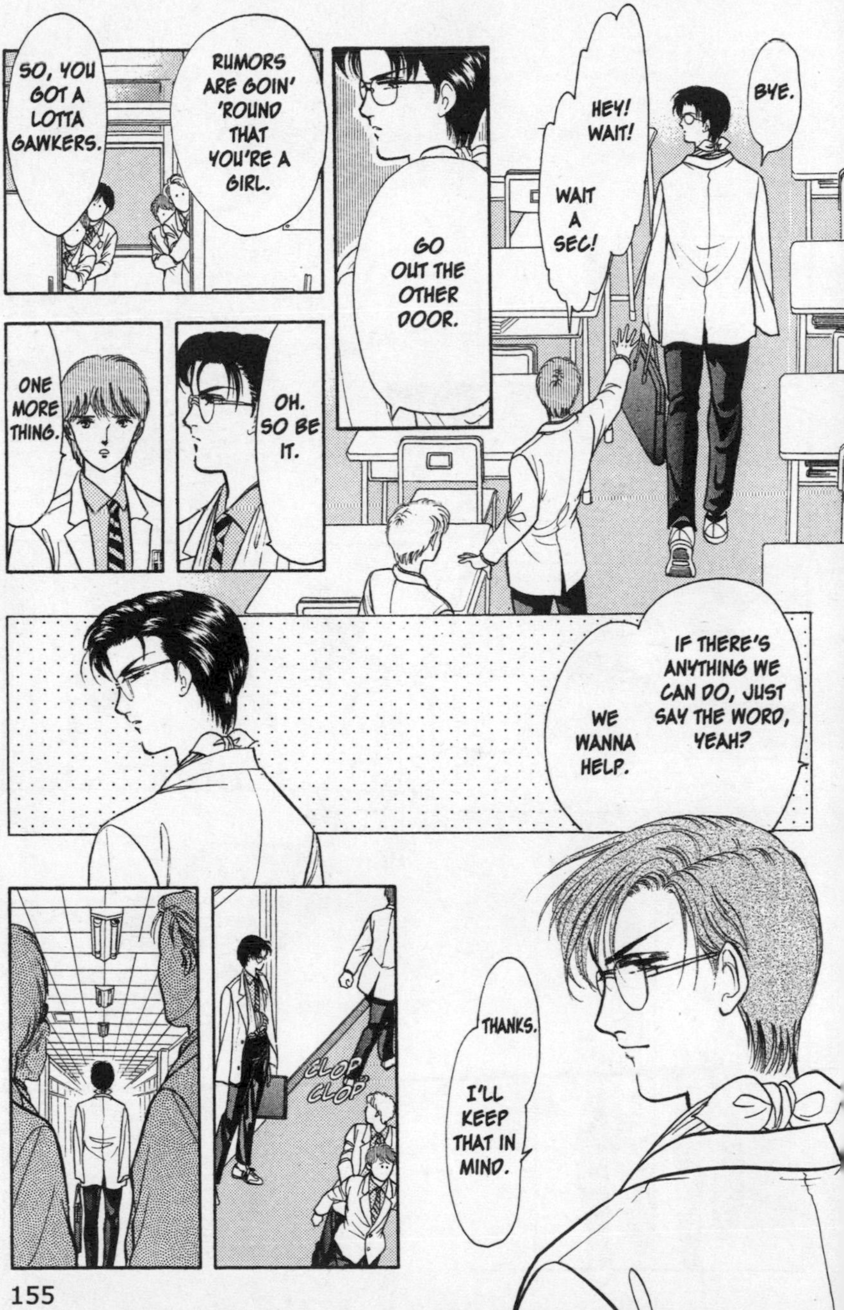
BYE.
HEY! WAIT!
WAIT A SEC!
GO OUT THE OTHER DOOR.
RUMORS ARE GOIN' 'ROUND THAT YOU'RE A GIRL.
SO, YOU GOT A LOTTA GAWKERS.
OH. SO BE IT.
ONE MORE THING.
IF THERE'S ANYTHING WE CAN DO, JUST SAY THE WORD, YEAH?
WE WANNA HELP.
THANKS.
I'LL KEEP THAT IN MIND.
CLOP CLOP

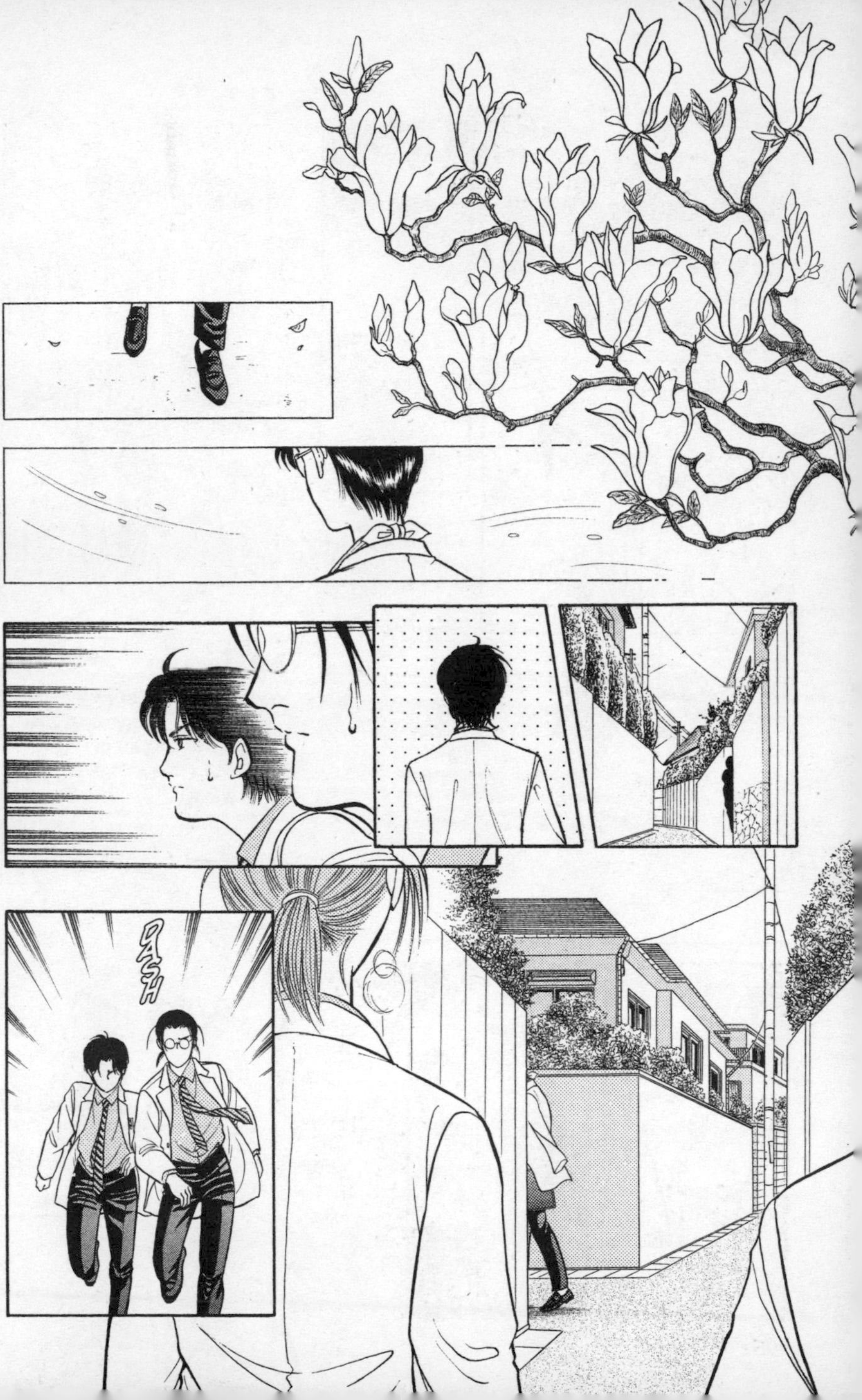
DASH

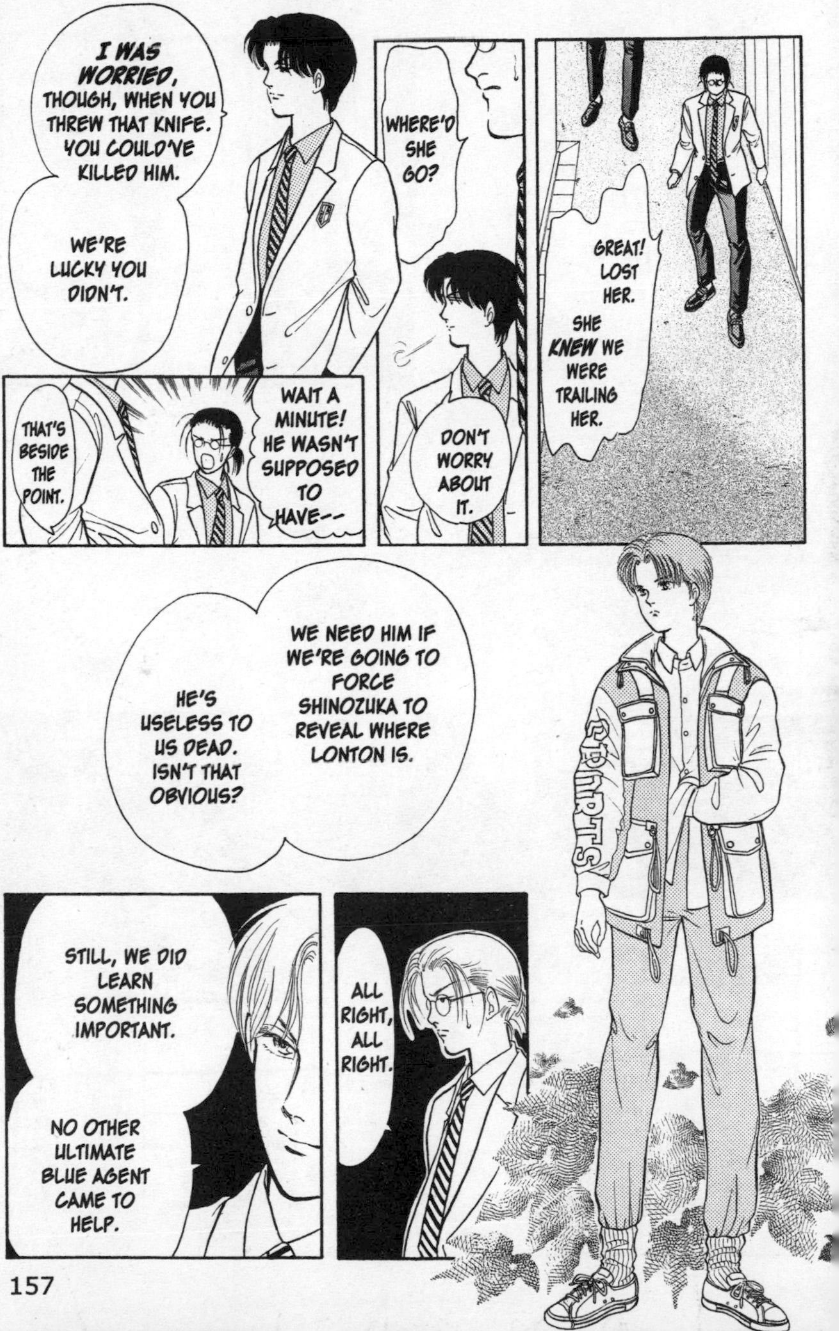
GREAT! LOST HER.
SHE *KNEW* WE WERE TRAILING HER.
WHERE'D SHE GO?
DON'T WORRY ABOUT IT.
I WAS WORRIED, THOUGH, WHEN YOU THREW THAT KNIFE. YOU COULD'VE KILLED HIM.
WE'RE LUCKY YOU DIDN'T.
WAIT A MINUTE! HE WASN'T SUPPOSED TO HAVE--
THAT'S BESIDE THE POINT.
WE NEED HIM IF WE'RE GOING TO FORCE SHINOZUKA TO REVEAL WHERE LONTON IS.
HE'S USELESS TO US DEAD. ISN'T THAT OBVIOUS?
ALL RIGHT, ALL RIGHT.
STILL, WE DID LEARN SOMETHING IMPORTANT.
NO OTHER ULTIMATE BLUE AGENT CAME TO HELP.

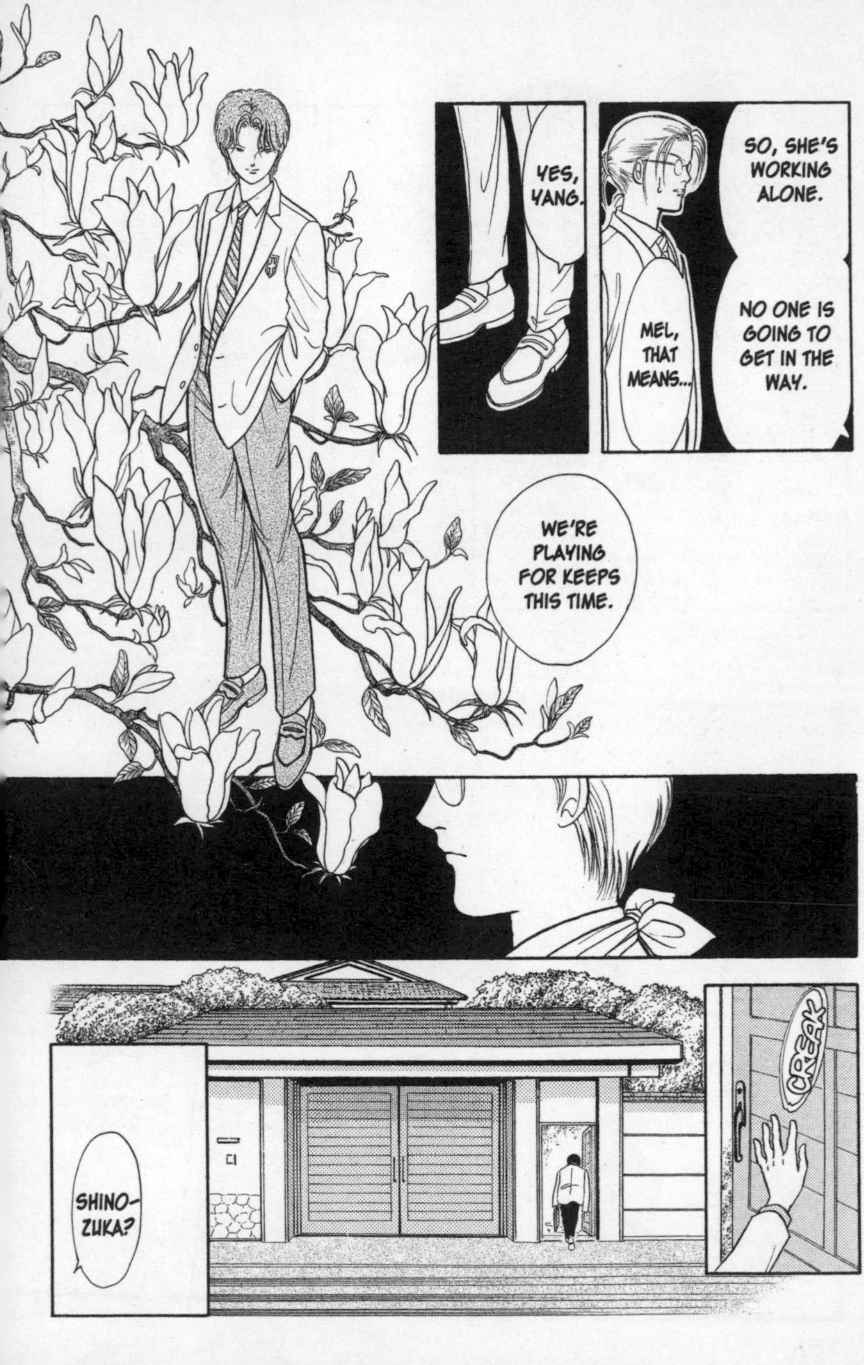
SO, SHE'S WORKING ALONE.
NO ONE IS GOING TO GET IN THE WAY.
MEL, THAT MEANS...
YES, YANG.
WE'RE PLAYING FOR KEEPS THIS TIME.
CREAK
SHINO-ZUKA?

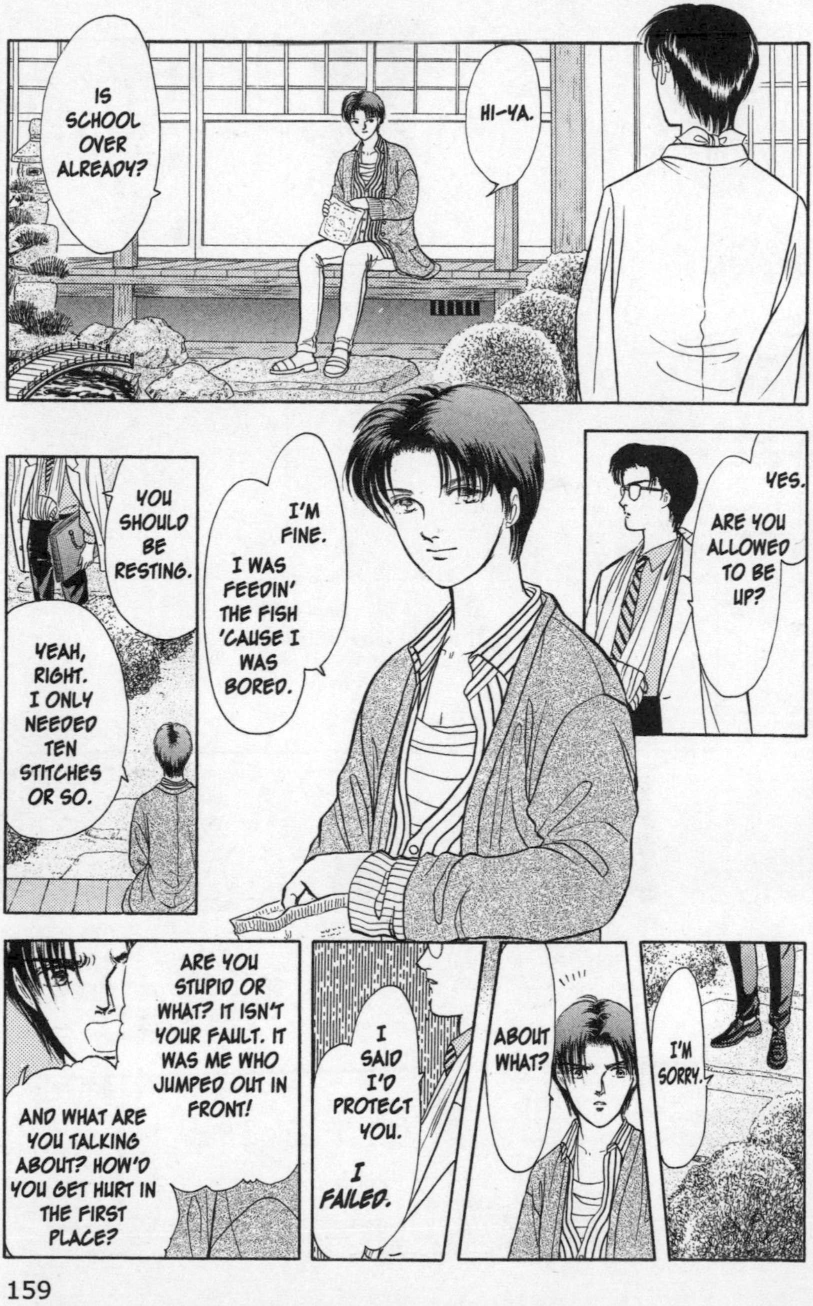
HI-YA.
IS SCHOOL OVER ALREADY?
YES. ARE YOU ALLOWED TO BE UP?
I'M FINE. I WAS FEEDIN' THE FISH 'CAUSE I WAS BORED.
YOU SHOULD BE RESTING.
YEAH, RIGHT. I ONLY NEEDED TEN STITCHES OR SO.
I'M SORRY.
ABOUT WHAT?
I SAID I'D PROTECT YOU.
I FAILED.
ARE YOU STUPID OR WHAT? IT ISN'T YOUR FAULT. IT WAS ME WHO JUMPED OUT IN FRONT!
AND WHAT ARE YOU TALKING ABOUT? HOW'D YOU GET HURT IN THE FIRST PLACE?

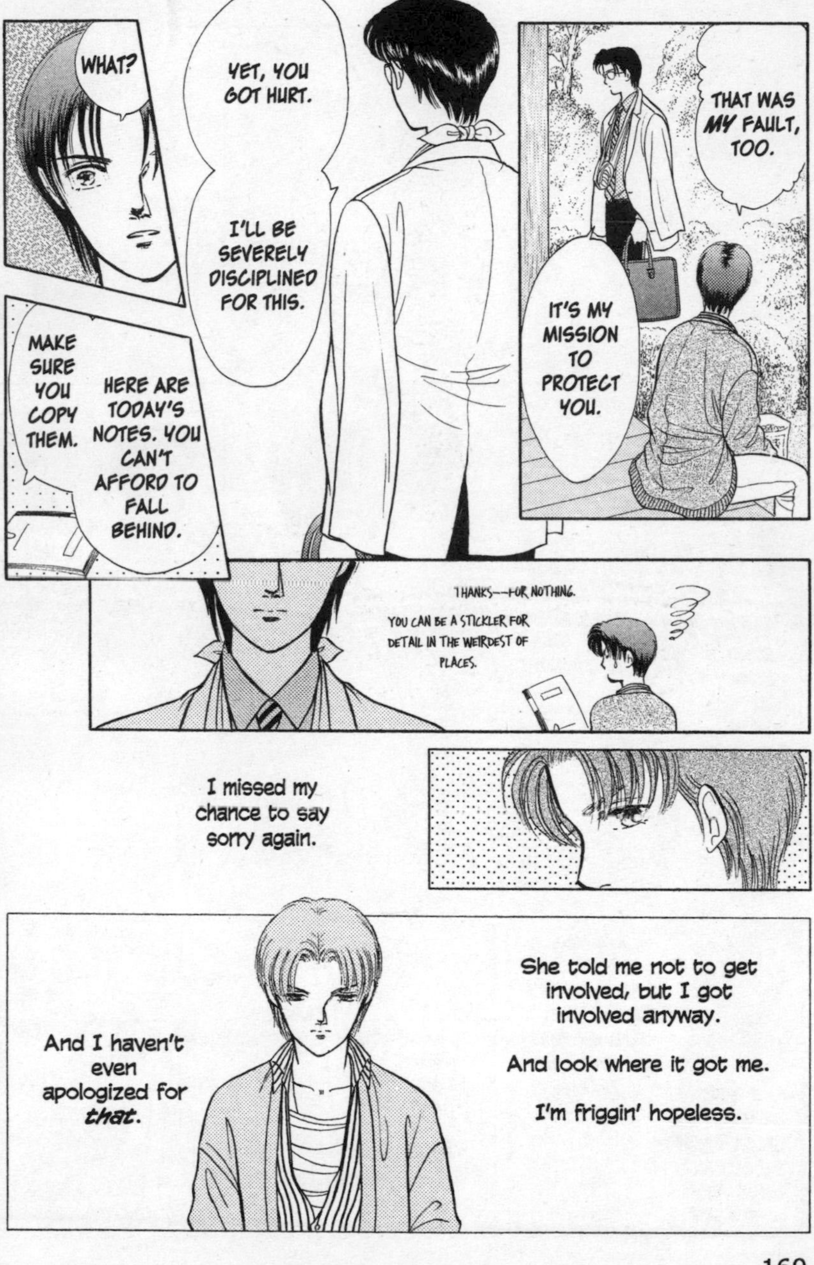
THAT WAS MY FAULT, TOO.
IT'S MY MISSION TO PROTECT YOU.
YET, YOU GOT HURT.
I'LL BE SEVERELY DISCIPLINED FOR THIS.
WHAT?
HERE ARE TODAY'S NOTES. YOU CAN'T AFFORD TO FALL BEHIND.
MAKE SURE YOU COPY THEM.
THANKS---FOR NOTHING.
YOU CAN BE A STICKLER FOR DETAIL IN THE WEIRDEST OF PLACES.
I missed my chance to say sorry again.
She told me not to get involved, but I got involved anyway.
And look where it got me.
I'm friggin' hopeless.
And I haven't even apologized for that.

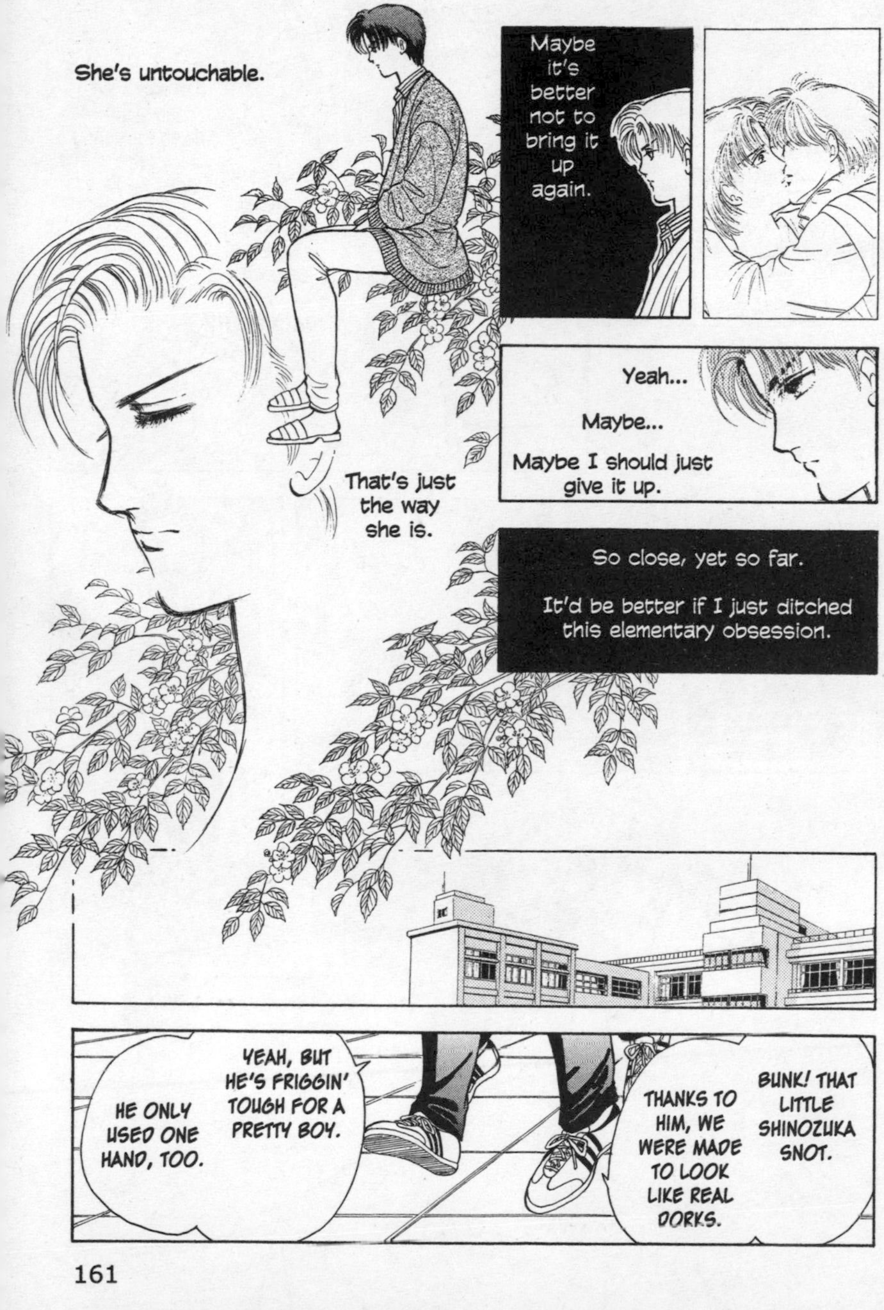
Maybe it's better not to bring it up again.
Yeah...
Maybe...
Maybe I should just give it up.
So close, yet so far.
It'd be better if I just ditched this elementary obsession.
She's untouchable.
That's just the way she is.
BUNK! THAT LITTLE SHINOZUKA SNOT.
THANKS TO HIM, WE WERE MADE TO LOOK LIKE REAL DORKS.
YEAH, BUT HE'S FRIGGIN' TOUGH FOR A PRETTY BOY.
HE ONLY USED ONE HAND, TOO.

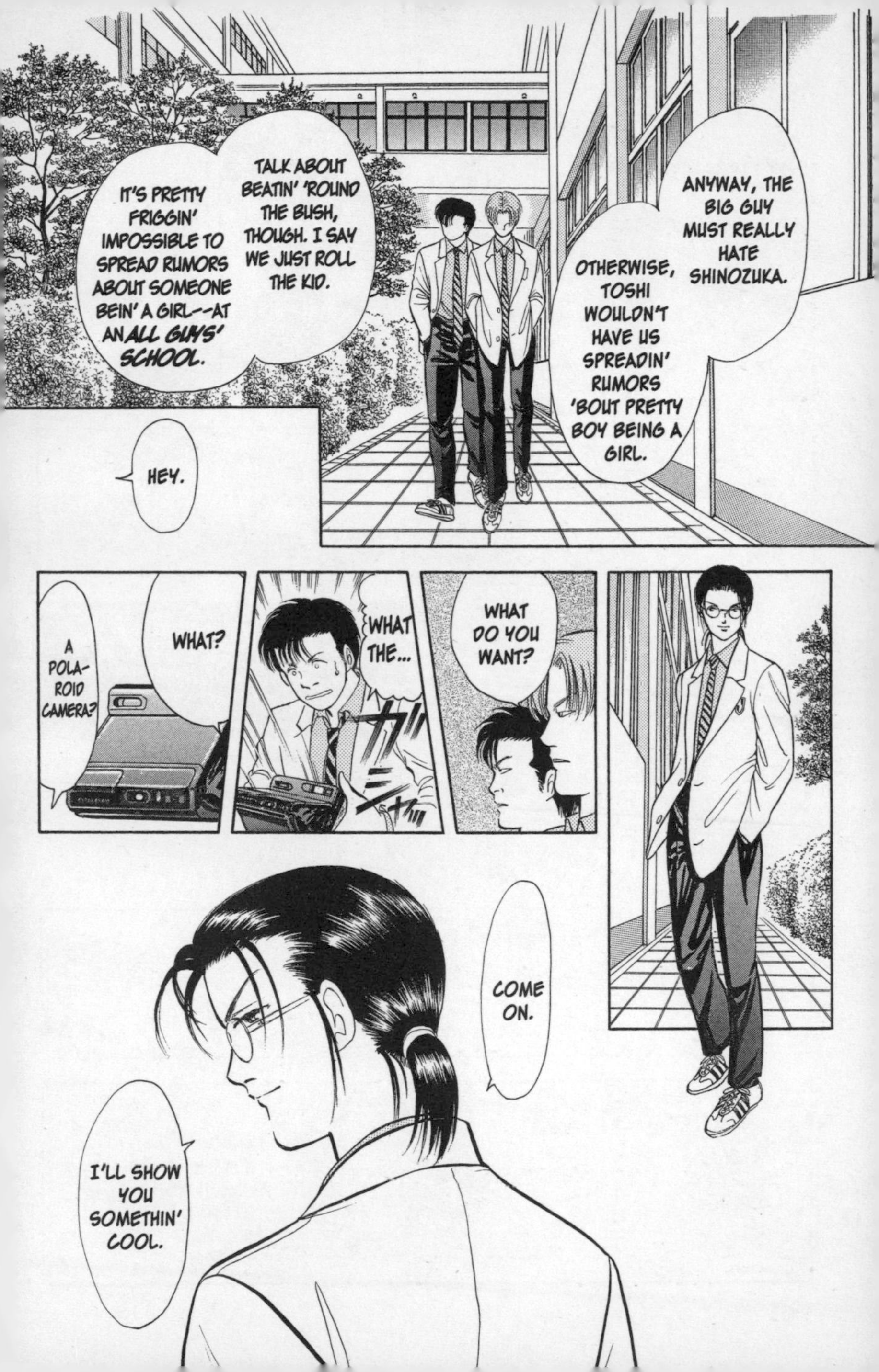
ANYWAY, THE BIG GUY MUST REALLY HATE SHINOZUKA.
OTHERWISE, TOSHI WOULDN'T HAVE US SPREADIN' RUMORS 'BOUT PRETTY BOY BEING A GIRL.
TALK ABOUT BEATIN' 'ROUND THE BUSH, THOUGH. I SAY WE JUST ROLL THE KID.
IT'S PRETTY FRIGGIN' IMPOSSIBLE TO SPREAD RUMORS ABOUT SOMEONE BEIN' A GIRL--AT AN ALL GUYS' SCHOOL.
HEY.
WHAT DO YOU WANT?
WHAT THE...
WHAT?
A POLAROID CAMERA?
COME ON.
I'LL SHOW YOU SOMETHIN' COOL.

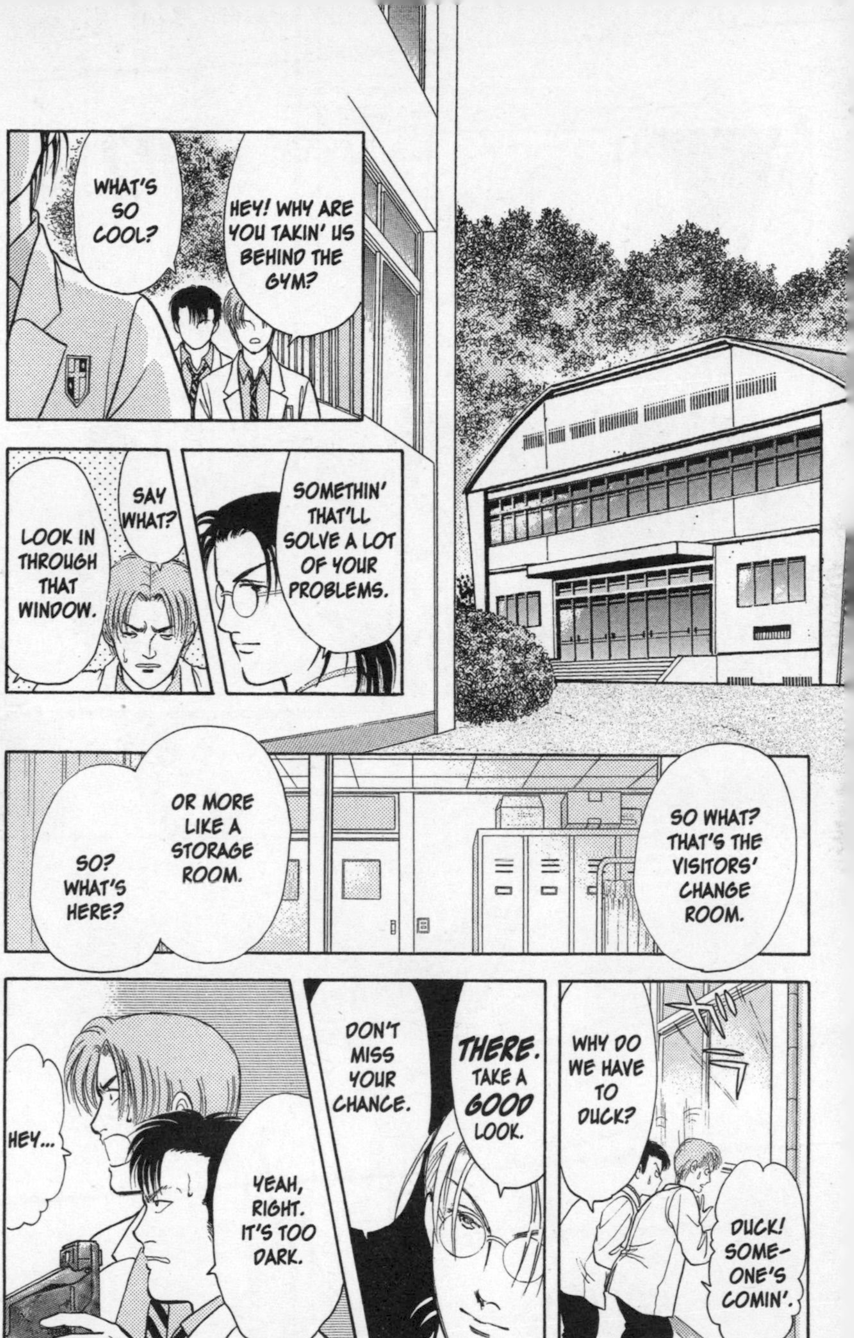
HEY! WHY ARE YOU TAKIN' US BEHIND THE GYM?
WHAT'S SO COOL?
SOMETHIN' THAT'LL SOLVE A LOT OF YOUR PROBLEMS.
SAY WHAT?
LOOK IN THROUGH THAT WINDOW.
SO WHAT? THAT'S THE VISITORS' CHANGE ROOM.
OR MORE LIKE A STORAGE ROOM.
SO? WHAT'S HERE?
DUCK! SOME-ONE'S COMIN'.
WHY DO WE HAVE TO DUCK?
THERE. TAKE A ***GOOD*** LOOK.
DON'T MISS YOUR CHANCE.
YEAH, RIGHT. IT'S TOO DARK.
HEY...

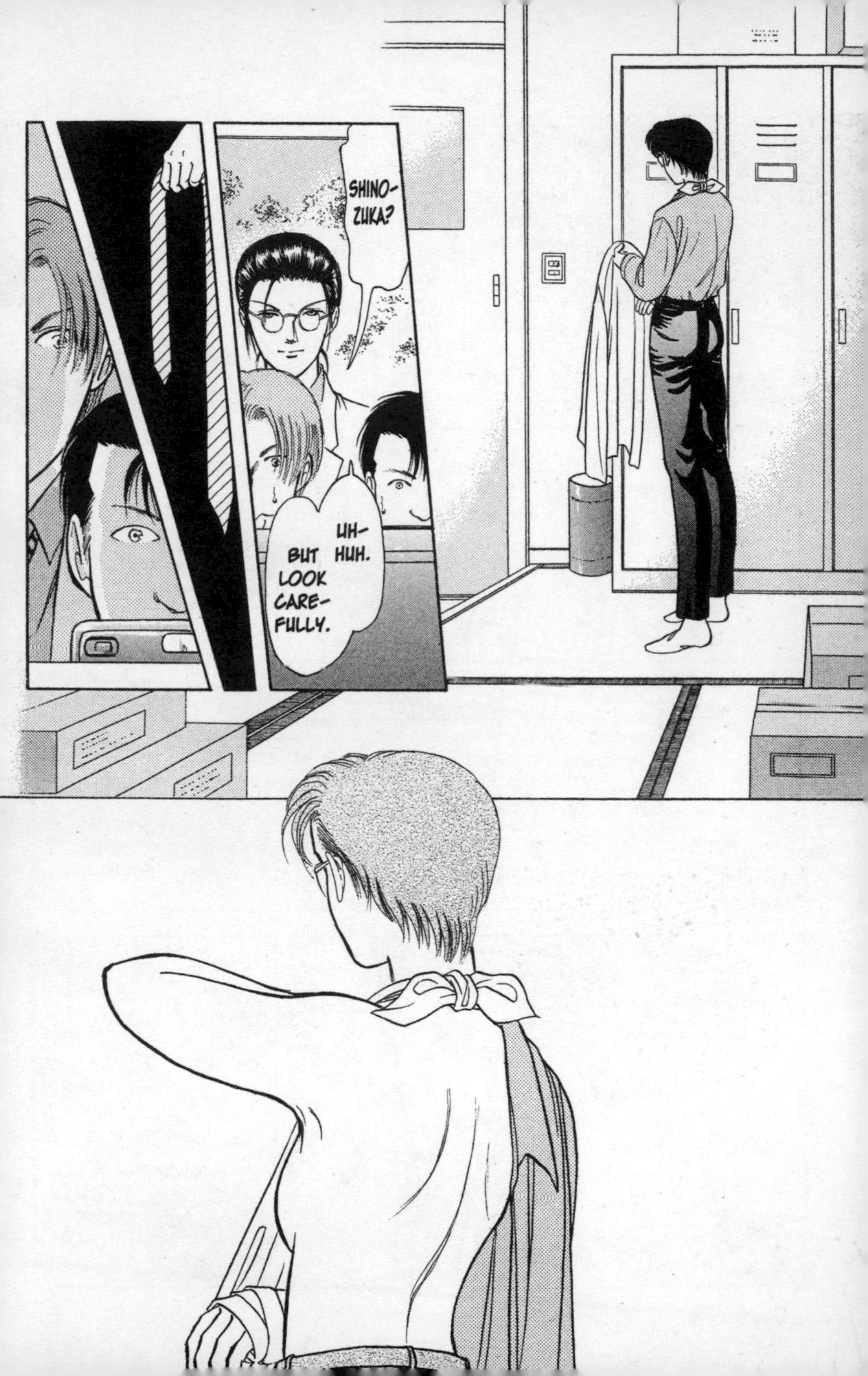
SHINO-ZUKA?
UH-HUH. BUT LOOK CARE-FULLY.

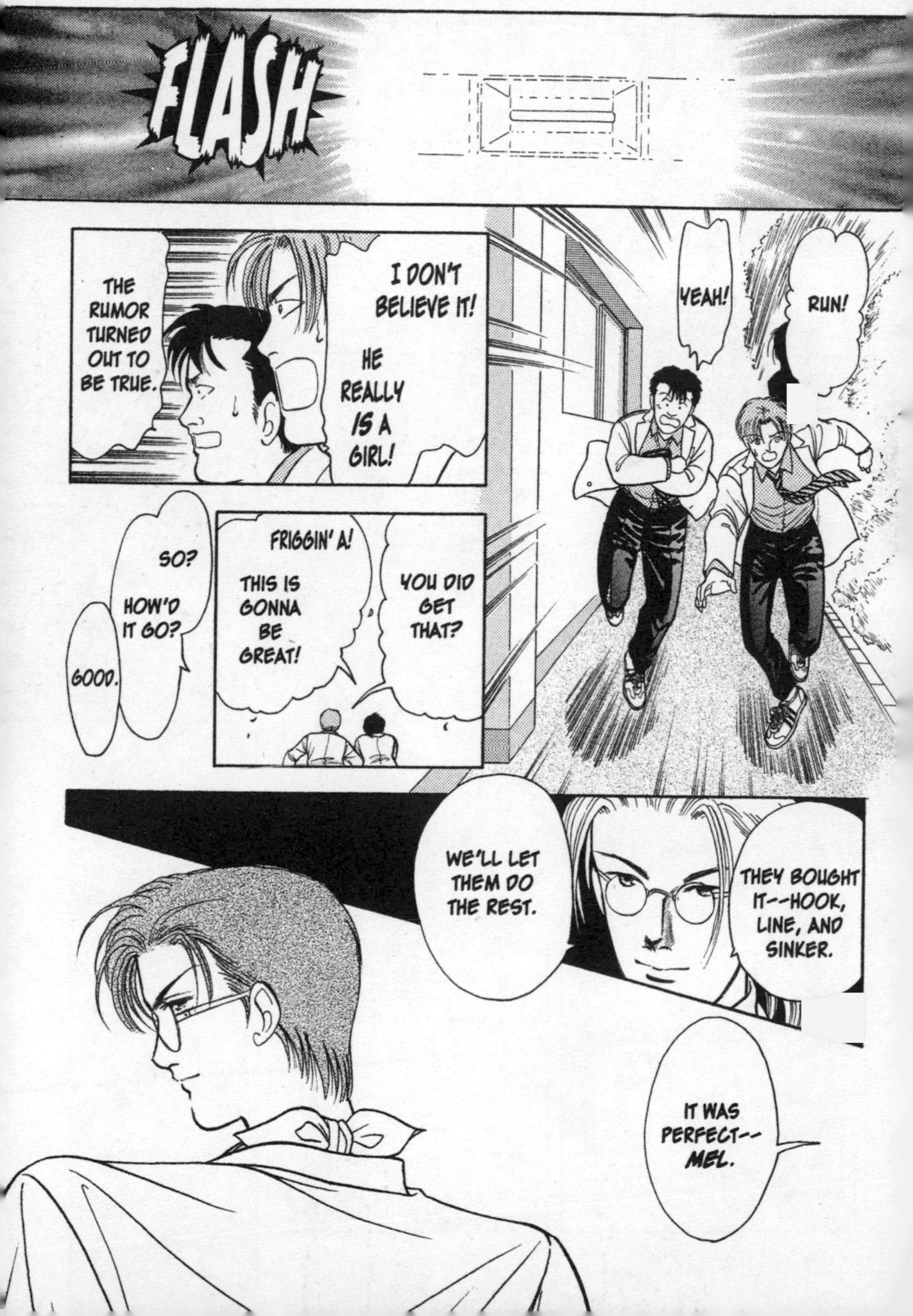
FLASH
RUN!
YEAH!
I DON'T BELIEVE IT!
HE REALLY IS A GIRL!
THE RUMOR TURNED OUT TO BE TRUE.
YOU DID GET THAT?
FRIGGIN' A!
THIS IS GONNA BE GREAT!
SO?
HOW'D IT GO?
GOOD.
THEY BOUGHT IT--HOOK, LINE, AND SINKER.
WE'LL LET THEM DO THE REST.
IT WAS PERFECT--MEL.

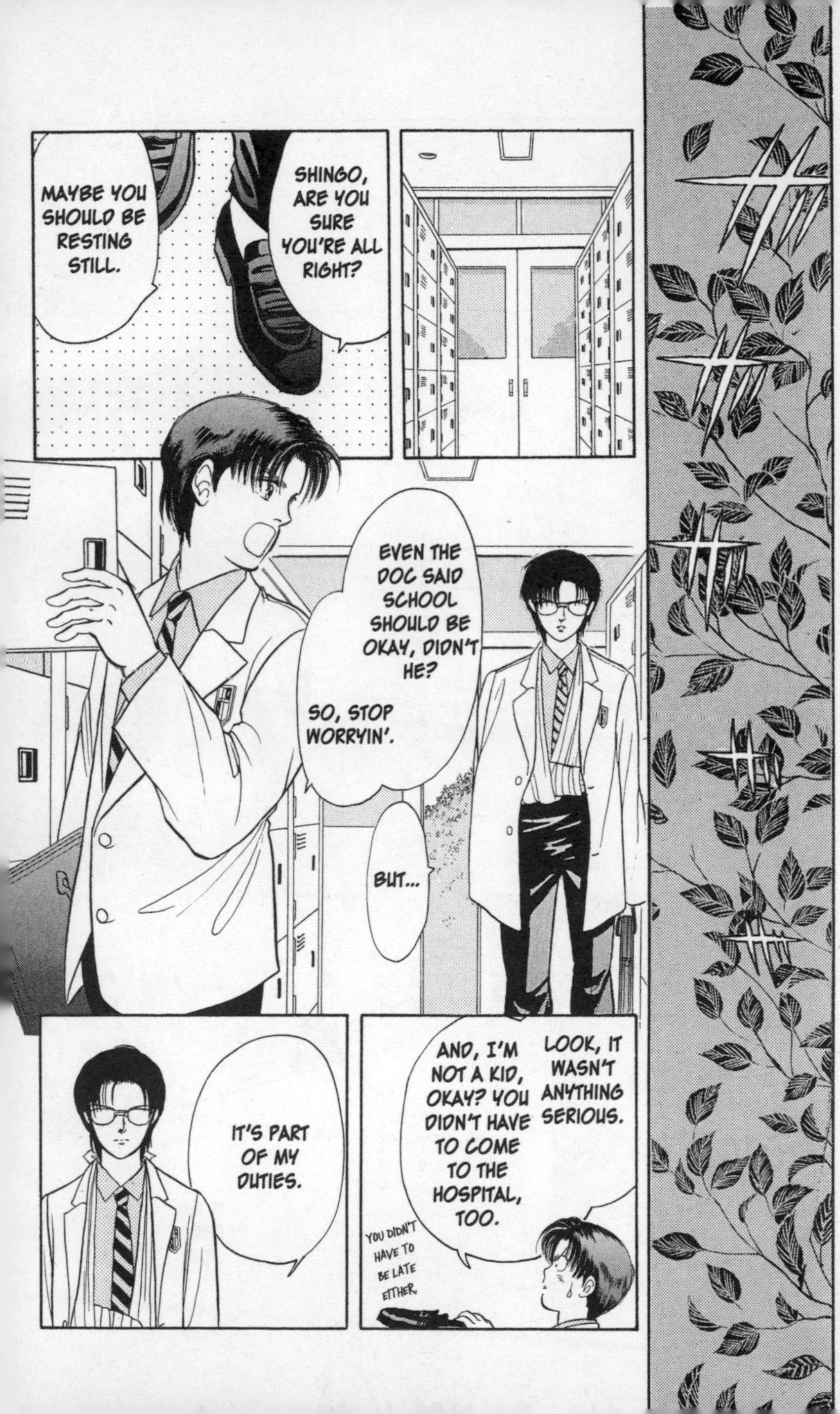
SHINGO, ARE YOU SURE YOU'RE ALL RIGHT?
MAYBE YOU SHOULD BE RESTING STILL.
EVEN THE DOC SAID SCHOOL SHOULD BE OKAY, DIDN'T HE?
SO, STOP WORRYIN'.
BUT...
LOOK, IT WASN'T ANYTHING SERIOUS.
AND, I'M NOT A KID, OKAY? YOU DIDN'T HAVE TO COME TO THE HOSPITAL, TOO.
YOU DIDN'T HAVE TO BE LATE EITHER.
IT'S PART OF MY DUTIES.

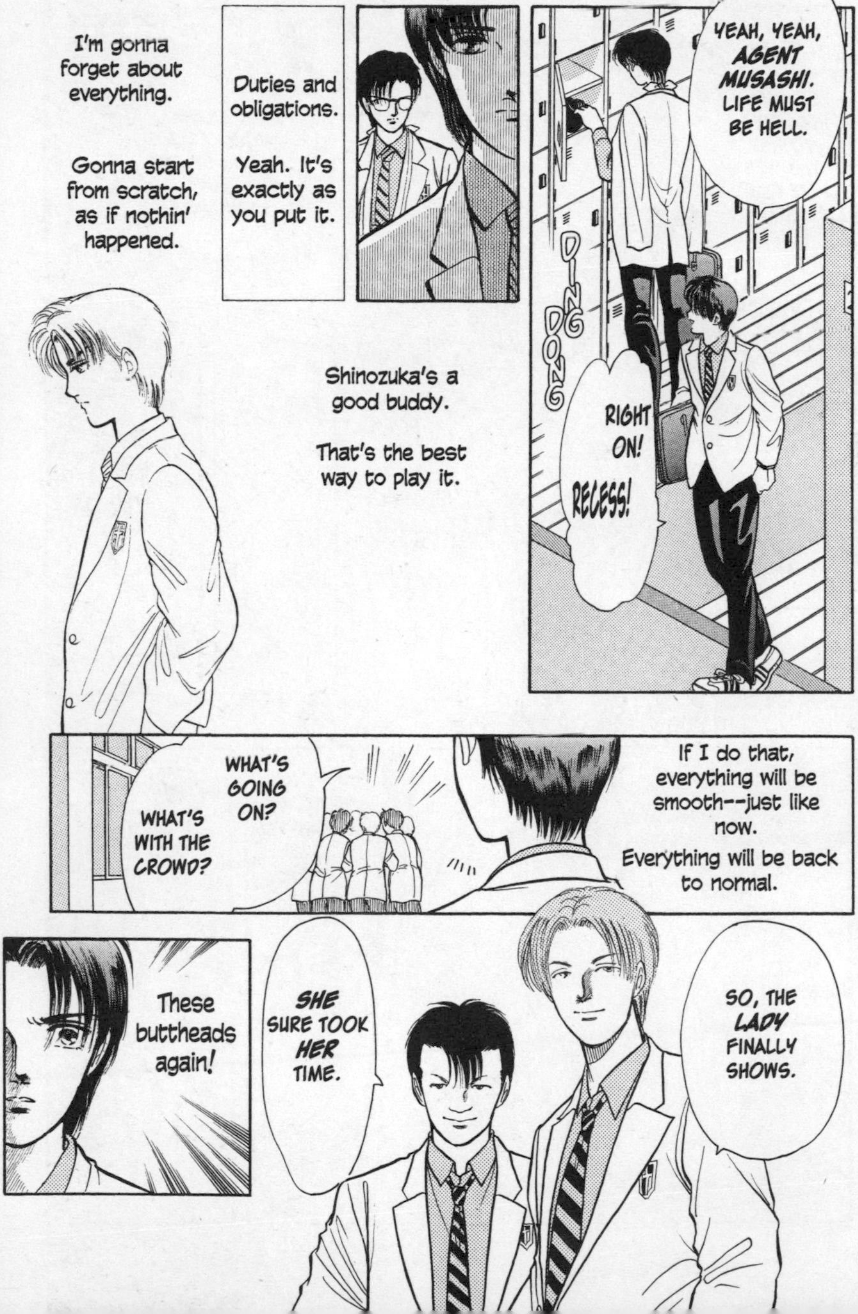
YEAH, YEAH, *AGENT MUSASHI.* LIFE MUST BE HELL.
DING DONG
RIGHT ON! RECESS!
Duties and obligations.
Yeah. It's exactly as you put it.
I'm gonna forget about everything.
Gonna start from scratch, as if nothin' happened.
Shinozuka's a good buddy.
That's the best way to play it.
If I do that, everything will be smooth--just like now.
Everything will be back to normal.
WHAT'S GOING ON?
WHAT'S WITH THE CROWD?
SO, THE *LADY* FINALLY SHOWS.
SHE SURE TOOK *HER* TIME.
These buttheads again!

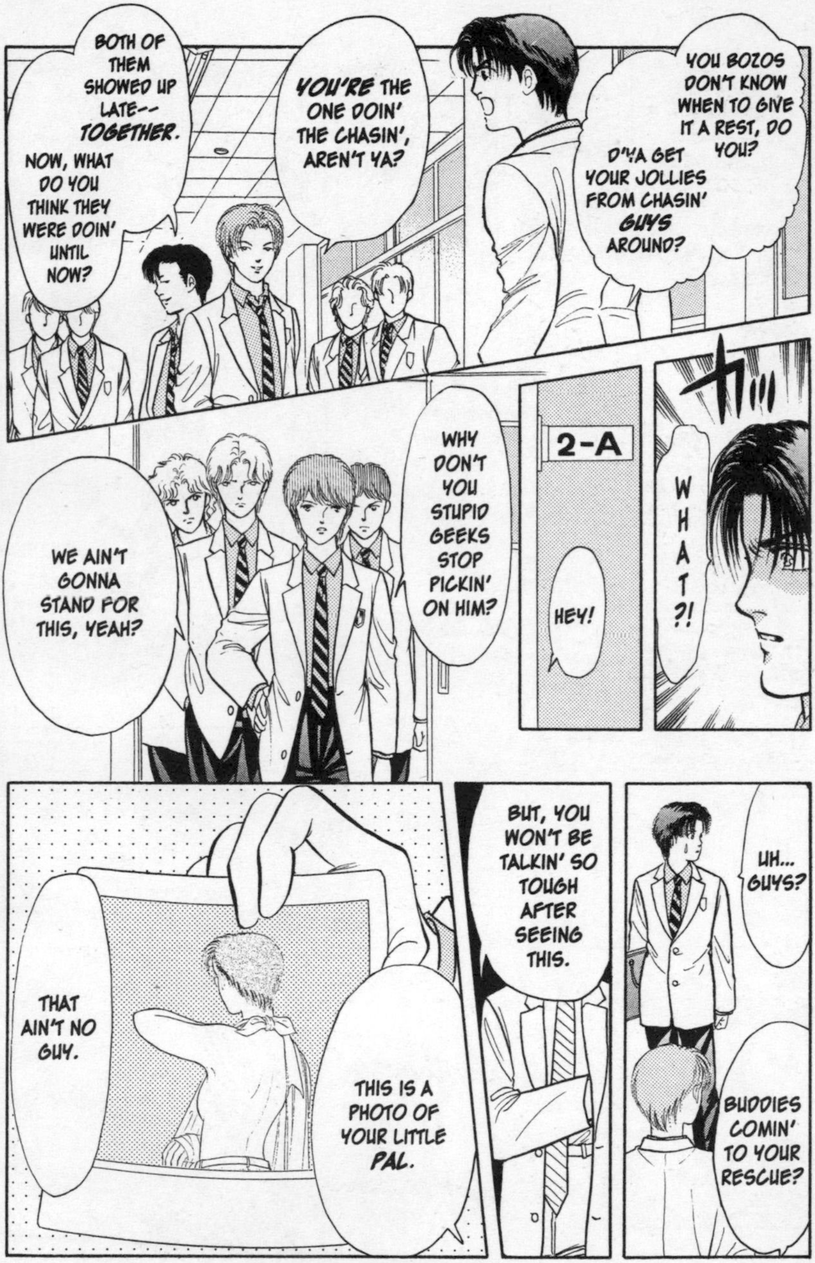
YOU BOZOS DON'T KNOW WHEN TO GIVE IT A REST, DO YOU?
D'YA GET YOUR JOLLIES FROM CHASIN' GUYS AROUND?
YOU'RE THE ONE DOIN' THE CHASIN', AREN'T YA?
BOTH OF THEM SHOWED UP LATE--TOGETHER.
NOW, WHAT DO YOU THINK THEY WERE DOIN' UNTIL NOW?
WHAT?!
2-A
HEY!
WHY DON'T YOU STUPID GEEKS STOP PICKIN' ON HIM?
WE AIN'T GONNA STAND FOR THIS, YEAH?
UH... GUYS?
BUDDIES COMIN' TO YOUR RESCUE?
BUT, YOU WON'T BE TALKIN' SO TOUGH AFTER SEEING THIS.
THIS IS A PHOTO OF YOUR LITTLE PAL.
THAT AIN'T NO GUY.

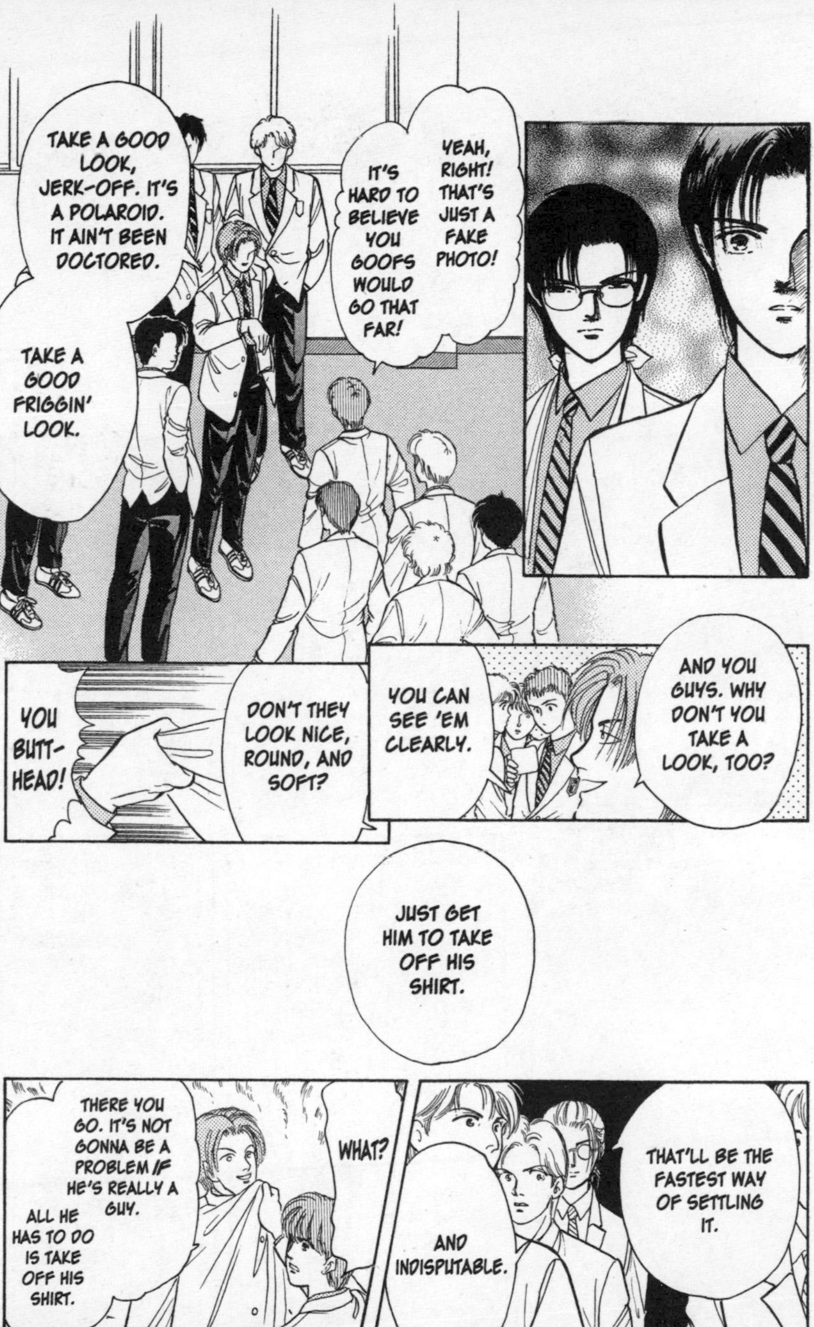
YEAH, RIGHT! THAT'S JUST A FAKE PHOTO!
IT'S HARD TO BELIEVE YOU GOOFS WOULD GO THAT FAR!
TAKE A GOOD LOOK, JERK-OFF. IT'S A POLAROID. IT AIN'T BEEN DOCTORED.
TAKE A GOOD FRIGGIN' LOOK.
AND YOU GUYS. WHY DON'T YOU TAKE A LOOK, TOO?
YOU CAN SEE 'EM CLEARLY.
DON'T THEY LOOK NICE, ROUND, AND SOFT?
YOU BUTT-HEAD!
JUST GET HIM TO TAKE OFF HIS SHIRT.
THAT'LL BE THE FASTEST WAY OF SETTLING IT.
AND INDISPUTABLE.
WHAT?
THERE YOU GO. IT'S NOT GONNA BE A PROBLEM IF HE'S REALLY A GUY.
ALL HE HAS TO DO IS TAKE OFF HIS SHIRT.

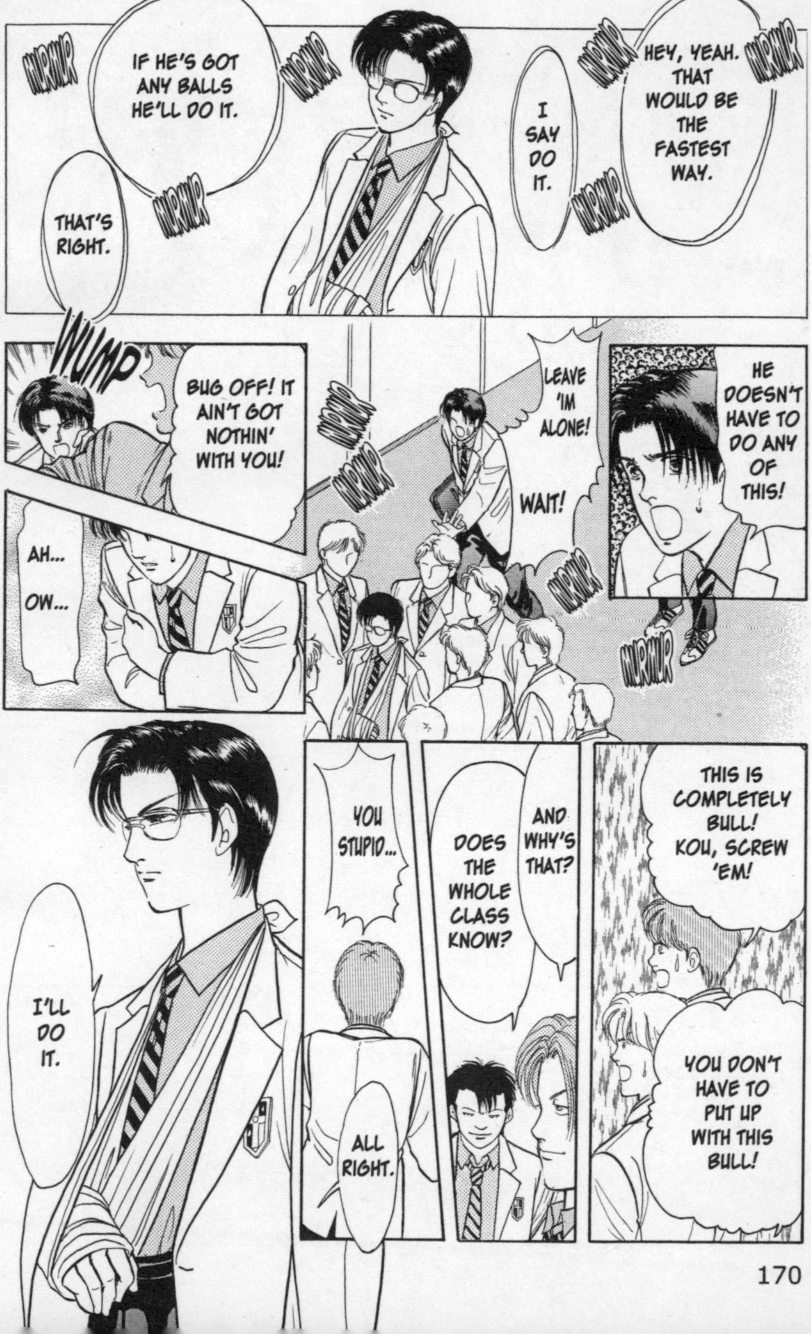
MURMUR
HEY, YEAH. THAT WOULD BE THE FASTEST WAY.
MURMUR
I SAY DO IT.
MURMUR
IF HE'S GOT ANY BALLS HE'LL DO IT.
MURMUR
MURMUR
THAT'S RIGHT.
HE DOESN'T HAVE TO DO ANY OF THIS!
MURMUR
LEAVE 'IM ALONE!
WAIT!
MURMUR
MURMUR
MURMUR
WUMP
BUG OFF! IT AIN'T GOT NOTHIN' WITH YOU!
AH... OW...
THIS IS COMPLETELY BULL! KOU, SCREW 'EM!
YOU DON'T HAVE TO PUT UP WITH THIS BULL!
AND WHY'S THAT?
DOES THE WHOLE CLASS KNOW?
YOU STUPID...
ALL RIGHT.
I'LL DO IT.

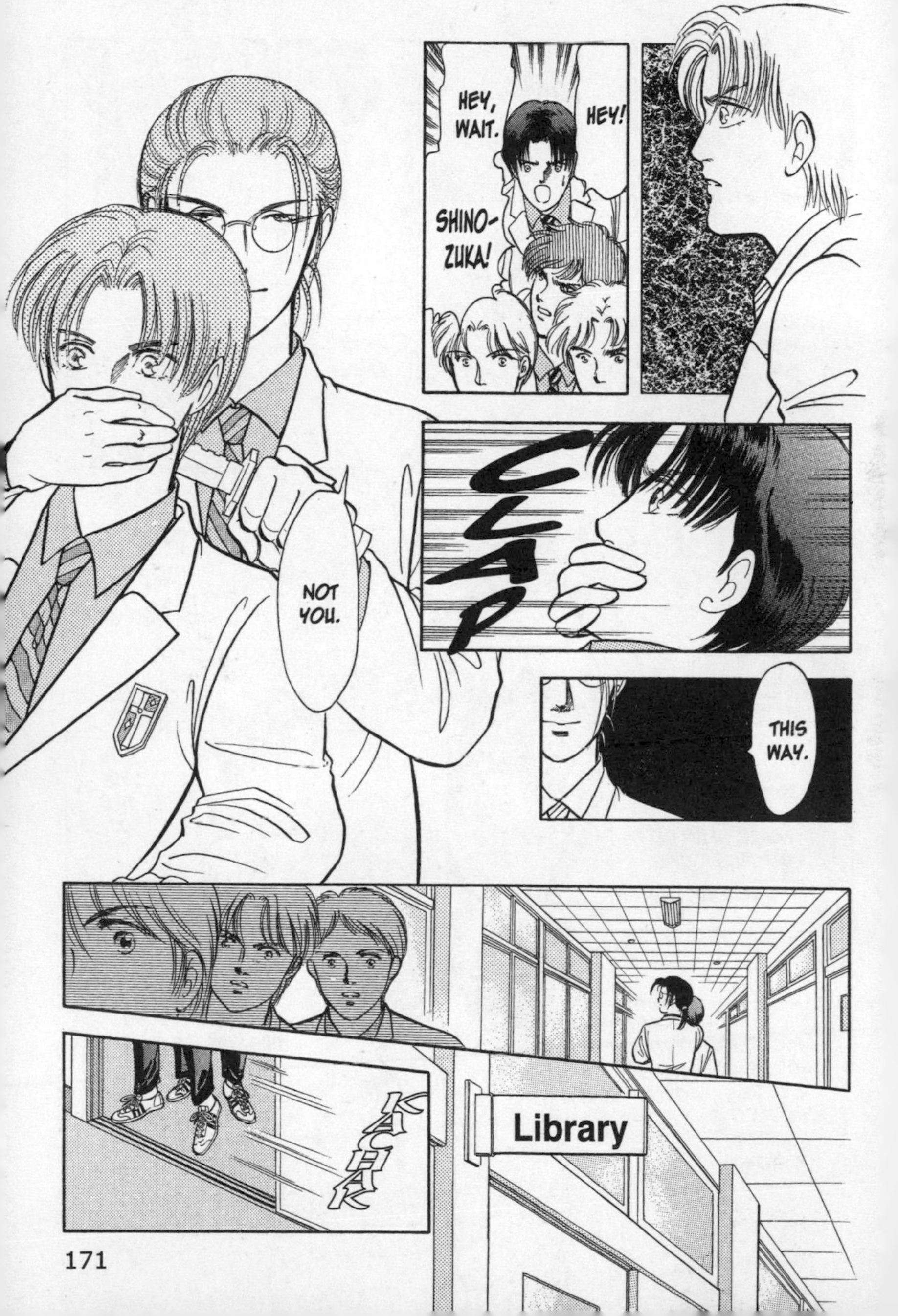
HEY!
HEY, WAIT.
SHINO-ZUKA!
CLAP
THIS WAY.
NOT YOU.
Library
KACHAK

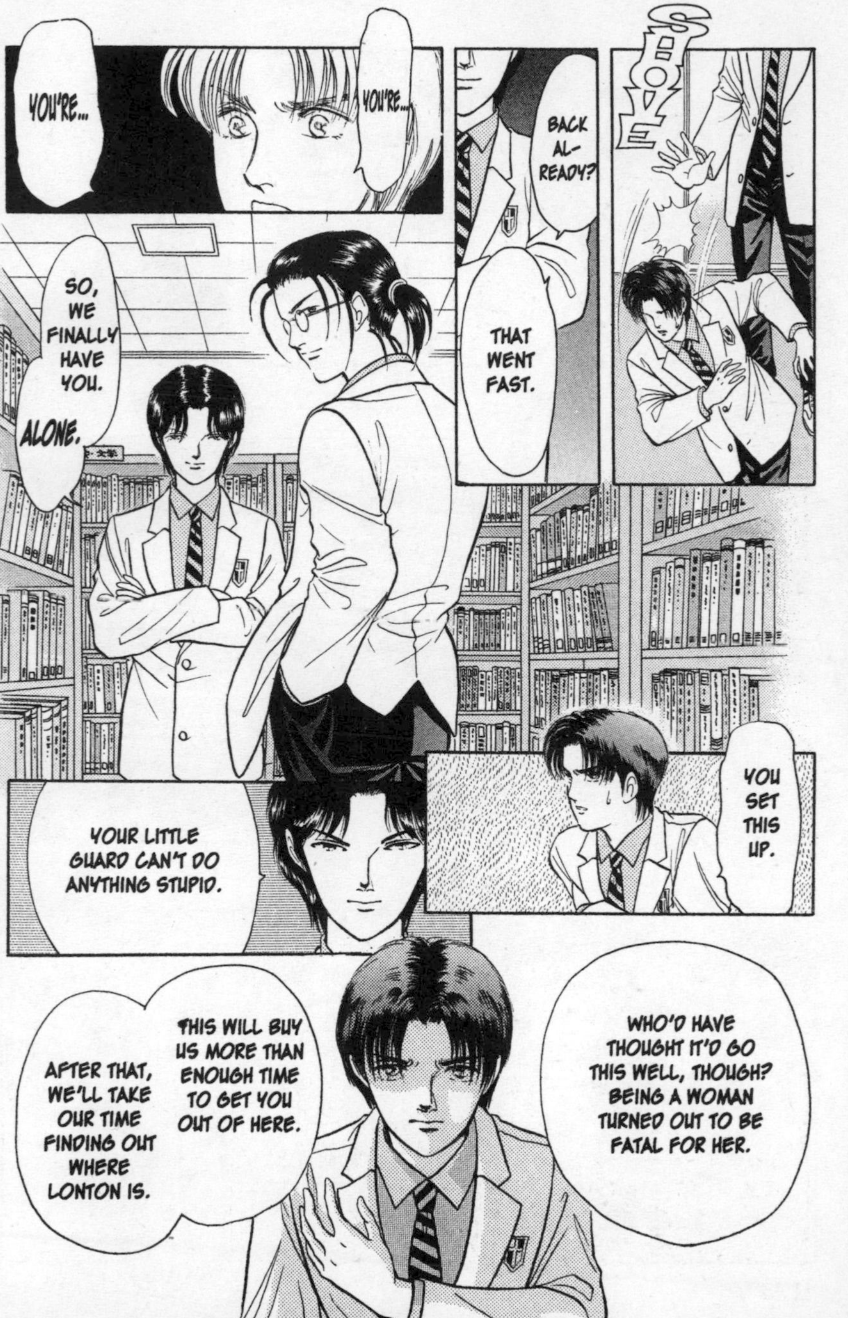
SHOVE
BACK AL-READY?
THAT WENT FAST.
YOU'RE...
YOU'RE...
SO, WE FINALLY HAVE YOU.
ALONE.
YOU SET THIS UP.
YOUR LITTLE GUARD CAN'T DO ANYTHING STUPID.
WHO'D HAVE THOUGHT IT'D GO THIS WELL, THOUGH? BEING A WOMAN TURNED OUT TO BE FATAL FOR HER.
THIS WILL BUY US MORE THAN ENOUGH TIME TO GET YOU OUT OF HERE.
AFTER THAT, WE'LL TAKE OUR TIME FINDING OUT WHERE LONTON IS.

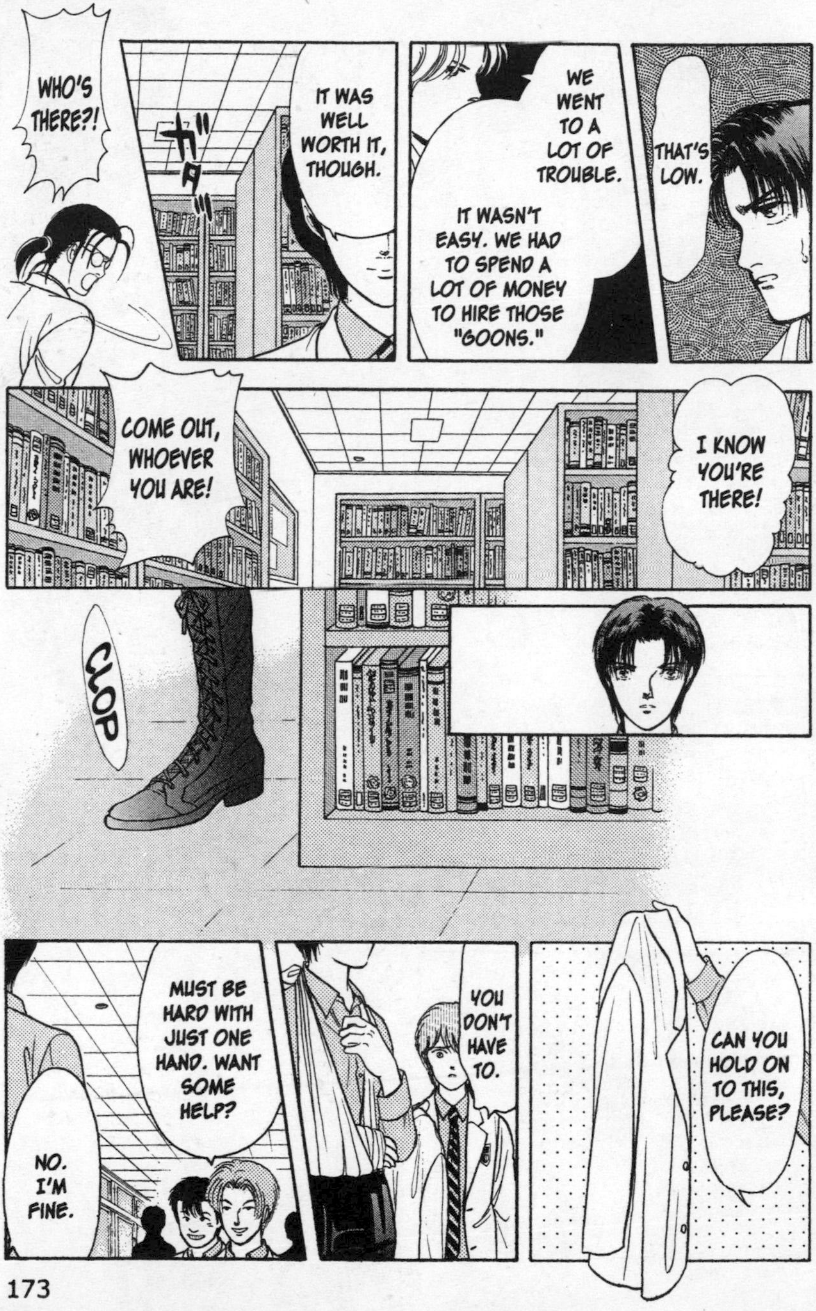
THAT'S LOW.
WE WENT TO A LOT OF TROUBLE.
IT WASN'T EASY. WE HAD TO SPEND A LOT OF MONEY TO HIRE THOSE "GOONS."
IT WAS WELL WORTH IT, THOUGH.
WHO'S THERE?!
I KNOW YOU'RE THERE!
COME OUT, WHOEVER YOU ARE!
CLOP
CAN YOU HOLD ON TO THIS, PLEASE?
YOU DON'T HAVE TO.
MUST BE HARD WITH JUST ONE HAND. WANT SOME HELP?
NO. I'M FINE.

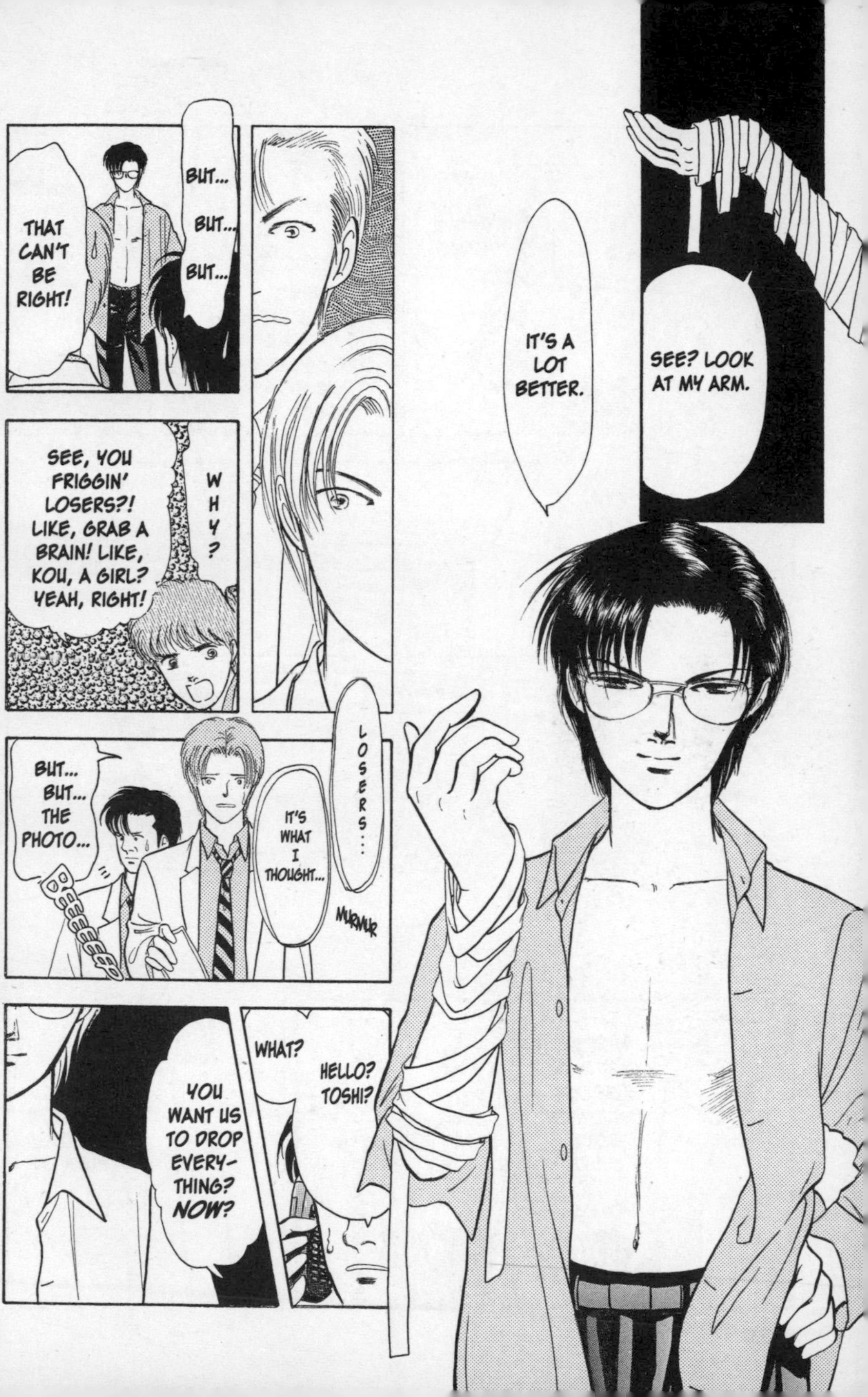

SEE? LOOK AT MY ARM.
IT'S A LOT BETTER.
BUT... BUT... BUT...
THAT CAN'T BE RIGHT!
WHY?
SEE, YOU FRIGGIN' LOSERS?! LIKE, GRAB A BRAIN! LIKE, KOU, A GIRL? YEAH, RIGHT!
LOSERS...
IT'S WHAT I THOUGHT...
MURMUR
BUT... BUT... THE PHOTO...
HELLO? TOSHI?
WHAT?
YOU WANT US TO DROP EVERY-THING? *NOW?*

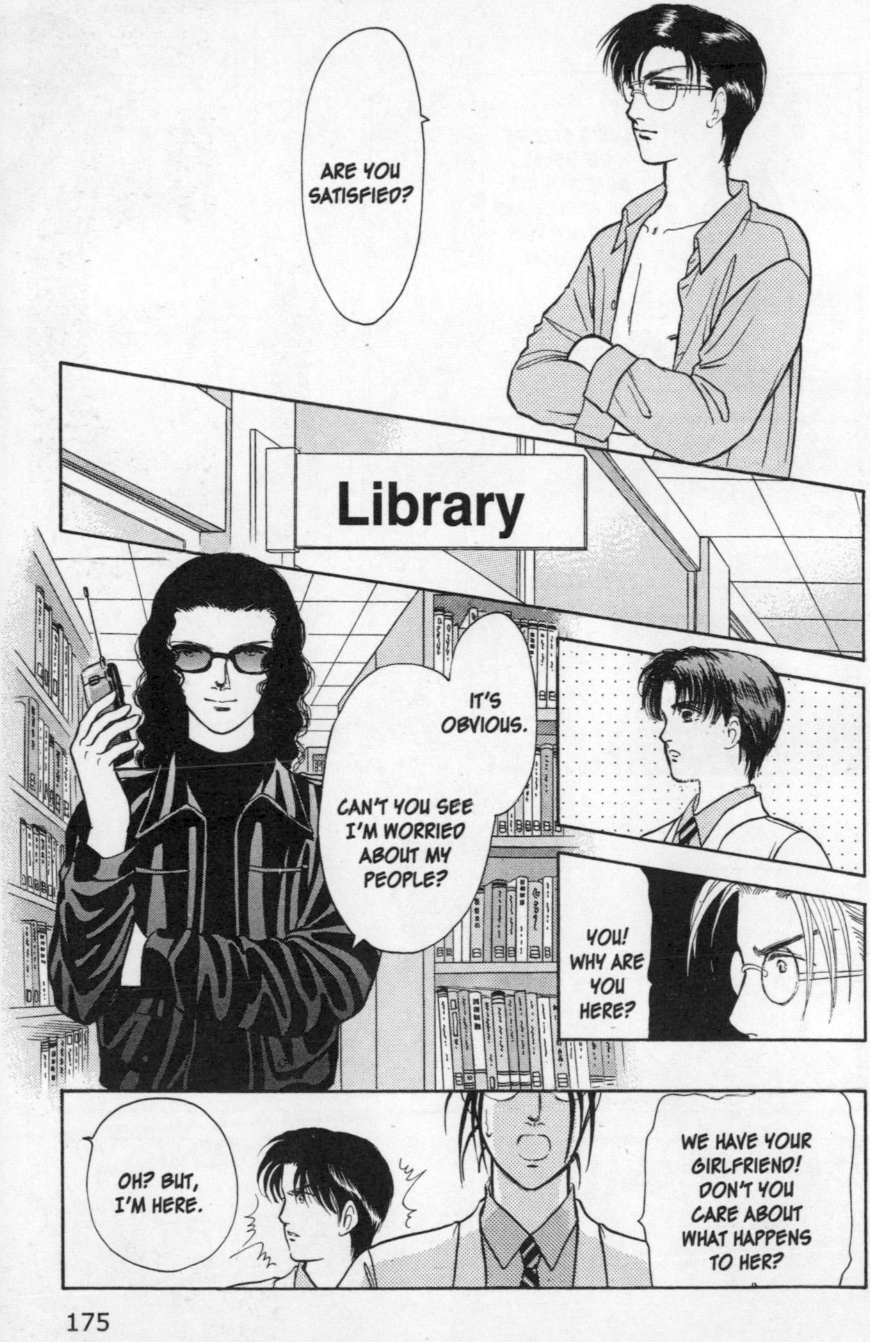
ARE YOU SATISFIED?
Library
YOU! WHY ARE YOU HERE?
IT'S OBVIOUS.
CAN'T YOU SEE I'M WORRIED ABOUT MY PEOPLE?
WE HAVE YOUR GIRLFRIEND! DON'T YOU CARE ABOUT WHAT HAPPENS TO HER?
OH? BUT, I'M HERE.

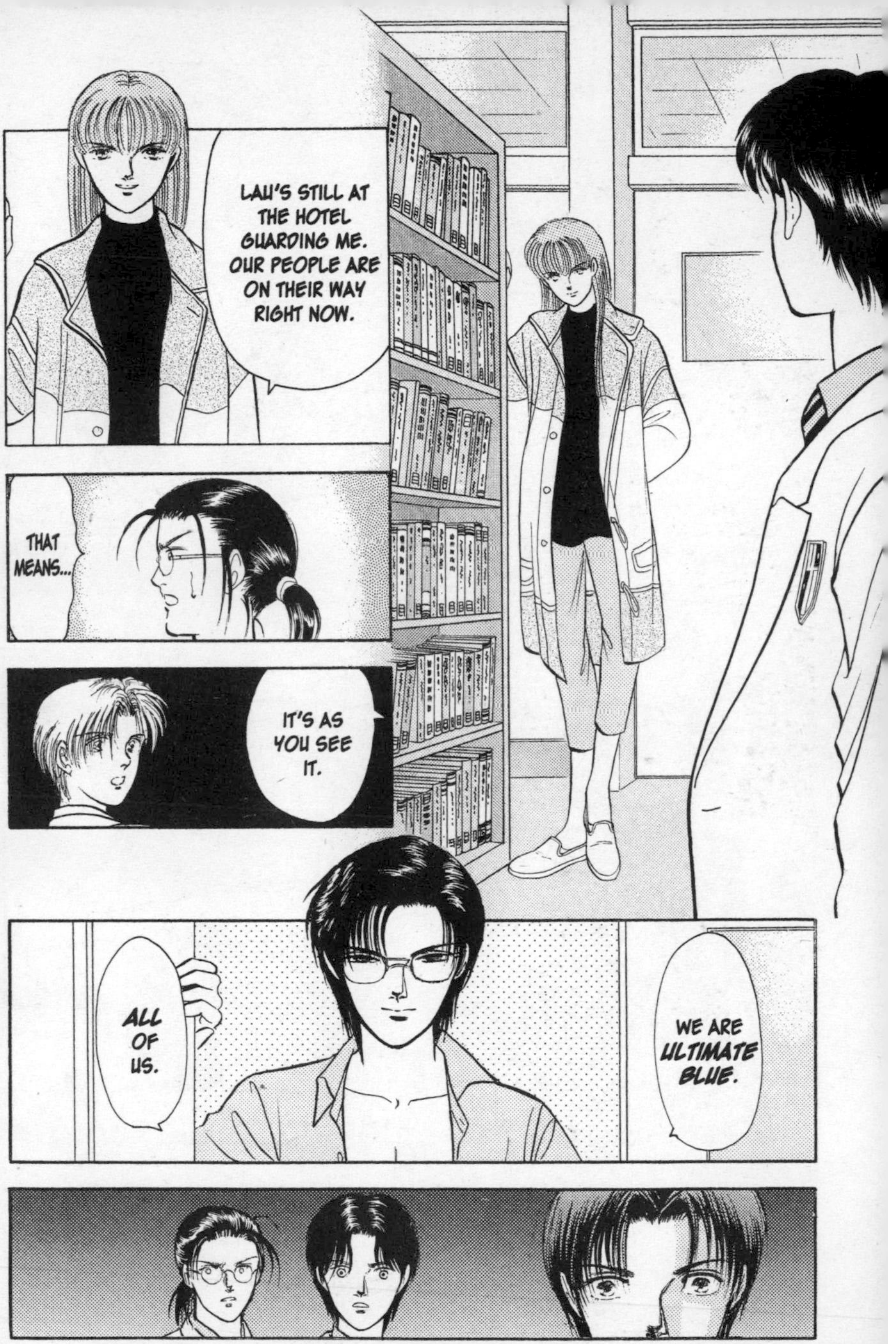
LAU'S STILL AT THE HOTEL GUARDING ME. OUR PEOPLE ARE ON THEIR WAY RIGHT NOW.
THAT MEANS...
IT'S AS YOU SEE IT.
WE ARE ULTIMATE BLUE.
ALL OF US.

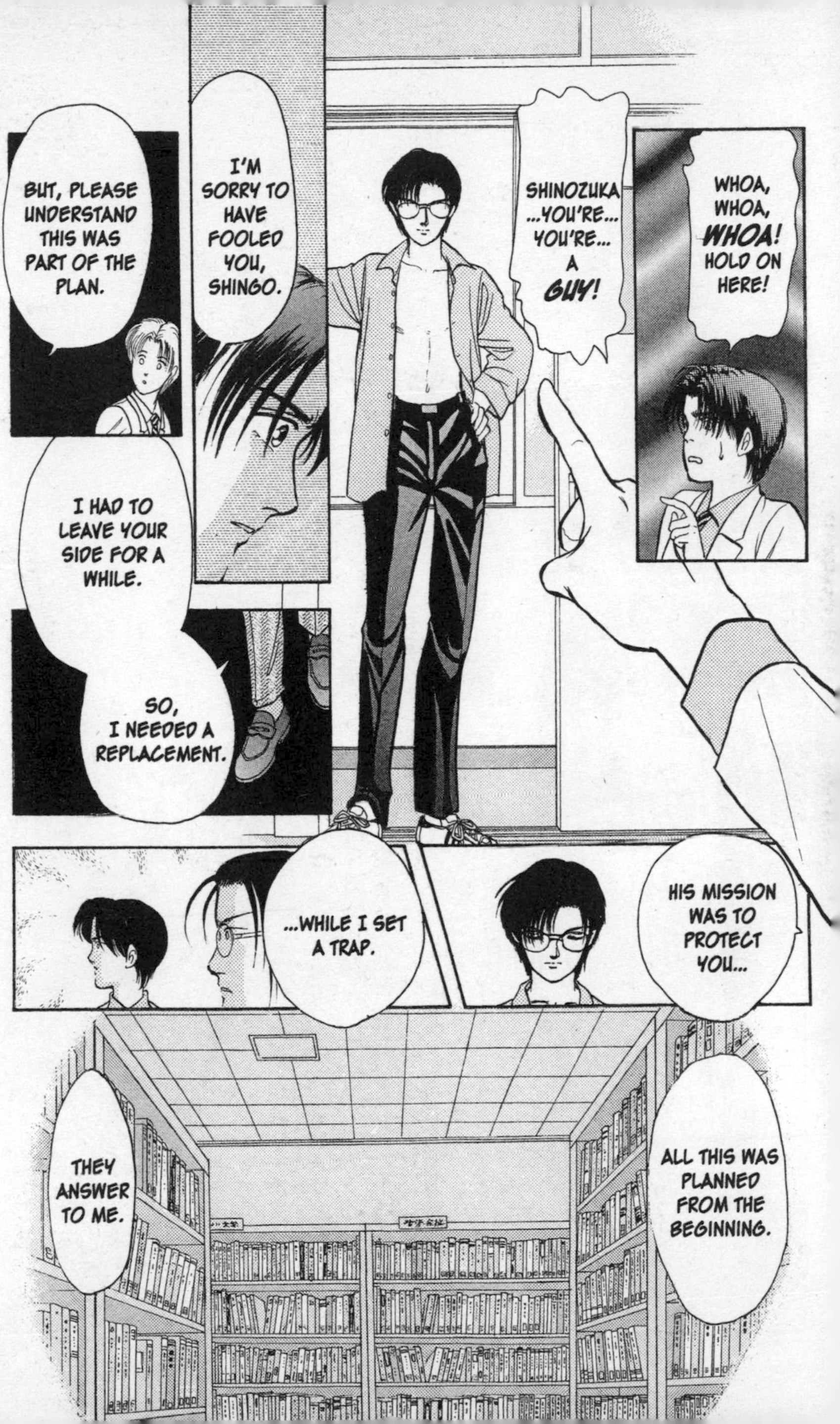
WHOA, WHOA, WHOA! HOLD ON HERE!
SHINOZUKA ...YOU'RE... YOU'RE... A GUY!
I'M SORRY TO HAVE FOOLED YOU, SHINGO.
BUT, PLEASE UNDERSTAND THIS WAS PART OF THE PLAN.
I HAD TO LEAVE YOUR SIDE FOR A WHILE.
SO, I NEEDED A REPLACEMENT.
HIS MISSION WAS TO PROTECT YOU...
...WHILE I SET A TRAP.
ALL THIS WAS PLANNED FROM THE BEGINNING.
THEY ANSWER TO ME.

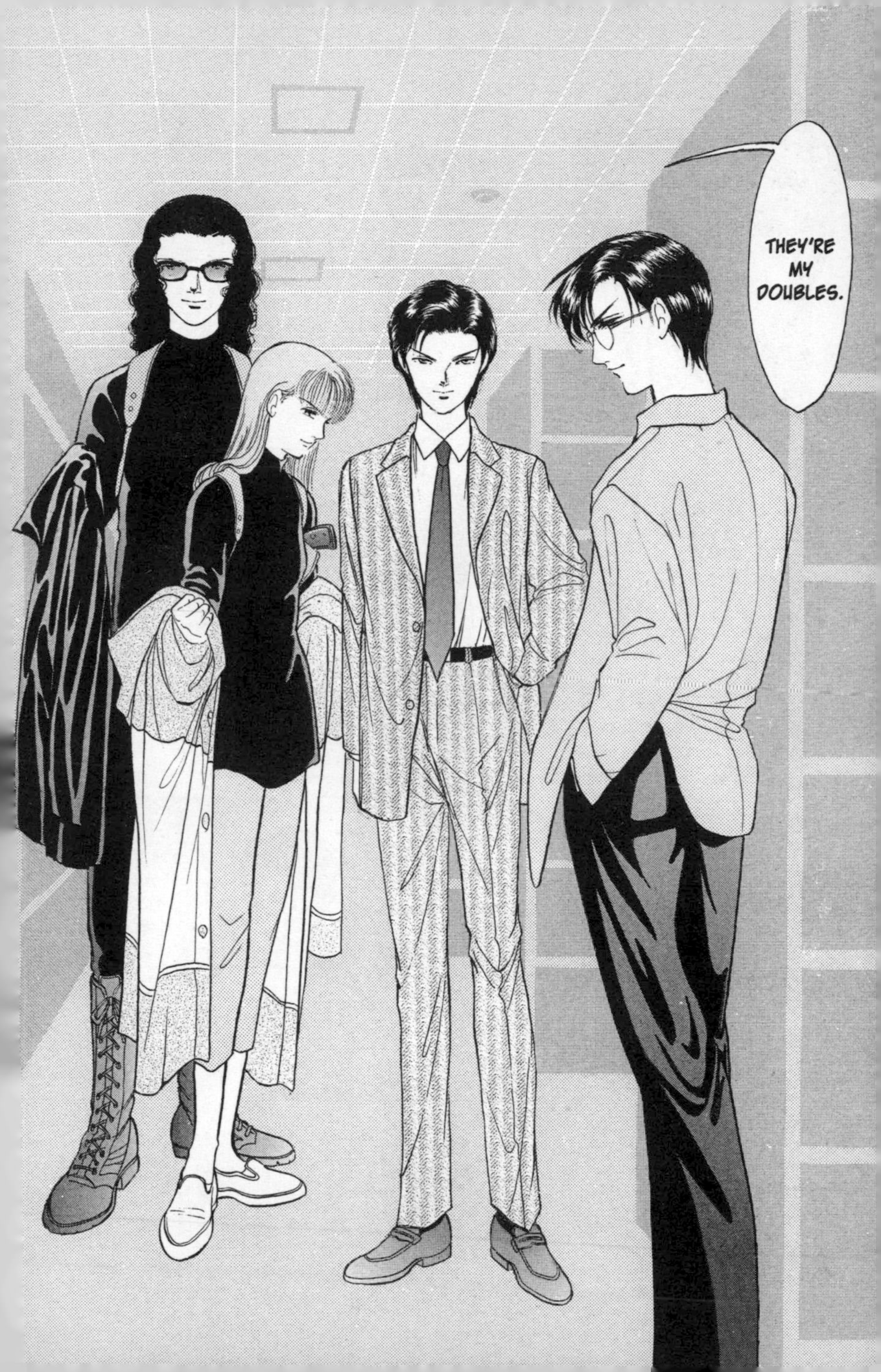
THEY'RE MY DOUBLES.

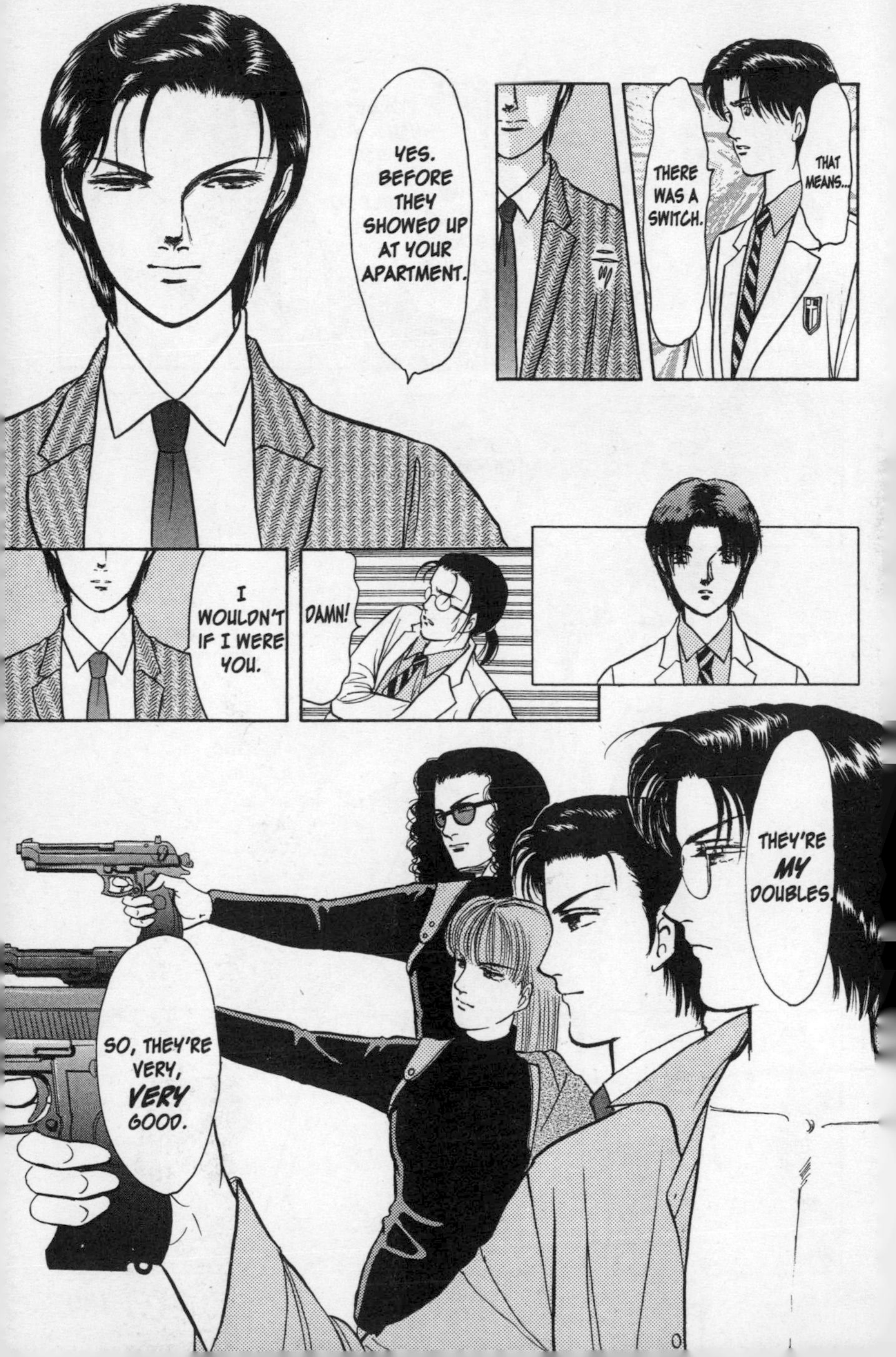
THAT MEANS...
THERE WAS A SWITCH.
YES. BEFORE THEY SHOWED UP AT YOUR APARTMENT.
DAMN!
I WOULDN'T IF I WERE YOU.
THEY'RE MY DOUBLES.
SO, THEY'RE VERY, VERY GOOD.

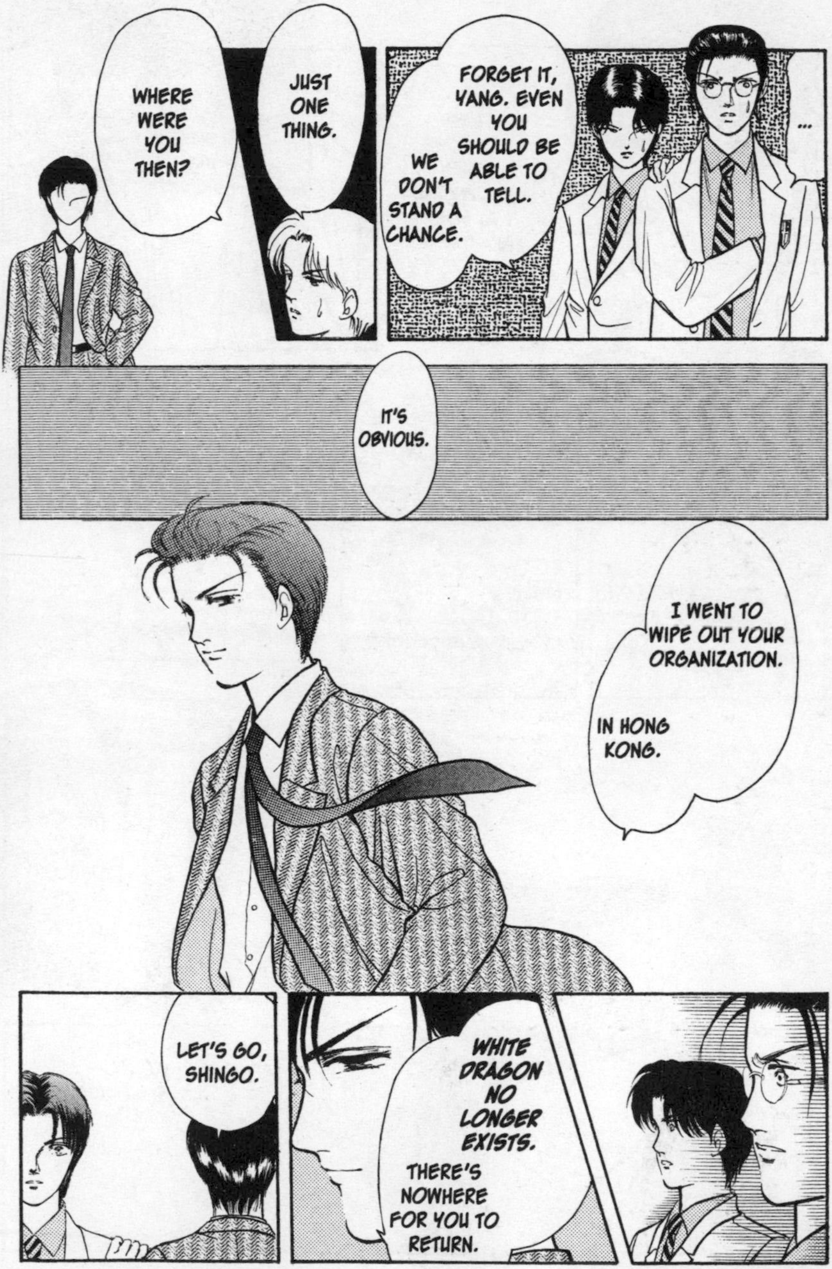
...
FORGET IT, YANG. EVEN YOU SHOULD BE ABLE TO TELL.
WE DON'T STAND A CHANCE.
JUST ONE THING.
WHERE WERE YOU THEN?
IT'S OBVIOUS.
I WENT TO WIPE OUT YOUR ORGANIZATION.
IN HONG KONG.
WHITE DRAGON NO LONGER EXISTS.
THERE'S NOWHERE FOR YOU TO RETURN.
LET'S GO, SHINGO.

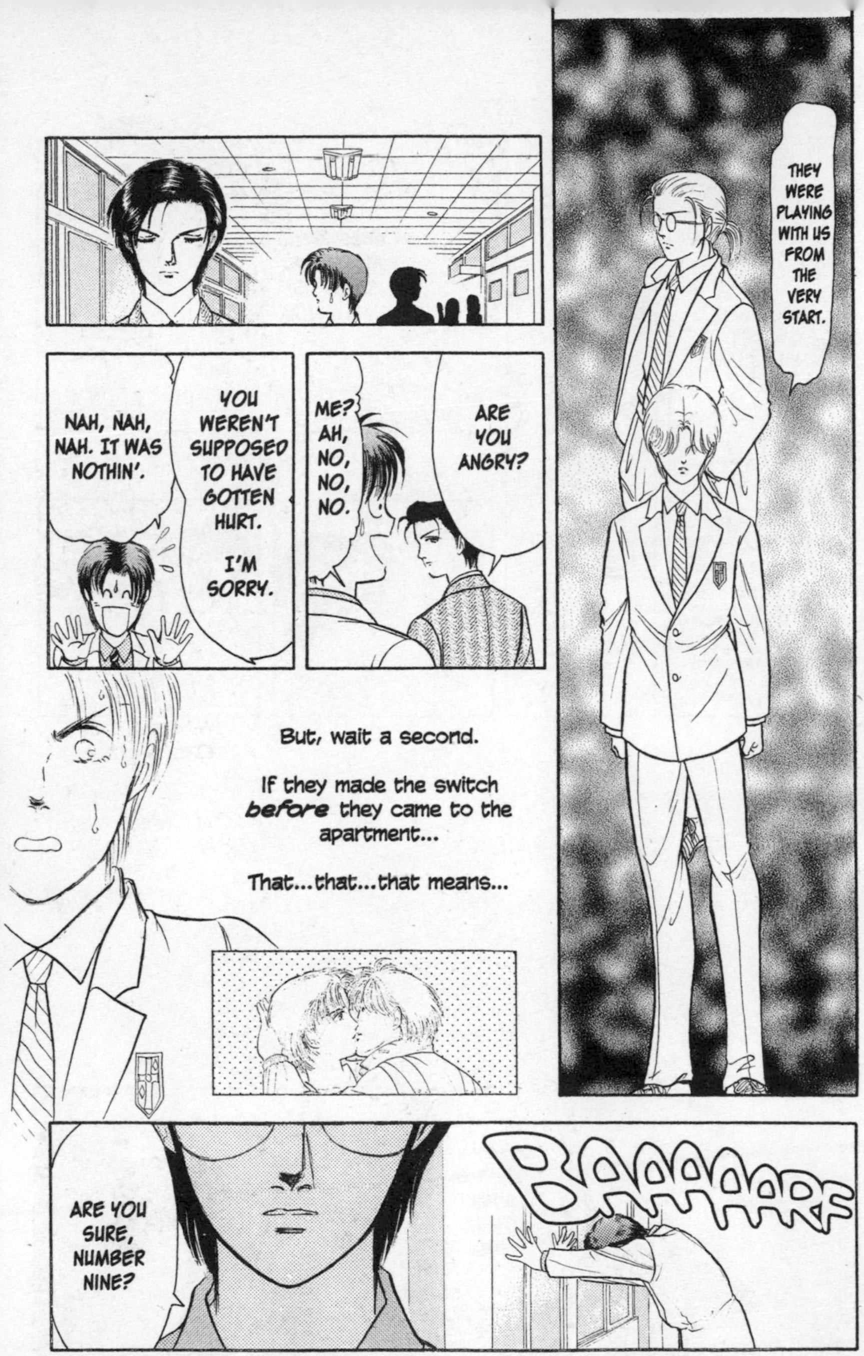
THEY WERE PLAYING WITH US FROM THE VERY START.
ARE YOU ANGRY?
ME? AH, NO, NO, NO.
YOU WEREN'T SUPPOSED TO HAVE GOTTEN HURT.
I'M SORRY.
NAH, NAH, NAH. IT WAS NOTHIN'.
But, wait a second.
If they made the switch ***before*** they came to the apartment...
That...that...that means...
BAAAAARF
ARE YOU SURE, NUMBER NINE?

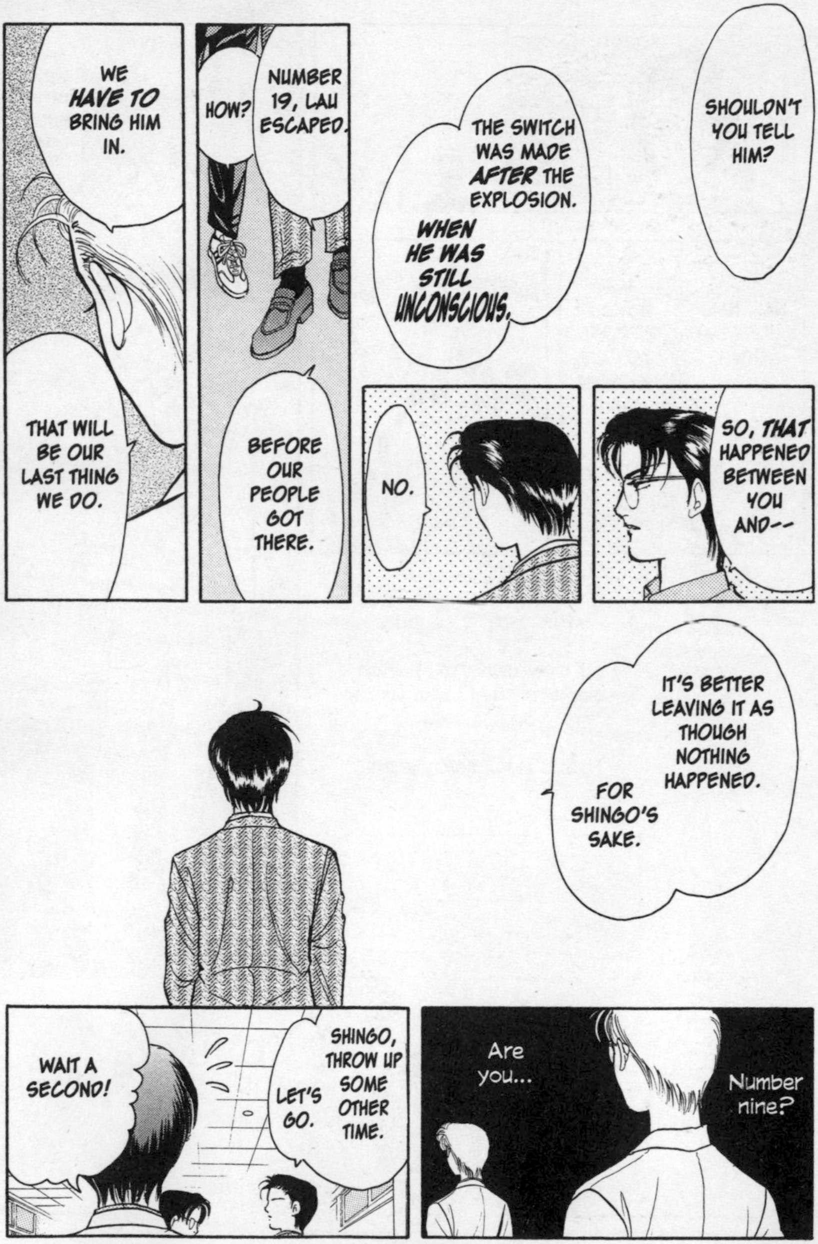
SHOULDN'T YOU TELL HIM?
THE SWITCH WAS MADE *AFTER* THE EXPLOSION.
WHEN HE WAS STILL UNCONSCIOUS.
SO, *THAT* HAPPENED BETWEEN YOU AND--
NO.
NUMBER 19, LAU ESCAPED.
HOW?
BEFORE OUR PEOPLE GOT THERE.
WE *HAVE TO* BRING HIM IN.
THAT WILL BE OUR LAST THING WE DO.
IT'S BETTER LEAVING IT AS THOUGH NOTHING HAPPENED.
FOR SHINGO'S SAKE.
Are you...
Number nine?
SHINGO, THROW UP SOME OTHER TIME.
LET'S GO.
WAIT A SECOND!

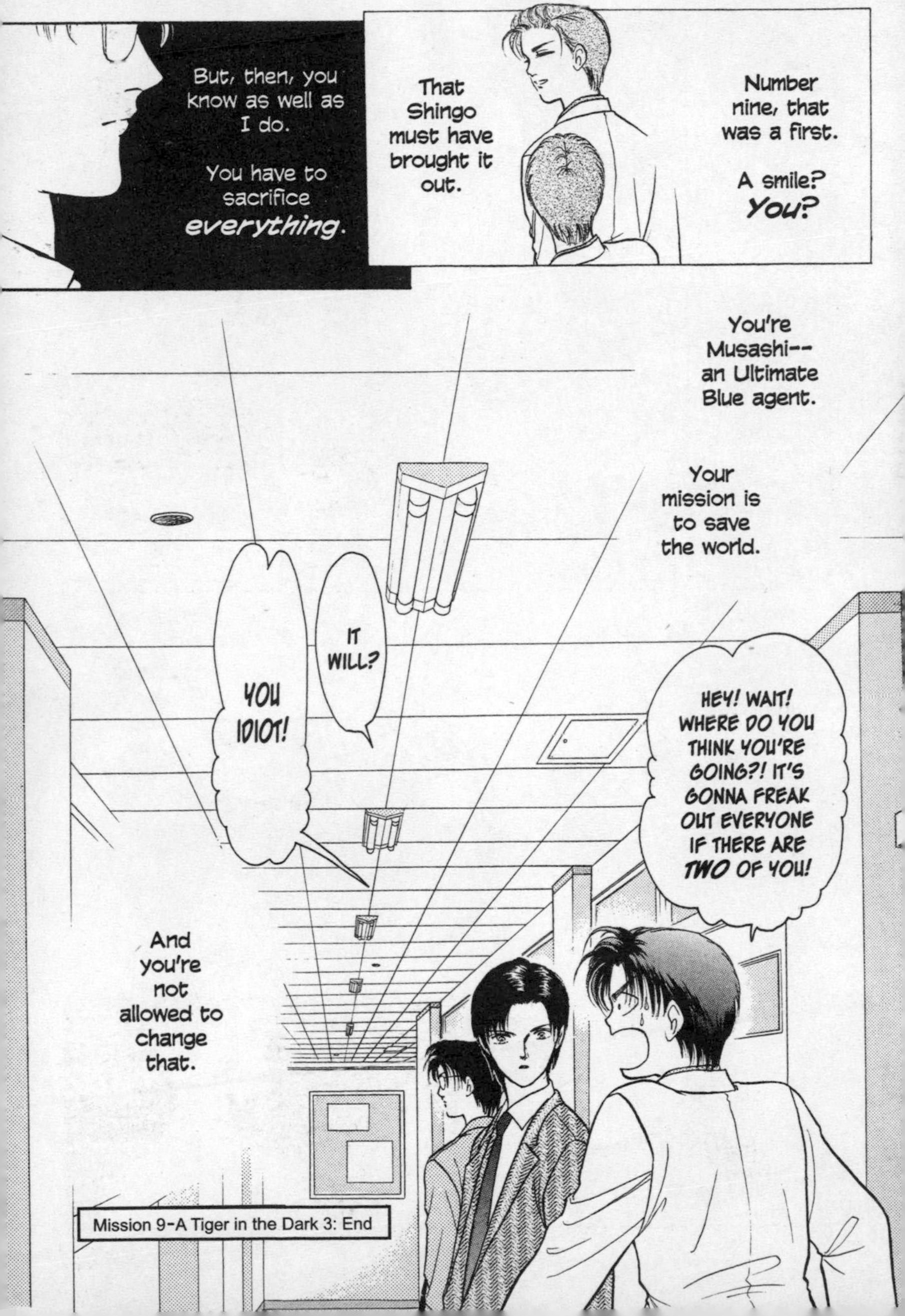
Number nine, that was a first.
A smile? *You?*
That Shingo must have brought it out.
But, then, you know as well as I do.
You have to sacrifice *everything*.
You're Musashi-- an Ultimate Blue agent.
Your mission is to save the world.
HEY! WAIT! WHERE DO YOU THINK YOU'RE GOING?! IT'S GONNA FREAK OUT EVERYONE IF THERE ARE *TWO* OF YOU!
IT WILL?
YOU IDIOT!
And you're not allowed to change that.

Mission 9-A Tiger in the Dark 3: End

cmx

Musashi #9 Vol. 4

By Takahashi Miyuki

Coming in August

Stolen launch codes of American ICBMs accidentally fall into the hands of a Japanese high school student vacationing in New York. When this news breaks and the enemy wants the codes back, Musashi 9 goes in alone to take action! But missions are never simple for the world's most lethal 16-year-old super agent. This innocent high school girl is not Musashi 9's only responsibility— she is already protecting a teenaged boy, whose affection for her is growing by the hour. Now, with two teens to guard, can Musashi # 9 complete her duty without becoming distracted by feelings she is unable to deny?

KYUBANME NO MUSASHI © 1996 by Miyuki Takahashi/AKITASHOTEN.

cmxmanga.com

CMX

Jim Lee
  Editorial Director
John Nee
  VP—Business Development
Jonathan Tarbox
  Group Editor
Paul Levitz
  President & Publisher
Georg Brewer
  VP—Design & Retail Product Development
Richard Bruning
  Senior VP—Creative Director
Patrick Caldon
  Senior VP—Finance & Operations
Chris Caramalis
  VP—Finance
Terri Cunningham
  VP—Managing Editor
Alison Gill
  VP—Manufacturing
Rich Johnson
  VP—Book Trade Sales
Hank Kanalz
  VP—General Manager, WildStorm
Lillian Laserson
  Senior VP & General Counsel
David McKillips
  VP—Advertising & Custom Publishing
Gregory Noveck
  Senior VP—Creative Affairs
Cheryl Rubin
  Senior VP—Brand Management
Bob Wayne
  VP—Sales & Marketing

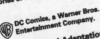
Translation and Adaptation by
Tony Ogasawara

William F. Schuch— Lettering
John J. Hill — CMX Logo & Publication Design
Larry Berry — Additional Design

ISBN: 1-4012-0542-9

FLIP IT!!

All the pages in this book were created—and are printed here—in Japanese RIGHT-to-LEFT format. No artwork has been reversed, so you can read the stories the way the creators meant for them to be read.

JAPANESE NAMES

Authentic Japanese name order is family name first, given name second. In the CMX books and on the covers, we will list the names of all characters as well as the manga creators in Japanese order, unless otherwise instructed by the author.

RIGHT TO LEFT?!

Traditional Japanese manga starts at the upper right-hand corner, and moves right-to-left as it goes down the page. Follow this guide for an easy understanding.

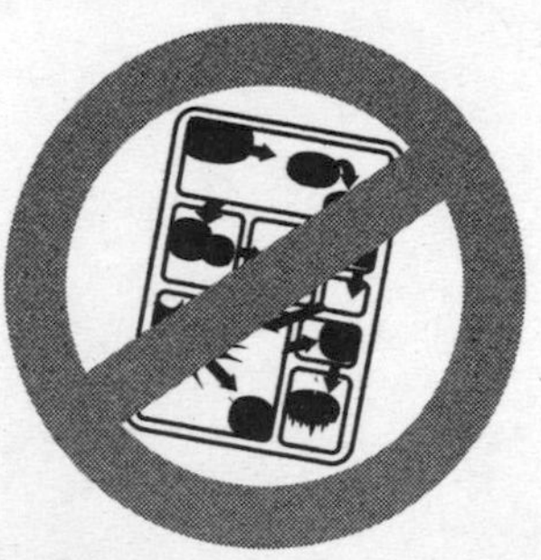

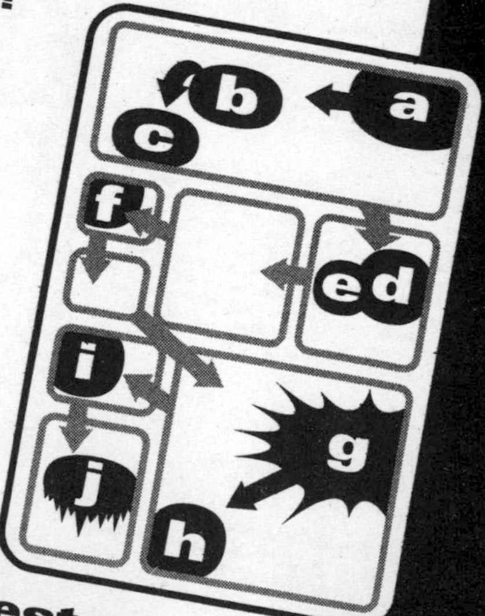
a
b
c
ed
f
g
h
i
j

Catch the latest at cmxmanga.com!